Exposing Privatization
Women and Health Care Reform in Canada

Exposing Privatization
Women and Health Care Reform in Canada

Pat Armstrong
Carol Amaratunga
Jocelyne Bernier
Karen Grant
Ann Pederson
Kay Willson

Garamond Press
Aurora, Ontario

Copyright © 2002 by the Authors. All rights reserved. No part of this book may be reproduced or transmitted in any form by any means without permission in writing from the publisher, except by a reviewer, who may quote brief passages in a review.

Printed and bound in Canada

Garamond Press Ltd.
63 Mahogany Court
Aurora, Ontario
L4G 6M8

National Library of Canada Cataloguing in Publication Data
Main entry under title:
    Exposing privatization: women and health care reform in Canada
(Health care in Canada)
Includes bibliographical references.
ISBN 1-55193-037-4

    1. Women's health services—Canada. 2. Health care reform—Canada.
3. Privatization—Canada. I. Armstrong, Pat, 1945-
II. Series: Health care in Canada (Aurora, Ont.)
RA564.85.E96 2001   362.1'082'0971   C2001-903126-2

This project was financially supported by the Centres of Excellence for Women's Health Program, Women's Health Bureau, Health Canada. The views expressed herein do not necessarily represent the views or the official policy of Health Canada.

Garamond Press gratefully acknowledges the support of the Department of Canadian Heritage, Government of Canada, for its publishing program, and of the Canadian Studies Bureau of the same Department for support of this specific publication.

Contents

Introduction 8
The Context for Health Care Reform in Canada 11
Introduction 11
The Aftermath of War 11
After the Welfare State 16
Canadian Reforms 29
Conclusion 41
Health Restructuring and Privatization from Women's Perspective in Newfoundland and Labrador 49
Introduction 49
Restructuring of the Health Care System 50
Privatizing Medical Services 61
The Impact of Privatization on Women as Care Providers 74
Shifting from Long-term Institutional to Home and
  Community-based Care 78
Health Reform, Privatization and Women in Nova Scotia 95
Introduction 95
Overview of Health Care Reform in Nova Scotia 96
Privatization Trends in Health Care Reform 101
Women and Health Care Reform 106
Women, Health Care and Privatization 110
Conclusion 116
What Price Have Women Paid for Health Care Reform? The Situation in Quebec 121
Introduction 121
Health Care Reform 122
The Price of Health Care Reform for Women in Quebec 139
Conclusion 151

Women, Privatization and Health Care Reform: The Ontario Case 163
Introduction 163
Hospitals 164
Long-term Care in the Community 178
Long-term Residential Care 187
Primary Care 192
Mental Health 198
Rehabilitation Services 199
Targeted Programs for Women 201
Health Information Technology 204
Conclusion 204

Missing Links: The Effects of Health Care Privatization on Women in Manitoba and Saskatchewan 217
Introduction 217
Privatization 223
The Impact of Privatization on Women 234
Conclusion 245

The Differential Impact of Health Care Privatization on Women in Alberta 253
Introduction 253
Gender-based Analysis in Alberta 254
The Evolution of Alberta Health and Social Policy 257
Public Participation 260
Privatization of Health Care in Alberta 263
Conclusion 281

The Information Gap: The Impact of Health Care Reform on British Columbia Women 287
The BC Process of Health Care Reform 287
Health Care Governance 288
Health Care Jobs 290
Nursing: The Burden of Care 295
Health Care Reform and Privatization 297
Hospital Reform 299
The Information Gap 303
Conclusion 309

Acknowledgments

This book is the product of many hands. Health Canada's Diane Ponée, Lynne Dee Sproule and Lorraine Pelot have continually provided support without censorship, keeping us on track but allowing us to follow where the research was taking us. Lesley Poirier, Sandy Bentley and Jennifer Howard were involved at the beginning of this project and played critical roles in the formation of the plans for the research. Carole Carbonneau, Heather Goodman and Kendra Kusturin did the critical coordinating and administrative work. Jane Springer's sensitive editing was critical in the transformation of the papers into a book.

Introduction

What is happening in Canadian health care reform? What does it mean for women? Given the government, academic and media concern with health care, you would think there would be an easily accessible answer to the first question. And given that women make up 80 per cent of health care providers, paid and unpaid, and a majority of patients, you would expect the question of the impact on women to be at the top of the agenda. But you would be wrong.

This is the conclusion we came to after investigating both issues. The we is the National Coordinating Group on Health Care Reform and Women, a collaborative group that brings together the five federally funded Centres of Excellence for Women's Health, the Canadian Women's Health Network and Health Canada's Women's Health Bureau. Our mandate is to coordinate research on health care reform, identify gaps in the research and take steps to fill those gaps, and finally, to translate this research into policies and practices.

The complexity of the task became obvious when we realized that all of us were talking about different reforms, depending on where we lived and what kind of work we did. Home care, for example, means one thing in Manitoba and another in Ontario. Who pays for, who delivers and who gets home care, under what conditions, are questions with different answers in each province – although the two provinces face similar pressures and often get similar advice. Moreover, reforms are significantly changing home care in both provinces and doing so at a rapid pace. Yet it is not easy to find out the precise nature and extent of these reforms, let alone what they mean in practice, especially for women.

In order to carry out our mandate, we first needed a better grasp of the nature, form and content of reforms across Canada. We also needed to know more about the global context and the pressures – as well as the models for reforms – coming from outside the country. Equally important was the question of the impact on women and indeed, whether or not reformers were investigating the issue at all. Because we could not find easily accessible answers to these questions, we decided to commission a series of papers.

In order to commission the papers, we had to develop a framework for the collection of information – a lens through which to select, sort and assess what was available from varied sources. After extensive discussion of many alternatives, we decided to use privatization as our central frame. Like health care reform, privatization has many meanings. In keeping with our objective to capture the central features of health care reform and its impact on women, we use the term more broadly than in the traditional economic sense.

For the purposes of this project, the privatization of health care refers to several different policy directions, all of which limit the role of the public sector and define health care as a private responsibility. According to our definition, the privatization of health care includes:

- privatizing the costs of health care by shifting the burden of payment to individuals;
- privatizing the delivery of health services by expanding opportunities for private, for-profit health service providers;
- privatizing the delivery of health care services by shifting care from public institutions to community-based organizations and private households;
- privatizing care work from public sector health care workers to unpaid caregivers; and
- privatizing management practices within the health system by adopting the management strategies of private sector businesses, by applying market rules to health service delivery and by treating health care as a market commodity.

Privatization in the health care system can occur both in the payment for health care services and in the provision of health care services. We defined services and providers broadly. For example, we included unpaid caregivers in the category of providers, the provision of medical supplies as a service and medications as an essential part of care delivery. By defining privatization in this way, we hoped to cover the entire range of reforms across the country.

Privatization was the frame for capturing health care reform but we also had to make clear what we meant by "women." Just as we recognize that there are considerable differences across the country in terms of reforms, we recognize that there are considerable differences among women in terms of the way they connect to health care. We know that women are the main providers of care, whether or not the care is paid, institutional or home-based. Women are also the main recipients of care, especially among the elderly. Although women are involved in much of the daily decision-making about health care, they are much less visible among senior policy-makers and managers. We are interested in what consequences reforms have for women as providers and patients, and their impact on women's participation in the decision-making process. At the same time, we are aware of the significant differences among women related to their physical, social, economic, cultural/racial locations and their age and sexual orientation. These, too, must be considered in assessing the consequences of reforms. Which women are affected, in what ways, by which reforms were central questions for our work.

Because we want to link research to change, we also asked the authors to search out both positive and negative reform strategies, keeping in mind that reforms may work for some and not others.

This book brings together the commissioned work to expose the many faces of health care privatization and what we know about its impact on women[1]. It begins with the international context for health care reform and then moves from coast to coast, setting out what we know about the reforms that are underway and about their impact on women. It is a survey based on the existing information and an analysis of the gaps in our knowledge. It is important to note that health care reform is an ever changing phenomenon. As this monograph goes to press, new policy changes are under way around the country. These reforms are not included in the discussions that follow, but the analyses here do reveal patterns that, in all likelihood, pertain to more recent policy changes. We hope it will not only inform but spur action in research, policy and practice.

Pat Armstrong
Carol Amaratunga
Jocelyne Bernier
Karen Grant
Ann Pederson
Kay Willson

---

1. The texts of the initial papers can be found on the Canadian Women's Health Network Website, www.cwhn@hn.ca.

The Context for Health Care Reform in Canada
Pat Armstrong

INTRODUCTION
Health care reform has seldom been a strictly local matter. Canada has developed some unique reform strategies and adapted others to suit its particular circumstances – and Canada is not without influence abroad, particularly in the areas of health promotion (Pederson, O'Neill and Rootman 1994) and gender-based analysis. But foreign influences and external pressures have seldom been absent. Health care reform, then, has to be understood within an international context.

This article seeks to contextualize current reforms, outlining some of the international and national pressures and influences that shape strategies to change health care in Canada. It then looks at the new paradigm for health care that is dominant in the international and national arenas.

THE AFTERMATH OF WAR
The International Stage
The Second World War set the stage for radical health care reform. Most countries involved in the war emerged from it with large state sectors, huge debts and a population that demanded better conditions in return for the sacrifices they had made for the war effort. As Malcolm Taylor put it, "There was a mood of rebellion against the universal risks of unemployment and sickness, disability and old age, widowhood and poverty."

Women were very much a part of this rebellion. In Canada, "CCF women, for example, demanded leadership training programs, publicly accessible birth control clinics and equal pay laws as early as the mid-1930s" (Bashevkin 1998, 19).

Although Allied governments feared massive revolt and a return to high unemployment in the aftermath of war, they were not driven simply by these fears. There was optimism about state intervention, based on Keynesian economics and the experiences of the war years. There was also a new view of cooperation among countries. For centuries, the increasingly global economy had prompted calls for some kind of international regulation. But it took the Second World War to convince decision-makers "that industrial countries, in particular, were too advanced, specialized, and interdependent to contemplate genuine, lasting improvements in economic welfare after the war without re-establishing some sort of new economic order" (Panic 1995, 38). Equally important, they saw the task as "too important and urgent for the postwar recovery to be left to the slow, haphazard processes of the markets, whose limitations had been exposed in the interwar period" (ibid.). Among the various women's movements, there was "great hope not just for women's advancement but also for social improvement via active good government" (Bashevkin 1998, 19).

According to one analyst of the period, "the powerful vested interests that might have resisted this successfully were too shell-shocked and marginalized by the disastrous turn of events in the 1930s and early 1940s to put up much of a resistance" (Panic 1995, 38). At the same time, there were multiple opportunities for investment and profit-making available in the wake of the war's destruction and with the development of new technologies, as well as generous government infrastructure support for business.

A variety of organizations resulted from the Bretton Woods agreements of 1946-47 and the establishment of the United Nations. The World Bank and the International Monetary Fund (IMF), officially specialized agencies of the United Nations, were intended to coordinate the international financial system. The World Health Organization (WHO), the United Nations Children's Emergency Fund (UNICEF), the United Nations Development Fund (UNDP) and the United Nations Population Fund (UNFPA) were designed to develop a range of health strategies throughout the world. As the Constitution of the World Health Organization made clear, there was a shared understanding that the "health of all peoples is fundamental to the attainment of peace and security, and is dependent upon the fullest cooperation of individuals and states" (in Koivusalo and Ollola 1997, 7).

Most industrialized countries developed or expanded public health care services, placing a particular emphasis in North America on the most expensive – hospital and medical care. By 1995, in 20 out of the 29 countries surveyed by the OECD "more than 70 per cent of total expenditure on health takes place in the public sector" and in seven of them, the public share was over 80 per cent (OECD 1992, 131). A significant sector of the labour involved in care was paid, and it included a growing number of women. Although critiques of the medical model were not absent, the primary issues were framed in terms of access to existing health care services that were assumed to provide quality care.

There was, in these health discussions, a recognition of different health needs for women, although women were not central participants in the international agreements or in the organizations they set up. At least one obvious women's issue was given priority – maternal and child health (WHO 1998, 11). This reflected the tendency to define women's health needs in terms of their reproductive capacities, and to address the issue more in terms of controlling women than of empowering them (see Stein 1997). In the dominant paradigm of the period, difference was often understood as biologically determined inferiority, and solutions offered in terms of a western medical model.

Matters related to women as paid and unpaid providers were not central concerns in these international debates, and it is difficult to find documentation of discussions at the international meetings about the division of labour within or outside health care services. Women did not simply passively accept the dominant paradigm, however. Many women benefited from the development of initiatives in such areas as public health and public care services, nutrition and sanitation initiatives, as patients, providers and decision-makers. Paid jobs in health care grew, and along with them, the strength of many women.[1]

Canadian Initiatives

It was in this context that Canada reformed postwar health care services. There was a strong federal state, buttressed by a Keynesian philosophy and by experience that supported state intervention. There were new technology- and hospital-based services that demonstrated the benefits of effective treatments and cures.

There was also a restless population demanding access to the health services that had become increasingly inaccessible in the prewar years and increasingly expensive in the postwar ones. And as employment expanded there was a labour movement growing in strength and numbers, a movement committed to a social wage that included health care. Various women's organizations were also part of the increasing pressure for public care, as women struggled to defend not only their own interests in terms of access to care but those of their families as well.

At the same time, there was a relative absence of for-profit services or even of insurance companies involved in health care. Nine out of ten hospitals were non-profit in 1955 (Dominion Bureau of Statistics 1957, 267). A significant proportion of insurance was also non-profit, with Blue Cross leading the pack. Large companies faced increasingly strong labour groups demanding health benefits and a public plan promised to reduce their direct costs. As a result, the corporate sector offered only limited opposition to state involvement.

There was strong evidence to support the need both for more services and for public care. Significant proportions of the population had no insurance coverage, and the uninsured stayed in hospitals longer than the insured, primarily because they went for care only when they were very ill. Given the high cost of care, the government often ended up paying for the uninsured.

Research on insurance indicated that even those with coverage had only part of their bill paid for by the company, particularly if the coverage was provided by a for-profit firm. At the same time, research found that voluntary insurance schemes added significantly to hospital expenditures (Taylor 1987, 111).

These pressures combined to set the stage for a public health care plan. Health care was defined more as a social good than as a market commodity. The discourse was about shared risks (Marsh 1975, 9-10) and "public responsibility for individual economic security and welfare" (quoted in Taylor 1987, 50).

There was, of course, controversy and compromise. The first postwar federal/provincial conference on health care failed to reach agreement. Foiled at the conference table, the federal government used its spending power first to fund research, training and hospital construction. Then it promised to pay half the cost of hospital insurance and later, medical insurance. Finally, the 1984 *Canada Health Act* brought hospital and medical insurance together, forbidding user fees and opening the door to care outside hospitals and doctors' offices. The provinces were far from universally supportive at any stage of these developments. The Conservative premier of Ontario went so far as to claim at one point that the new "Machiavellian scheme" was "one of the greatest frauds that has ever been perpetrated on the people of this country" (ibid., 375).

Such opposition encouraged the development of a plan based on principles set out at the federal level rather than on a detailed plan that each province would follow. In the end, the *Canada Health Act* is only thirteen pages long, and that includes text in both official languages. As a result, there is not one system but many systems, each with the possibility of adapting to local needs. The provinces and territories have used their spending power to shape regional, municipal and organizational developments, but significant choices remain at each level.

Opposition from various quarters also encouraged the development of a plan based on an insurance model rather than a provider model. The government responded to the concerns of provider organizations by leaving services in their hands. Under this model, "private insurance is implicitly or explicitly forbidden and there is no opting out of paying taxes for the public system" (National Forum on Health 1997b, 16). Although the insurance plan must be publicly administered, there is no requirement in the *Canada Health Act* that the services be provided by a non-profit firm.

Another result of public health insurance was the expansion of choice, especially given the additional criteria of universality, accessibility and comprehensiveness. Because governments funded services rather than individuals, and did not provide services directly, there was a range of options available for many women. Patients could choose among service providers and seek consultations from more than one kind of service. Coverage was thus portable for service to service and job to job, and alternative means of delivering care were available in many areas. This was particularly important to women because they often encounter providers who dismiss their symptoms or respond in ways that reflect stereotypes and cultural values that are inappropriate to an individual woman's needs. Moreover, women are more likely to have short-term employment and portability from job to job is critical to ensure continuity in care.

Medicare also led to an enormous expansion in access to services. Access improved for those most in need (Enterline *et al.* 1973), and the majority of these were women. At the same time, the number of jobs for women grew dramatically. Between 1951 and 1961, the number of women in the health services labour force increased from 107,063 to 205,284 (Dominion Bureau of Statistics 1966, table 12B). By 1991, more than a million women worked in health and social services, representing 16 per cent of the entire female labour force (Statistics Canada 1993, table 1). This expansion in the broader public sector contributed to the development of strong professional and union organizations among women – organizations that have successfully fought for better conditions and relations at work and for the recognition and defence of the skilled nature of their labour (see Armstrong, Choiniere and Day 1993; Armstrong 1993).

A women's health movement also emerged. Women were active in public and occupational health, in demanding access to services, in offering health education and in promoting self-regulation, as well as better conditions, for paid care providers. They stressed what today would be called the determinants of health and health promotion, albeit often framed by middle-class women for the poorer classes. By contrast, much of the initial focus of the postwar movement was on a critique of medicine, in terms of the emphasis on a medical model, on medical power and on institutional care. Self-help, empowerment through shared knowledge, and alternative therapies were central strategies in the movement that began in the 1960s (see, for example, Kleiber and Light 1978; McDonnell and Valverde 1985; Montreal Women's Health Press 1968). It expanded to challenge the entire paradigm dominant in health services and the assumptions made not only about women's bodies and women's relations but also about their work.

Empowerment, community, self-help, alternative therapies, disease prevention and health promotion and rights have all been central to the discourse around the women's health movement. The movement began to stress both sameness and difference (Bacchi 1990), both women as actors and women as a group who have few choices to make. The emphasis has been increasingly on connections rather than on isolated individuals, on emotions as well as on reason, on needs as well as on wants, on multiple rather than on single strategies, and on the concrete along with the abstract or general (see, for example, Harding 1986, 1991). Context matters. So do relations with others. These relations, and locations, are understood to have a profound impact on health in general, and on choice in particular.

While these could be described as the main features of the dominant paradigm in the women's health movement, it should be recognized that there is no single, unified movement. Controversy, debate and new theories have been central to the critiques of existing practices and to proposals for the future. These differences become most evident around specific issues such as the introduction of midwifery programs and of new reproductive technologies.

AFTER THE WELFARE STATE
The Emerging Paradigm

For 25 years after the Second World War, what has been described as the postwar consensus largely held (Bashevkin 1998, 19). But by the early 1970s, the international agreements that reflected a Keynesian approach had begun to unravel. Both the United States withdrawal from the gold standard and the increases in petroleum prices marked a major turning point in philosophy and practices at the international and national level. While there is disagreement over the cause of this change, there is little dispute that a new philosophy guided international development (Mendelson 1997).

In contrast to the Keynesian approach, the new neo-liberal paradigm placed its faith in a "free economy and a strong state" (Alan Walker quoted in Martin 1993, 46). The theory called for a dismantling of the welfare state, but not for a weak state in such areas as control of the money supply or moral authority. As Martin points out in his exploration of public sector reform, it "is not *whether* or not the state intervenes in the economy that has changed but *how*, and to whose benefit" (Martin 1993, 48). The emphasis on free markets required positive intervention by the state to maintain the conditions for the free market and for social order. This means deregulating much of economic activity and regulating more of labour and personal activities. Margaret Thatcher, for example, argued that social decay required strong government to support a return to principled morality (Bashevkin 1998, 22). "Special interests" such as women's groups were often seen as part of this decay (Shields and Evans 1998, 17). At the same time, the belief in market mechanisms supported the move to privatize public corporations or contract out services in the public sphere and to apply for-profit principles to the public sector that remains. It assumed that because of competition, the for-profit sector is necessarily efficient and effective – in contrast to public sector organizations, which are defined as bloated, bureaucratic and ineffective.

In this paradigm, the market is seen "as a provider of economic efficiency and as a guarantor of a sense of individual freedom and responsibility" (Taylor quoted in Martin 1993, 48). Each firm and each individual, pursuing their own interests, would stimulate the economy, eliminate waste and expand choice. Unlike Keynesian theory, which assumed shared risks and the right to collectively provided supports, the neo-liberal approach focused on freedom from economic interference. Equity was the result of each person facing the same market conditions. The benefits would "trickle down" to the disadvantaged, providing far better results than universal programs that were defined as encouraging dependency and stifling choice (Bashevkin 1998, 28). However, under these strategies large numbers of women throughout the world have seen their conditions deteriorate, while only a minority has experienced the trickle (Sparr 1994).

The new stress on the private sector coincided with failures in and critiques of the public sector. The OECD, for example, lists as factors leading to "the reappraisal of the rationale for government intervention" both "a perception that the public sector performance was inferior to that of the private sector" and "citizens' demands for improved responsiveness, choice and quality of service" (OECD 1995, 19). The collapse of the Soviet Union, and the accompanying notion that state expansion was a central cause, helped fuel this development. In their influential book, *Reinventing Government* (1992), David Osborne and Ted Gaebler maintained that "market-oriented governments" should 'steer', not 'row' or run things" (281). In this new framework, citizens are increasingly described as customers "who can choose in a market-like fashion between different service providers" and community choices are defined mainly as individual consumer ones (Pierre 1995, 56).

Women's groups were among the most active critics of government services. For instance, they objected to the medicalization of daily life supported by a government-funded hospital and physician system. Although both physicians and hospitals remained outside government hands in many countries, state policies clearly played a critical role in how care was delivered and in the extent to which, and the manner in which, women participated in decision-making. Medical schools and other forms of education for health providers came under attack for both the exclusion of women and for the way women were included. Similarly, the male bias in the definitions, content, methods and models in state-supported medical research was exposed. The quality of care became a central concern as women pointed to the considerable variations in such areas as caesarian rates and the failure to monitor physician practices. At the same time, policies and practices seldom took differences between women and men, or those among women, into account. The effectiveness and appropriateness of treatment became a central concern. Women were critical of governments' failure to support alternative therapies and alternative ways of delivering care, as well as of the limited attention paid the determinants of health and primary care. Lack of integration and continuity in services was also raised as an issue, along with the White, European, male health model that dominated care services. Equity that involved recognition of differences, especially in terms of context, capacity and power – not simply equal treatment – was a major goal. So was social justice, and women's groups pointed out it did not always result from public intervention (see, for example, Boyd 1997; Brodie 1997).

Although women were amongst the most critical of public sector health interventions, they did not necessarily support private sector solutions. Susan Sherwin, for example, persuasively argued "that the institution of medicine has been designed in ways that reinforce sexism, and the effects of medical practice are often bad for women" but remained committed to "reforming rather than rejecting" many (although not all) existing health care arrangements

(Sherwin 1992, 6). Women's groups particularly objected to the role for-profit companies played in drugs and devices, demanding greater government control (see, for example, McDonnell 1986; Overall 1993; Rehner 1989). They demonstrated that interventions had a differential and often inappropriate impact on women as citizens, patients, providers and decision-makers. And they have been successful in demanding a gender-based analysis of all such interventions.

Their success is not without contradictions, however. Take the example of reproductive rights. Rosalind Petchesky (1995) argues that the 1994 Programme of Action of the Cairo International Conference on Population and Development,

> enshrines an almost feminist vision of reproductive rights and gender equality in place of the old population control discourse and retains a mainstream model of development under which that vision cannot possibly be realized (152).

She goes on to explain that the Programme represents the success resulting from years of effort by women's groups around the world to "gain recognition of women's reproductive and sexual self-determination as a basic health need and human right" (ibid.). Yet the Programme not only failed "to address the real implications of privatization" (156), but went so far as to make a commitment to "increase involvement of the private sector" (157). In Petchesky's words,

> the Cairo document promotes the very privatization, commodification and deregulation of reproductive health services that, by its own admission, have led to diminished access and increasing mortality and morbidity for poor women, who constitute "the most vulnerable groups" in both developing and developed countries. (ibid.)

Another contradiction has to do with both the discourse surrounding reform and the demand for change. As Rekart (1993) makes clear, there is a great deal of overlap in the language used by a range of groups involved in reform. Those seeking to dismantle the public system and those seeking to preserve it, albeit through changing forms, share a discourse around community and health promotion, continuity and integration, informed consent and self-help, accountability and empowerment, quality and effectiveness, primary care and local control, choice and equity. Yet both groups mean quite different things by these concepts. The risk is that, in the context of a dominant paradigm that promotes market methods and delivery along with individual responsibility, it will not be women's understandings that prevail. Instead, women's language and critiques may be used to encourage support for strategies that deny their goals. Just as those involved in the reform of mental health services found their critiques used to justify de-institutionalization that left many without care and those that remained in care with often worse services (see Simmons 1990), so are women's groups seeing their arguments used to justify market solutions to health service problems (Armstrong 1996).

The Debt/Deficit Pressure

Debt and deficits emerged as a major problem during the post-welfare state period. Governments throughout the industrial world were spending more than they were taking in each year, leaving them with deficits on an annual basis and debt loads over time. Undoubtedly the situation was serious, as more and more tax dollars went to pay interest on the debt.

There have been great debates about what caused these fiscal problems. In the dominant theory, we need look no farther for the explanation than the welfare state itself. The debt was caused by inefficient state bureaucracies (see Ruggie 1996, ch. 1), as well as by what the OECD described as "demands of public sector staff" (OECD 1995, 19). Public choice analysts in particular saw bureaucrats protecting their own interests rather than protecting the public. The theory assumes such interests inevitably lead to expansion, although the significant variation among states in terms of expansion would tend to deny this claim (see, for example, Sainsbury 1996; Ruggie 1996). Certainly the for-profit sector has these tendencies. Indeed, because the aim of the for-profit sector is growth, it is difficult to see how privatization will lead to contraction. It is the case that unionization spread in the public sector during this period. Brought together in large, public sector workplaces, women in particular had demanded better wages and conditions of work. However, they had started from very low levels indeed and wages, especially at the top, are often significantly lower in the public sector than in the for-profit one.

The dominant theory also found the explanation for the debt in overspending on social services, services that simultaneously created dependencies while undermining the incentive to work. Too many people saw the social wage as a right and benefits were too generous. Abuse was rampant, especially among lone-parent women and the users of health care, the majority of whom are women. There was not enough emphasis on responsibility and individual initiative. At the same time, regulation of the market and high taxes, combined with strong labour and high wages, acted as a disincentive to investment. Yet two economists examining the growth in debt in Canada concluded that "Expenditures on social programs did not contribute significantly to the growth of government spending relative to the GDP" (Mimto and Cross 1991, 1). Instead, the debt was largely the result of the way it was financed, of interest rates and of the reduction of taxes on some areas. Moreover, Canada has quite low employment taxes compared to other industrial countries and our overall tax rates compare favourably with those in the United States, suggesting high taxes cannot explain much of the debt in industrial countries (Armstrong and Armstrong 1998, table 6.5).

It is nonetheless important to note that unemployment rose throughout the industrial world after changes in monetarist policies in the 1970s. This in turn contributed to rising social expenses. But it is debatable whether or not this rise was caused by the welfare state alone. In *Public Sector Change and the*

Crisis of Governance, the authors argue that it was "the contradictions of monetarist fiscal policy mixed with the Keynesian welfare state system that necessarily produced the political economy of public debt" (Shields and Evans 1998, 23). Whatever the cause, the rising unemployment rates also served to limit the strength of labour and women's movement demands on both governments and corporations.

Certainly health expenditures continued to grow, as they had throughout the postwar period, and these expenditures are not as directly related to unemployment. According to the OECD, it was "the pace of technological development in the health sector, and the demands of governments to constrain both total spending and the rising expectations of consumers" that were major factors leading to health care reform (OECD 1996, 7). But the data also indicate that the most rapidly rising costs were those related to sectors dominated by for-profit management and those that involved private, rather than public, expenditures. Indeed, public health systems have been the most successful at cost control (Brouselle 1998, 52). This would suggest that the problem was not exclusively to be found in the welfare state expenditures. Employment and labour costs did rise, although not at the same rate. This money, moreover, cannot be treated simply as an expense. The mainly female labour force contributes directly to the economy by spending their earnings and paying their taxes.

The debt, combined with new pressures to compete globally as a result of liberalized trade policies, is frequently offered as a reason to reduce public expenditure on health care, especially now that deficits seem to have largely disappeared. However, as economist Harold Chorney demonstrates, debt burdens were not nearly as high as they were in the immediate postwar period when governments chose to develop the welfare state (Chorney 1996, 358). There are still choices today, as the variations in national strategies attest (see Sainsbury 1996).

The Limits to Care

Another factor encouraging reform was a growing conviction about the limits of public care (Blomqvist and Brown 1994). This idea about limits took at least two forms. The first had to do with the notion that the demands on health care were unlimited, especially in the face of an aging population (Lawrence 1996, 12). According to Struthers, the issue is far from new. As early as 1941, Toronto hospitals started discharging elderly patients into nursing homes as a way of saving money. Politicians began talking about the "astounding increase in the number of persons living beyond 65 years of age," describing it as "the greatest social problem of our day" (Struthers 1997, 174, 196). The same language is being used four decades later to talk about the need for restraint (OECD 1996, 11). Yet Henry Aaron points out in his presentation to the OECD that "the aging of populations cannot account for much of the growth of health care spending" and the effect varies significantly from country to country (Aaron 1996, 52). Countries have had significant numbers in the oldest age groups without bankrupting their public systems. Aaron argues that the "most important demographic influence behind rising costs is declining birth rates" (ibid.) because of the impact it has on the ratio of elderly to non-elderly. The majority of those in the elderly population and all of those who bear children are women – so policy that looks to these demographic factors for explanations of rising costs is necessarily looking to women.

Few of these discussions about the unlimited demand for care link this demand to advertisements produced by the for-profit sectors promising wonder cures for everything from memory loss to sexual dysfunction, from cancer and infertility to incontinence and hot flushes. More common is a focus on doctors and the claim that they use their power to create demand in order to enhance their incomes. As the OECD document on *Health Care Reform* notes, "government efforts to control costs have been hampered by a reluctance to withdraw the power conferred on doctors to decide what medical care is necessary and appropriate" (OECD 1996, 7). Women's groups too have been critical of over-treatment, linking this to fee-for-service payment as well as to the medical model.

Another limit that is increasingly part of health care reform discussions relates to the determinants of health and the impact of health care on health. As the Preface to *Why Are Some People Healthy and Others Not? The Determinants of Health Of Populations* puts it, "the effectiveness of traditional medical care as a determinant of health and well-being has been coming under increasing scrutiny" (Evans, Barer and Marmor 1994, xii). Women's groups have been particularly active in pointing out the need for policies that look not only at the prevention of disease and the promotion of health but at conditions such as poverty and employment that have a profound impact on health. They have also been central to a critique of current health practices. The risk here is that the arguments will be used to reduce investment in health care without either changing the way the remaining care is delivered or addressing the determinants of health inside or outside the health care system (Robertson 1998).

Technology

Technological change has helped treat more diseases and prolong life. The consequence of this may be greater medical costs, as more people survive with significant medical problems that are treated with expensive technologies and care. Women's groups have been ambivalent about these technologies, especially in the area of reproduction (Rehner 1989).

While on one hand, they may create possibilities; on the other, the technologies may limit opportunities for healthy lives not only for patients but for providers. Technologies have an equally contradictory impact on cost. The increased intensity of services is a major factor in rising health costs. And estimates indicate that "one third of the increase in intensity was due to new technology and two-thirds was due to small technological improvements" (Abel-Smith 1996, 27). At the same time, technologies have helped reduce institutional costs by making more ambulatory care possible. Technologies have also contributed to the shortening of patient stays, in that new methods have made possible less invasive surgery as well as more care in the home.

However, as women in particular have pointed out, the cost savings may be mainly realized through a shifting in care responsibilities from publicly funded institutions to private homes, where it is mainly women who provide the care (see, for example, Armstrong *et al.* 1994; Aronson and Neysmith 1997; Chappell 1993; Glazer 1993). In addition, the shifting of care to the home sends the risks of care to the home, along with the expenses. Both providers and patients may be at risk. For the patients, untrained providers may inadvertently provide inadequate or inappropriate care. Home conditions may be unsafe, not only in terms of exposure to bacteria and viruses, but also in terms of a hostile environment. For providers, lack of training may result in injuries, and increased stress. Even those providers who have the skills may find themselves at risk in isolated environments, with few technical or social supports. Moreover, technologies have important implications for how health care is conceptualized and for power and control as well as for ethics and access. As Abby Lippman (1998) points out in her discussion of geneticization,

> While research, services, and policy networks that validate women's experiences as a way to promote their health are set in motion (for example, the five recently funded Centres of Excellence for Women's Health Research in Canada), parallel developments associated with geneticization are likely to present a formidable challenge to maintaining health issues as collective and political rather than individual and medical. (65)

Increasingly, choice in health care is being talked about in terms of consumer preferences and customer satisfaction surveys. The discourse in the new paradigm is that of the market, with talk of one-stop shopping becoming commonplace. In a book subtitled *A Blueprint for Canadian Health Care Reform*, for example, the authors recommend that "The Physician should shop on behalf of his [sic] patient to provide the best possible service at the most effective cost" (Jerome-Forget and Forget 1998, 15).

Health Care as a Business

The new paradigm in a host of international organizations and agreements is exemplified by the fact that the World Bank, rather than the World Health Organization, has increasingly taken the lead in health sector development (Koivusalo 1997, 18). Debts incurred in the wake of the 1973 rise in petroleum prices and of lending, borrowing and investment practices left many countries faced with structural adjustment programs established by the World Bank and International Monetary Fund (IMF). The imposed guidelines promote market-oriented, open economies, reduced state support and privatization of services (see ibid.; Scarpaci 1989). Even the guidelines for gender-based analysis that are increasingly part of the international package specify privatization as a basic tenet of health care reform.

Searching for new areas for investment and profit growth, corporations have found that health care is in many ways an "unopened oyster" (Peterson 1997, 299; see also Fuller 1991 and Nelson 1995). In many countries, most services have been provided by the state or by non-profit organizations, leaving plenty of room for expansion by for-profit firms. Until relatively recently, the United States also had a large proportion of public and non-profit organizations involved in health care. But this has changed rapidly. "By 1994, for-profit health maintenance organizations had more enrollees than their not-for-profit counterparts, which had previously dominated the scene." Hospitals too increasingly became for-profit, often as part of a Managed Care package. Hospital saw their aggregate profits increase by 25 per cent in 1996, with aggregate profits rising from $5.6 billion in 1988 to $21.3 billion in 1996 (Bellandini 1998, 68). The profit growth reflects the movement of large corporations into the health sector and the mergers and consolidations that have taken place as they seek to eliminate the competition through both vertical and horizontal integration. In the United States, over half the population enrolled in HMOs are in the four largest firms (Thorpe 1997, 343). Similar patterns are evident in the very profitable drug industries: industries that have been the subject of extensive critiques for their impact on women.

This kind of consolidation, especially under a paradigm that favours markets, gives such corporations significant power. In his introduction to a special issue of the *Journal of Health Politics, Policy, and the Law*, Mark Peterson (1997) points out that:

> At the table of health care decision-makers, capitalists – investors, shareholders, and the managers of capital markets – thus demand greater recognition, and by the nature of their activities, wield increased control over both public and private policy agenda. (299)

At the same time, choices are reduced for both providers and patients as firms seek greater control over costs. Their influence is evident not only within the United States but also within the international organizations such as the World Bank, where the United States has significant power. It is evident as well in international trade agreements that stress the liberalization of markets, including those covering health care, and that limit state intervention in health services.

Models for Health Care Reform

Efficiency and Choice

While reform is not new, what marks the difference between current reforms and those of the past is a paradigm shift. The new paradigm is a business paradigm, based on a belief in market strategies and for-profit managerial techniques. It assumes a definition of health as a market commodity and of patients as consumers. Although it is acknowledged that "the health care sector lacks some of the basic features of a 'free' market," it is assumed that "the introduction of market-like mechanisms creates incentives for improving efficiency, and possibly also effectiveness and quality, depending on the competence and expertise of the purchaser" (Christie 1996, 14). The imperfections of the health care market can be addressed by "managed competition," defined by the OECD (1992) as

> government regulation of a health care market which uses competition as the means to achieve efficiency objectives within a framework of government intervention designed to achieve other policy objectives such as equity. (10)

There is, then, an acknowledgment that markets do not lead to equity when left on their own and that not only state intervention but public financing is required. It is also recognized that "systems based on market principles, notably the United States system, are far from optimal when it comes to allocating resources" (Jönsson 1996, 8). At the same time, this recognition is combined with an assumption that efficiency produced by competition is necessarily good and results in both greater choice and efficiency.

A popular response to these contradictory concepts, at least among those supporting a business approach, is an internal market, where funds and some regulation would still come from government but more of the rest would be privatized and allocated by market mechanisms (Jerome-Forget and Forget 1998, 12). Within this internal market model, privatization takes various forms.

One form is the separation of purchaser from provider; that is, governments no longer provide services. Instead, they purchase them from competing providers. This is intended to increase efficiency by encouraging providers to compete with each other for the health care market and to provide governments as well as patients with choices. Canada already has such a separation, given that governments do not directly provide most services and doctors are not employees of the state. However, there has not been a tradition of competition among these providers for patients or financing.

There are several problems with this competitive model in addition to the ones of equity acknowledged by the promoters. First, competitive behaviour "may not always make medical or scientific sense, since close co-operation with a broad range of colleagues over a broad range of areas is necessary for goods results" (Christie 1996, 14). Women in particular have stressed the need to develop teams in an effort to address the full range of health issues, and such competition could undermine cooperation of this sort. The lack of competition among Canadian health providers has also supported coordination activities across services. Second, competition is more expensive. It increases administrative and other costs, as the American system demonstrates (Himmelstein and Woolhandler 1994). Deber et al., for example, conclude that "competition and markets for services perceived as necessary appear to increase costs, rather than constrain them" (Deber et al. 1998). Third, competition encourages unnecessary duplication. It requires a host of providers who do the same thing and thus means there are extra services that can lose the competition. Fourth, competition can lead to monopolies, as the winning providers eliminate the competition (Jönsson 1996, 39). In many areas of countries such as Canada, there will not be a range of providers to compete in the first place. Indeed, the problem is not one of selecting among services but one of encouraging services to locate there, especially in rural and northern areas. Fifth, competition often means lack of continuity. It can result in fluctuations in the supply of services and in the provider. Sixth, the privatization of services often creates the need for greater government regulation, as well as the need for governments to continue to operate in the unprofitable areas and provide for people that the private sectors avoid. Those most likely to be left out are poor women and those with disabilities. It thus may mean more rather than less government intervention and less choice. Equally important, it may lower quality because "the producer with the lowest price may not necessarily be the one who gives best value for the money" (ibid.)

Another form of privatization – one that could also be classified as a purchaser/provider split – is the contracting out of services. In this approach, hospitals or governments contract out all or part of a service to those who bid on the job. Contracting out has all the problems of the purchaser/provider competitive model. In addition, there is no reason to believe that contracting will lead to savings in the long run. While competition and the transfer of services to private providers may reduce short-term costs, there is evidence to suggest this is short-lived. As Starr so succinctly puts it, "the contractors could scarcely be expected to exert less pressure for higher spending than do the much maligned public employees" (Starr 1987, 5). Instead, contracting may primarily lead to rising demands and increasing influence from for-profit firms. Struthers' research on Ontario long-term care facilities certainly bears this out (Struthers 1997). Moreover, the contracting out of services can undermine both continuity and institutional memory. Loyalty to the main organization is also harder to maintain. And while contracting out can increase flexibility, it may reduce the capacity to monitor performance and reorganize overall service processes (Starr 1987, 7).

Partnerships are yet another form of privatization. Instead of, or in addition to, selling state organizations or contracting out services to the lowest bidder, governments promote partnerships between public and private sector organizations. These may be voluntary and non-profit or for-profit. The idea is that shared expertise and resources can be brought to bear on service organization and delivery. As Rekart (1993) points out, such partnerships can push voluntary or public agencies to conform more and more to for-profit practices. This could have some positive results but the emphasis may be on cost more than on service, and alternative ways of providing care that have been promoted particularly by women could be eliminated. Partnerships also shift the balance of power. This too could be positive and/or negative for providers and patients. The partner with more resources is likely to end up with more power, and this more powerful partner is more likely to be a for-profit organization, especially in the context of a business paradigm.

An additional problem with partnerships is confidentiality. Because they are assumed to operate in a competitive setting, organizations may resist making decisions and information public. Public accountability is more difficult when organizational practices are not readily transparent.

In searching for efficiency under the new reform paradigm, health care organizations are also adopting management techniques developed in the for-profit sector. Indeed, the problems are frequently seen as managerial ones that can be solved through the expertise of managers. Women's groups have been among those concerned about the lack of continuity and integration in the health care services. They have also suggested there was waste and inappropriate hierarchy in the system. Better management could help address these concerns.

However, there is not a great deal of evidence to support the assumption that the for-profit techniques are necessarily more efficient or that they are applicable to the health sector (Armstrong *et al.* 1997). And there is growing scepticism about the downsizing, flexible labour practices, just-in-time production and flattened-hierarchy strategies many private firms have adopted. There is, however, evidence to indicate that costs savings are achieved primarily through lower wages, poorer quality care and a shifting of costs along with responsibility to patients (Glazer 1993; Deber *et al.* 1998). Private, for-profit providers are also less likely to have unionized staff and often hire part-time or casual labour (Starr 1978, 7). This should not be surprising, given that most of service costs are labour ones and that for-profit firms need to add on profit to their bill. Equally important, their efficiencies are sometimes achieved through a denial of care, or through a careful selection of the least demanding patients. In short, the savings result more from paying the mainly female providers less, offering them less training or transferring care to the unpaid, usually female providers in the home than they do from the elimination of waste.

Central to the new paradigm is the notion that governments should not do what the private sector could do. Combined with pressure to cut government expenditures and eliminate unnecessary care, it has led to state withdrawal from some areas of care and to the failure to cover some new areas or technologies. In the absence of the state, private and often for-profit organizations move in to fill the gap. This form of privatization goes beyond the purchaser/provider split because the cost is borne entirely either by private insurance or by the individual.

Effectiveness and Accountability

Just as governments have increasingly looked to market mechanisms and market management for solutions to perceived problems with efficiency and choice, so too have they looked to market mechanisms and the for-profit sector for methods designed to increase effectiveness and accountability within the public sector.

One such method is the use of direct payments for services, variously called co-insurance, cost-sharing or deductibles. The assumption is that patients will value services more and use them more wisely if they have to pay something for the service. User fees are thus supposed to reduce abuse while bringing more money into the system. In a similar vein, parallel private and public services are promoted as a means of reducing waiting lists, making the rich pay and increasing resources in the public system. Economist Robert Evans refers to such user fees as "zombies," strategies that were discredited long ago yet keep arising in spite of their inadequacy (Evans *et al.* 1994).

A series of Canadian studies have demonstrated that user fees neither reduce abuse nor lead to more effective use of health services (see especially Barer *et al.* 1994). The main reason is that:

> health care isn't like other products and the "market" for health care cannot be analyzed the same way as the market for shoes and VCRs....people do not often have sufficient notice in advance to make correct judgements about necessity. This is precisely why they consult physicians. (Stoddart *et al.* 1993, 7)

What user fees do is tax the sick, the disabled and the frail elderly, a majority of whom are women and many of whom are poor women. They increase administrative costs and bureaucratic processes and sometimes put more money in doctors' hands, without changing much about the way health care is delivered.

Nor do parallel private and public systems reduce cost, bring more money to the system or even increase access. Research in Manitoba on cataract surgery found that private clients served to increase costs without significantly improving access. Moreover, they tended to decrease efficiency, at least in terms of physicians who worked in both the private and public systems (DeCoster and Brownell 1997). British research indicates that "far from improving access, privately financed care appears to worsen it" (Deber and Swan 1998, 335).

Another important approach to effectiveness that has emerged in recent years is evidence-based decision-making. Throughout the OECD countries, there is increasing stress on scientific evidence and on accountability defined in terms of numerical measurement. In the new paradigm, "effectiveness means doing the right thing, at the right time and in the right way," based on the assumption that it is possible to determine scientifically precisely what that is (Christie 1996, 13). Managerial practices assume "if you can't measure it you can't manage it," based on the assumption that everything that is important can be counted and can be counted accurately (Newcomer quoted in WGHSU 1994, 16). What counts is what can be counted, or measured or determined through randomized trials. Management science is united with medical science, to allow greater control over providers and patients alike.

There is little dispute that such evidence is essential in both clinical and policy decisions. Indeed, women's groups have frequently called for more evidence and used such evidence in making arguments for reform. But evidence, and the new emphasis on evidence-based decision-making, is a gender issue for a variety of reasons.

What constitutes evidence is a gender issue, as are the problems or areas addressed, the definitions as well as the methods used and the conclusions drawn. Two kinds of evidence are privileged in health reform. The numerical data of the sort that measures such things as number of beds and nurses per population, such processes as length of stay, required nursing time and outcomes, and such attitudes as patient satisfaction. But no number is innocent, as Deborah Stone (1997) so succinctly put it. What is counted, how it is counted, how it is processed and what is done with what is found are value-laden choices, ones that are frequently biased against women or at least fail to take their interests, their locations and their critiques into account. Indeed, the very privileging of quantitative data conflicts with gender-based analysis.

The second kind of privileged evidence is clinical. Here the gold standard is the randomized clinical trial. But as those who argue for gender-based analysis have demonstrated, the standard has too often been set on trials conducted with a 70 kilogram male (Laurence and Weinhouse 1997, 5). More attention has been paid to this bias than to the bias in the numerical data, perhaps because it is so obvious. However, efforts to address the problems have too often been restricted to including women in trials, and the bias that arises from problem selection, methodologies and the categories used for analysis have been a much less frequent concern (Oakley 1990).

Yet both kinds of evidence are assumed to be objective. Central to gender-based analysis is a critique of objectivity, both as an ideal and as a practice. Of course, feminists are not alone or even original in their contention that all evidence is socially constructed by social beings, based on culturally bound notions of value and limited by the particular context in which the evidence is developed. What is much less common is the positive value feminists place on recognizing the locations of the researchers, their personal experiences and knowledge acquired though experience. Nor are feminists original in their suspicions of numbers. Like other critical theorists, feminists have recognized the complexity of social phenomena and attached particular importance to the context in which data are collected. Feminists move beyond the kind of criticism such theorists make, however, when they stress the gender-specific nature of the scientific gaze and the critical aspects of health care rendered invisible by the emphasis on quantitative methods (see, for example, Armstrong 1998; Moss 1996; Stein 1997; Sherwin 1998).

A gender-based analysis, then, does not reject evidence. Nor does it restrict concepts and methods for evidence gathering to those associated with qualitative approaches or to what Nelson calls "the socially created cognitive category of 'feminine'" (Nelson 1995). Indeed, calls for gender-based analysis often draw on quantitative sources to demonstrate the need for such analysis. For example, statistics have been used to establish the female domination of care work, the connections between reductions in public services and the expansion of women's unpaid care work, the preponderance of women among patients and those who take family members for care, and the unequal position of women in the health care field. Statistics have also been used to reveal the systemic discrimination imbedded in the market and to show that women enjoy better access in public health systems. However, feminists see "the pursuit of precision alone, without richness, as a vice" (Davis and Hersh quoted in Nelson 1995, 30). In the feminist perspective, there is rarely a single, right way, right time or right thing to be done.

The issue in evidence-based decision-making is larger than the problem of limited methods and subjects. It is also the transformation of the evidence available into formulas for care. Such formulas not only undermine the provider's decision-making power – as indeed they are often intended to do – they increase the likelihood that equity will be defined in terms of sameness, with everyone subjected to uniform care. Feminists in particular have stressed the importance of recognizing context and differences, history and values, in making the health care decisions that are as much art as science. Within the context of a business paradigm, evidence may be used more to control and limit than to improve quality of care based on individual locations and choice.

Basing everything on evidence has the additional risk of transforming what are political choices into technological ones to be made by experts; in other words, to revert to the model women have been so critical of in the past. There is, of course, a problem with stressing diversity and individual decision-making to the extent that no generalization is possible. In gathering evidence, "the issue then is not that all intervention is bad but rather what kind of intervention was involved, when, for what reasons, on what women and performed by whom" (Mitchinson 1998, 136, 138). The evidence should then be used as the basis of decision-making, not as the decision itself.

CANADIAN REFORMS

Canada has been an active participant in these international developments, sharing many of the assumptions and values that are central to the new paradigm. Like other nations, it has been faced with a large and growing public debt, along with large and growing health care costs. By 1995, the debt load represented 26 per cent of federal spending, while "federal program spending net of transfer payments was only 19 per cent" (Swimmer 1996, 1). Provinces and territories too had debts and deficits. And a much bigger share of their budgets went to health. Such debts have been an important catalyst in, and justification for, reform.

The solutions in Canada, like those internationally, were sought in market and management mechanisms. As Gene Swimmer (1996), in *How Ottawa Spends*, says, the cuts

> have been portrayed as a change in philosophy toward reducing the role of the federal government by devolving responsibilities to other levels of government and to the private and voluntary sectors; reducing transfer payments to provinces, individuals, and businesses; applying

private sector management techniques to those federal government activities that remain. (1-2)

Like the authors of *Reinventing Government*, the Canadian federal finance minister in 1995 made a commitment to "getting government right" (Martin 1995). The Program Review undertaken by all government departments had a "partnership test" that asked, "What activities or programs should or could be transferred in whole or in part to the private or voluntary sector?" (Paquet and Shepherd 1996, 25). Provinces such as Alberta and Ontario went further than the federal government in stressing that individuals should be responsible for their own welfare (ibid.). Governments in all jurisdictions in Canada, however, have regularly reaffirmed their commitment to the *Canada Health Act*. Paradoxically, "getting government right" through private-sector managerial strategies and some privatization has frequently been presented as the only way to save the public system in the face of rising costs, rising demands and the limits of care. But there remains a significant remnant of the philosophy that guided the welfare state in the platforms of political parties. And women in particular continue to show strong support for their public health care system.

International Agreements

State support for trade liberalization and privatization, combined with a continuing commitment to some form of public involvement in health care, is evident in the negotiations of trade agreements.

There is some disagreement about the extent to which health care falls under the trade agreements. According to Judy D'Arcy, president of CUPE, the union that represents a large number of female health care workers, the original Free Trade Agreement (FTA)

> explicitly allows for American private sector management of all hospitals (general, children's, psychiatric, or extended care), ambulance services, various types of clinics, nursing homes, homes for the disabled, single mothers and the emotionally disabled, together with all aspects (i.e., not just the management) of other social services like medical labs. (D'Arcy 1998, 19)

The FTA permits the management of any public health care service by American-owned profit-making groups, even when most of the money still comes from the Canadian taxpayer.

Monique Bégin, former Minister of Health and Welfare Canada, has argued that this means "any American business could come and buy Canadian hospitals and take over their management. Hospitals are not government services and are not excluded from the free trade agreement" (Bégin 1998). In areas such as nursing homes, rehabilitation services and medical laboratories where for-profit services are already established, the door is wide open to American firms. Indeed, such corporations have moved quickly to expand in all these areas. Colleen Fuller (1993) maintains that private management firms have not yet taken over the hospital sector primarily because the *Canada*

Health Act's requirement for public administration has provided some protection. However, with the federal government collapsing funding for health care into the Canada Health and Social Transfer, the *Canada Health Act* may provide less protection against for-profit takeovers in the future.

While the federal government was altering the funding for health care, it negotiated a new free trade deal that supersedes the provinces. NAFTA "will eventually bind provincial and municipal levels of government to its rules" (Maher 1993, 13). The proposed Agreement on Internal Trade was intended to help this process by eliminating trade barriers among provinces. Under such an agreement, opening one province to for-profit American firms could mean that every province was open to such business. British Columbia has been particularly hostile to this development, fearing that a move by one province to welcome for-profit health care or professional groups would mean that no province could resist (McKenna 1996, B1; Fuller 1995, 11).

Although NAFTA seemed to protect areas designed for a public purpose, it also set up a process to review excluded services such as health, "to determine the extent to which they constitute indirect subsidies to Canadian trade" (Maher 1993). Given that cars cost more to produce in the United States in large measure because of health care benefits, it is possible that Canadian medicare could be defined as an unfair subsidy. Under NAFTA, governments had until March 31, 1996 to submit a list of programs and services they wanted to shield from NAFTA rules. Fearing that market principles would prevail in the very lucrative health care field, the Canadian Health Coalition launched a campaign to protect medicare. They were joined by several provincial governments. But perhaps the most effective advocacy came from a legal opinion commissioned by the Coalition. Bryan Schwartz, an advocate of free trade, challenged the federal claim that health care would be protected under NAFTA. According to this Winnipeg professor of law,

> To the extent that NAFTA applies to a health sector, it would permit for-profit United States enterprises to enter and operate in Canada. Annex II of NAFTA shields health care from the full force of NAFTA, but only to the extent that "it is a social service" that is maintained or provided "for a public purpose." (Schwartz 1996, 1)

As long as services are fully funded from the public purse, they may be protected. As soon as services are de-listed or even when user charges are allowed, "NAFTA may guarantee the right of United States commercial enterprises to enter the market or expand their presence" (ibid.). The "grey" areas such as physiotherapy that involve both public and private money are particularly at risk. This opinion was supported by Barry Appleton, a Toronto-based international trade lawyer, and by a variety of community groups as well.

The campaign by this coalition of church groups, seniors' organizations, student federations, anti-poverty organizations, women's organizations and unions was successful in drawing attention to the danger of the reservation clause. In response, the federal government entered negotiations with the NAFTA partners to reach agreement on the general reservation. According to this agreement, all reservable provincial and state laws and regulations, with the exception of financial services, are protected under NAFTA. Existing public health and social services are to be excluded from NAFTA foreign investment rules, so the individual services did not have to be specified before the March 31 date. The letter of agreement demonstrated that the trade deals are not irrevocable and that politics can make a difference. But it did not provide any protection from privatization within Canada, nor did it protect these privatized services from NAFTA rules. According to former senior Canadian government trade negotiator Mel Clark,

> For practical purposes, NAFTA gives the United States the absolute right to countervail any Canadian export on the grounds that its production was subsidized by medicare, and that this right nullifies the imprecise, conditional limited Canadian rights contained Annex I and II of NAFTA. (Clark 1999, 11)

Trade liberalization, as Marjorie Cohen (1987) in particular has demonstrated, has an impact on whether women have paid work, and what kind of paid work they have. It may also have an impact on whether or not they have access to health care, and on what kind of care they have access to.

The liberalization push did not end with NAFTA. Canada was also an active participant in the attempt to introduce the Multilateral Agreement on Investment (MAI). The definition of investment included subsidies to health care, education, child and elder care. "By signing the MAI, nation states would cede the right to regulate foreign corporations in all these areas" (Clarke and Barlow 1998, 11). For now, this agreement is on hold, in part as a result of protests from various citizen groups around the world, not least the Council of Canadians headed by Maude Barlow. However, the new free trade agreement being negotiated to include the south and Latin America puts health care on the table once again.

Downsizing and Devolution

The federal government has led the way in downsizing health care. The provinces have followed suit, especially in the wake of the cuts in federal transfers to the provinces when support for health, education and social services were rolled together and dramatically reduced in the 1995 Canada Health and Social Transfer.

Government cutbacks on public sector employment and wage controls have had a profound philosophical impact and a profound impact on the gender balance of employment (see Day and Brodsky 1998). Five major industries (government services, communication and other utilities, education, health, and social services) account for over 93 percent of female public sector employees and over three-quarters of all unionized female workers (Akyeampong 1998, 31). These industries have provided women most of their best jobs. Union members are more likely to have permanent employment and, when they do have part-time jobs, to have more hours of work each week (ibid, 34). Their wages and benefits are significantly better than those of non-union employees, and those of public sector workers are significantly better than those in the private sector (CCSD 1997).[2] Although many women in the broader public sector are not direct employees of the state, they are often lumped together with government employees and tax dollars pay most of their wages, even when their employer is a for-profit organization. In making cuts to the public sector, the federal government has established a model for reform that is undermining many of the gains women have made and has reinforced a philosophy that blames public sector employees. Some of the provinces have gone farther and even taken a lead in undermining labour gains and thus women's advancements through the public sector. There is already evidence that the result is both job and wage loss as the public sector becomes more like the private one (Akyeampong 1998, app.).

Federal cutbacks to health started long before those in the civil service. The federal government began reducing its financial contributions to health care only a decade after public medical insurance was introduced. In 1977, the Liberal government moved away from the commitment to pay half of all provincial costs, introducing instead a formula designed both to make the contribution more predictable and to reduce the federal contribution. The Established Program Financing scheme put a limit on growth but continued to allow for some increase and to equalize payments among provinces. It also expanded the definition of care to make it possible for provinces to include more than hospital and doctor expenses. In 1986 and again in 1989, the Conservative government limited transfers. A total freeze was introduced in 1990. A further reduction came in 1995, when the Liberal federal government announced the Canada Health and Social Transfer (CHST). The introduction of the CHST meant it was no longer possible to determine how much the federal government contributed to health care, and the provinces had much greater leeway in how they spent the transfer dollars.

In consequence, it became more difficult for the federal government to enforce the principles of the *Canada Health Act*. The Social Union Agreement among the federal and provincial/territorial governments (except Quebec) includes a commitment to the five principles of the *Canada Health Act*, but no enforcement mechanism (Canada 1999). The provinces and territories promised to spend any new money on health, but there is no guarantee that the increased federal allocations for health are being spent in a manner that conforms to the principles.

Provinces and territories responded to these reductions in federal funding with a variety of strategies. As is the case at the federal level, such strategies do not simply reflect the pressure to cut costs. They also reflect a new philosophy about government responsibility, about the involvement of the for-profit sector and about health care limitations. In the 1970s, the provinces and territories mainly introduced global budgets for service organizations. In the 1990s, the strategies were quite different. Reports commissioned in virtually all the provinces stressed the limits of health care and the importance of health promotion. But reform was framed primarily as a managerial issue. Care delivery was to be relocated from hospitals to homes and other institutions, and coordinated for the most part through regional bodies and primary care. Both the reorganization of work within institutions and the coordination of services outside them were based on private sector management techniques. The emphasis is on what the management literature calls core competencies. In health terms, this means focusing on "basic insurance services" and leaving the rest to supplemental health insurance, private payment and private delivery (for a summary see Angus 1992; Deber, Mhatre and Baker 1994).

The strategies were summarized as "spending smarter and spending less" (Sutherland and Fulton 1994), with a new emphasis on evidence and outcomes, effectiveness (Dorland and Davis 1996) and care "closer to home" (BCRCHC 1991). In many ways, the various reports picked up on women's critiques of health care reform. The recommendations for the shift from institution to community, from centre to region and from physician to non-physician seemed to address their concerns, especially when combined with primary care, greater integration, more local control through regionalization and more continuity though integration. Most reports also considered the working conditions and the morale of providers, although seldom in terms of care in the home.

Hospitals have been a major target for reform, not surprisingly, given their high consumption of tax dollars, the attacks on their practices and their heavy reliance on a unionized, female labour force. Technologies have helped shorten patient stays, and increase ambulatory care and day-surgery. They have also been used to reorganize work, monitor providers and transfer labour to workers with less formal training. As is the case in the for-profit sector, hospital services have been vertically and horizontally integrated. Hospitals have also been redefined to focus exclusively on acute care. Acute care has in turn been more and more narrowly defined to include only the most severe and short-term illness or injury. This redefinition has important implications for patients and providers, not the least of which is a renewed emphasis on the medical model.

The patients that providers deal with now are all very sick and require intensive care services. As a result, the work is not only harder and more intense, but there is less time to get to know the patients or feel the satisfaction that comes from helping individuals recover their health (Armstrong *et al.* 1997, 2000). Combined with the managerial emphasis on measurement and monitoring, the result is often a loss of control for the providers. For the patient, the redefinition means that care under the protection of the *Canada Health Act* is short-lived, given that it fully covers only hospital and doctor care. Those who remain in hospital for more than a very short period are increasingly described as abusers or bed blockers. Most of these "abusers" are women. As for those who are forced to leave hospital "quicker and sicker," the impact is only now being described by research. Given that the extent of public involvement in both the funding and delivery of home care and long-term care varies significantly among the provinces and territories, it is likely that the impact on women will vary as well. And it will vary from woman to woman, depending on their location, capacities and resources.

Cutbacks in hospitals have significantly reduced employment opportunities for registered nurses in particular. While employment for nurses grew by 36 per cent between 1966 and 1971, the growth declined with budget reductions and came to a halt in 1992. Between 1993 and 1996, nearly 8,000 positions disappeared. And because these data count nurses rather than jobs, they understate the number of full-time jobs that disappeared. They also understate the extent to which nurses work on contract, either as individuals or as employees of nurse registries, and thus with less security and fewer benefits, and perhaps lower pay. During the 1993-94 period, the total number of RNs in Canada remained unchanged, a reflection of both the education cutbacks and the poor job prospects for nurses (Ryten 1997, table 3). This has, in turn, led to what is now recognized as a shortage of RNs. Meanwhile, more of the work is being done by women with less formal training. Sometimes this is appropriate, but the use of what are often called "generic" workers with little if any training may put both providers and patients at risk (Sky 1995).

Within hospitals, non-nursing jobs are being privatized. Some of the work of cleaning, food preparation and maintenance has been redefined as "hotel services" and contracted out to the lowest bidder. Such a redefinition flies in the face of a determinants of health approach and the research that demonstrates that good food and clean environments are critical to health. It is mainly women who do this non-nursing work, and they have long defined themselves as health care workers, not hotel workers (White 1990). As is the case with other managerial decisions, this contracting out is only now being examined in terms of its impact on quality and cost. The results available suggest that neither efficiency nor effectiveness improve (CHEPA 1997).

Governments have also entered into partnerships with for-profit firms to deliver services previously delivered by the public sector. Laboratories are one example of shared services. The assumptions leading to this strategy are the same as for privatization; namely that the for-profit sector is more efficient and that the public sector should not do anything the private sector can do. The effects are often similar to other forms of privatization – job loss or lower wages for the mainly female workers and little long-term gain cost-benefits or quality.

Regionalization and decentralization strategies have been undertaken in many jurisdictions, on the assumption that decentralized structures will be more responsive to local needs and more effective in care delivery. However, there are important advantages in central planning and coordination, as well as in a collective determination of political principles. "Such decentralization may make the achievement of equity, efficiency, and cost control across the nation less easy" (Maynard 1996, 3) and could serve to undermine the principles of the *Canada Health Act*. Women's collective strength may well be less at the local and regional level than it is at the national one.

The devolution of care to the community has, in some instances, meant more emphasis on clinics providing primary care. Provinces have also moved to provide "one-stop shopping," single entry points for an array of home and long-term care services. Both strategies may be a mixed blessing for women. On the one hand, they may mean more coordinated and continuous care. On the other, the sole entry point may be used to cut back services as well as to extend them, especially in a context of budget reductions. And formulas for eligibility may serve to exclude many women, especially if these formulas fail to take important differences among women into account. Equally important, local authorities with shrinking budgets may have to sacrifice the public health measures that have been so important to women in favour of responding to the immediate demands for home and long-term care. Indeed, there is little evidence of new initiatives in the areas of traditional public health and some talk about privatizing services such as water as a means of bringing more money into local governments.

The last link in the devolution chain is the home, one place where women do most of the labour. Illnesses and treatments that were once restricted to institutions on the grounds that they required skilled care in a special environment have been transferred to the home, with mixed results for patients and providers. The transfer of care to the home is often presented not simply as a cost-saving measure, but as a response to people's preferences and as a means of providing more holistic care. But in their study of home-based care, Lesemann and Nahmiash (1993) conclude that

> these systems are under considerable pressure to resolve the financial constraints of large hospital institutions. Such pressure is unnatural for services which promote a different rationale for care and caregiving. It discourages a family and community dynamic which would pursue objectives of health, quality of life and well-being rather than respond to pathological problems and services caught up in the spiralling costs. If the institutional rationale does not undergo a major shift, the relief provided by the home care system to this clientele may only be temporary. (96)

Similarly, Aronson and Neysmith found that "home care workers' ability to deliver high quality, personalized care is compromised by organizational practices that speed up and intensify their work" (Aronson and Neysmith 1996). It is also compromised by the low value placed on the work, a value that reflects both the setting of the job and the sex of the workers. In other research on home care for the elderly by the same authors, they maintain that:

> the historical record suggests that it will be women from low income households who will be hired to provide most home care services. Thus the greatest risks will be carried by frail old persons and low income workers. In other words, it will be marginalized groups of

women who both deliver and receive the programs. (Neysmith and Aronson 1996, 12)

Especially in large metropolitan areas, these home care workers are often immigrant women who must deal daily with "racist attitudes and behaviour from clients and their families" (Neysmith and Aronson 1997, 497). And like other home care workers, they deal with the problems of isolation that expose them to the risk of violence and injury.

Many of these home care workers are employed by for-profit firms. Some forms of for-profit home care have always existed for private purchase but provincial governments have been experimenting with funding more for-profit care, even in the face of evidence that such care is significantly more expensive than that provided by government agencies (Shapiro 1997).

Although many women might prefer their own homes to the increasingly oppressive hospital environment, we cannot assume this to be the case for all women. As feminists have long made clear, many homes are not havens in a heartless world (McLeod 1980; Chappell, Strain and Blandford 1986). There are far too many women without safe homes to go to once they are discharged from institutions. And a larger number do not want to be a burden to their daughters, mothers or partners even when they have a home, and such homes are clean and comfortable. A Montreal study concluded that "maintaining the elderly in the community at all costs might in fact be at the expense of their caregivers" (Jutras and Veilleux 1991, 50). The same might be said of all caregiving, most of whose providers are women.

Yet another kind of devolution is evident in the health care provisions for Aboriginal peoples. The federal government has been transferring care services to the control of Aboriginal peoples themselves. Provinces too have been transferring control, or at least including Aboriginal peoples in decision-making bodies and developing strategies to make care delivery more culturally sensitive (Health Canada 1999). It remains to be seen whether these services will have sufficient resources and whether they will be sensitive to Aboriginal women's concerns.

Regulation, Liberalization and Partnerships

Consistent with international developments, Canada has combined the removal of regulations in some areas with more regulation in others. Drug regulation is a good example.

As a result of the trade negotiations, the Conservative federal government introduced Bill C-91 in 1993. This legislation eliminated compulsory licencing that allowed companies to manufacture and sell patented drugs once the companies that developed them had several years of exclusive sales. Under compulsory licencing, the company with the patent received a royalty to compensate for research, development and lower profits. Compulsory licencing was introduced after research demonstrated what the Quebec Royal Commission termed "the abusive prices of drugs" resulting from both foreign control of the drug industry and "a form of collusion in price setting" (quoted in Lesemann 1984, 145). Under compulsory licencing profits remained high, but pressure to remove this limit on patents was strong (ECIPI 1985). First in 1987, and then in 1993, Canada extended patent protection to brand name drugs for at least 20 years. Paradoxically, in the wake of free trade, pharmaceutical companies have been granted extensive monopolies through heavy state intervention.

The trade agreements have already had an impact on women's access to drugs by raising prices (CDMA n.d.). The effect of such patent legislation "is to limit competition and raise prices, and industry profits, thus contributing to the overall escalation of health costs in Canada" (National Forum on Health 1997a, 5). Some of these increased prices are paid for from tax dollars, given that the *Canada Health Act* requires that the medications necessary during hospital stays be covered by the public plan. But drugs are one of the factors making shorter patient stays and day surgery possible. And dehospitalization means more of the costs of drugs are covered by individuals, either through their insurance companies or out of pocket. As the National Forum on Health reports, private drug insurance is correlated with income. Only 7 per cent of those earning below $20,000 a year have private insurance to cover drug costs (ibid.). In 1995, 56 per cent of all women with labour force income earned less than $20,000 (Statistics Canada 1997, table 2). It is women, then, who are most likely to have to pay the full cost of these rising prices themselves.

Some provinces have responded to rising drug prices by introducing drug plans that favour both bulk purchasing and the least expensive drugs. The "reference-based pricing" system in British Columbia has helped to increase access and reduce costs, especially for the most vulnerable (Fitz-James 1996, 12). In addition, all provinces have long covered at least part of the costs of drugs for those on welfare and for the elderly, most of whom are women. However, the Forum concludes that governments are not doing enough to provide access to essential drugs, to control costs or encourage research (National Forum on Health 1997a, 7).

The Forum also concludes it is the pharmaceutical industry, rather than the government, that is steering research. According to the Forum, "'Partnerships' between the industry and particular granting agencies do not help; their research focus is still on drugs. The transfer must be arm's length, with no strings" (ibid., 8). It may well be that strings are attached in many partnerships – partnerships that are increasingly promoted by governments as the way research should or even must be done. Combined with the reductions in allocations for research and for educational institutions, the emphasis on partnerships may encourage researchers to shape their agendas to those of the partners with the money.

While trade liberalization has meant increased regulation in terms of drugs, it has promoted the freer movement of health care professionals across the border between Canada and the United States. NAFTA made "temporary status in the United States much simpler and quicker to obtain" (De Vortz and Laryea 1998, 9) and temporary status "has become a back door to permanent emigration." According to research conducted for the C.D. Howe Institute, the number of nurses who emigrated to the United States in 1993-94 was equal to 40 per cent of the 1991 graduating class (ibid., table 5). With cutbacks, many of these nurses had little choice but to leave Canada. Now many of these nurses are being wooed back with hospitals facing severe shortages. It should be noted, however, that Canada is more selective, and less liberal, when it comes to admitting nurses from countries other than the United States (Wotherspoon 1990).

Provinces and territories have also been looking at the regulation of health professions and of labour unions. In terms of professions, the tendency seems to be towards deregulation. More public input into the regulation of professions has been a common theme, as has change in the scope of practice legislation to reduce professional monopolies. The introduction of midwifery legislation is one example. As is the case in many areas, there are contradictory possibilities for women in these developments. On the one hand, women have argued for greater control over medical practices; Registered Nurses (RNs) argue that they could do much of what a physician does and Licenced or Registered Practical Nurses (LPNs) that they could do some of the work now done by RNs. On the other hand, the consequence could be that managerial decisions become more important than professional ones and that the lowest skilled or lowest paid workers are used.

In terms of unions, the tendency seems to be towards more regulation, or at least towards limits on union practices and scope. Unions may be further undermined by the contracting out of previously unionized work to the private sector, where regulations and conditions make unionization more difficult. Moreover, some of the legislative protections such as pay equity that women have won apply only to the public sector. So privatization may move women out from the protection of some rights legislation as well.

Like the federal government, other jurisdictions have been extending regulations in some areas and liberalizing them in others. For example, Ontario has introduced compulsory competitive bidding in aspects of home care, accompanied by an extensive set of regulations designed to ensure that the for-profit sector has a place. And, while the Ontario government removed employment equity legislation in the name of reducing state intervention, it also established a Commission with the power to close non-government owned hospitals. Similarly, the expansion of home care also expanded the rights of the state to require information from individual households and to inspect household finances.

Health protection activities offer another example of deregulation. The federal government has reduced the size and scope of its Health Protection Branch. With fewer researchers employed by the government to assess the safety of food, drugs, air, water and technologies, the government relies more on the organizations producing the products for evidence of their risks and effectiveness, and more on the corporations' financial contributions to fund the investigations. Again, popular pressure from women's groups and others may be forcing the government to reverse practices. The 1999 federal budget contained provision for the restoration of some of the Health Protection Branch cuts and pressures continue to mount for reregulation.

Some of the provinces have taken similar actions in areas under their jurisdictions. Health protection is a women's issue not only because women too breathe, eat, drink, use medical devices and take drugs but because women have long been active in efforts to protect the food, water, air, devices and drug supplies. Deregulation, cost recovery or the failure to take action in new areas of regulation such as genetically altered products and new technologies create particular risks for women. Health Canada explicitly recognized the gender-specific impact in their consultations on health protection (Health Canada 1998). Yet in the context of greater reliance on corporations to police themselves, it is unclear how gender issues will be taken into account or how a gender-based analysis will be effectively used.

Accountability, Information and Quality

The 1999 federal budget promised "report cards" on the health care system, committing $95 million to the project. The term "report cards" is a short form for what is variously described as an "accountability system" (Walker 1999, A7), providing details on "how well the health care system is working" (McIlroy 1999, A4), responding to a "need to know more about what we're getting for our money" (Toronto Star 1999, A6) and assessing quality. A wide range of data is to be collected and standardized, with a view to influencing policy development and implementation.

There is little dispute about whether or not such data could be useful for health care decision-making. Indeed, much has already been collected, and some has been used to promote women's issues. Women's groups have been among the most vocal in the call for more transparent decision-making and better research on quality. However, there is no guarantee that the new report cards will address women's concerns or provide them with the kind and quality of data they need.

The Advisory Council on Health Infostructure recommended to the health minister that the standards for information systems be set by the Canadian Institute for Health Information (CIHI) (ACHI 1999). Bringing together tasks previously carried out by Statistics Canada, Health Canada and various hospital associations, CIHI already exists as an independent agency intended to "define and adopt emerging standards for health care informatics" (CCIHI n.d.).

On its membership form, CIHI promises members "influence on the direction of national health care standards" and CIHI is described as having "substantial representation from the private sector" on its board of directors (Toronto Star 1999, A6). It is perhaps not surprising that private sector firms involved in the health care or health information business would be interested in membership, given this promise and the potential for profit growth in the information industry. It is more surprising that they are invited, given the potential for a conflict of interest. The representation from women's organizations or from the women who provide care in and out of the home may well be limited by the fact that voting memberships require contributions beginning at $1,000. The decisions made by this agency are not simply technical, although they are often presented as such. How categories are created and catalogued, processed and published can have a fundamental impact on care. In order to reach the objective of "public accountability and transparency" identified by *A Framework to Improve the Social Union for Canadians* (Canada 1999, 2) membership and transparency in the organization that sets the standards for the accounts is critical. It is also essential that it take women's critique and concerns into account.

The quality of information depends upon the context as well as on the power relations involved in all aspects of information development and use. As Susan Sherwin points out, the new emphasis on information for consumers is "built on a model of articulate, intelligent patients accustomed to making decisions about the course of their lives." Yet she questions "how much control individual patients really have over the determination of their treatment within the stressful world of health care services" (Sherwin 1998, 24). This is particularly the case in the context of massive changes in the health system, changes in which women as citizens have had little say. The report cards risk becoming formulas for care, rather than information to be used in providing care, formulas that replace professional judgement and patient choice while enhancing managerial power.

The report cards also have the risk of transforming what are fundamentally value decisions into expert ones. Women may be invited on boards and research teams as experts, and they may be able to influence how numbers are developed. This is necessary but insufficient to take women's concerns into account. The choices have to remain public choices that are recognized as value-laden, with women playing a major role in decision-making at all levels.

The discussions around information technologies are often presented as if they are mainly about clinical choices, patient satisfaction and scientific truth. It is important to recognize that information technologies are central to the new managerial paradigm in terms of controlling work and reorganizing where, when and how care is delivered and by whom. Most of these technologies have been developed by the for-profit sector that has built for-profit managerial techniques into them. They are based on assumptions similar to those of the medical model, and have all the same problems for women of the medical model. More information is useful to women, but only if its limits and the value choices imbedded in it are recognized.

CONCLUSION

Reform in health care is not new. What is new is the context. In the postwar period, the dominant paradigm at the international and national levels supported government intervention in the funding and provision of health services, leaving the determination of how, where and when these were delivered largely to the male doctors who dominated medical care and to the demands from patients. Health care was defined as a public good and a human right, based on a recognition of shared risk and shared responsibility. This approach has undoubtedly improved access to services, especially for women, and allowed for a distribution of care based more on need than on ability to pay. Paid work in the broader public sector expanded, unions flourished and many women held relatively protected health care jobs.

What was perpetuated and strengthened during the postwar period, however, was a medical model and hospital-based care. The emphasis was on cure rather than prevention, and there were problems in transferring from service to service and in continuity of care. Women's groups and researchers on women were among the most vocal critics of health care services – services that were not only insensitive to women's varied concerns but often inappropriate or ineffective. They were equally critical of how research was done and used. Women's own research clearly demonstrated that health care is a women's issue, and that all aspects of care had a differential impact on women, an impact that varied depending on women's location. Such criticisms have played an important role in the new reforms.

The early 1970s marked the rise to dominance of a new paradigm at the international and national levels. The welfare state and public sector workers came to be defined as part of the problem. Solutions were sought in market mechanisms and for-profit management techniques. Increasingly, health care was defined as a consumer commodity and as a business that could be a source of profit. In the name of cost control, efficiency, effectiveness, accountability, integration, continuity and choice, governments began to intervene more in the organization of health care. Somewhat paradoxically, privatization has often been the strategy or the result. Women seldom promoted privatization in terms of the adoption of for-profit techniques or services, but much of the discourse around privatization appeared to address their concerns.

Privatization has been promoted in spite of a 1985 study by the federal government's Health and Welfare Canada concluding that "the often asserted benefits of privatization were largely absent, or were unknown and possibly suspect" (Health and Welfare Canada 1985, 68). This study focused primarily on privatization in terms of coverage and delivery transferred to mainly for-profit firms. The notion of privatization has been expanded since then, increasingly involving a reliance on market mechanisms. Yet as economist Robert Evans makes clear, "international experience over the last forty years has demonstrated that greater reliance on the market is associated with inferior system performance – inequality, inefficiency, high cost and public dissatisfaction" (Evans 1997, 428).

Why, given this evidence, are market mechanisms so popular? Evans' answer is that "market mechanisms yield distributional advantages for particular influential groups" (ibid.). These influential groups include the for-profit providers and insurers and the wealthy, who can purchase better access while sharing less of the overall costs. Most of those who benefit are men, albeit a small minority of men; most of those who bear the burden and express dissatisfaction with the market solutions are women. While some of the reforms have improved the way health care is delivered to and by some women, there is growing evidence that many women have suffered from the reforms. In spite of an emphasis on gender-based analysis, the context for reform often makes it difficult for gender concerns to be addressed in ways that will take women, and the differences among them, into account.

Notes

An earlier version of this article appears as the first chapter in Pat Armstrong et. al, 2000.
1. See OECD (1998), for data on the growth of nursing work. While there are variations in terms of both growth and the female domination of the occupation, the number of jobs increased significantly between 1985 and 1995, and the overwhelming majority of nurses in all countries surveyed were women.
2. There are somewhat different definitions used for private and public sector in the reports by Akyeampong and the Canadian Council on Social Development. This is the case even within the reports themselves. As a result, the data are not strictly comparable. Nonetheless the patterns are clear.

References

Aaron, Henry. 1996. "Thinking About Health Care Financing: Some Propositions." In Organization for Economic Cooperation and Development. *Health Reform: The Will To Change*, 47-58. Paris: OECD, 1996.

Abel-Smith, Brian. 1996. "The Escalation of Health Care Costs: How Did We Get There?" In Organization for Economic Cooperation and Development. *Health Reform: The Will To Change*, 17-30. Paris: OECD, 1996.

Advisory Council on Health Infostructure. 1999. *Canada Health Infoway: Paths to Better Health. Final Report*. Ottawa: Minister of Public Works and Government Services.

Akyeampong, Ernest B. 1998. "The Rise of Unionization Among Women." *Perspectives on Labour and Income* 10 (4): 30-41.

Angus, Douglas A. 1992. "A Great Canadian Prescription: Take Two Commissioned Studies and Call Me in the Morning." In Raisa B. Deber and Gail G. Thompson, eds., *Restructuring Canada's Health Services System: How Do We Get There From Here?* Toronto: University of Toronto Press.

Armstrong, Pat. 1993. "Professions, Unions or What? Learning from Nurses." In Linda Briskin and Patricia McDermott, eds., *Women Challenging Unions: Feminism, Democracy, and Militancy*. Toronto: University of Toronto Press.

—. 1994. "Closer to Home: More Work for Mother." In Pat Armstrong *et al.*, *Take Care: Warning Signals for Canada's Health System*. Toronto: Garamond.

—. 1996. "Unraveling the Safety Net: Transformations in Health Care and Their Impact on Women." In Janine Brodie, ed., *Women and Canadian Public Policy*, 129-49. Toronto: University of Toronto Press.

—. 1998. "Women and Health: Challenges and Changes." In Nancy Mandell, ed., *Feminist Issues: Race, Class and Sexuality*, 249-66. Scarborough: Prentice-Hall.

Armstrong, Pat, Jacqueline Choiniere and Elaine Day. 1993. *Vital Signs: Nursing in Transition*. Toronto: Garamond.

Armstrong, Pat, et al. 1997. *Medical Alert: New Work Organizations in Health Care*. Toronto: Garamond.

—. 2000. *Heal Thyself. Managing Health Care Reform*. Toronto: Garamond

Armstrong, Pat and Hugh Armstrong. 1998. *Universal Health Care: What the United States Can Learn from Canada*. New York: The New Press.

Aronson, Jane and Sheila Neysmith. 1996. "The Work of Visiting Homemakers in the Context of Cost Cutting in Long Term Care." *Canadian Journal of Public Health* 87 (6): 422-25.

—. 1997. "The Retreat of the State and Long-Term Provisions: Implications for Frail Elderly People, Unpaid Family Carers and Paid Home Care Workers." *Studies in Political Economy* 53(Summer): 37-66.

Bacchi, Carol. 1990. *Same/Difference*. Sydney: Allen and Unwin.

Barer, Morris, Vanda Bhatia, Greg Stoddart and Robert Evans. 1994. "The Remarkable Tenacity of User Charges." Toronto: The Ontario Premier's Council on Health, Well-Being and Social Justice.

Bashevkin, Sylvia. 1998. *Women on the Defensive: Living Through Conservative Times*. Toronto: University of Toronto Press.

Bégin, Monique. 1998. "Free Trade Will Destroy Our Precious Medicare." *The Toronto Star*, October 28.

Bellandi, Deanna. 1998. "Health Care Industry Gets Clean Bill of Health." *Modern Health Care* (March 16): 68-74.

Blomqvist, Ake and David M. Brown, eds. 1994. *Limits to Care: Reforming Canada's Health System in an Age of Restraint*. Toronto: C.D. Howe Institute.

Boyd, Susan, ed. 1997. *Challenging the Public/Private Divide: Feminism, Law and Public Policy*. Toronto: University of Toronto Press.

British Columbia Royal Commission on Health Care and Costs. 1991. *Closer to Home: A Summary Report*. Victoria: BC Royal Commission on Health Care.

Brodie, Janine, ed. 1997. *Women and Canadian Public Policy*. Toronto: University of Toronto Press.

Brouselle, Astrid. 1998. "Controlling Health Expenditures: What Matters." In National Forum on Health. *Striking a Balance. Health Care Systems in Canada and Elsewhere*. Sainte-Foy: Multimondes. 39-84.

Canada. 1999. *A Framework to Improve the Social Union for Canadians*. An Agreement between the Government of Canada and Governments of the Provinces and the Territories, 4 February.

Canadian Council on Social Development (CCSD). 1997. *Public Sector Downsizing: The Impact on Job Quality in Canada*. Ottawa: CCSD.

Canadian Drug Manufacturers' Association (CDMA). n.d. *The Review of Bill C-91*. North York: The Canadian Drug Manufacturers' Association.

Canadian Institute for Health Information. n.d. "A Partnership Invitation." Ottawa.

Centre for Health Economics and Policy Analysis. 1997. *'The Part of the First Part...' Contracting in Health Care*. Hamilton: CHEPA.

Chappell, Neena L. 1993. "Implications of Shifting Health Care Policy for Care-Givers in Canada." *Journal of Aging and Social Policy* 51 (1/2): 39-55.

Chappell, Neena L., Laurel A. Strain and Audrey Blandford. 1986. *Aging and Health Care: A Social Perspective*. Toronto: Holt, Rinehart and Winston.

Chorney, Harold. 1996. "Debts, Deficits and Full Employment." In Robert Boyer and Daniel Drache, eds., *States Against Markets: The Limits of Globalization*, 357-79. London: Routledge.

Christie, Werner. 1996. "Keynote Address." In Organization for Economic Cooperation and Development, *Health Reform: The Will to Change*, 11-16. Paris: OECD.

Clark, Mel. 1999. "Chrétien Government Killing Medicare System It Promised to Save." *CCPA Monitor* 5 (9): 11.

Clarke, Tony and Maude Barlow. 1998. *MAI. Round 2*. Toronto: Stoddart.

Cohen, Marjorie. 1987. *Free Trade and the Future of Women's Work: Manufacturing and Service Industries*. Toronto: Garamond.

D'Arcy, Judy. 1988. "A Futuristic Nightmare." *Healthsharing* (Fall).

Day, Sheila and Gwen Brodsky.1998. "Women and the Equality Deficit: The Impact of Restructuring Canada's Social Programs." Ottawa: Status of Women Canada. March.

De Vortez, Don and Samuel A. Laryea. 1998. *Canadian Human Capital Transfers: The United States and Beyond*. Toronto: C.D. Howe Institute.

Deber, Raisa and B. Swan. 1998. "Puzzling Issues in Health Financing." In National Forum on Health, *Striking a Balance. Health Care Systems in Canada and Elsewhere*. Sainte-Foy: Editions Multimondes, 310-42.

Deber, Raisa, Sharmila Mhatre and G. Ross Baker. 1994. "A Review of Provincial Initiatives." In Ake Blomqvist and David M. Brown, eds., *Limits to Care: Reforming Canada's Health System in an Age of Restraint*. Toronto: C.D. Howe Institute.

Deber, Raisa *et al.* 1998. "The Public-Private Mix in Health Care." In National Forum on Health, *Health Care Systems in Canada and Elsewhere*, 423-545. Sainte-Foy: Editions Multimondes.

DeCoster, Carolyn A. and Marni D. Brownell. 1997. "Private Health Care in Canada: Savior or Siren." *Public Health Reports* 112 (July/August): 299-305.

Dominion Bureau of Statistics. 1957. *Canada 1957*. Ottawa: Queen's Printer.

—. 1966. *Labour Force, Occupation and Industry Trends*. Ottawa: Minister of Trade and Commerce.

Dorland, John L. and S. Mathwin Davis, eds. 1996. *How Many Roads...? Regionalization & Decentralization in Health Care*. Kingston: Queen's School of Policy Studies.

Eastman Commission of Inquiry on the Pharmaceutical Industry (ECIPI). 1985. *Report*. Ottawa: Supply and Services Canada.

Enterline, Philip, Allison McDonald, J. Corbett McDonald and Nicholas Steinmetz. 1973. "The Distribution of Medical Services Before and After Free Medicare." *Medical Care* 11 (4): 269-86.

Evans, Robert G. 1997. "Going For the Gold: The Redistribution Agenda behind Market-Based Health Care Reform." *Journal of Health Politics, Policy and Law* 23 (2): 428-65.

Evans, Robert G., Morris L. Barer and Theodore R. Marmor. 1994. *Why Are Some People Healthy and Others Not? The Determinants of Health of Populations*. New York: Aldine De Gruyter.

Evans, Robert *et al.* 1994. "Who are the Zombies and What Do They Want?" Toronto: The Ontario Premier's Council on Health, Well-Being, and Social Justice

Fitz-James, Michael. 1996. "Happy Birthday, Reference-Based Pricing." *Canadian Healthcare Manager* 3 (6).

Fuller, Colleen. 1991. *Caring for Profit*. Ottawa: Canadian Centre for Policy Alternatives.

—. 1993. "A Matter of Life and Death: NAFTA and Medicare." *Canadian Forum*. (October):14-19.

—. 1995. "The Conspiracy to Implement NAFTA and End Medicare." *Canadian Perspectives* (Autumn).

Glazer, Nona. 1993. *Women's Paid and Unpaid Labor: The Work Transfer in Health Care and Retailing*. Philadelphia: Temple University Press.

Harding, Sandra. 1986. *The Science Question in Feminism*. Ithaca: Cornell University Press.

—. 1991. *Whose Science? Whose Knowledge? Thinking from Women's Lives*. Ithaca: Cornell University Press.

Health and Welfare Canada. 1985. *Privatization in the Canadian Health Care System: Assertions, Evidence, Ideology and Options*. Ottawa: Health and Welfare Canada.

Health Canada. 1998. *Shared Responsibilities: Shared Vision*. Ottawa: Health Canada.

—. 1999. *Health Reform Data Base Overview by Province, 1998-99*. Ottawa: Health Canada.

Himmelstein, David U. and Steffie Woolhandler. 1994. *The National Health Program Book*. Monroe, ME: Common Courage Press.

Jerome-Forget, Monique and Claude E. Forget. 1998. *Who Is The Master? A Blueprint for Canadian Health Care Reform*. Montreal: The Institute for Research on Public Policy.

Jönsson, Bengt. 1996. "Making Sense of Health Reform." In Organization for Economic Cooperation and Development, *Health Reform: The Will To Change*, 31-45. Paris: OECD.

Jutras, Sylvie and Frances Veilleux. 1991. "Informal Caregiving: Correlates of Perceived Burden." *Canadian Journal on Aging* 10 (1): 45-55.

Kleiber, Nancy and Linda Light. 1978. *Caring for Ourselves: An Alternative Structure for Health Care*. Vancouver: BC Public Health.

Koivusala, Meri and Eeva Ollila. 1997. *Making a Healthy World. Agencies, Actors and Policies in International Health*. New York: Zed Books.

Laurence, Leslie and Beth Weinhouse. 1997. *Outrageous Practices: How Gender Bias Threatens Women's Health*. New Brunswick, NJ: Rutgers University Press.

Lawrence, Carmen. 1996. "Opening Statement." In Organization for Economic Cooperation and Development, *Health Reform: The Will to Change*. Paris: OECD.

Lesemann, Frederic. 1984. *Services and Circuses: Community and the Welfare State*. Montreal: Black Rose.

Lesemann, Frederic and Daphne Nahmiash. 1993. "Home-Based Care in Canada and Quebec." In Frederic Lesemann and Claude Martin, eds., *Home-Based Care: The Elderly, the Family and the Welfare State: An International Comparison*, 81-99. Ottawa: University of Ottawa Press.

Lippman, Abby. 1998. "The Politics of Health: Geneticization Versus Health Promotion." In Susan Sherwin, ed. *The Politics of Women's Health. Exploring Agency and Autonomy*, 64-82. Philadelphia: Temple University Press.

Maher, Janet. 1993. "Healthcare in Crisis." *Healthsharing* (Fall/Winter): 17-21.

Marsh, Leonard. 1975. *Report on Social Security for Canada 1943*. Toronto: University of Toronto Press.

Martin, Brendan. 1993. *In the Public Interest? Privatization and Public Sector Reform*. London: Zed Books.

Martin, Paul (Finance Minister). 1995. "Budget Speech." February 27. Ottawa, Ontario.

Maynard, Alan. 1996. "United Kingdom" In John L. Dorland and S. Mathwin Davis, eds., *How Many Roads...? Regionalization & Decentralization in Health Care*. Kingston: Queen's School of Policy Studies.

McDonnell, Kathleen. ed. 1986. *Adverse Effects: Women and the Pharmaceutical Industry*. Toronto: Women's Press.

McDonnell, Kathleen and Mariana Valverde. 1985. *The Health Sharing Book*. Toronto: Women's Press.

McIlroy, Ann. "Canadians' Medical Data Should Be On Computer, Panel Says." *The Globe and Mail*, 4 February, B1.

McKenna, Barrie. 1996. "Provinces Take Steps to Shield Health Care." *The Globe and Mail*, 26 March, B1.

McLeod, Linda. 1980. *Wife Battering in Canada: The Vicious Circle*. Ottawa: The Canadian Advisory Council on the Status of Women.

Mendelson, Michael. 1997. *The Capitalist Models: Where They Came from and Where They May Go*. Ottawa: Caledon Institute of Social Policy.

Mimoto, H. and P. Cross. 1991. "The Growth of the Federal Debt." *The Canadian Economic Observer* (June):1-17.

Mitchinson, Wendy. 1992. "Agency, Diversity, and Constraints: Women and Their Physicians, Canada 1850-1950." In Susan Sherwin, ed., *No Longer Patient: Feminist Ethics and Health Care*, 122-49. Philadelphia: Temple University Press.

Montreal Women's Press. 1968. *The Birth Control Handbook*. Montreal: Montreal Women's Press.

Moss, Kary L. 1996. *Man-Made Medicine: Women's Health, Public Policy and Reform*. Durham: Duke University Press.

National Forum on Health. 1997a. "Directions for a Pharmaceutical Policy in Canada." In *Canada Health Action: Building on the Legacy*. Vol. 2. *Synthesis Reports and Issues Papers*. Ottawa: Minister of Public Works and Government Services.

National Forum on Health. 1997b. "Striking a Balance Working Group Synthesis Report." In *Canada Health Action: Building on the Legacy*. Vol. 2. *Synthesis Reports and Issues Papers*. Ottawa: Minister of Public Works and Government Services.

Nelson, Joyce. 1995. "Dr. Rockefeller Will See You Now." *Canadian Forum* (January/February): 7-11.

Newcomer, Lee N. 1994. Quoted in Working Group on Health Services Utilization, "When Less Is Better: Using Canada's Hospitals Efficiently." Paper presented at the Conference of Federal, Provincial, Territorial Deputy Ministers of Health, 19.

Neysmith, Sheila and Jane Aronson. 1996. "Home Care Workers Discuss Their Work: The Skills Required to Use Your Common Sense." *Journal of Aging Studies* 10 (1): 1-14.

—. 1997. "Working Conditions in Home Care: Negotiating Race and Class Boundaries in Gendered Work." *International Journal of Health Services* 27 (3): 479-99.

Oakley, Ann. 1990. "Who's Afraid of the Randomized Controlled Trial? Some Dilemmas of the Scientific Method and Good Research Practice." In Helen Robert, ed., *Women's Health Counts*. London: Routledge.

Organization for Economic Cooperation and Development. 1992. *The Reform of Health Care: A Comparative Analysis of Seven OECD Countries*. Paris: OECD.

—. 1995. *Governance in Transition: Public Management Reforms in OECD Countries*. Paris: OECD.

—. 1996. *Health Reform: The Will To Change*. Paris: OECD.

—. 1998. *The Future of Female Dominated Occupations*. Paris: OECD.

Osborne, David, and Ted Gaebler. 1992. *Reinventing Government: How the Entrepreneurial Spirit is Transforming the Public Sector*. New York: Plume.

Overall, Christine. 1993. *Human Reproduction: Principles, Practices and Policies*. Toronto: Oxford University Press.

Panic, Mica. 1995. "The Bretton Woods System: Concept and Practice." In Jonathan Michie and John Grieve Smith, eds., *The Global Economy*, 37-54. Oxford: Oxford University Press.

Paquet, Gilles and Robert Shepherd. 1996. "The Program Review Process: A Deconstruction." In Gene Swimmer, ed., *How Ottawa Spends: Life Under the Knife*. Ottawa: Carleton University Press.

Pederson, Ann, Michel O'Neill and Irving Rootman. 1994. *Health Promotion in Canada: Provincial, National and International Perspectives*. Toronto: Harcourt.

Petchesky, Rosalind Pollack. 1995. "From Population Control to Reproductive Rights: Feminist Fault Lines." *Reproductive Health Matters* (6):152-61.

Peterson, Mark A. 1997. "Introduction: Health Care Into the Next Century." *Journal of Health Politics, Policy and the Law* 22 (2): 291-313.

Pierre, Jon. 1995."The Marketization of the State: Citizens, Consumers, and the Emergence of the Public Market." In B. Guy Peters and Donald J. Savoie, eds., *Governance in a Changing Environment*. Montreal: McGill-Queen's University Press.

Rehner, Jan. 1989. *Infertility: Old Myths, New Meanings*. Toronto: Second Story Press.

Rekart. Josephine.1993. *Public Funds: Private Provision. The Role of the Voluntary Sector*. Vancouver: UBC Press.

Robertson, Ann. 1998. "Shifting Discourses on Health in Canada: From Health Promotion to Population Health." *Health Promotion International* 13(2):155-66.

Ruggie, Mary. 1996. *Realignments in the Welfare State: Health Policy in the United States, Britain, and Canada*. New York: Columbia University Press.

Ryten, Eva. 1997. *A Statistical Picture of the Past, Present and Future of Registered Nurses in Canada*. Ottawa: Canadian Nurses Association.

Sainsbury, Diane. 1996. *Gender, Equality and Welfare States*. Cambridge: Cambridge University Press.

Scarpaci, Joseph, ed. 1989. *Health Services Privatization in Industrial Societies*. New Brunswick, NJ: Rutgers University Press.

Shapiro, Evelyn. 1997. *The Cost of Privatization: A Case Study of Manitoba*. Ottawa: Canadian Centre for Policy Alternatives.

Shields, John and B. Mitchell Evans. 1998. *Shrinking the State. Globalization and Public Administration "Reform"*. Halifax: Fernwood.

Schwartz, Dr. Bryan. 1996. "NAFTA Reservations in the Areas of Health Care." Opinion prepared for the Canadian Health Coalition, Winnipeg, MB. File No. 24703.

Sherwin, Susan. 1992. *No Longer Patient: Feminist Ethics and Health Care*. Philadelphia: Temple University Press.

Sherwin, Susan, ed. 1998. *The Politics of Women's Health. Exploring Agency and Autonomy*. Philadelphia: Temple University Press.

Simmons, Harvey. 1990. *Unbalanced: Mental Health Policy in Ontario 1930-1989*. Toronto: Wall and Thompson.

Sky, Laura. 1995. "Lean and Mean Health Care: The Creation of the Generic Worker and the Deregulation of Health Care." Working paper 95-3, Health Research Project, Ontario Federation of Labour, June.

Sparr, Pamela, ed. 1994. *Mortgaging Women's Lives: Feminist Critiques of Structural Adjustment*. London: Zed Books.

Starr, Paul. 1987. "The Meaning of Privatization." In Sheila B. Kamerman and Alfred Kahn, eds., *Privatization and the Welfare State*, 15-48. New York: Harper Collins.

Statistics Canada. 1993. *91 Census, Industry and Class of Worker*. Ottawa: Minister of Industry, Science and Technology. Cat. No. 93-226.

—. 1997. *Earnings of Women and Men. 1995*. Ottawa: Minister of Industry.

Stein, Jane. 1997. *Empowerment and Women's Health Theory, Methods and Practice*. London: Zed Books.

Stoddart, Greg, Morris Barer Robert Evans and Vanda Bhatia. 1993. "Why Not User Charges? The Real Issues." Toronto: The Ontario Premier's Council on Health, Well-Being and Social Justice.

Stone, Deborah. 1997. *Policy Paradox*. New York: W.W. Norton.

Struthers, James. 1997. "Reluctant Partners: State Regulation of Private Nursing Homes in Ontario, 1941-72". In Raymond B. Blake, Penny E. Bryden and J.Frank Strain, eds., *The Welfare State in Canada. Past, Present and Future*, 171-92. Concord: Irwin.

Sutherland, Ralph and Jane Fulton. 1994. *Spending Smarter and Spending Less: Policies and Partnerships for Health Care in Canada*. Ottawa: Canadian Hospital Association Press.

Swimmer, Gene. 1996. "An Introduction to Life Under the Knife." In Gene Swimmer, ed., *How Ottawa Spends: Life Under the Knife*, 1-17. Ottawa: Carleton University Press.

Taylor, Malcolm. 1987. *Health Insurance and Canadian Public Policy*. Kingston: McGill-Queen's University Press.

Thorpe, Kenneth E. 1997. "The Health System in Transition: Care, Cost and Coverage." *Journal of Health Politics, Policy and the Law* 22 (2): 339-61.

Toronto Star. 1999. "Report Cards' Proposed for Health-Care Services." February, A6.

Walker, William. 1999. "PM Forging Ahead on Health Accord." *The Toronto Star*, 27 January, A7.

White, Jerry. 1990. *Hospital Strike: Women, Unions, and Public Sector Conflict*. Toronto: Thompson.

World Health Organization (WHO). 1998. *The World Health Report 1998*. Geneva: World Health Organization.

Wotherspoon, Terry. 1990. "Immigration, Gender and Professional Labour: State Regulation of Nursing and Teaching." Paper presented to the CSAA 25th Annual Meeting, May, Victoria, BC.

Health Restructuring and Privatization from Women's Perspective in Newfoundland and Labrador

Ingrid Botting, with support from Barbara Neis, Linda Kealey and Shirley Solberg

INTRODUCTION

Since the early 1990s, Newfoundland and Labrador has experienced extensive reform and restructuring of its health care system. The cornerstone of the reform initiative was the regionalization of health care delivery and management, which has largely meant a transfer of direct responsibility for service provision and delivery from the state to the recently established regional Community Health and Institutional Boards. Another significant aspect of reform and restructuring has been the adoption of a population health approach, which implies a shift towards prevention through a focus on health determinants such as income, education, employment and gender. A population health model has required a more holistic approach to policy development. For example, the movement of some social services, such as child welfare and youth corrections, from the Department of Human Resources and Employment to the Community Health Boards has furthered the province's efforts at integrating health care and social services.[1] The provincial government also released a Strategic Social Plan (1996) – to address social and economic issues in an integrated manner – which considers the input of community groups (Government of Newfoundland and Labrador 1998).[2] The reform of primary care has also been on the agenda for health care reform, but little substantive change has taken place in this area. While the province remains the main provider of funding, the Department of Health and Community Services (before 1998, the Department of Health) is now mainly involved in policy development and financing the health care system.[3]

One of the hidden aspects of health care reform in Newfoundland and Labrador, as elsewhere, has been the transfer of some financial responsibilities from the state to the private sector, and to individuals and families. Another has been the individualization of responsibility for one's health, which in some cases has meant a transfer of caregiving work onto individuals and families, which has the potential to land on the shoulders of women.

Since a population health approach implies a shift towards prevention through a focus on health determinants, and gender is a known health determinant, policy should be shaped by gender-informed, evidence-based decision-making processes. In the course of changes to the health care system over the past decade in Newfoundland and Labrador, it is apparent that not enough attention has been paid to the potential for differential effects of reform and restructuring on the women, men and children of this province; nor has enough attention been paid to addressing questions of access and equity. The gap that exists between the models of reform (many of which are promising in regard to meeting women's diverse health care needs) and what has actually occurred, especially in regard to women's health, has prompted this review.

RESTRUCTURING OF THE HEALTH CARE SYSTEM

In Newfoundland and Labrador, the process of health care restructuring began when the Progressive Conservative government of Brian Peckford sponsored a Royal Commission on Hospital and Nursing Home Costs in February 1984. After several consultations with key stakeholders, the Royal Commission made 232 recommendations, most of which have since been adopted – even though many of the recommendations took years to address. The report suggested that if government were to fully implement its recommendations, which included shorter hospital stays, more day surgery, an increase in chronic care facilities and decrease in acute care, a reduction of hospital beds per 1,000 population from 5.4 to less than 4, the transformation of cottage hospitals into clinics, the maximum use of part-time and casual nurses, the deinstitutionalization of mental health patients and the physically disabled, reform would result in a substantial reduction of the overall health care budget (Government of Newfoundland and Labrador 1984).

According to a 1994 report on health care reform published by the Department of Health, "Responding to Changing Health Needs," the government did not begin its full-fledged restructuring process until 1990 (Government of Newfoundland and Labrador, Department of Health 1994, 1). In response to an anticipated 14 per cent shortfall in health care funding in 1990, the government established a Resource Committee to review the system. While the committee did not produce any public documents, the 1994 report explained that the committee recommended: 1) resources should be moved away from certain sectors and into other areas; 2) all programs funded by the Department of Health should be subject to review; 3) quality of care should be a primary factor in the decision-making process; and 4) duplication of services in the health system should be addressed (ibid., 2).

Participants in the committee, such as the Association of Registered Nurses of Newfoundland and Labrador (ARNNL), whose membership is dominated by women frontline workers, have advocated an increased role for nurses and other women workers in the decision-making process. Yet six years later, in 2000, the ARNNL emphasized that their views had not been adequately represented (Kelly 2000). Even though women's organizations and health care professionals have supported the transformation of the health care system from a focus on acute care towards a focus on illness prevention, it appears that government adopted these measures as part of a cost-cutting reform agenda instead of as part of a commitment to making the system more accessible and equitable.

A 1992 *Globe and Mail* feature on health care reform highlighted Newfoundland's efforts, which initially focused on budget cutting and bed closures. According to the newspaper report:

> What Newfoundland did last year, as part of the severest budget in the province's history, was launch an unprecedented cost-cutting assault on its health-care system. When the smoke cleared, 450 of the province's 3,000 acute-care beds (15 per cent) had disappeared, and so had 850 jobs. Yet one year later the system seems to have survived. (*Globe and Mail* 27/4/92)

By 1994, the ratio of acute care beds per 1,000 population had been reduced to 3.58. The ratio of acute care beds per 1,000 population does not reflect seasonal fluctuations in access to health care services. For example, in summer months the number of beds is even lower to accommodate shortages in staff due to summer vacations.

In furthering its reform and restructuring agenda, between 1993 and 1995 the government established Institutional Boards that consolidated the management and financing of hospitals and began the process of regionalization. Around the same time, the Department also established Community Health Boards, which were mandated to assume responsibility for a number of social services, long-term care, home support, and illness prevention and health promotion issues.

Regionalization

The Newfoundland and Labrador government began thinking about hospital restructuring in the early 1980s, when it started closing cottage hospitals in rural regions or transforming them into health clinics focusing on chronic care. While many of these facilities were no longer viable and were desperately in need of costly renovation and repair, communities experienced a loss of control of their own infrastructure. Thus, when the government proposed further restructuring in some communities only a few years after the loss of their cottage hospitals, they responded negatively.

During the 1980s, the government also gave the St. John's Hospital Council a mandate to plan for restructuring hospital facilities in the St. John's region. In 1989 the council released a report to the province outlining its plan for hospital amalgamation and restructuring, which it anticipated would cost $300 million. The Minister of Health did not adopt the recommendations in the report. Instead, he encouraged the council to consider relocating the Janeway Children's Hospital to the Health Sciences Centre and to consider redeveloping the obstetrical and gynaecological facilities for the province. The minister's recommendations served as the basis for future restructuring of hospitals in the St. John's region.

In 1992, as part of the hospital restructuring process, Minister of Health Chris Decker announced the government intended to review the number of provincial hospital boards operating under the *Hospitals Act*. Decker appointed Lucy Dobbin (past CEO of St. Clare's Mercy Hospital) to chair the Commission. Dr. Arthur May (future president of Memorial University) chaired the Advisory Committee, which conducted consultations in Newfoundland and Labrador as well as in Saskatchewan and New Brunswick. Dobbin's final report, *Report on the Reduction of Hospital Boards,* released in March 1993, recommended that the existing independent hospital and nursing home boards throughout the province be collapsed into six or seven regional boards. The reduction was considered in light of principles such as the "effective and efficient utilization of scarce human and fiscal resources"; "opportunities to take advantage of economies of scale that can be achieved by alternate board structures"; and the "impact on quality of services provided."

Dobbin also stated that because of the challenge of geography (a small population and a vast territory), her intention was to keep primary care services as close to the people as feasible, and ensure that secondary services were available in each region, and that tertiary care services were available only in St. John's (Dobbin 1993, 3). The government adopted most of Dobbin's recommendations, which focused on hospital closures (mainly in St. John's), amalgamations of budgets and administration, and the amalgamation of the boards themselves. The first two Institutional Boards were set up in 1995.

Questions of access and equity were not addressed in detail in the report, nor was there mention of the ways in which the regionalization process might have differential effects on men, women and children from different parts of the province. For example, the issue of who pays for travel and transportation costs for patients and their families (discussed below), was not addressed. Further bed closures, staff reductions and other reforms within individual hospitals would now be the responsibility of the boards and not of the provincial government. When the Institutional Board on the west coast of the island closed 22 beds in 1995, Premier Clyde Wells said the government had not given the board that directive (*Evening Telegram* 2/8/95).

The largest hospital restructuring project in the province took place in St. John's and is yet to be completed. Despite resistance from individual hospital boards in St. John's, Dobbin recommended that the Janeway Child Health Centre and the Children's Rehabilitation Centre be merged and that one board for all acute institutions be established, amalgamating the Janeway, General Hospital, Grace, St. Clare's, Waterford, and Dr. Walter Templeman Hospital on Bell Island. Significantly, Dobbin mentioned that the Waterford Hospital had already started to de-institutionalize mental health patients and to move them into a community-based model of care.

On April 1, 1995, the Health Care Corporation of St. John's assumed responsibility for eight health care facilities in the St. John's region, three schools of nursing, Central Laundry facilities and the Regional Ambulance Service. Some key aspects of the restructuring in St. John's were the adoption of one budget for all institutions, the closure of the Salvation Army Grace Hospital, the closure of the Janeway (Pleasantville site) and the construction of a new children's hospital at the Health Sciences site. Hospital restructuring in the St. John's region was meant to cost $130 million, which was considerably less than the St. John's Hospital Council's 1989 figure of $300 million.

According to Eileen Young, Chairperson of the Health Care Corporation of St. John's, the amalgamation of obstetrical services and pediatric services will be most effective, meaning "new mothers will no longer be separated from sick newborns requiring medical attention" (Government of Newfoundland and Labrador, Department of Health 1996d). Little publicly accessible documentation exists on the potential positive and negative effects of these changes on women's health as care recipients and as paid workers. In April 2001, however, a St. John's family doctor launched a letter-writing campaign to protest the reduction in the number of semi-private and private rooms for new mothers (reduced from 28 to 16) and cramped quarters in the wards since the Health Care Corporation moved the obstetrical unit from the Grace Hospital to the Health Sciences Centre. The doctor stated that new mothers are being released too soon after giving birth, with many giving up breastfeeding, and that cramped quarters in the wards have made it difficult for staff to work in these areas (*Evening Telegram* 30 April 2001).

Furthering the regionalization of service delivery and management, in 1993 the department announced the establishment of regional Community Health Boards (CHBs), which were mandated to provide a comprehensive range of community health services including "health promotion, health protection, single point of entry for home care, home support services as well as entrance to personal care and nursing homes, continuing care, drug dependency, and mental health services" (Government of Newfoundland and Labrador, Department of Health 1994, 3). In St. John's, for example, the CHB came out of the merging of the St. John's Home Care Program, the St. John's Drug Dependency Services and the St. John's and District Health Unit. Within the next year, three other CHBs were established in the province (Eastern, Central and Western) as well as two Integrated Boards, which combined Community Health and Institutional boards on the northern peninsula and in Labrador.

The government's rationale for establishing the CHBs was their commitment to emphasize "wellness over illness, empowering communities, and one-stop shopping" (Government of Newfoundland and Labrador, Department of Health 1994). The minister also noted that the boards' objective would be to promote "individual responsibility for one's own health" (Government of Newfoundland and Labrador, Department of Health 1993b). As a result of the regionalization process, the department's role changed to focus primarily on policy direction, funding and monitoring (Government of Newfoundland and Labrador, Department of Health 1993a).

Since 1995 the province has furthered the devolution of power and responsibility for certain social services and health care services. On April 1, 1998 Child Welfare and Community Corrections, as well as Family and Rehabilitative Services, which were delivered by the Department of Human Resources and Employment, were integrated with the Department of Health, which was renamed the Department of Health and Community Services. According to the Newfoundland and Labrador Health Boards Association, even more social services will be shifted to the CHBs (Peddle 2000). In 1998 the province drafted a new *Child, Youth and Family Services Act*, which "provides the framework for the development of prevention and early intervention strategies with services delivered by Health and Community Services and Integrated Boards, and community- based agencies. It will also expand services to youths aged 16 and 17" (Government of Newfoundland and Labrador, Department of Health 1999c).

The Newfoundland and Labrador Health Boards Association (NLHBA) represents the boards in the province, providing group purchasing services, labour relations advice and some research and monitoring of the situation.[4] The NLHBA has raised serious questions about the transferring of social services to the CHBs without proper planning and funding. One of the effects, according to the NLHBA, has been the privatization of the delivery of some health and social services (NLHCSA 2000).

In March 1998, the Department of Health added $2 million to the budget for the regional CHBs. However, $300,000 of the total was allocated to a vaccination budget for school children and the remaining $700,000 was allocated for protection, promotion, prevention and early intervention, mental health, addictions and continuing care (Government of Newfoundland and Labrador, Department of Health 1998a). It is difficult to analyze changes over time in funding to the CHBs, because of the scope of the boards' responsibility for administering non-acute care in the "community" as well as prevention and promotion. While overall funding for the CHBs has increased from 3.14 per cent in the early 1990s to around 15 per cent in 2000-01, many new services, previously dealt with by other government departments, have come under the jurisdiction of the boards.

The Changing Role of the Department of Health
The devolution of power and responsibility, as well as the scope of change (from around 30 individual boards to eight) means that tracking and monitoring the impacts of restructuring is extremely difficult.

Over the past decade, the provincial government has explained its further integration of services into the CHBs in terms of providing better continuity of care and avoiding duplication (Government of Newfoundland and Labrador, Department of Health 1993c). In effect, however, as part of the restructuring process, the Department of Health has moved away from its past role as a health service provider towards a focus on policy development. One of the most significant changes in terms of government's role has been the movement of health services out of its area of responsibility and into the jurisdiction of the boards. Prior to the reforms, the Department administered 18 to 19 cottage hospitals – which they closed or replaced with community health centres – as well as most of the major institutions. A dramatic change in terms of the impact on women as unpaid care providers, care recipients and paid health care workers has been that personal home support services, once administered directly by department employees, have come under the administration of the CHBs. Outside of institutions, home support work is done primarily by non-unionized, low-paid, untrained women workers.

The provincial government has retained some control over the boards insofar as they are appointed and not elected. In provinces such as Saskatchewan, where health board members are elected, the number of women directly involved in decision-making has increased substantially (see Kay Willson and Jennifer Howard's article in this volume).

For the first time ever, in May 1997, the government held a Provincial Health Forum, chaired by Roger Grimes, former Minister of Health. The forum was organized primarily to respond to the changes that restructuring had created for the newly established boards, for patients and for frontline workers. Some of the issues addressed included: the need for a better integrated health system, doctor shortages in rural communities, emergency room doctor shortages, workload stress among frontline workers, waiting times for cardiac surgery and other health services, the pace of reform and the need for a more coordinated role for health professionals, increased emphasis on prevention and public education, and more evidence-based decision-making. The participants, who included a number of stakeholders, stated that "if government plans to make further changes in health service delivery, they should know with some certainty that improved service will be the outcome" (Government of Newfoundland and Labrador, Department of Health 1997).

In response to the problems raised at the public forum, the department introduced the following measures: an improved compensation package for emergency room doctors ($5.3 million), implementation of Workload Measurement Systems for nurses, the establishment of Primary Service and Teaching Units in Twillingate and Port aux Basques, the formation of an Advisory Committee on health issues, and an injection of $20 million into the

Institutional Boards (ibid.) This reactive, project-based, targeted-initiative rationale has characterized the government's planning and funding of the health care system since 1995. Reactive strategies such as these have a high potential to threaten sustainability, universality and continuity of care for women and men.

Frontline workers, reform-oriented community groups and women's groups have all supported the principles underlying the Department's new approach to policy and program development. These include less focus on treatment and more on disease prevention and health promotion; less focus on institutions and more on community; and a primary health care approach, which supports the decentralization of decision-making (Tucker 1996, 9). However, the reform process has been characterized by a lack of consultation and a lack of planning, according to associations of health care professionals and community groups. One of the department's most obvious shortcomings is that it has not had the time or the resources to produce an annual report since 1995, which raises serious questions about accountability.

The provincial Medical Association (NLMA), the Newfoundland and Labrador Nurses' Union (NLNU), and the Association of Registered Nurses (ARNNL) have been particularly vocal about the reorganization of primary care. While doctors have been concerned mainly with maintaining their role as gatekeepers of primary care, nurses' groups have argued for an enhanced role in the health care system. Both groups have argued that such restructuring requires research and planning. For instance, the NLMA argued that the cost effectiveness of primary care provided by physicians and other providers should be studied thoroughly before any major changes are made to the system (NLMA 1996). Nurses, however, have adamantly argued that they have not achieved the level of input into decision-making they should have had in the process (Vivian and Carol 2000; ARNNL 2000).

In 1995 the NLNU commissioned a study on primary care reform, "Community Health Centres: The Better Way to Health Reform, NLNU's Perspective." Conducted by Dr. Michael Rachlis (Professor of Medicine at McMaster University) and Carol Kushner, the report argued that if nurses, doctors and allied health professionals worked as a team at the point of entry, patients "would get more services up front at a stage when they can, in fact, manage their medical condition" (*Evening Telegram* 14/9/95). Debbie Forward, president in 1996 of the NLNU, said the NLNU supported the community health centre model because it uses an expanded role for nurses and there is extensive documentation to support the fact that a nurse is a cost-efficient and qualified health care deliverer (*Evening Telegram* 28/10/96). The NLNU also presented government with a document titled, "Action Plan to Develop Community Health Centres in Newfoundland and Labrador" in 1996 (Government of Newfoundland and Labrador, Department of Health, 1996a).

The Danemark-Newfoundland primary care demonstration project on the southern shore of the Avalon Peninsula used community consultations to determine the health care needs of the local population. According to an ARNNL representative, women cited increased stress levels due to the closure of the fish plant in the community and other lifestyle issues (ARNNL 2000). The project, co-sponsored by the World Health Organization, officially lasted for two years; however, one of the region's community health nurses has continued to work within the project's framework and has begun to see profound change in the community after a number of years. Demonstration projects such as these are potentially useful if the funding continues and if they are used to inform policy in other regions.

Public/Private Sector Spending

In Newfoundland and Labrador, just as in other provinces, the public and private sectors are both involved in the financing and delivery of health care. As outlined in the *Canada Health Act*, public health, hospital services, services to status Indians and Inuit, and physician services are publicly funded. Privately funded health care expenditures usually encompass insurance premiums, out-of-pocket health care costs, drugs, dental service, vision care and complementary medicines and therapies. The Canadian Institute for Health Information (CIHI) projected that in 1999, on average, each Canadian would spend around $850 per year on health care and that 23 per cent of health care spending in Newfoundland and Labrador would come from private sector sources. Compared with other jurisdictions, Newfoundland and Labrador's private spending percentage is relatively low. For example, Ontario's proportion was highest in Canada at 34 per cent, followed by Alberta, PEI and New Brunswick at around 31 per cent (CIHI 2000a, 19). Other CIHI figures indicate that per capita private health care spending (in current dollars) in Newfoundland and Labrador increased from $381.53 in 1990 to a forecasted figure of $603.25 in 1999 (CIHI 2000b, Attachment 9). Lower private expenditures may be more a consequence of relatively low incomes in the province than a reflection of the adequacy of public services. Poorer people tend to underutilize health care services relative to their actual health status.

In 1999, Newfoundland and Labrador spent (private and public) $2,037 per person on health care (CIHI 2000a, 16) and ranked fifth in terms of overall spending on health care. Generally speaking, provinces with smaller populations and a large geographical distribution spend more public monies on health care per capita than those with more populated areas. Newfoundland and Labrador and the Territories have the highest portion of GDP spent on health care (NLHCSA 1999, 10). Throughout the 1990s, Newfoundland and Labrador, however, had the lowest care per capita health care expenditures in the country (CIHI 2000b, Attachment 5).

In Newfoundland and Labrador the cost of health care has also been rising dramatically, with increased costs of new technology, new prescription drugs, new equipment, new medical specialists, and the integration of social services programs into the health care boards. Public funding has not kept pace with these changes, according to the NLHCSA (NLHCSA 2000, 6).

The provinces and territories are responsible for administering the bulk of the public sector health care budget, a portion of which is financed through federal transfers of cash and tax points (CIHI 2000a, 18). Newfoundland and Labrador is one out of seven provinces that receives equalization funding from Ottawa. The federal government's eradication of Established Programs Financing and CAP (cost-sharing funding for health care and other social services transfers) in 1995, and its introduction of the Canada Health and Social Transfer (CHST) block funding scheme in 1996 has meant a dramatic reduction in federal health care funding to the province. Since the CHST was introduced, it has been difficult to document where the federal dollars have been spent because the provinces and territories are free to allocate the CHST to health, education and other social programs according to their individual priorities. The National Union of Public and Government Employees (NUPGE) has also noted that "because the point of entry into the health care system in Canada is increasingly community-based rather than institution-based, there is no guarantee that the provinces will put extra CHST/Social Union bonus money into the health care system" (NUPGE 2000).

According to the NLHCSA, Newfoundland and Labrador was hit particularly hard by the changes to federal funding: "For Newfoundland and Labrador, the reduction in health transfers, at -12.8% between 1985 and 1995, has been greatest among all the provinces and territories, and is well below the national average of -8.7%" (NLHCSA 1999b, 10). One factor that sets Newfoundland and Labrador apart is the current system of tax point transfers – whereby the federal government reduces its tax rate, allowing provincial governments to increase their tax rate without changing the "bottom line" a taxpayer pays (CIHI 2000a, 18). These transfers are less valuable to poorer provinces with high unemployment and a less active economy. The federal government's change of funding from needs-based to a per capita funding scheme (Government of Canada, Department of Finance 2000) also hurts poorer provinces like Newfoundland and Labrador. It was within this context that the NLHCSA lobbied against the provincial government's proposal to cut taxes, stating that the health care system would suffer as a consequence.

In 1996-97 the NLMA noted that the provincial government spent 26.8 per cent of its budget on health care. "However, in comparing real per capita spending on health to other provinces, Newfoundland and Labrador ranks lowest" (NLMA 1997, 1). The NLMA also pointed out that the provincial health budget was frozen for three years (1994-97), and found that 92 per cent of the public believe that smaller communities are having increased difficulty finding and keeping good physicians (ibid., 2).

In its 2000 budget, the government allocated 60 per cent of the health care budget to hospitals and nursing homes, 15.6 per cent to community health, 15.6 per cent to MCP-Physician services and 5.3 per cent for medical and drug subsidies. The only item geared specifically to women's health was $2 million allocated to a Comprehensive Breast Health Centre at St. Clare's hospital (Government of Newfoundland and Labrador 2000). Significantly, Newfoundland has the lowest level of mammogram use in the country. Only 43 per cent of women between 50 and 69 received mammograms in 1996-97, increasing to 48.2 per cent in 1998-99 – compared with the national average of 63.1 per cent and 66.2 per cent respectively (CIHI *Health Indicators 2000* in CIHI 2000a). In light of the CIHI figures, this targeted program for women appears to be reactive rather than proactive.

It has yet to be determined whether the regionalization of health care has been cost-effective. However, evidence from a number of sources underlines the serious financial difficulties that the Institutional and Community Health Boards are facing. According to John Peddle, executive director of the Newfoundland and Labrador Health Care Association, the province's health care sector is supposed to have yearly budgets, which has made long-term planning next to impossible. In 1995 the Institutional Boards were asked to find $27 million "to help the province out of its $60 million deficit" (*Evening Telegram* 8/4/96). In 1997, following the recommendations of the Public Health Forum, the provincial government gave the boards an additional $20 million. In 1998 the boards' financial problems continued to persist, and the department allocated an extra $10 million to the boards (Government of Newfoundland and Labrador, Department of Health 1998b).[5] Lack of information about government plans and the direction of reform and restructuring efforts have created a great deal of uncertainty throughout the institutional and community sectors (Tucker 1996, 13).

Gender and Rural-Urban Disparities

Despite restructuring, access to some health care services for women, men and children living in remote areas continues to be an issue, although the extent and nature of the impacts require more research. A community needs assessment done for the Grenfell Regional Health Services, which has responsibility for Southeast Labrador, the Labrador Straits, and the St. Anthony, Flowers Cove and Roddicton areas found a relatively high level of overall satisfaction with regional health services. Satisfaction was highest with clinic and public health nursing services. It was lowest with allied health professional services, long-term care and mental health services. Discontent with allied health professional services was related to the absence of such services within the region and limited availability of others. Mental health services were also considered to be inadequate. In all areas in the region the need for more home care and home support for the elderly was a major concern. Lengthy waiting lists, limits on the coverage available in the evenings and on weekends, and the cost of home care were issues. Some regions lacked basic facilities for long-term care and where such facilities did exist, there were too few and staffing levels were insufficient. At 4.4 visits per person per year health service utilization in the region appeared to be below the Canadian average of 5.2 per person per year. Unfortunately, interview findings on health care utilization and satisfaction are not fully broken down by gender in the report on the community needs assessment (Bavington *et al.* 1999).

Numerous communities have questioned the centralization of services and boards have stressed their own inability, due to financial constraints, to deliver the services of their communities' need. Changes to the health care system have taken place during a period in which many small communities have been losing their younger population to outmigration, as well as losing their tax base, their provincial funding from the Department of Municipalities and their sense of cohesion. As one NLNU representative stated, "almost the day after the government announced its regionalization scheme, trucks came into small communities to pick up medical equipment that was going to be relocated to the larger centre. These communities had fundraised for the equipment they were losing" (Vivian and Carol July 2000)!

At a community meeting held in 1999 in Labrador West, residents and health care workers highlighted several problems of access related to cuts in available services, particularly in the areas of physiotherapy and occupational therapy; the movement of the site administrator at the Labrador City hospital to Goose Bay; a general downgrading of services; and a decline in visiting specialists. In short, residents argued that regional boards in the northern regions of the province should get more funding because of their relative isolation and increased costs associated with remoteness (*Western Star* 4/10/99).

In 1998, Minister of Health Joan Marie Alyward signed a Memorandum of Understanding with Division Surgeon 1 of the Canadian Air Force to bring air force physicians into the provincial health care system on an emergency basis. According to the minister, "while the Air Force medical teams are not a permanent solution to the ongoing challenge of physician recruitment, they will provide relief for physicians and other health professionals and enhance health care in under-serviced areas of the province" (Government of Newfoundland and Labrador, Department of Health 1998c). Practices such as these demonstrate the acuity of the situation as well as a lack of planning.

In terms of women's health, there are a number of issues involving uneven access to care, especially for those living in remote regions of the island. Regional nurses have worked effectively in northern areas where they can treat patients for the common cold, ankle sprains, urinary tract and vaginal infections, and conduct Pap smears. Many female patients feel more at ease having Pap smears with a female health care worker (*Evening Telegram* 25/02/97). While a Nurse Practitioner Act was passed in 1998, nurses have argued that nurse practitioners have been underused. Access to sexual and reproductive health prevention and promotion in certain areas of the province is another serious equity issue. Teen pregnancy, sexually transmitted diseases and increasing risks of cancer in women because of lack of testing are expensive for the health and social services system in the long run, but the supports for these services have not been put into the regionalized system (Matchim 2000).

The regionalization of medicine has also meant increased reliance on long distance telephone services. Phone lines to rural areas are constantly blocked from 6 pm on and, as a result, health care providers have difficulties getting assistance. For instance, in December 1998, blocked telephone lines resulted in the deaths of two patients (one in Labrador and the other on the Bonavista Peninsula) because health care workers couldn't get through to the poison control centre in St. John's (*Evening Telegram* 9/12/98).

PRIVATIZING MEDICAL SERVICES
Reducing Public Coverage of Health Services

As in other provinces, over the past decade, in Newfoundland and Labrador public coverage for certain medical services has been privatized. Who pays for services, such as vision care, dental, prescription drugs and physiotherapy, has in some cases shifted from the state to individuals and households. Factors such as the regionalization of health care service provision, a shift from acute care in hospitals to care in the "community," more day surgery and federal and provincial legislative and policy changes have changed the nature of health care costs (e.g., the transportation costs associated with accessing services have increased), as well as who pays for them. These changes have a particularly dramatic effect on women, who are more likely to use the health care system than men, whose incomes are on average lower, and whose employment status is likely to be more precarious. The transfer of some costs to individuals and households through out-of-pocket payments, increased co-payments, and increased deductibles from private health care insurance has the potential to exacerbate women's vulnerability to poverty and to illness particularly as care recipients and unpaid care providers.

Medical Care Plan and De-listing

During the 1990s the provincial government de-listed some medical services that were once covered under the provincial Medical Care Plan (MCP). While services that fall under the *Canada Health Act* must be covered by public insurance plans, the province has control over coverage for other medical services listed in the *Medical Insurance Act,* such as prescription drugs, optometry and some physician services. The province has some power to decide on what it deems as "medically necessary" but it is difficult to find out exactly how this is currently defined. The NLMA has also pressured government to de-list some services that are supplied by physicians.

In 1988 the Department of Health began to reduce the amount of vision coverage under the provinces' medical plan, providing one insured service per patient in a 24-month period instead of every 12 months. Responding to pressure from optometrists and others, in 1990 the government brought back 12-month coverage for persons under the age of 18 and over 64. Vision care is a service that has now been de-listed altogether. This restriction ignores the many eye problems that women experience with aging.

The process of de-listing other services continued into 1991, when the NMLA announced its doctors would begin billing patients for services not covered by MCP, but for which patients had not generally been charged in the past, including medical examinations for employment or a driver's licence;

medical advice over the phone; absent-from-work forms; and the cost of dressings and bandages for casts and splints.

Joyce Hancock, then executive director of the Bay St. George Status of Women Council, criticized the decision, stating "many of the council's clients seek medical advice in the quickest way possible – and that may mean picking up the phone and saying their child has a temperature of over a hundred." Hancock was also concerned that people "won't do things for their own health if it costs money," arguing as well that women working in stores and offices may be required to get a verification form from the doctor if they miss a day of work. Hancock also noted that women may end up going to work sick and spending the money on their children, rather than paying for the verification. Rev. Christina Oosthuizen, also of the west coast of the island, asked how a person on social assistance looking for work could pay $60 or $70 for a pre-employment medical. Such measures also have a high potential to hurt the working poor, as the minimum wage has not been indexed to inflation in Newfoundland and Labrador (*The Georgian 17/12/91*). The minimum wage was increased to $5.50 an hour from $5.25 in 1999, but Newfoundland and Labrador's rate remains the lowest in the country. A study of minimum wages in Canada concluded that 64 per cent of all minimum wage earners in the country are women (Goldberg and Green 1999, i).

In May 1995, the government announced that it would no longer insure medical exams required for seniors upon renewal of a driver's licence. This meant that the cost of a medical exam, which elderly drivers at 70 years were required to take every two years, and after 80 every year, would be shouldered by the individual driver. The cost of the exam was around $40 in 1995 (Government of Newfoundland and Labrador, Department of Health 1995).

Currently, the Newfoundland and Labrador Medical Care Commission, which came under the jurisdiction of the Department of Health on 1 April 2000, has a Surgical-Dental Program, which covers a limited range of surgeries, a Dental-Health Plan (DHP) and a Medical Insurance Plan (MIP).

While other provinces have recently reduced dental health coverage for children or eliminated the program altogether, children up to and including the age of 12 in Newfoundland and Labrador are covered for examinations at six-month intervals; cleanings at 12-month intervals; fluoride applications at 12-month intervals; x-rays; and fillings and extractions (NMCP n.d.). Parents of children using the plan must, however, pay an amount directly to the dentist for each service provided. This fee differs from dentist to dentist. Phone calls to various dentist offices in St. John's revealed that a cleaning can involve a co-payment of anywhere between $4 and $12 and a filling can cost from $12 to $40. Parents without private insurance pay the full amount.

In Newfoundland and Labrador, Social Assistance recipients from 13 to 17 years of age receive the same basic services as children under the DHP. Adult recipients of Social Assistance are eligible for emergency care and extractions only. Thus, if those over the age of 18 prefer to have a cavity filled rather than wait until their teeth need to be extracted, they must cover the cost privately (ibid.).

In December 1996, in reviewing the MCP's Annual Report, the House of Assembly noted savings of 2.4 per cent in the province's DHP because some services were no longer covered (Government of Newfoundland and Labrador, Department of Health 1996g). While the legislature did not specify the source of the savings, it appears that surgical dental procedures such as wisdom teeth removal were no longer covered even though the administration of general anaesthesia was covered if the procedure was done in hospital.

Under the *Medical Care Insurance Act*, the following services are currently insured for all persons in facilities approved by the commission, (i.e., hospitals) physician services, surgical-dental treatment, group immunizations, diagnostic and therapeutic x-ray and laboratory services. Services rendered by practitioners such as optometrists, chiropractors, podiatrists, osteopaths, denturists, psychologists, physiotherapists, audiologists and paramedical personnel are not covered under the Act (*Medical Care Insurance Insured Services Regulations under the Medical Care Insurance Act*).

Complementary Medicines and Alternative Therapies

Complementary medicines and alternative therapies are not covered under the provincial health plan in this province, but they are being increasingly used for treatment and prevention by a number of women. According to a CIHI study, women are 50 per cent more likely to use complementary medicines such as acupuncture, naturopathy, massage and homeopathy than men. The same report indicated that Newfoundlanders and Labradorians are the least likely of all Canadians to use complementary and alternative medicine, which includes chiropractic care (CIHI 2000a, 38). Less than 4 per cent use complementary therapies. Perhaps the fact that complementary medicines and alternative therapies are not publicly insured explains the low percentage of users in this province. This lack of coverage could be viewed as government not keeping up with the coverage of new and readily used services for those who cannot afford to pay.

Drugs

Medications received as part of institutional care are publicly insured and accessible to all patients. Payers include governments, through pharmacare programs; hospitals; private insurers, including insurance companies; employers and unions; and patients paying out-of-pocket. There is no universal provincial drug plan in Newfoundland and Labrador, unlike in provinces such as Manitoba and Saskatchewan, where individuals pay a yearly deductible (see Willson and Howard in this volume). In Newfoundland and Labrador only some seniors and people on social assistance are provided with a drug card, which covers a number of prescription medications and a few over-the-counter drugs.

Increases in the cost of prescription drugs and the use of expensive drug treatments for certain illnesses have meant that individuals carry more and more of the financial costs of drugs. National policy changes over the past 10 years have contributed to these increases. According to Colleen Fuller, in 1993, on the eve of signing NAFTA, the federal government enacted Bill C-91, which granted 20-year patent protection to expensive, brand-name drugs, most of "which were manufactured and distributed by the powerful US-based pharmaceutical industry." Bill C-91 has also meant a marked increase in the cost of prescription drugs – which went up 93 per cent from 1987 to 1996 (Fuller 1991, 191).

In addition, more outpatient surgery and the de-institutionalization of the mentally and physically disabled have meant that more and more people are having to pay for their drugs while being cared for at home. For example, the average length of stay in hospital dropped from 8.1 days in 1992-93 to 7.5 days in 1993-94 (Government of Newfoundland and Labrador, *Annual Reports*, 10-11)]. This increase in cost for prescription medications is especially prohibitive for women workers who are low income, part-time earners and not covered under private medical insurance policies.

Access to coverage for drugs for those who do not have private insurance or work-related health plans is minimal in Newfoundland and Labrador. The province offers a senior citizens' drug subsidy program for all residents over 65 years of age who are in receipt of the Guaranteed Income Supplement from the federal government and who are registered with Old Age Security. These are generally the poorest of poor seniors. Elderly women who do not qualify for the provincial drug subsidy are hardest hit by this exclusionary policy.

People in receipt of social assistance are provided free coverage for prescription drugs. However, in 1996, the government capped coverage for dispensing fees at $3.50 for social assistance recipients. The minister noted that

> the rate of $3.50 is all government can afford to pay in light of the province's fiscal position. It was never government's intention to implement a co-pay for social services clients as is the case in most other provinces. If, however, some pharmacies choose not to dispense within the set rate then I acknowledge their decision to implement a co-pay and the market will establish the rate. (Department of Newfoundland and Labrador, Department of Health 1996b)

In May 2000, the Minister of Human Resources and Employment used the drug card as an incentive for getting people off social assistance and into the workforce. He announced the extension of drug card benefits to single persons and families without children who move off welfare and into the workforce, stating that "for many clients, the loss of health benefits is a disincentive to taking employment" (Government of Newfoundland and Labrador, Department of Health 2000b). Families with children already receive drug card benefits for six months when they move into the workforce. Individuals with serious illness or children in need of medication, who only have access to low wage jobs, may not be able to afford to work even under the new incentive plan.

Physiotherapy

In the early 1980s, the majority of physiotherapists were employed in large centres or in hospitals. Community services were supplied by only two physiotherapists in 1983. The Newfoundland and Labrador Branch of the Canadian Physiotherapy Association said then that access to physiotherapy in small communities was limited by the fact that the local physiotherapist (such as in Trepassey) was not funded to travel, and that while some patients were funded to travel (those with Veterans Affairs or on social assistance), others were not. The association argued that the situation was not cost-effective because patients were referred to larger centres (CPA 1983). There is no evidence to suggest that the problems that the association identified in 1983 have been alleviated.

The president of the Allied Health Care Professionals Association has said that restructuring has not made a huge impact on her membership in terms of layoffs or complaints because most of the job loss has been through attrition. Migration to the private sector has increased substantially over the last 10 years (King 2000). Private practice physiotherapists are often paid better ($65 an hour compared to $23) and have better access to training and other benefits than those working in the public sector. Physiotherapists working in private practice often deal with patients who have third party insurance coverage, as well as injured workers. The newly named Workplace Health and Safety Compensation Commission's "get injured workers back to work as quickly as possible" initiative has resulted in an increase in use of private clinics.

Access to physiotherapy because of shortages and the inability to pay for travel to a centre where those services are available, remains a huge concern for residents of rural communities. Shortages of physiotherapists in some regions, such as on the west coast of the island, may delay women's and men's recovery from their workplace injuries.

The Health Boards Association identified the expansion of privately operated health services as a consequence of increases in "unfunded health needs, such as physiotherapy" and recommended that government establish a financial plan for the health system with adequate long-term funding to ensure a continuum of health services in the system (NLHCSA 2000, 10).

Ambulance and Patient Travel

The Health Care Corporation of St. John's has a tertiary care mandate for the entire province. According to the Department of Health, "The idea is to have major surgery done in St. John's with the patient being transferred as quickly as possible to the regional or secondary level and then back to the local community for home-based care" (*Evening Telegram* 24/8/96). Patients from rural communities must travel to St. John's for all major surgeries, radiation treatments and some other testing. Regionalization of services and the centralization of tertiary care in St. John's have raised serious issues of access and equity for those from rural communities. A recent community needs assessment for northern Newfoundland and southern Labrador found that roughly 20 per cent of visits per person per year to health facilities involved travel to a facility in the region, province or outside the province. This travel was to see specialists, for tests or treatments, and, in 8 per cent of cases, to see a general practitioner (Bavington *et al.* 1999, 21-23).

Local newspapers have reported on patients from rural communities who have suffered because of bed closures and cutbacks on top of the centralized system. For instance in 1999, a 93-year-old woman was put back into an ambulance for a five-hour drive after receiving a pacemaker in St. John's that afternoon. She was having difficulty, so the ambulance picked her up once again, and she arrived in St. John's at 6 AM in the morning (*Evening Telegram* 30/7/99).

The Department of Health administers the Emergency Air Ambulance Program for the transportation of patients within the province and to hospitals outside the province. Users are required to pay co-payment charges. Residents who travel by commercial air to access medically necessary insured services, which are not available within their area of residence or within the province, may qualify for financial assistance under the Medical Transportation Assistance Program (Health Canada n.d.).

Program applicants pay a $500 deductible in any 12-month period from the date of initial travel. Once the deductible is paid the remaining balance of expenditures is shared at 50 per cent. When the program was announced, the Department of Health did not address the issue of how low-income patients were going to pay for air transport if they did not have the $500 deductible. The cost of plane tickets from Labrador or the Northern Peninsula often exceed $500, and the cost incurred by a spouse or companion travelling with the patient is almost never covered.

Ambulance services are covered when an inpatient of one hospital is conveyed to another hospital for special tests or treatment but remains an inpatient of the first hospital. Some coverage of transportation costs is available under the Ground Emergency Ambulance Program and the Emergency Air Ambulance Program.

It appears that the government is further privatizing the province's ambulance services, without guaranteeing that private operators will adequately service remote areas. The Community Ambulance Association has raised concerns about increased funding to private, for-profit ambulance companies rather than to community-based services run by volunteer labour. Private ambulance companies keep 80 per cent of patient fees, yet many of the companies do not even operate in the communities they are supposed to cover (NDP Caucus 2000). For example, in St. John's in 1999, there were only two ambulances to cover between 200,000 and 300,000 people on nights and weekends. This compared unfavourably with the ambulance coverage in the much smaller region of Conception Bay South, where there were two ambulances and drivers covering the region, seven days a week, 24 hours a day (NAPE 1999).

Access to dialysis services has also been an ongoing problem for rural residents. If dialysis is not available for patients in a remote region of the province, then the patient and his/her spouse who need the service three times a day would have to relocate to St. John's at their own expense (*Northern Pen* 8/2/99).

User Fees and Hospitals

While under the *Canada Health Act*, institutional care in hospitals for medically necessary procedures must be publicly insured for all patients, in the 1970s and early 1980s, patients in Newfoundland hospitals paid a $5 per night user fee. This fee was eliminated in 1984, when the *Canada Health Act* came into effect, but the fee's elimination was met with opposition from the provincial department (*Evening Telegram* 7/1/84). Since then, patients have been required to pay user fees for a number of services they require in hospital, such as ambulance costs, some crutches, extra x-rays from the lab department, and photocopies of health records. There has always been a cost for semi-private and private rooms, but insurance companies are no longer covering it (Government of Newfoundland and Labrador, SCPAHCC 1999, 37, 39). Thus, the costs for private and semi-private rooms, based on rates set by the province, have been increasing for those who can afford to pay.

Yet hospital user fees are prohibitive to many patients who require certain services. Patients owed the St. John's Health Corporation $4.6 million in 1997-98. The corporation said that it rotates the claims between five collection agencies and "if one company is unsuccessful in getting the money we turn it over to another collection agency" (ibid., 37). The corporation has also adopted a policy of asking for a deposit when patients are admitted to hospital. What about low- income patients who are not able to establish a credit rating? The extent to which hospitals continue to take deposits from patients is an area that requires further research.

The percentage of day surgeries increased substantially between 1992-93 and 1994-95, from 41 per cent to 57 per cent of all surgeries (Government of Newfoundland and Labrador, *Annual Reports*).[6] Some operations, such as those for cataracts and gallbladder, can now be done using day surgery. Since services and drugs that are insured in hospital are not covered in the "community," the shift to outpatient care and day surgery entails transferring more of these costs from government to patients and their families. For example, many patients who require IV treatment, which can be administered at home, must try to take it in hospital where this expensive medication is covered. There is little evidence that patients are being consistently admitted to hospital so they can avoid having to pay these costs. The Health Boards Association noted, for example, that among the unfunded services that have been privatized in the recent past are "home support or private blood testing/ cholesterol testing/blood sugar testing offered in the home." There is no charge for these services in hospital (NLHCSA 2000, 10). Shorter hospital stays have led to some privatization of costs. In some instances, shorter hospital stays may increase the burden on unpaid care providers; however, much more study needs to be done in this area.

Midwifery: Who Will Pay?

The transformation of midwifery into a public service is still underway in Newfoundland and Labrador, but the question of who will pay for the service is an open one. In 1993, the government established an Advisory Committee on Midwifery whose final report was presented in May 1994. In February 1999, the government appointed a multi-disciplinary Midwifery Implementation Committee (in Ontario, the implementation process began in 1989). The committee's task is to provide advice to government on the development of legislation related to midwifery and the implementation of midwifery services in the province. It is also responsible for recommending the scope and standards of midwifery practice, midwifery education and registration requirements, and eventually the establishment of a board (college) (ACM 1994).[7]

In provinces where midwifery has been legislated, such as Manitoba, Ontario and Saskatchewan, the main issue is who will pay for the services (see Kay Willson and Jennifer Howard's article on Manitoba and Saskatchewan and Pat Armstrong and Hugh Armstrong's on Ontario in this volume). According to the Armstrongs, the use of midwives has been proven to be a cost-effective measure of delivery, if publicly funded.

Abortions and Private Clinics

In Newfoundland and Labrador abortions are publicly insured in hospitals. However, there is a long history of problems of women's access to timely abortions in their local areas. A private, non-profit Morgentaler clinic is established in St. John's. Women's groups have supported the concept of private (non-profit) clinics for abortions because there is inadequate access to the procedure in hospitals, the way in which abortions are done in hospital has not always met individual women's needs and there is a lack of other support throughout this potentially traumatic process. Women's groups have also argued that abortions in all settings should be publicly insured.

In 1995 then Federal Health Minister Diane Marleau announced that if provincial governments did not pay patients' user fees for private medical clinics, they would receive reductions in transfer payments. Newfoundland and Labrador refused to comply. At the time, abortions were publicly insured when done at the Health Sciences Centre, which was the only hospital in Newfoundland and Labrador that did the procedure (Matchim May 2000).[8]

When abortion was removed from the Criminal Code in a Supreme Court of Canada decision in the 1990s, it was added to the *Canada Health Act* as a medical procedure. The standard patient user fee for an abortion ranged from around $400 to $600, depending on the point in the gestation period. At this time the St. John's Morgentaler Clinic did about 400 abortions a year. The provincial Minister of Health held the position that the government would only pay the physician's fees, which amounted to around $85 through Medicare at the Morgentaler clinic, leaving women patients a bill of around $400. That same year, the General Hospital, where there was no user fee, did about 400 to 450 abortions a year.

In response to the province's refusal to comply with federal government policy, Peggy Keats, then manager of the Morgentaler Clinic stated: "we feel the province has an obligation to pay the fees...it's something they've been advocating for years, because private clinics are safer, more economical, cost effective, and less emotional for the patient" (*Evening Telegram* 3/9/95). Keats argued that private clinics are better able to offer confidentiality to patients as well as additional counselling services such as family planning and testing related to HIV and other sexually transmitted diseases. Equally important, the waiting lists for abortions in private hospitals are two to three weeks compared to one week at the Morgentaler Clinic (*Evening Telegram* 22/1/98).

In 1998, buckling under pressure from the federal government, the province agreed to pay patients' facility fees at the Morgentaler Clinic. The government's decision did not involve increased expenditures because it had been losing between $8,000 and $11,000 a month in penalties. While this has eliminated financial barriers to free, accessible and safe abortions, it has not eliminated the barrier of high transportation costs for women outside the St. John's area.

Workplace Health, Safety and Compensation

Significant changes in the Newfoundland and Labrador workers' compensation system in recent years have resulted in the privatization of some services, reductions in benefits and the transfer of greater responsibility for recovery and re-employment to workers and their families. In 1984 a new wage loss system of workers' compensation came into effect, designed to provide a worker injured on the job with income replacement in line with his or her pre-injury earnings. The Newfoundland and Labrador Workplace Health and Safety Compensation Commission (WHSCC), as it is now called, has since 1984, made a number of complex changes to the way the system operates most of them driven by a will to reduce the commission's unfunded liability.

In 1990, the commission announced it intended to undertake an organizational structure review in 1991 "in an effort to reduce unnecessary program expenditures" (WCC 1990, 3). Following the review, the provincial government made legislative changes to reduce benefit replacement levels for injured workers and levied a surcharge on employers. The commission also directed some care to non-traditional medical therapy (WCC 1991)[9] and pushed workers back to work quicker by queue jumping. For example, in the early 1990s the Medical Services branch of the Commission arranged for 797 injured workers to receive priority appointments with orthopaedic surgeons by paying a premium (WCC 1990, 9). In some cases the Commission has also paid to open hospital beds.

Between 1990 and 1998 the Commission began to focus on health promotion and prevention of workplace injuries. This shift took place within the context of swift budget cuts and additional reforms, including the integration of the claims and rehabilitation departments, and the adoption of a case management approach to claims management. The Commission also transformed the

Miller Centre multi-disciplinary assessment program for diagnosis and counselling from a residential to an outpatient system. In an effort to get workers back to work sooner, the Commission introduced "ease back to work" programs. Prior to this, vocational rehabilitation was introduced when an injured worker achieved maximum medical recovery. Another dramatic change to the system was the implementation of "experience rating" in 1995.[10] Experience rating means that employers pay lower premiums if they have fewer reported injuries. This often leads employers to deal with injured workers outside of the system. These factors have contributed to a near-complete transformation of outpatient rehabilitation. The new focus on prevention has placed more of the responsibility onto injured workers.

Reduced benefit levels have forced workers to shoulder a larger proportion of the lost wages associated with removal from work – a potentially greater problem for lower income workers than higher income workers. Commission queue-jumping may have contributed to general delays in accessing important medical procedures for non-work related illnesses. Experience rating may be placing particular pressure on workers vulnerable to layoff or demotion (many of whom are women) to resort to private health schemes or the public health care system for treatment and, in some cases, to do without the rehabilitative support they need.

Privatizing Non-medical Services

The privatization of non-medical services has been dramatic in Newfoundland and Labrador, in the outsourcing of dietary, laundry and housekeeping services in hospitals, as well as in the area of health information. Any shift from public sector provision of health care services to the private sector has the potential to affect women as care providers, whose jobs are transformed from more secure and possibly unionized positions in publicly funded institutions to often less secure jobs in the private service sector. Care recipients are also at risk where there is inadequate legislation to protect their privacy, and in terms of food quality and cultural appropriateness issues associated with the standardized, centralized food production of multinational food franchises.

Dietary, Laundry and Housekeeping Services

There has been a direct link between cutbacks to the health care system, government downloading of responsibility to the regional Institutional and Community Health Boards, and the contracting out of some services. In 1996, the St. John's Health Care Corporation announced the first of three phases of "expenditure reductions in dietary, housekeeping and laundry services." Since September 1996, Nova Services has been managing dietary and central laundry services, and Versa Services has been managing housekeeping for the corporation. Since 1996, changes in the preparation and delivery of food for city area hospitals have resulted in $1.4 million in savings. Food services in the hospital cafeteria have been contracted to major franchises such as Tim Hortons. Patients staying in the hostel at the Health Sciences Centre in St. John's, for which they must pay a nightly rate, have few other options than to eat their breakfast, lunch and supper at Tim Hortons, while other franchises complete their construction phase at the facility. Access to nutritious meals is jeopardized – despite the recognition by the determinants of health literature of the importance of good nutrition to good health.

The contracting out and centralization of laundry and dietary services have meant significant job losses. In 1996, the St. John's Health Care Corporation planned to eliminate 143 full-time equivalent positions. The second and third phases were to result in the loss of another 100 positions (*Evening Telegram* 23/10/96). The corporation planned the job losses through attrition, a voluntary retirement program and by cutting hours of temporary workers. The housekeeping unit at St. Clare's was hit particularly hard when 51 employees lost 24.7 full-time equivalent positions. CEO Sister Elizabeth Davis told the Strategic Social Plan Advisory Committee that we are "putting a lot of people on unemployment or social assistance" (*Evening Telegram* 26/10/96).

Questions about food quality associated with centralized cooking facilities have been raised in various regions. In 1997 the Central East Health Board requested an independent review of the planning, preparation and delivery of food to residents of Lakeside Homes in Gander after resident complaints about quality. Following the results of the review, the government ordered the kitchen re-instated.

Biomedical Waste Management

Since 1995 the government has reduced the number of incinerators operating in health facilities in the province from 24 to eight. In 1997, the province gave a private for-profit company a five-year, $3 million contract to provide biomedical waste, transportation, treatment and disposal services to health care facilities in the province. The government had earlier stated that it hoped it would "result in a private sector company setting up a single incinerator site to take care of biomedical waste from every hospital in the province" (*Evening Telegram* 7/9/96).

Financing of Hospital Construction and Privatization

The money the government extends to the regional health care boards has not been adequate to meet their infrastructure renovation needs. Over the past few years it has come up with new ways of funding capital projects, which have often resulted in further privatization. In 1998, the provincial government took $25 million out of the Immigrant Investment Fund to finance hospital construction and renovation in various parts of the island. The Public Accounts Committee raised questions about this new funding practice (Government of Newfoundland and Labrador, Department of Health 1998b). The Immigrant Investment Fund is supposed to provide incentives for private companies to set up businesses in Newfoundland and Labrador, to create jobs and bring capital into the economy. In the case of hospital construction, it appears the government is handing the buildings over to private companies, who take the risk, and then the government leases the buildings back from them (Government of Newfoundland and Labrador, Public Accounts Committee 2000).

When the government could not finance the construction of a new hospital facility in Melville, it entered into a partnership in 1996 with Voisey's Bay Nickel Company, a subsidiary of INCO, to build a hospital at Happy Valley-Goose Bay. Each partner was to contribute 50 per cent of the funding for the project. President Stewart Gendron stated, "Voisey's Bay Nickel Company is a long term corporate citizen of Labrador...we have to ensure there are adequate health and medical facilities for our employees, something we are accustomed to doing in communities where we have operations such as Thompson, Manitoba, Sudbury, Ontario, and Soraoka, Indonesia" (Government of Newfoundland and Labrador, Department of Health 1996f).

Health Information Systems

One example of shifting non-medical health services to for-profit corporations in Newfoundland and Labrador has been the creation of a private health information system known as SmartHealth, a joint venture between EDS Canada Inc (51 per cent) and the Royal Bank (49 per cent). EDS is a global consortium, partly owned by Ross Perrot, with registered profits of around $18 billion last year. EDS has also been involved in welfare privatization in the United States (Brown 1999). Manitoba, under the leadership of former Conservative Premier Gary Filmon, was the first province to enter into an agreement with SmartHealth, but Newfoundland and Labrador is the first province to follow through on this partnership. (The Manitoba deal fell through just before the 1999 provincial election.) The development of a private health information system in Newfoundland and Labrador has been key to the restructuring process. Government has proceeded without first adopting privacy legislation to protect individuals whose health information will soon be in the hands of private companies.

> The Newfoundland and Labrador Centre for Health Information was established following the recommendations of the Health System Information task force in 1993 to "bring various existing health information systems together to establish an integrated and comprehensive information technology system for health and social services." The task force recommended the development of a unique personal identifier (UPI), on the basis that "Quality information is not only important for improving the health of the population, it has become a commodity." The task force also recommended that the province adopt privacy standards, and that health informatics be identified as a priority strategy for the Provincial Economic Recovery Plan (Government of Newfoundland and Labrador, Department of Health 1996e). The health information industry has since become one of the province's targeted economic diversification schemes.[11]

According to the CEO of the St. John's Health Care Corporation, which is involved in the development of a unique identifier, "the biggest concern...is confidentiality and privacy. That is why in this Province we are working with SmartHealth because SmartHealth was created by the Royal Bank and we know we trust a lot of our information to banks and they have the capacity to keep that confidential, they have those kinds of systems developed" (SCPAHCC 1999, 36).

According to government, the database linkages possible with UPI will enable service providers to evaluate the relationship between program costs, outputs and outcomes, and to determine the most cost-effective use of resources in the system (Government of Newfoundland and Labrador, Department of Health 1999a). In May 2000 the province said the development of a UPI registry was underway as the first phase of eight in a provincial Health Information Network, which will be "comprehensive, integrated, person-centred...and will assist in the direct provision of health care services and research" (Department of Newfoundland and Labrador, Department of Health 2000b).

Genetics Research for Profit

The province's unique history of settlement and migration, coupled with its relatively small population base, has made this island, like others such as Iceland, a haven for genetic researchers in universities and in the private sector. New technologies and scientific methods have outpaced the development of privacy legislation to protect the individuals involved.

Dermatologist Dr. Wayne Gulliver has established Newfound Genomics in St. John's, a company founded by Lineage Biomedical of St. John's and Gemini Holdings of Cambridge, England. From his research on psoriasis, Gulliver determined that the skin disease was often passed down from generation to generation and he saw an opportunity to conduct genetic research. In an interview with CBC radio in April 2000 Gulliver said that "he hopes other companies come here to research Newfoundland's genes...genetic research could also bring in pharmaceutical companies and research dollars to Memorial University" (Gulliver 2000). He noted that a genetics industry in Newfoundland and Labrador could create up to 500 jobs. Gulliver stated that Newfound Genomics would share one per cent of any profits with a non-profit organization for psoriasis sufferers and that those individuals who give him their genetic information will retain their right to their DNA. Gulliver stated that "at a time when the government is struggling to find money for health care and education, genetic research is better left to private companies" and that Newfound will "generate revenue by licensing the new therapies and pharmaceutical applications that come out of its research" (*Evening Telegram* 22/4/00). Gulliver also hopes that the government will contribute seed money to his company.

The Department of Health has begun to consider the ethical and privacy issues involved in this new initiative. In a position paper on research, ethics and privacy presented to the department in 2000, Dr. Verna Skanes, past Assistant Dean of Research and Graduate Studies (Medicine) at Memorial University, emphasized that ethical and privacy protection mechanisms have not been put in place to deal with industry-sponsored clinical research. University-based research is bound by the *Tri-Council Policy Statement for*

Research Involving Human Subjects. However, ethics reviews of research carried out by researchers who are not affiliated with academic medical centres are generally carried out by for-profit review boards, which are not bound by the same guidelines (Skanes 2000).

According to Skanes, most of the genetics research in this province has taken place in academic settings, and has focused on single-gene disorders under the Tri Council Ethics policy. These types of diseases are relatively rare and have not interested private companies (ibid., 3). Skanes noted that new technologies developed as outcomes of the Human Genome Project have made possible the study of complex genetic disorders, such as rheumatoid arthritis and Type I diabetes, which are known to cluster in families. This is the type of disease that interests Gulliver, and the private sector more generally.

Skanes argues that Newfoundland and Labrador lagged behind provinces such as Alberta, Saskatchewan, Manitoba and Ontario in terms of privacy legislation relating to the protection of health information. She cautioned that the profit motive, and industrial culture which requires "patenting, secrecy, nondisclosure of research results etc., are in contrast to the sharing of data, collaboration, publication etc." of most university-based research (ibid., 8).

THE IMPACT OF PRIVATIZATION ON WOMEN AS CARE PROVIDERS

In Newfoundland and Labrador women make up a large proportion of paid employees in the health care sector. Over the last decade 80 per cent of health care workers have been women.[12] In some occupations such as nursing and in the home support sector, women make up an even larger proportion of paid employees. Thus, cuts to jobs in the health care sector and the ways in which working conditions have changed over the course of the restructuring process have been particularly relevant to women's experiences as paid workers. While all women health care workers have been negatively affected over the course of rapid change, most of the job loss has occurred in the lowest paid sectors of the health care system, which has increased these women's vulnerability to poverty.

Women's Employment

As elsewhere in Canada, government cutbacks in health care and restructuring of the delivery of health care in Newfoundland and Labrador have led to layoffs of women employed in health care occupations. The downsizing of support staff positions, middle management and the transfer of some institutionally based jobs to the private sector through outsourcing, have created a ripple effect throughout the entire system. Furthermore, the loss of jobs has been felt unevenly in different regions of the province.

Unlike other provinces, Newfoundland and Labrador did not lose nursing jobs through restructuring. Between 1994 and 1999, the Northwest Territories, Nova Scotia and Ontario experienced the greatest declines in the number of registered nurses per capita employed in nursing, whereas the Yukon and Newfoundland experienced the greatest increases (CIHI 2000c). Despite this trend, however, the Newfoundland and Labrador Nurses' Union (NLNU) and the Association of Registered Nurses of Newfoundland and Labrador (ARNNL) have repeatedly argued that there is a nursing shortage, and that at least 400 new nursing positions are needed in the province (NLHCSA 1999a, 8). Acute shortages of health care professionals over the summer months in places like Corner Brook, where 63 acute care beds were closed in the summer of 2000 because of nursing shortages, are an indication of a shortage and can have devastating effects.

The cost-saving measures of the St. John's Health Care Corporation, the largest industry in the province next to the government, have been geared towards reducing staff. Cost savings have been achieved through the transformation of full-time permanent positions to part-time, temporary or casual ones.

The casualization of the nursing workforce in Newfoundland and Labrador happened rapidly (see Table 1). In 1992, 11.9 per cent of the nursing workforce was casual. By 1998, 24.3 per cent, or 1,300 of the NLNU's 4,500 members worked on a casual basis. As one NLNU representative remarked, "There was a generation of nurses waiting by the telephone" (Vivian and Caroll n.d.). Of the 137 graduates of the 1997 nursing class who were working in the province in 1998, only one had a permanent position. As of 1998, casual nurses did not receive sick leave, vacation benefits or compassionate leave, and they did not qualify for maternity benefits under the collective agreement, but received 14 per cent of their salary in lieu of those benefits.

Prior to the 1999 nurses' strike, after which they got a seven per cent increase, nurses had not received a pay increase since 1991. Since the strike (the first since 1979), the provincial government has made an effort to restore permanent nursing positions. In March 1999 it announced that it would convert 75 casual nursing positions to permanent status (full-time and part-time) and create 125 new permanent positions (NLHCSA 1999a, 8).

Table 1: Number of Women Employed (Full Time and Part Time) in Health Occupations, Newfoundland and Labrador, 1990 and 1999

Women in Health Occupations	Full Time 1990	Full Time 1999	Part Time 1990	Part Time 1999
Professional occupations in health, nurse supervisors and registered nurses	3,800	5,500	1,000	1,000
Technical, assisting and related occupations	3,700	4,800	0	900
Total	7,500	10,300	1,100	1,900

Source: Statistics Canada, *Labour Force Historical Review*, 1999

This reversal of the casualization of nursing positions by government came on the heels of massive protests and public support for the nurses. Other issues that emerged during the strike remain unresolved. For example, the NLNU noted that health care workers who are represented by the Newfoundland and Labrador Union of Public and Private Employees (NAPE) have better family leave provisions in their collective agreement than the NLNU, whose membership is female-dominated (Vivian and Caroll 2000).

The NLNU and the ARNNL have argued repeatedly that nurses were not included in the decision-making processes that led to reform, and that when they were brought in, it was too late (Vivian and Caroll 2000; ARNNL 2000). Nurses have pressed for an increased role for RNs as entry points into the system and for more money to be shifted into the communities, especially for older people with complicated illnesses. They have also noted that shorter hospital stays mean patients who are sent home are ending up back in hospital. They are also seeing more pressure put on family members to look after their relatives while they are in hospital because nurses' workloads are too high – as a result, even care within hospitals is being privatized.

Other health care sector workers, such as support staff, LPNs and cleaning, laundry and dietary workers have experienced substantial job loss as a consequence of restructuring (Furlong July 2000). These women are the lowest paid in the health care sector and the most vulnerable to poverty in an economy where there is high unemployment and an over-representation of non-unionized service sector jobs.

The Health Care Corporation estimated that substantial staff reductions through restructuring would result in annual savings of about $14.5 million. Other ways the corporation has attempted to keep its budget in line are through integrating the administrative and support departments and outsourcing housekeeping, central laundry and food services. There is little evidence of job loss in the other regional Institutional Boards; however, the loss of even one or two positions in smaller centres can have devastating effects on the staff, community and on the quality of care (Vivian and Caroll July 2000). Many of those initially laid off in the St. John's region were in managerial positions, with transferable skills. However, women working in dietary, laundry and housekeeping services would not have had access to comparable employment in the private sector once they were laid off (SCPAHCC 1999, 20).

Working Conditions
In a population health model, which has been adopted by the province, income and working environments are important determinants of health. Over the past decade nurses and other hospital workers have outlined the negative effects of reform such as high levels of stress, increased workloads, rapid change with little input from frontline workers, understaffing, and workplace health and safety issues (Kelly June 2000)

Although the NLNU's membership had not received a wage increase since 1991, the 1999 nurses' strike was about more than higher wages. Nurses went on strike because they believed that more nursing positions were required in hospitals, long-term care facilities and in the community; their workloads were increasing at an alarming rate, as were workplace injuries; and that quality of patient care was at risk (*The Georgian* 9/2/99). The government's lack of commitment to contributing to the nurses' pension plan on a consistent basis, and other short-sighted health care policies were also factors in the strike (*Evening Telegram* 2/7/93).

The most traumatic restructuring initiative in the province occurred in St. John's, where the Health Care Corporation changed the model of health care delivery, flattened hierarchies and brought in program-based management in order to cut costs and streamline operations. For example, the six departments of physiotherapy in St. John's hospitals in 1995 were eliminated. Physiotherapists are now integrated into the medicine program or the cardiac program.

The impact of the shift to program-based management on women workers and women care recipients does not appear to have been examined, though some of these studies (if they exist) may not be readily accessible. However, women's health services appear to have provided a model for this approach. Sister Davis stated, "I can honestly say some programs were, from the beginning easier: women's health for example. Because St. Clare's had transferred obstetrics in the early 1990s, women's health was already pretty much functioning as a program" (SCPAHCC 1999, 31). Frontline workers indicate that the program approach is based on a business model, which does not necessarily work well in the health care system because the concept of patients as individuals gets lost and staff nurses lose their leadership at the unit level. From the nurses' perspective, these reforms have destroyed women's workplace culture and professional identities.

Restructuring has brought job reclassification. The nature of work has changed for many health-related professionals and the current classification system does not properly reflect the complexity of their work (Government of Newfoundland and Labrador, Department of Health 2000b). The government reclassified the management positions first and stalled the reclassification of other professions (NAPE 1998) which tend to be dominated by women. It has recently agreed to reclassify nurses.

A province-wide survey conducted by the NLNU found that 91 per cent of respondents agreed the role of nurses should involve more emphasis on educating patients and the community on illness prevention and health promotion (*Evening Telegram* 18/1/98). However, frontline workers charge that the government is only paying lip-service to the shift to community-based care. Over the past 10 years nurses have experienced powerlessness, no input, lack of clinical support and fewer opportunities for continuing education. Community health nurses have few opportunities to enhance their skills through continuing education, even though their roles have changed (Kelly June 2000).

In March 2000 the NLNU denounced Alberta's Bill 11 and asked the federal government to commit to funding increases, expand medicare to include home care and community care, impose a moratorium on public-private partnerships in health care, and declare that health care and social services be excluded from all trade agreements (*Northern Pen* 13/3/00).

Occupational Health and Safety

Occupational health and safety issues have been a major concern for nurses over the past decade. A study released at the NLNU's 1996 convention revealed that 85 per cent of nurses experience some kind of abuse at work. It indicated a direct link between restructuring and the abuse of nurses by patients: "Nurses feel that they're seeing more abuse because the cutbacks mean patients have to wait longer to receive care" (*Express* 30/10/96).

Only two years into its mandate, the Health Care Corporation of St. John's began acknowledging the increasing levels of stress on workers by introducing an occupational health system. However, two years later, the corporation proposed a "new sick-leave policy for nurses that would require nurses to waive their rights of patient-doctor confidentiality in order to avail themselves of sick-leave benefits." John Vivian, executive director of the NLNU, said the union is asking the corporation to redirect its energies to addressing the underlying causes of sick leave, rather than adding more stress to an already overstressed work environment (*Evening Telegram* 19/8/99).

Policy and legislative changes to the workers' compensation system have also had a dramatic effect on women workers in the health care sector. Legislated cutbacks in benefits to injured workers have been devastating to the NLNU membership. Nurses, like other injured workers, are now entitled to only 80 per cent of their pre-injury salaries. The NLNU mentioned that some injured workers have had to declare personal bankruptcy because of difficulties in making ends meet while on compensation (NLNU July 2000).

SHIFTING FROM LONG-TERM INSTITUTIONAL TO HOME AND COMMUNITY-BASED CARE

The shift away from institutional care in hospital to care in the community has opened the door for privatization on a number of fronts. While medical services, and pharmaceuticals are publicly insured under the *Canada Health Act* for patients in hospital, once a patient moves into the community these services are no longer fully covered. Long-term care in the community can be accessed through home support services, personal care homes, which are mainly privately run nursing homes, and other caregiving services in the home. Thus, hospital bed closures, shorter hospital stays and increases in outpatient surgery have meant that more and more families are having to confront the issue of financing their short- and long-term care at home, or in long-term care institutions. The cost for such care is increasing. In addition, the shift to community-based care, while supported in principle by women's organizations, has been built on the assumption of women's traditional roles as unpaid care providers. All too frequently the burden of this shift has fallen onto women; we do not, however, know the extent to which this has occurred in the absence of provincially based research on women's unpaid work. Long-term care also represents an aspect of health care delivery that is open to privatization. As elsewhere, access to privatized services in the home, such as personal nurses, home support and homemaking (in locations of the province where these services exist) are limited to those who can afford to pay. Other essential services such as transportation services for the physically disabled and elderly have been privatized.

Institutional Long-term Care

There has been a shift in thinking in terms of how the chronically ill are cared for. Throughout the restructuring process, the demands on long-term care institutions have increased due to cutbacks to acute care provision in hospitals. As more expensive acute care beds have been closed, new personal home care and nursing home beds have been opened. Beds in smaller hospitals in some small communities were converted into long-term care beds as these hospitals became health centres. Unlike in other provinces, such as Manitoba, where clients are assessed on a sliding scale, home care and long-term care are not insured services in Newfoundland and Labrador. There has been a steady increase in user fees for long-term care for those who can afford to pay the full amount, and a decrease in the subsidy for those who require government assistance.

According to the Department of Health, 2,920 men and women receive institutional long-term care services in 19 nursing homes and 18 community health centres in the province (Government of Newfoundland and Labrador 2000a). No breakdown by sex of these clients is available, but given sex differences in life expectancy and potential differences in the capacity and willingness of spouses to care for each other, the majority are probably women. In Newfoundland and Labrador, institutional long-term care, primarily for persons 65 and older and persons with debilitating diseases, is administered in community health centres and nursing homes. These institutions are now primarily administered by Regional Health Boards. However, seven nursing homes continue to operate under independent boards.

According to the Department of Health, a universal rate for long-term care was first established in 1984 at $1,400 per month, or approximately 70 per cent of the full cost at that time. The 1984 rate increased to $1,510 per month in 1986. Following a policy review in 1996, Health Minister Lloyd Matthews implemented a new rate structure for residents of long-term care institutions, the first adjustment since 1986. The 1996 rate for long-term care was set at $2,800 a month (Government of Newfoundland and Labrador, Department of Health 1996c). The Department rationalized its steep increase because of increasing pressures on the system related to an aging population, and a climate of fiscal restraint:

> currently there are 58,000 seniors in the province, but in the next 15 years there will be some 88,000 seniors.... those who have some ability to pay for nursing home care either through pensionable income, RRSPs and RRIFs as well as savings, should be required to make a contribution. Otherwise the ability of government to offer a long term care program in the future is seriously threatened. (ibid.)

Generally speaking, therefore, in 2000, if you had $5,000 or more at the time of the financial assessment, you paid $2,800 per month for residential long-term care (St. John's Nursing Home Board July 2000). If you had less than $5,000, all your income went towards paying the monthly rate, but you were able to keep a personal allowance of $125 per month.

The rate for personal allowance for residents in facilities such as nursing homes, personal care homes and residential settings such as Emmanuel House increased 10 years later in 1999, up a mere $15 per month, in honour of the Year of Older Persons (Government of Newfoundland and Labrador, Department of Health 1999b).

The 1996 rate structure often impoverished the spouses of individuals in institutional long-term care who remained at home. Until May 2000, only a client's private income could be transferred to the spouse remaining at home, which meant that old age security and guaranteed income supplements were clawed back. In response to pressure from community groups, this policy was reversed in March 2000, allowing the spouse at home to keep some or all of the client's total private and federal maintenance income.

Palliative Care

Recipients of palliative care have also experienced negative effects from the restructuring process. According to a 1999 report on palliative care in Canada, the Department of Health in Newfoundland and Labrador is conducting a provincial survey, followed by the development of a Provincial Framework for Palliative Care Services (SSCSAST 2000). Only limited data on palliative care are currently available.

On April 1, 1998 the mandate of the four Health and Community Services Boards and two Integrated Boards was broadened and they began to receive global funding for palliative care in the community. The Health Care Corporation of St. John's has the most extensive palliative care program in the province, with an eight-bed, in-patient unit. According to the St. John's Health Care Corporation, palliative care is not covered for doctors by MCP. Therefore the only hospital in the province with a palliative care unit – St. Clare's Mercy Hospital – pays physicians a subsidy for working with patients in the unit. In 1997-98 the Health Care Corporation allocated $50,000 a year for the subsidy, but stated that they were trying to reduce that expenditure (SCPAHCC 1999, 50).

Other boards have limited access to palliative care resources, and in many cases patients requiring palliative care outside of their homes have to go to long-term care facilities where they pay. The Newfoundland and Labrador Cancer Treatment and Research Foundation has a palliative care service, which conducts outpatient pain and symptom management clinics.

In June 2000, a Senate Sub-Committee released a report that argued that the state of palliative care in Canada was a disgrace (SSCSAST 2000). According to the National Union of Public and General Employees (NUPGE), the report concluded that "[a]ccess to, and the successful delivery of, quality end-of-life care, where it exists, was described as the 'luck of the draw's rather than basic entitlement." While the report did not include a gender analysis, many of the issues raised about the quality and access to palliative care were relevant to women in Newfoundland and Labrador.

The Senate Sub-committee raised several issues relating to privatization, including the fact that although some of the palliative care services are paid for in hospital, in long-term care facilities, residents must pay varying amounts. The committee's national survey also found that selected aspects of home-based palliative care may be paid by provincial health plans as part of a home care program, but these plans do not always include the cost of drugs and equipment such as pain pumps, oxygen and commodes. Some patients are thus forced to seek admission to hospital (if this is possible). The survey also found that some plans pay for only a limited number of hours of professional and home support services. Consequently, people may need to use private insurance, personal savings or contributions from social agencies and service clubs to cover costs. The Senate Sub-committee recommended that the "federal government immediately implement income security and job protection for family members who care for the dying" (ibid.).

Home Care

Home care is a health care issue of particular relevance to women, because women are more likely to rely on home care services than men, they make up the vast majority of home care workers and they are also expected to provide more unpaid care to relatives.

The Policy Context

Newfoundland's public spending on home care increased from 2.2 per cent of total public health spending in 1990-91, to 5.1 per cent in 1997-98 (Health Canada 1975-76/1997-98). Since 1984, the budget for home support alone has increased from $1 million to $30 million in this province.*

Home support started in the early 1970s in St. John's under the St. John's Home Care Program. Initially, services were contracted out to private providers (for-profit and non-profit) and were available to seniors only. Since then the home support program has become province-wide and has been extended to physically disabled persons under the age of 65. In 1996, the Department of Health assumed responsibility for the Provincial Home Support Program. Currently, the program has three components, including: the Continuing Care Division, which administers long-term care assessment for those over 64 (including home care and institutional placement); Family and Rehabilitative Services, which administers the assessment for those under 64 with disabilities; and the Child Welfare Division, for children in care or on protection caseloads (IAPP 1999).

The Department of Health has transferred the management of home support services to the Regional Health and Community Services Boards. In effect the province has divested itself of direct involvement in the administration and

---

* Home support and home care are terms that the Government of Newfoundland and Labrador used interchangeably.

regulation of the home support sector. For example, while the government once granted operating licences (under a provincial licencing board) to home support agencies, it has since abolished the board and delegated the task of licencing to the Regional Health Boards (William Shallow and Associates 2000, 39).

Throughout the restructuring process the department has not provided clearly defined standards for the sector, nor has it allocated appropriate resources to the regional boards to monitor the quality of care (ibid., 38). Some rural regions lack the number of case managers they need. In such instances, the home support sector is highly unregulated. In addition, in 1998, the government passed the *Self-Managed Home Support Services Act*. This Act declares that the person "to whom home support services are being provided is considered to be the employer of the person who provides the home support services." The bill's objective is to make clear that the government takes no responsibility for workplace issues (apart from labour standards legislation) for home care workers in self-managed care.

Three major studies done on home care in the province have determined that the home support sector is in a state of crisis. In January 1999, Health and Community Services commissioned the Institute for the Advancement of Public Policy to conduct a review of the Home Support Program to determine "the extent to which the program components are consistent in philosophy, orientation, and benefits extended to clients" (IAPP 1999, 1). Although the Institute's report did not include a gender analysis, its findings are relevant to understanding the impact of privatization on women. It determined that pressure on the home support program is increasing substantially for a number of reasons: government policies have increasingly promoted care in the "community" and the home; the population is aging; and outmigration and rural-to-urban migration have meant that fewer informal, unpaid caregivers are available in the community (ibid., 35). Second, the Canadian Research Institute for the Advancement of Women (CRIAW) published a gender analysis of home care issues comparing the St. John's region of Newfoundland to Winnipeg, Manitoba (Morris *et al.* 1999, 15). The study linked home care directly to women's vulnerability to poverty as care recipients, care providers and as paid workers. The third study, conducted by the Employers' Council of Newfoundland and Labrador, focused on issues related to home support agencies (William Shallow and Associates 2000). In Newfoundland and Labrador, home care is done through agencies or the self-managed model.

Access to aggregate data on the number of home care providers and recipients in Newfoundland and Labrador is lacking. According to the Employers' Council study, the Centre for Health Information does not collect data on home support and aggregate information is not consistently collected by all the regional boards. This presents a major obstacle to monitoring the situation, let alone to conducting a gender analysis.

Women as Recipients of Care and as Unpaid Care Providers

The CRIAW study found that women outnumbered men by a substantial margin in their need for home support services. For example, in St. John's 416 elderly women used home care in 1998 compared with 160 men. The CRIAW researchers found a more even gender distribution in home support services to the physically disabled.

The demand for home support services is expected to increase exponentially over the next decade. For example, the CRIAW study determined that in the St. John's region in 1996 there were 17,075 men and women over the age of 65. If the proportion of women were the same as it is province-wide (57% of the population over age 65) then the gender breakdown of seniors in the St. John's region would be 9,733 women and 7,342 men. In 1998, only 1.2 per cent (or 203) of these seniors qualified for subsidized care. The number of seniors receiving subsidized care dropped from 800 in 1994 to 203 in 1998 (ibid., 15, 50).

As the use of home support services increases, more and more of the costs are being shouldered by individuals. In Newfoundland and Labrador, there is no universal funding for home support services. Private clients can pay for their home support personally or through private insurance. Those who cannot afford the cost can apply for government subsidies. Subsidized clients are given the choice of using care provided by agencies (both not-for-profit and for-profit) or they can hire their own home support under the self-managed care model and become employers themselves. In general, seniors over the age of 65 living in urban centres use agencies and recipients under 65 (with physical disabilities) and those living in rural areas use self-managed care.

Since 1996 the ceiling for funding for seniors requiring home care has been $2,268 per month. Depending on their income, seniors might be required to pay from 10 per cent to 90 per cent of this amount. This funding is equivalent to about nine hours per day of home support, which does not include professional nursing care, physiotherapy, social work or occupational therapy, which are covered under the Health and Community Services Boards in rural and urban areas. Long waiting lists mean that recipients who have insurance usually use it for these services (ibid., 15). In the St. John's region, on average, seniors contribute around 12 per cent. If their income and assets are above the threshold then they have to turn to private care at $10 an hour for home support and $15 an hour for an LPN.

The government's rationale for the ceiling of $2,268 is to "allow approximately 8-10 hours of complementary care per day which would accommodate the working hours of families." In other words, the ceiling presupposes family support (IAPP 1999, 36). CRIAW cited a Department of Health representative who stated that "we don't measure it here but we estimate that informal family support amounts to 80 per cent of care. This is a national statistic" (Morris *et al.* 1999, 26). In addition, in the province, the financial assessment tool includes an inquiry into the extent of family support. This has major ramifications for women, whose services are taken for granted by the system and who are the likely providers of these services. In addition, many prospective clients have to wait for up to six months for their funding, during which time they have to pay for their own care (William Shallow and Associates 2000, 44).

A review of home support in the province criticized financial assessment criteria, arguing that it is difficult for almost all individuals (except those on social assistance) to access government-funded home support because "eligibility is based on levels of income that are below the national poverty line. Those applicants who are just above the income limit, or have fixed assets such as their home but few liquid assets, feel this most acutely" (IAPP 1999, 39). The reviewers also found the guidelines for assessment to be inflexible and did not take into account factors such as variations in the cost of living in different parts of the province, the seasonal nature of the economy and fluctuations in income levels. The review found evidence of families who have been forced to separate in order to qualify for home support services. Low-income working people who are supporting a disabled person or a senior family member often do not qualify for home support services, though they have willingly accepted responsibility for the care of their family member (ibid., 47).

The CRIAW study found that some seniors were left without enough money for food, and that several workers and agency staff said they regularly took food to their clients at their own expense (Morris *et al.* 1999, 28). It also concluded that "as family members, women are expected to supplement home care services for no pay at great expense to their health and economic well-being." Many unpaid care providers have to take time off work. As a consequence they lose benefits, seniority, incur out-of-pocket expenses and become more prone to injury and stress.

Home Care Workers

In 1997, there were more than 3,500 home care workers in the province working for individuals, agencies or voluntary non-profit organizations, over 95 per cent of them were women (Statistics Canada 1999). Many home care workers are former employees of health care institutions, laid off as a consequence of restructuring of the health care system (NLFL 1997). The CRIAW study argued that "the move from institutional care to home care is transforming an overworked and underpaid, mainly female labour force into an even more underpaid and isolated female labour force." It found that home care is vulnerable to de-professionalization and that nurses and LPNs were being paid less than half the wages they would have received in institutions (Morris *et al.* 1999, 17).

Home care workers are not adequately protected under labour standards legislation in the province. The Federation of Labour found that it is not unusual for a home care worker to report for work only to be sent home without pay because a family member had made other plans. Many home care workers work one-hour shifts, with eight shifts per day, stretching from 8:30 am to 10:30 pm. Many work for 12 days and then get two days off. Some work up to 50 hours per week. At least half of home care workers have other home care work, and some hold down three jobs (ibid., 44). Home care workers do not have adequate sick leave benefits, nor do they have access to injury prevention programs and little access to equipment while on the job. In terms of enforcing labour standards legislation, the Department of Environment and Labour operates on a "complaints driven" basis, and home support workers rarely lodge complaints. They quit instead (William Shallow and Associates 1999, 48).

Workers incur many out-of-pocket expenses, including professional licences and fees ($95 per year for an LPN in St. John's); updating first-aid and CPR courses; immunizations including hepatitis A and B ($100); gas expenses and buying food for poor clients. Workers also have to pay for their letter of conduct, and if they transport their clients in their own vehicles, they must pay for special insurance coverage themselves (ibid., 57). Recipients sympathized with the financial situation of home support workers (Morris *et al.* 1999, 46).

Home support workers are poorly paid. Their average wage in Newfoundland and Labrador in 2000 was $6 an hour, sharing with New Brunswick the status of being the lowest in Canada. Health care workers in institutions earn double for similar work and experience. As one home care worker stated in 1999: "I've been a home support worker since 1988. My son who works in a fast food outlet, and my daughter, who works in a clothing store in the mall, bring home more money than I do" (William Shallow and Associates 2000, 56).

Home care workers employed by agencies require 120 hours of training within six months of becoming employed but recent studies have determined that this is not always enforced. There are no guidelines or monitoring for training self-managed care home support workers (Morris *et al.* 1999, 47). Changes to Federal Human Resources and Development policy for retraining, which emphasizes EI eligibility, has also been prohibitive to most of the women who work as home support workers. Twelve-week training programs are sponsored by the provincial Department of Education at private and public training institutions, but the cost is $2,000 (William Shallow and Associates 2000, 48).

The unionization of home care workers in self-managed care is a complex issue. Community organizations have opposed unionization because they believe that individuals' needs would not be met. They have also raised the issue of continuity of care due to factors such as seniority rights. With self-managed care, the client is allocated a level of government funding, then becomes the employer and hires a home care worker to do the tasks he or she deems necessary. According to the Canadian Association of Retired Persons, self-managed care is more widespread in Newfoundland and Labrador than anywhere else. For people with disabilities, approximately 80 per cent of services are provided through self-managed care. For seniors there is a 75-25 split (CARP 1999, 49-50).

Home care workers in self-managed care are ineligible for workers' compensation, unless their employers purchase insurance out-of-pocket. There are no provincial regulations that state employers must provide workers' compensation benefits. Individual recipients of home support care are thus personally liable in the event of a workplace injury. In 1997, the provincial budget committed $1 million to extend coverage to home care workers in self-managed care but "this has yet to be implemented" (IAPP 1999, 54).

Drastic change to the home support sector in this province is needed.[13] The CRIAW study's recommendations for change were particularly aimed at improving economic and social conditions for women within the sector. The study recommends that provincial governments eliminate all fees for service; establish provincial professional associations for home care workers; eliminate gender bias in assessment process; require public and private agencies receiving government funds to be transparent and accountable to the public; and invest in respite care.

Other Community Care Issues

Mental Health

At a national level, a majority of depression sufferers are women. Between 1993 and 1998, diagnoses of depression increased by 38 per cent and the cost of prescription drugs for depression nearly doubled (McDaniel 1999, 200). According to Moyra Buchan, Executive Director of the Newfoundland and Labrador Branch of the Canadian Mental Health Association, the de-institutionalization of mental health patients began in the 1960s. While mental health advocates supported this shift to the "community," they did so under the assumption that proper support would be available. In Newfoundland and Labrador individuals with serious mental illness still have to travel to St. John's to the Waterford Hospital.

The major issues in the mental health system in the province parallel problems in other aspects of health care reform, according to Buchan. This includes regional disparities, distance from services, lack of community supports, outmigration of younger people, an aging population, difficulties in recruiting and retaining mental health professionals in rural areas, centralization of specialized services, and a crisis orientation rather than one of prevention and intervention (Buchan 2000). Another issue may be the offloading of drug costs onto individuals and families through de-institutionalization and greater reliance on outpatient treatment.

Since early intervention and prevention is particularly important for those experiencing mental health issues, any cuts to community groups and other organizations that provide emotional support as an adjunct to counselling and psychotherapy may have devastating affects. According to Buchan, there is not sufficient money going into the community. The restructuring process has also meant a lack of coordination of services.

Since the establishment of regional Community Health Boards in 1994 there has been a small increase in the number of community-based mental health counsellors and mental health programs in rural areas. In the private sector, there is a growing number of fee-for-service practitioners. While private health insurance programs and employee assistance programs often assist with part-payment of fees, many people who need services do not have access to these programs. In addition, people living with mental illness do not qualify for home support. They may qualify if they have an additional health-related illness or disability but not based on their mental illness alone (William Shallow and Associates 2000, 53).

In 1994, the *Profile of Women's Health in Newfoundland and Labrador* found that many women had limited access to mental health services. Barriers to access included limited programs and personnel, distance, responsibilities as caregivers, inappropriateness of existing services and the over-medicalization of women's health (WGWH 1994, 47). Mental issues are particularly significant for Aboriginal women in the province. These were highlighted in a 1997 report generated by the Tongamiut Inuit Annait Ad Hoc Committee on Mining in Labrador. The report recommended studying "the mental health of women and families due to the effects of long-distance commuting fathers," and "the impact on women's physical and mental health of the stresses of teenage and unwanted pregnancies, increased abortion rates, single parenthood" (Tongamiut Inuit Annait Ad Hoc Committee on Mining in Labrador 1997).

Women's Health and Women's Organizations within a Population Health Framework

The policy shift towards prevention, intervention and promotion, which has not been adequately funded by provincial or federal governments, has placed an extra burden on private non-profit organizations. In addition, the federal government's change from core to project funding for women's organizations has drastically affected their capacity to provide ongoing input into health care at the grassroots level.

Newfoundland and Labrador has faired relatively poorly in terms of indicators for women's health. Newfoundland and Labrador has the highest hysterectomy and caesarian-section rates in the country – 25 per cent of all births are caesarian. The life expectancy for women is the lowest in the country, with the exception of the territories. While Health Canada and the Department of Health have developed some programs targeted at women' health, they are minimal. At the provincial level, they focus on issues such as smoking cessation, child welfare, cervical and breast cancer screening, and violence prevention. These programs have been welcomed by women's communities, but it is unclear whether funding will be sustained. Project-based support arguably threatens sustainability, universality, and equity in access to the health care system. In addition, targeted programs do not address the need for gender-informed research and analysis, which considers all aspects of women's health status as paid employees, unpaid care providers and care recipients.

Planned Parenthood, a health centre that serves the province but is based in St. John's, has seen its role change in the context of health care reform and restructuring. Established in the 1970s, it has been able to survive while other branches in the province struggled to stay afloat and eventually closed. In 1981, the federal government stopped funding Planned Parenthood, which then had to rely completely on community support. The organization was saved by a private donor. In 1998, the provincial Department of Health began to provide $30,000 per year. Executive Director Peggy Matchim says there is considerable stress on the organization's resources because the government has done little to develop a sexual and reproductive health program in the province (Matchim 2000). The situation is particularly bad for young women living in rural communities and lesbians. Access to birth control is limited for many young women in the province. They may find their way to Planned Parenthood in St. John's, but more resources are needed in rural communities.

The Women's Health Network of Newfoundland and Labrador has benefited from special programs such as the Centres of Excellence in Women's Health that have provided some funding for research and action related to women's health. However, when the Network approached Health Canada for funding for its annual forum, which is on women's self care and cultural diversity, it responded curtly, stating, "we do not fund community groups any more" (Malone 2000). Health Canada only funds larger organizations to develop proposals that focus on long-range and policy issues. The Women's Health Network retorted that most policy change begins with the grassroots and argues that the federal government must demonstrate respect for the non-profit sector.

Newfoundland did not have a breast screening policy in 1992, and women were faced with long waiting lists for diagnostic breast screening. After a three-year pilot project, the government allocated $2 million in the 2000-2001 budget for a Breast Screening Centre in St. John's (*Women's Wellness* 1998). The centre coordinates provincial diagnostic activities and is the administrative hub for the breast health program for the whole province, yet expenses for women travelling to St. John's for this service are not covered.

A recent prevention and promotion initiative was the announcement of the launch of the Healthy Newfoundland and Labrador website, a site of consumer health information around the province. The local resources posted on the website for women include two breastfeeding support groups, the Women's Care Centre (since closed down), Planned Parenthood, the Urban Aboriginal Women's Group and the Women's Health Network. All of these resources are St. John's-based with the exception of one of the breastfeeding support groups. Groups such as the Urban Aboriginal Women's Groups which runs out of the Native Friendship Centre in St. John's, has not been able to secure government funding for any of its projects. In addition, many women around the province do not have access to the internet. The website exemplifies the way in which the government attempts to deal with prevention and promotion with the least amount of resources.

As a result of a joint federal/provincial National Child Benefit initiative, Newfoundland and Labrador was allocated $10.5 million per year in 1998. The province has used the money to improve and expand licenced child care, provide additional family resource project sites and develop a coordinated regional youth service network. However, the government rationalized these expenditures, which included a related Provincial Reinvestment Plan, by stating that they would "assist families in making the transition to work" and introduce "income support measures that address disincentives to employment" (Government of Newfoundland and Labrador, Department of Health 1998b). Limiting access to social assistance has the potential to negatively impact the health and well-being of single mothers and children if adequate well-paying jobs and other supports are not provided. In 1998, the government funded eight National Child Benefit and Family Resource Centres across the province as part of this venture. There is no guarantee that these centres will remain open.

Other private, non-profit organizations like the Women's Centres have been hurt by cuts in core funding from the federal government. The amount allocated to Women's Centres through the provincial government is only $30,000 per year. These centres often provide vital services for women in the community, such as lay counselling, referrals and early intervention.

The federal and Newfoundland and Labrador governments have not integrated a gender analysis into their health care restructuring processes. The few programs targeted at women are often announced and re-announced. They have focused primarily on reproductive illnesses, child welfare and violence prevention. Too often they are project-based and difficult to sustain, underfunded and too restricted in scope to ensure that women's health is promoted rather than jeopardized by policy initiatives.

Notes

This project could not have been completed without the invaluable assistance of numerous individuals and organizations, nor without the financial assistance of the Women's Health Bureau, Health Canada, the National Network on Environments and Women's Health (NNEWH), York University, and the "Coasts Under Stress Project." The author wishes to thank the Social Sciences and Humanities Research Council of Canada (SSHRC), and the Natural Sciences and Engineering Research Council of Canada (NSERC) who have provided the major funds for the "Coasts Under Stress" Project through the SSHRC Major Collaborative Research Initiative (MCRI) program. Funding was also provided by the host universities: Memorial University of Newfoundland, the University of Victoria and the University of Calgary. A list of those who provided insight is too long to include here, but I am thankful to all those who contributed. Any errors or omissions in the final document, however, are my own. I would like to thank the project's supervisors Drs. Barbara Neis, Linda Kealey and Shirley Solberg, of Memorial University of Newfoundland, for guiding the research and for their sound editorial advice. I am grateful to Barbara Neis for doing a thorough edit of the report and for conceptualizing and helping write the final section. Thank you to Cathy King of the Coasts Under Stress Project for formatting the document on such short notice.

1. Community groups speculate that more social services (e.g., social housing), will come under the jurisdiction of the health boards in the near future.
2. The Strategic Social Plan stemmed from the recommendations of the Social Policy Advisory Committee (SPAC), contained in two reports: SPAC, *Volume I: What the People Said* (March 1997); and SPAC, *Volume II: Investing in People and Communities, A Framework for Social Development* (April 1997).
3. I have used the Department of Health throughout the document in referring to the Department of Health (pre-1998) and the Department of Health and Community Services (post-1998).

4. The NLHBA started off in the early 1960s as the Newfoundland Hospitals Association. In 1987 the Association changed its name to Newfoundland Hospital and Nursing Home Association, to be more reflective of its membership, which now includes nursing homes. In 1995 its mandate was broadened to include community-based health services and Community Health Boards were added to the membership. In accordance with these health care reforms the organization changed its name to the Newfoundland and Labrador Health Care Association. In 1998 its mandate changed again to integrate child welfare, family and rehabilitation, and community/youth corrections into the health system. The Community Health Boards became the Health and Community Services Boards and the Association became the Newfoundland and Labrador Health and Community Services Association. In 2000, the Association Aðreviewed the many attempts to match the name of the Association with the evolving mandate of the health system and voted for a final comprehensive change, choosing a name that is clear, distinctive, and flexible enough for future change." (Newfoundland and Labrador Health Boards Association <ww.nlhba.nf.ca> [17 May 2000]).
5. The problems were said to have resulted from "increased patient acuity; increased workload in emergency and outpatient services; aging population with multiple health and social needs; pay equity; new high cost drug therapies, such as chemotherapy and antibiotics; inflation on supply costs; new technology; and increased maintenance costs due to the aging of the equipment and facilities."
6. There were no *Annual Reports* published after 1994-95, so the data is unavailable.
7. For the most up-to-date information available on midwifery in the province see Newfoundland and Labrador Midwives' Association at <http://www.ucs.mun.ca/'pherbert/>.
8. Abortions are still only available in St. John's.
9. See also Government of Newfoundland and Labrador, *1991 Workers' Compensation Statutory Review*. For further discussion of coverage for alternative medicines and therapies under WCC, see Government of Newfoundland and Labrador, *Report of the 1996-97 Statutory Review Committee on the Workers' Compensation Act: Time to Refocus*, May 1997, 82-83.
10. For a criticism of experience rating, see Newfoundland and Labrador Federation of Labour, "Evaluations and Recommendations: A Review of Workers' Compensation," presented to the Workers' Compensation Review Committee, 27 May 1991, 24-25.
11. See also "Recommendations" in The Health Industry Sector Development Strategy Working Group and the Economic Recovery Commission (1995), *Health Industry Sector Development Strategy*, 67-71.
12. These percentages are based on calculations from Statistics Canada (1999), Labour Force Historical Review. CD-ROM.
13. In March 2001, the provincial government increased home care workers' wages from $5.84 per hour to $7.01 per hour effective 1 June 2001 (Newsrelease, 22 March 2001).

References

Advisory Committee on Midwifery (ACM). 1994. *Final Report of Provincial Advisory Committee on Midwifery*. Presented to the Department of Health.

Association of Registered Nurses of Newfoundland and Labrador (ARNNL). May 2000. Personal communication with author. Used with permission.

Bavington, B. *et al*. 1999. *Community Needs Assessment for Grenfell Regional Health Services*. St. John's: Memorial University of Newfoundland Health Research Unit, Division of Community Medicine, Faculty of Medicine.

Brown, Bev. 1999. "Stop Making 'Decentralization to the Community' A Code Phrase for Cutthroats and Cutbacks!" Paper presented to the 10th Annual National Social Policy Conference, June, Montreal, QC.

Buchan, Moyra. May 2000. Personal communication with the author.

Canadian Association of Retired Persons (CARP). 1999. *Putting a Face on Home Care: CARP's Report on Home Care in Canada*. Toronto: CARP.

Canadian Physiotherapy Association (CPA), Newfoundland and Labrador Branch. 1983. "Brief to the Royal Commission on Hospital and Nursing Home Costs." October.

Dobbin, Lucy C. 1993. "Report on the Reduction of Hospital Boards." Presented to Hon. Dr. Hubert Kitchen, Minister of Health, Government of Newfoundland and Labrador.

Canadian Institute for Health Information (CIHI). 2000a. *Annual Report*. Ottawa: CIHI.

—. 2000b. *National Health Expenditure Trends (1975-1999) Report*. "Attachment 9." <http//.www.cihi.ca/medrls/nhexdec/attac9.htm>. 16 May 2000.

——. 2000c. "Canadian Institute for Health Information Reports Continued Drop in Registered Nurses Per Capita in Aging Workforce." *Newsrelease* (19 July).

Fuller, Colleen. 1991. *Caring for Profit*. Ottawa: Canadian Centre for Policy Allernatives.

Furlong, Carol (NAPE). 12 July 2000. Personal communication with the author. Used with permission.

Goldberg, Michael and David Green. 1999. *Raising the Floor: The Social and Economic Benefits of Minimum Wages in Canada*. Vancouver, B.C.: Canadian Centre for Policy Alternatives.

Government of Canada. Department of Finance. 2000. "Budget Plan – Chapter 6 'Improving Quality of Life of Canadians and their Children.'" <http://www.fin.gc.ca/budget00/bpe/bpch6_1e.htm>. 17 May 2000.

Government of Newfoundland and Labrador. 1984. *Report of the Royal Commission on Hospital and Nursing Home Costs to the Government of Newfoundland and Labrador*, Chair David B. Orsborn; Paul Patey and Garfield Pynn. St. John's: Government of Newfoundland and Labrador.

—. 1998. *People, Partners, and Prosperity: A Strategic Social Plan for Newfoundland and Labrador*. St. John's: Government of Newfoundland and Labrador.

—. 2000. *Budget 2000: for the Health of our People*. <www.gov.nf.ca /Budget2000/default.htm>. May 2000.

Government of Newfoundland and Labrador. Department of Health. A*nnual Report 1992-93; Annual Report 1993-94; Annual Report 1994-95*. St. John's: Department of Health.

Government of Newfoundland and Labrador. Department of Health. 1993a. *Newsrelease* (2 April).

—. 1993b. *Newsrelease* (2 September).

—. 1993c. *Newsrelease* (24 November).

—. 1994. "Newfoundland's Department of Health Reform Initiatives, Responding to Changing Health Needs." St. John's: Department of Health.

—. 1995. *Newsrelease* (1 May).

—. 1996a. *Newsrelease* (1 May).

—. 1996b. *Newsrelease* (16 July).

—. 1996c. *Newsrelease* (19 July).

—. 1996d. *Newsrelease* (4 September).

—. 1996e. *Newsrelease* (8 October).

—. 1996f. *Newsrelease* (22 November).

—. 1996g. *Newsrelease* (4 December).

—. 1997. *Newsrelease* (10 May).

—. 1998a. *Newsrelease* (25 March).

—. 1998b. *Newsrelease* (26 March).

—. 1998c. *Newsrelease* (5 June).

—. 1999a. "Improving the Ability to Use Information in the Health System." August 20.

—. 1999b. *Newsrelease* (22 March).

—. 1999c. *Newsrelease* (4 October).

—. 2000a. *Newsrelease* (15 February).

—. 2000b. *Newsrelease* (15 May).
—. 2001. *Newsrelease* (22 March).
Government of Newfoundland and Labrador. Public Accounts Committee. 2000. <http://www.gov.nf.ca/house/pac/feb700.htm>. 7 February.
Gulliver, Wayne. 2000. Interview. "News," CBC Radio, 21 April. Transcript courtesy of Newfoundland and Labrador NDP Caucus.
Health Canada. n.d. "Health Insurance – Medicare – Newfoundland." <www.hc.gc.ca/medicare/nfld-e.htm>. 17 May 2000.
Health Canada. 1975-76/1997-98. "Public Home Care Expenditures in Canada, 1975-76 to 1997-98." <www.hc-sc.gc.ca/datapcb/datahesa/E_home.htm>. 16 May 2000.
Institute for the Advancement of Public Policy (IAPP). 1999. *A Review of the Home Support Program*. St. John's.
Kelly, Colleen (ARNNL Consultant). 20 June 2000. Personal communication with author. Used with permission.
King, Sharon. April 2000. Personal communication with the author. Used with permission.
Malone, Donna. 12 July 2000. Personal communication with the author. Used with permission.
Matchim, Peggy. May 2000. Personal communication with author. Used with permission.
McDaniel, Susan. 1999. "Untangling Love and Domination: Challenges of Home Care for the Elderly in a Reconstructing Canada." *Journal of Canadian Studies* 34 (2).
Medical Care Insurance Insured Services Regulations under the Medical Care Insurance Act. OC 96-132, secs. 3 and 4. Consolidated Newfoundland Regulation 21/96.
Morris, Marika *et al*. 1999. *The Changing Nature of Home Care and its Impact on Women's Vulnerability to Poverty*. Prepared for the Canadian Research Institute for the Advancement of Women (CRIAW). Ottawa: Status of Women Canada.
National Union of Public and General Employees (NUPGE). 2000. "Backgrounder: Women in Health Care." Prepared for the National Union's Advisory Committee on Women's Issues." May.
New Democratic Party (NDP) Caucus of Newfoundland and Labrador. May 2000. Personal communication with author. Used with permission.
Newfoundland and Labrador Federation of Labour (NLFL). 1997. "Submission by the NFL to the Social Policy Committee of Newfoundland and Labrador on Home Care Workers." 4 March.
Newfoundland and Labrador Health and Community Services Association. (NLHCSA). 1999a. "Nursing Recruitment and Retention: National Efforts, Information and Summary Gathered at the 1999 National Labour Relations Conference." Winnipeg, MB: NLHCSA.
Newfoundland and Labrador Health and Community Services Association (NLHCSA). 1999b. "Tax Cuts and Health Funding." Presentation to the Premier's Advisory Council on the Economy and Technology." <http://www.nlhba.ca>. 28 September.
—. 2000. "Presentation to the Minister of Finance on Budget 2000." 1 March.
Newfoundland and Labrador Medical Association (NLMA). 1996. "Review of The Draft Model for a Redesigned Health Care System in Newfoundland and Labrador." <http://calloso.med.mun.ca/~nlma/nwslet/nlhca.htm>. 17 May 2000.
—. 1997. "Pre-Budget Consultation Brief." <http://calloso.med.mun.ca/~nlma/nwslet/bud97.htm>. 17 May 2000.
Newfoundland and Labrador Nurses' Union (NLNU). July 2000. Personal communication with author. Used with permission.
Newfoundland Association of Public Employee (NAPE). 1998. *Newsrelease* (22 July).
—. 1999. *Newsrelease* (6 August).
Newfoundland Medical Care Plan (NMCP). n.d. "Dental Health Plan." <http://www.gov.nf.ca/mcp/dental.htm>. 17 May 2000.
Peddle, John. May 2000. Personal communication with author. Used with permission.
Skanes, Dr. Verna. 2000. "Issues Arising From Commercialization of Human Genetics Research: A Report and Some Recommendations for Discussion." Paper presented to the Department of Health, February. St. John's, Newfoundland.

St. John's Nursing Home Board. June 2000. Personal communication with the author.

Standing Committee of Public Accounts on the Health Care Corporation (SCPAHCC). 1999. *Report of the Standing Committee of Public Accounts on the Health Care Corporation of St. John's.*

Standing Senate Committee on Social Affairs, Science and Technology. (SSCSAST). 2000. *Final Report: Quality End-of-Life Care: The Right of Every Canadian.*

Statistics Canada 1999. *Labour Force Historical Review.* CD-ROM.

Tongamiut Inuit Annait Ad Hoc Committee on Women and Mining in Labrador. 1997. *52% of the Population Deserves a Closer Look: A Proposal for Guidelines Regarding the Environmental and Socio-economic Impacts on Women from the Mining Development at Voisey's Bay.* <http://www.innu.ca>.

Tucker, Sheila. 1996. "Increasing Efficiency in the Health Sector: A Case Study of the Newfoundland and Labrador Department of Health."

Vivian, John and Karen Caroll. 6 July 2000. Personal communication with author. Used with permission.

William Shallow and Associates. 2000. *Home is Where the Care Is: Home Support Agencies Beyond 2000.* St. John's: Newfoundland and Labrador Employers' Council Home Support Sector.

Women's Wellness: Report on the Development and Implementation of the Breast Screening Program. 1998. Prepared for Newfoundland and Labrador Department of Health and Community Services.

Workers' Compensation Commission. 1990. *Annual Report.* St. John's: WCC.

—. 1991. *Annual Report.* St. John's: WCC.

Working Group on Women's Health. 1994. *A Profile of Women's Health in Newfoundland and Labrador.* St. John's: Department of Health.

Health Reform, Privatization and Women in Nova Scotia

Barbara Clow

INTRODUCTION

Despite the important place of publicly funded health care in the Canadian psyche and despite the profound health and care implications of reform in the 1990s, analysis of provincial reform initiatives has been limited. Few researchers have examined the evolution of policy and planning, or the impact of privatization. Moreover, gender issues and gender analysis have been conspicuously absent in many policy and academic discussions, despite the fact that women represent the largest proportion of health care workers and consumers in this country. This analysis of health reform in Nova Scotia aims to improve our understanding of the reform process at the provincial level – the site of health care delivery – and its implications for women.

The discussion begins with an exploration of the reform landscape of Nova Scotia in the 1990s, using the lens of privatization. This section highlights the challenges that reform poses for some of the smaller provinces, most of which have fewer resources to weather federal cuts and escalating costs. Although various governments in Nova Scotia have envisioned fundamental changes in the health care system, political leaders have found it difficult, if not impossible, to simultaneously reduce and re-deploy health care spending. The second half of the discussion locates both women and women's issues in the reform landscape of Nova Scotia, again with special attention to the nature and impact of privatization. As we might expect, privatization of health care has proved especially taxing for women in the province, despite some effort by government to include women and women's issues in the reform process.

Overview of Health Care Reform in Nova Scotia*

Throughout the 1970s and 1980s, Nova Scotia was "one of the most traditional of provinces in its approach to the health care system"(Bickerton 1999,166; Boase 1994, 101). While some other provinces elected to diversify their health care spending or their approaches to health care delivery during this period, governments in Nova Scotia remained committed primarily to treatment of illness rather than health promotion, and to hospital-based care and physicians' services rather than home or community care (Bickerton 1999, 179). In 1989-90, for example, doctors and hospitals accounted for more than 80 per cent of the operating budget of the Department of Health and Fitness, compared to just 2 per cent devoted to wellness and prevention programs (NS Dept. of Health 1990b, 13). As a result, Nova Scotia found itself in an especially difficult position during the late 1980s and early 1990s, when the need for restructuring of health care became more urgent. Having invested heavily in hospitals and doctors – rather than in less expensive programs and providers, such as home care and nurse practitioners – the government could not easily cut existing staff and services without jeopardizing access to and quality of health care. At the same time, the effort to devise effective reform strategies called into question the nature of health care governance. According to political scientist James Bickerton, "fundamental reform of this system involved a core choice between a more centralized, hierarchical system and a decentralized, participatory system" (Bickerton 1999,168). Through the 1990s, provincial governments were repeatedly advised to adopt the latter approach to health care reform – to rationalize services through regionalization and democratization of health care planning and spending. Cautious moves in these directions are slowly modifying the structure of health care delivery in Nova Scotia as the province strives to balance budgets and offset reductions in staff and services.

As rising health care costs and declining financial support from the federal government in the 1970s and 1980s began to strain provincial resources, the government was forced to re-evaluate Nova Scotia's health care priorities. In 1987, the premier struck a Royal Commission on Health Care, the Gallant Commission, to evaluate the health care system and recommend strategies for fiscal restraint. Although the government appears to have been mainly interested in saving money, the Commission stressed the need for more comprehensive reforms that would improve the quality of care as well as reduce costs (ibid.,167). The Gallant report proposed first a shift of health care spending priorities from disease management to health promotion, with an attendant reallocation of resources from hospitals and doctors to public health programs (Boase 1994, 87). Second, the Commission urged the government to rationalize the delivery of services and enhance public participation

---

* Because researchers have paid relatively little attention to the reform process in Nova Scotia, this section draws heavily on a small selection of studies, particularly the work of James Bickerton, author of an especially fine analysis of health care governance in the province.

through the creation of four Regional Health Authorities (RHAs). These boards, granted fiscal autonomy and staffed by "qualified and committed community members, including consumers and providers of health care," would not only eliminate duplication of existing services, but ensure that each region received health care appropriate to the needs of its residents (NS Royal Commission on Health Care 1989, 41-43). Finally, the Gallant Commission recommended a streamlined Department of Health and the creation of a Provincial Health Council (PHC) to advise the government.

The work of the Royal Commission on Health Care Reform embodied a new vision for health care and health care governance in Nova Scotia, and it served as a model for provincial reformers throughout the 1990s. But the immediate reaction to the report was not promising. Although the government recognized the need for restructuring and retrenchment, the degree of decentralization and democratization proposed by the Commission seemed too radical a solution for Nova Scotia's health care woes. Consequently, the premier established the Provincial Health Council in 1991, while other reforms recommended by the Gallant Commission fell by the wayside. Ironically, the PHC "soon became a vocal critic of the pace and content of health reform," prodding the government to move more swiftly in the direction of decentralized, democratized health care planning and delivery (Bickerton 1999, 170).

The election of a new government in 1993 seemed to presage a revival of the reform process: health care had figured prominently in election campaigns and party leaders had made political capital out of the premier's declaration that "community-based care" would be too costly (ibid., 171). After the election, the new premier also chose an outspoken and reform-minded physician as his Minister of Health. The Minister's Action Committee on Health System Reform, also known as the Blueprint Committee, was established to evaluate the state of health care in Nova Scotia. Like the Gallant Commission before it, the Blueprint Committee concluded that "the health system doesn't just need a new paint job, it needs to be redesigned and modernized" (NS Minister's Action Committee 1994, 8). Although Committee members accepted the necessity of cutting costs, they were equally interested in fundamental restructuring that would improve the quality of care. "Deficit reduction," concluded the final report, "is not health system reform" (ibid., 20). Specifically, the Blueprint Committee advised the government to shift health care spending priorities from curative to preventive services (ibid., 35). Committee members also favoured decentralization and democratization of health care delivery through the creation of a "network of Community Health Boards (CHBs), four Regional Health Boards (RHBs), and a Provincial Programs Advisory Committee (PPAC)" (ibid., 26). To ensure accountability and responsiveness in this new system, the Committee further proposed that RHBs be comprised of two-thirds CHB representatives and one-third ministerial appointees. Moreover, two-thirds of RHB members and one half of CHB members would be health care consumers rather than providers. The PPAC, staffed by representatives of the RHBs, the Department of Health and other stakeholders, would provide guidance in policy development and implementation. Finally, the Blueprint Committee stressed the importance of giving community boards "the maximum degree of responsibility and decision-making power," including control over budgets (Bickerton 1999, 172).

The government responded promptly to these recommendations, setting up four interim Regional Health Boards to "kick-start the reform process" (NS Minister's Action Committee 1994, 27). These RHBs, appointed by the Minister of Health, were given a mandate to provide primary health care, rationalize services and facilitate the establishment of Community Health Boards. In keeping with the recommendations of the Blueprint Committee, the government also proposed to alleviate pressures on expensive hospital services by providing better home care, including "single entry" coordination of regional and community resources (NS Dept. of Health 1994, 11-13). Having taken these first steps toward decentralization, however, the government stopped short of democratization. For example, while the Blueprint Committee had given top priority to the formation of CHBs, "to ensure we do not centralize at the regional level," the Department of Health hesitated to devolve responsibility further from the regional boards to the communities (NS Minister's Action Committee 1994, 27). As a result, the RHBs – rather than the CHBs – became the cornerstone of reformed health care governance in Nova Scotia, setting health care priorities, establishing and administering budgets, managing hospitals and controlling community input. RHBs also continued to be staffed exclusively through ministerial appointments, rather than from the CHBs, attenuating local representation and accountability.

Meanwhile, according to Bickerton, cuts to the Department of Health's budget "overwhelmed the reform initiative," necessitating not only "hospital and bed closures, salary rollbacks, layoffs and pharmacare cuts," but a strategic retreat from investment in "alternative services or community-based programs"(Bickerton 1999, 173-74). Despite the vision of the Gallant Commission and the Blueprint Committee, and despite the willingness of the government to reform health care, it proved too difficult to make cuts and salutary changes at the same time. As a result, spending priorities remained largely unchanged even after the government promised that "the provincial budget will transfer some resources from institutions to home care" (NS Dept. of Health 1995, 11). Between 1994 and 1996, for example, hospital costs and doctors fees claimed nearly 70 per cent of health care resources while other professionals and services received slightly more than 10 per cent (CIHI 1998, 274).

By 1996, health care reform had reached an impasse and Nova Scotians were beginning to lose patience, particularly in the face of continued cuts to health care following the inception of the Canada Health and Social Transfer. Doctors and nurses in the province warned about the dire consequences of health reform centred on reduction of existing services (Canadian Press

Newswire 20 May 1996 and 16 September 1996). A government poll likewise found that 62 per cent of Nova Scotians felt the quality of their health care had worsened during the 1990s (Canadian Press Newswire 27 July 1996). To alleviate pressure on the health care system – and the government – the Minister of Health announced an infusion of cash. An additional $65 million, he maintained, demonstrated that "this government is continuing its commitment to provide quality health care, and to the vision of health care renewal expressed in Nova Scotia's Blueprint for Health System Reform" (NS Dept. of Health News Release 15 August 1996). Not only was this a tiny sum compared with the $1.5 billion budget for health expenditures, but most of the money was used to defray traditional costs (hospital services and doctors' fees) rather than to create health care alternatives as recommended by the Blueprint Committee (CIHI 1998, 273; Bickerton 1999, 176). Other government decisions also tempered the process of decentralization and democratization. For instance, the Department of Health "proposed an extended transition period," which slowed the formation of CHBs and continued the policy of ministerial appointments for RHBs (Community Health Planning 1998, 27). Although the provincial government had approached health care reform with enthusiasm and determination, by 1997 the process was once again stalled.

Nova Scotia's next government took up the challenge of health care reform along with the vision of the Gallant Commission and the Blueprint Committee. Following the 1999 election, the Minister's Task Force on Regionalized Health Care in Nova Scotia was established to "study the strengths and weaknesses" of regionalized health care delivery and to recommend improvements to the system (NS Minister's Task Force 1999, 4). After extensive consultation with consumers and providers, the Task Force concluded that although Nova Scotians approved of decentralized health care, they did not understand existing arrangements and blamed regionalization for diminished quality of care. Moreover, many Nova Scotians felt that communities did not have sufficient representation in planning or delivery of health care services and that, as a result, local needs and opinions were being ignored. Some felt that they had lost ground when the management of community hospitals was transferred to the Regional Health Boards (NS Minister's Task Force 1999, 9, 18). The final report of the Task Force consequently emphasized the need to "complete" decentralization of health care delivery so that all Nova Scotians could experience "the benefits of a fully integrated, community-based health care system" (ibid., 9). In particular, the Task Force urged the government to define the status of the CHBs in law, ensuring adequate local representation at the regional level, and to proceed with the devolution of responsibility for health care to these revamped boards.

In keeping with these recommendations, the government introduced legislation to clarify and codify the roles of regional and community health boards. In 2000, the four RHBs were replaced by nine District Health Authorities (DHAs) appointed by the Minister of Health (NS Dept. of Health News Release

1 February 2001). The DHAs were mandated to "a) govern, plan, manage, monitor, evaluate and deliver health services in a health district ... in order to i) maintain the most beneficial allocation of health-care resources, ii) avoid duplication of health services, and iii) meet the needs of the health district, ... and b) to endeavour to maintain and improve the health of residents" (Govt of NS 2000, Clause 19). CHBs, in contrast, were defined as advisory bodies: they would develop health plans for each community, but would have no control over funding or delivery of services. While two-thirds of DHA members would be drawn from people nominated by the CHBs, the Minister of Health retained the right to make appointments to the DHAs and to request additional names where it was deemed "necessary to have a larger group of nominees to consider" (ibid., Clauses 11 and 52). In other words, the Community Health Boards and the people they represent still lack real power over the reform and delivery of health care in Nova Scotia.

Although decentralization has apparently reached a plateau, other reform initiatives hint at changing health care priorities. For example, in 1999 the government established a pilot project in primary care that relies on nurse practitioners working in community health centres, rather than on doctors based in hospitals (NS Dept.. of Health April 1999). The same year, the Department of Health announced plans to organize midwifery in the province as a "self-regulated primary health care profession"(NS Dept. of Health News Release 25 June 1999). In 2001, the government increased respite services for informal caregivers and set up a single-entry access system for home and chronic care, a system originally proposed by the Blueprint Committee (NS Dept. of Health News Release 14 February and 22 January 2001). Although these initiatives are encouraging, they are also fairly modest. As in the past, doctors and hospitals continue to absorb the lion's share of health care resources and, in many instances, the medical profession continues to enjoy a privileged relationship with the government (CIHI 2000). Although midwifery may become a self-regulating profession, nurse practitioners in the primary care pilot project work under the supervision of family doctors rather than as independent caregivers (NS Dept. of Health April 1999). Moreover, recent investments in health care alternatives have not kept pace with cuts to existing services. Fiscal realities have made it impossible to offset reductions in the number of hospital beds, nurses and support staff with serious financial commitments to developing long-term care or cultivating other health providers, such as midwives and nurse-practitioners. Saving money remains the government's top priority. As the Minister of Health observed in February 2001, "make no mistake, difficult decisions will need to be made. ... We have to control costs in a health care system that doubles its spending every 15 years. At this rate, future generations won't be able to afford quality health care. This government won't allow that to happen"(NS Dept. of Health News Release 1 February 2001).

Historic commitments to doctors and hospitals, escalating costs and diminishing resources, and the need for concurrent restructuring and retrenchment have long hampered the reform process in Nova Scotia and they remain formidable obstacles today. After more than a decade of consultation, reorganization and legislation, Nova Scotia has taken only the most tentative steps away from traditional funding priorities toward a novel system of devising and delivering health care. This fact has not been lost on the people of the province. In a recent survey conducted by the Provincial Health Council, Nova Scotians "indicated that they are tired of being asked the same questions over and over again; and they are very skeptical that anything will come of their comments and suggestions"(NS Provincial Health Council 2000, xiii).

PRIVATIZATION TRENDS IN HEALTH CARE REFORM

Privatization in health care appears in many guises: the adoption of corporate management techniques to ration and rationalize services; the expansion of opportunities for private, profit-oriented health service providers; the transfer of responsibility for health care delivery from publicly funded institutions to home and community settings; the shift of financial burdens for care and caregiving from the state to individuals. Provincial administrations in Nova Scotia have utilized many of these privatization strategies during the 1990s in their quest to improve health care and control health care spending.

From the inception of the Gallant Commission, reform initiatives bore the imprint of corporate language, perspectives and expertise (Chin-Yee 1997, 23). For example, while governments in the 1970s turned to the medical profession for advice about health care priorities, at the end of the 1980s the premier appointed an accountant, J. Camille Gallant, to spearhead the investigation of health care and make recommendations for improvements to the system (Boase 1994, 118). The Commission's report stressed the economic imperatives for restructuring, elaborating the implications of escalating expenditures on pharmacare, hospitals, doctors and ambulance services in light of decreased federal spending (NS Royal Commission 1989, 17-34). Even the health benefits of reform were cast in cost-benefit terms. "The challenge," concluded the commissioners, "is to devise a New Health Strategy that maximizes the impact of health expenditures by establishing a cost-effective health system that not only treats illness, but also prevents disease and promotes well-being" (ibid., 16). The Royal Commission also drew heavily on the corporate model to evaluate health care delivery and health care costs. Utilization rates, in particular, provided a standard of efficiency as well as a rationale for reallocation of resources (Chin-Yee 1997, 21). For example, the commissioners noted that "Nova Scotia's occupancy rate of 75 per cent for general hospital beds ... suggests a surplus ... and an opportunity for reallocating resources to other types of services"(NS Royal Commission 1989, 24). Interestingly, over-use as much as under-use could lead to the same solution: downsizing. The Commission justified cuts to pharmacare on the grounds that the cost of the program in Nova Scotia was already 32 per cent higher than the national average, largely due to "over-medication" of seniors and "the misuse of prescription and over-the-counter drugs by Nova Scotians"(ibid., 25, 67).

The solutions proposed for the health care crisis similarly emphasized better "management" of existing resources. According to the report of the Royal Commission, doctors were to be transformed from caregivers to "resource managers"(NS Royal Commission 1989, 55). Some of these strategies represented novel approaches to restructuring and restraint. For instance, the Gallant Commission suggested that physicians' fees be controlled through capitation, payment on a per-patient rather than a per-procedure basis, or through the creation of salaried positions. But these types of corporate solutions were not necessarily feasible. Although physicians' services represented an obvious target of reform across the country, the medical profession in Nova Scotia was especially liable to oppose changes that threatened professional incomes because doctors in the province had traditionally enjoyed a privileged and protected position in the health care system. The Commission also recommended that health care funds be diverted from tertiary to primary care without considering how this might be accomplished in a province that had previously made limited investments in home or community care.

Throughout the 1990s, a corporate mentality remained prominent in reform agendas. In 1995, for example, the government introduced legislation to amalgamate four Halifax hospitals into a single complex, the Queen Elizabeth II Health Science Centre, through which "all adult tertiary care in the province will be managed, coordinated and delivered." The Minister of Health told the press that the merger was an "excellent move" because it would "mean more effective health care and more efficiency of service" (NS Dept. of Health News Release 23 November 1995). The following year, the government also formalized a merger between the Izaak Walton Killam (IWK) Children's Hospital and the Grace Maternity Hospital. "It is necessary," concluded the Minister of Health, "to help streamline operations to enhance health services for the children, women and families in Nova Scotia and the Maritimes" (NS Dept.. of Health News Release 17 May 1996). In keeping with the corporate model, the government assumed that amalgamation of hospitals would save money by eliminating expensive management positions and the duplication of personnel and services. While cost containment and recovery were undoubtedly achieved through these consolidations, Fiona Chin-Yee points out that most savings arose from "reducing staff and out-sourcing work" (1997, 23). Nursing and support staff, in particular, were laid off, paid off, or simply not replaced in the amalgamation process and some services previously offered through the hospitals were "off-loaded onto other segments of the health and social services system" that could ill afford them (ibid., 24). For example, as government officials and hospital administrators sought to decrease dependence on hospital beds, through the use of day surgeries and shortened stays, the pressure on home care intensified (NS Dept. of Health April 1995, 17-18). At the same time, private companies took advantage of hospital restructuring to provide health care services. Following the creation of the QE II Health Sciences Centre, a

Halifax firm took over the training and management of 600 nurses working for the hospital as casual employees (Halifax Hospital Outsources 4 November 1996). During 1996, the Victorian Order of Nurses, a charitable organization providing 75 per cent of Nova Scotia's home care, likewise faced intense competition from private agencies for government contracts (Canadian Press Newswire 16 September 1996; *Halifax Chronicle-Herald* 17 October 1996).

One of the most persistent features of reform in Nova Scotia, as elsewhere in the country, has been decentralization of health care planning and delivery. From the Gallant Commission in 1989 to the Minister's Task Force on Regionalized Health Care in 1999, successive governments have prescribed regionalization as a cure for many health care ills. Supporters of decentralization, like advocates of hospital mergers, claim that significant savings can be achieved through regional restructuring of health delivery (NS Dept. of Health February 1998, 5-7). According to a 1998 report, regionalization saved the province $2 million by replacing 36 hospital presidents and directors with eight CEOs governing the Regional Health Boards and the newly merged hospital complexes. Additional savings of more than $2 million resulted from economizing on "middle management and support services" for "finance, payroll, laundry, housekeeping, and food services" (NS Dept. of Health February 1998, 16-18). Although these gains appear impressive, they represent only a tiny fraction of Nova Scotia's health care budget: between 1994 and 1998, the Department of Health spent nearly $8 billion on health care (CIHI 1998, 273). Whether or not regionalization facilitated cost recovery, it undoubtedly promoted cost containment. Although the government insisted "there have been no hospital closures due to regionalization," both health care services and personnel suffered drastic cuts through the latter half of the 1990s (NS Dept. of Health February 1998, 9). Moreover, the Minister of Health publicly acknowledged that economic "'modifications'" would continue. "We're in a budget crunch," he told the press in June 2000 (Canadian Press Newswire 7 June 2000).

Regionalization not only facilitated the privatization of health care delivery, it embodied the privatization of health care governance. Chin-Yee maintains that the "corporate agenda within the public health sector" has led to a downward shift of responsibility, "with more accountability resting on the shoulders of lower level workers, with none of the corresponding control" (1997, 23). Decentralization of health care planning and delivery in Nova Scotia reflects this trend as successive governments have demanded more and more from regional and community health boards without granting them authority commensurate with their responsibilities. CHBs, for instance, have been mandated to establish health care priorities but have no power to administer health care budgets. As a result, they have no guarantee that their recommendations will be heard or heeded by the DHAs or the Department of Health. Although the DHAs have greater control over health care planning and spending, being responsible for the delivery of services in their regions, their work is constrained by the fact that "funding envelopes" are determined provincially (Bickerton 1999, 173). Not only must DHAs work with the resources allotted to them by the Department of Health, whether or not funding levels are adequate to regional needs, but they are closely accountable for the administration of their budgets. Under the terms of the *Health Authorities Act*, DHAs are allowed to retain budget surpluses gleaned from cost-cutting measures, but they may not carry a deficit for more than a year (Govt of NS 2000, Clause 31). Similarly, DHAs are not permitted to invest in capital items, such as equipment or buildings, unless these expenditures have been previously approved by the Department of Health (ibid., Clause 30). In other words, decentralization in the interests of retrenchment has not fostered democratization of the reform process or the delivery of health care. As Nova Scotia's auditor general told the press, "many of the problems the health boards experience have more to do with the operation of the Department of Health than with any inadequacy on the part of the board itself. 'When boards are not informed of funding decisions on a timely basis and told they must maintain services and cannot implement initiatives until approved, then the boards are effectively paralyzed'"(Moulton 1999, 6).

In the same way, decentralization has served to divert criticism away from the Department of Health by shifting accountability for health care to regional and local authorities. In other words, the structure of the regional, district and community boards has allowed governments to retain close control of health care spending while conveying the impression that the Department of Health is not directly responsible for health care cuts. Although many Nova Scotians appreciate the formidable challenges facing RHBs, they have nonetheless criticized both the RHBs and the Department of Health for loss of jobs and services. The RHBs were so unpopular that in 1999 the premier pledged to dismantle the system (ibid.). In replacing four RHBs with nine DHAs, the government promised that the new system would be "more responsive to the needs of Nova Scotians ... and will strengthen the relationships between individuals, providers, and health care organizations"(NS Dept. of Health 1 November 1999, 4) Whether or not the new health authorities will be more responsive to the public remains to be seen, but they are already absorbing some of the hostility that formerly would have been reserved for the provincial government (*Halifax Chronicle-Herald* 16 July 2000; Walker 2000, 57).

Reform and decentralization have also encouraged "classic" privatization – a growing dependence on personal resources, financial and otherwise, for the provision of health care. For example, while public expenditures on health care have remained stable or increased marginally over the last decades, private spending in Nova Scotia has soared dramatically, from less than $100 per capita in 1975 to nearly $800 per capita in 2000 (CIHI 1998, 273; CIHI 2000). The largest share of private funds go to pay for drugs or the services of health care professionals other than physicians (CIHI 1998, 225). At the same time, because cuts to existing services have not been offset by investment in health care alternatives, Nova Scotians have had to shoulder the costs of health care delivery through the provision of unpaid services, notably home and chronic care for needy relatives. Critics questioned this growing dependence on privately funded and informal health care. Was it good for patients, they asked, or simply good for budgets? *(Halifax Chronicle-Herald* 24 January1998, B5). In response, the government portrayed home care not just as an effective strategy for cost containment, but as a healthier alternative to hospital or institutional care. A 1994 report, for instance, recommended that expanded home care services be available only to those who lacked "natural support systems"comprised of family and friends, as if state-sponsored care was somehow "unnatural" (NS Dept. of Health 1994, 8). "Normalizing" family and community responsibility for home care has helped the government to resist demands for financial compensation in the form of pay, tax breaks or pension benefits for unpaid caregivers (Campbell 1998, 5, 23).

Even in the realm of health care planning, governments in Nova Scotia have actively pursued privatization by encouraging unpaid work. Members of the District Health Authorities, for example, volunteer their time and services (Govt of NS 2000, Clause 15). Private initiatives in health promotion have similarly received the approbation of the government. In 1997, for example, the Minister of Health presented a Public Health Award to the Kiwanis Club of Truro for its efforts in maintaining a local park that "contributed greatly to people's health." A public health nurse in Kentville was similarly honoured for her efforts to establish sex education programs for adolescents (NS Dept. of Health News Release 7 July 1997). The minister's involvement in the ceremony, and the decision to announce the ceremony as Department of Health news, were particularly illuminating because the awards themselves were sponsored by the Public Health Association of Nova Scotia (PHA), a voluntary organization of health professionals committed to promotion of wellness and prevention of illness. By praising and participating in the efforts of a private, voluntary organization to reward private, voluntary initiatives in the promotion of public health, the government contributed to the privatization of health care in Nova Scotia.

Privatization, in its various manifestations, has thus become embedded in Nova Scotia's response to the health care crisis of the 1990s: successive administrations have embraced corporate models and solutions; profit-oriented companies have emerged to compete for health care contracts and provide services; private spending on and responsibility for health care have increased. At the same time, the government has tried to convince the public that privatization is not only necessary and effective, but "natural" and desirable. Popular and professional protests against cuts to health care spending, staff and services suggest that Nova Scotians remain skeptical about the need for or advantages of privatization. As Chin-Yee concluded from her survey of Nova Scotians' attitudes, "In 1997, 97 per cent of respondents felt that privatization initiatives would erode equity of access to health services. The poor, the unemployed, the old and those with low paying or part time work would be hardest hit" (1997, 111). But it is surely noteworthy that a Department of Health news release could quote the president of the Public Health Association in support of the ideals of personal responsibility and private initiative in health care. "All of us," she concluded, "in our everyday lives, have a part to play in making the public healthy" (NS Dept. of Health News Release 7 July 1997). After more than a decade of reform, privatization is more than just state policy – it may have become a state of mind for some Nova Scotians.

WOMEN AND HEALTH CARE REFORM

During the 1990s, provincial reformers have been mindful of the need to integrate women and women's health issues into the reform process. The Gallant Commission's insistence that reform planning and policies must be based on a "comprehensive understanding" of the health status of Nova Scotians inspired a 1993 survey of women's health (NS Dept. of Health 1993, 1). Similarly, a general health survey conducted two years later compared the health status of men and women living in Nova Scotia (NS Dept. of Health 1996). Provincial administrations have also paid scrupulous attention to the gender mix of committees and agencies dealing with health care reform, striving for a balance of male and female members. But while more women are advising the government and more women are being questioned about their health, awareness of the gendered dimensions of health, health care and health care reform seems fairly limited.

The first and, to date, the only government survey of women's health was released in September 1993: *The Health Status of Women in Nova Scotia*. Influenced by the reform vision of the Gallant Commission, the survey not only evaluated women's health status using biomedical indices such as hospitalization, morbidity and mortality rates, it also outlined the social, economic and demographic profile of women living in Nova Scotia (NS Dept. of Health 1993, 1). The report assembled an impressive and unprecedented amount of information about women and health, but it provided few analytical insights. For example, the survey revealed that women in Nova Scotia had lower incomes than women elsewhere in the country and that older women in the province were especially likely to be living in poverty. But beyond noting the association between low incomes and compromised health – and expressing concern – the authors made no attempt to correlate poverty with illness among Nova Scotian women (NS Dept. of Health 1993, 9-10, 47). The report also ignored differences among women and their impact on health status. No mention was made of the experiences of women of colour or women living in rural settings, nor was any attempt made to compare those experiences with white, urban women. At the same time, the exclusion of men from the survey made it impossible to evaluate the impact of gender on women's health status. Were men healthier than women or were they suffering similar rates of illness and unhappiness, and could differences or similarities be linked to employment rates and income levels?

Two years later, the Department of Health in collaboration with Heart Health Nova Scotia, released a second overview of health in the province (NS

Dept. of Health 1995). While the earlier report had attended to the social and economic determinants of health, these factors took a back seat to biomedical criteria in the subsequent survey. Public health nurses measured weight, blood pressure and blood cholesterol in survey subjects and questioned participants about their drinking, smoking, eating and exercise habits. Analysts later correlated these quantitative data with rates of illness, specifically cardiovascular diseases. Discussion of ethnic and regional variations in health status was absent from the study while the impact of class alluded to in the first survey had largely disappeared from the second. Indeed, poverty as a predictor of health status was displaced in this report by personal perceptions of wellness. "How individuals feel about their own health," the authors noted, "is usually a reflection of their physical, mental and social well-being.... Self-rated health has been found to correlate well with symptoms and actual health measures as well as use of health services. It is also a good independent predictor of longevity" (NS Dept. of Health 1995, 7). Personal attitudes rather than social conditions became the new yardstick. The *Nova Scotia Health Survey* thus reflected both a retreat from the Gallant Commission's vision of health care assessment and the trend toward privatization in health care reform.

The 1995 report did improve on the earlier survey by providing data on both women and men in different age groups, thereby facilitating a comparative analysis of health and health care in the province. But while the survey relayed information about men's and women's health, it seldom attempted to analyze gender differences. For example, the report expressed concern about high depression rates among younger women without exploring the causes of this phenomenon. The authors also made no mention of the fact that women in all age groups experienced depressive symptoms more frequently than men (NS Dept. of Health 1995, 13, 60). The report sometimes dismissed gender as an explanation for differences between men and women, as in the case of personal perceptions of wellness. The survey revealed that older men were most satisfied with their health and older women were least satisfied, but the authors concluded: "While this signals a difference between older men and women based on sex, the difference is more likely due to age. Women tend to live longer and therefore may be more likely to experience discomforts associated with aging" (NS Dept. of Health 1995, 14). This explanation reflected demographic trends and assumptions about the gendered experience of aging. However, in this instance the data presented did not demonstrate that the female seniors were, in fact, older than the male seniors in the survey (NS Dept. of Health 1995, 7). More important, in a report that stressed the correlation between personal perceptions of health and health status, no mention was made of the health and care implications of high rates of dissatisfaction among older women.

In 1996, the IWK-Grace Health Centre and a group of researchers at Dalhousie University led by John LeBlanc produced a new health survey, *Women and Children's Health in Nova Scotia*. Although the report was not technically a government document, the study was undertaken "to complement existing surveys," including *Health Status of Women in Nova Scotia* (1993). More important, the study was clearly framed by the government's reform agenda, as it aimed to provide information "at the county and health region level, thereby allowing comparisons at a level of use to local and regional health professionals and administrators as well as residents of Nova Scotia counties" (LeBlanc 1996, 1-1). It is therefore worth comparing the presentation of women's health in this report with earlier government surveys. Not surprisingly, women's health continued to be cast in terms that limited the possibility of gender-sensitive reforms.

Like the 1995 survey, LeBlanc's report focused on biomedical criteria almost to the exclusion of other determinants of health. Although information on social and economic factors, such as rates of poverty and suicide, appeared at the end of the report, they were imported wholesale, without comment or clarification, from the 1993 study commissioned by the Department of Health. And while the researchers analyzed suicide and addiction rates as well as disease and hospitalization rates by county, they did not investigate regional levels of unemployment or income. Without a comparable breakdown of economic status by county, it was difficult to conceive of or evaluate the impact of poverty on women's and men's health. Moreover, the biomedical appraisal of women's health was itself problematic. Men were excluded from the survey, as they had been in the 1993 study, making gender analysis impossible. More important, the report seemed to focus on gender-specific conditions regardless of their statistical impact on women's health. For example, according to the 1993 report, cancer was the leading cause of death among Nova Scotian women, followed very closely by heart disease and, at some distance, by strokes (LeBlanc 1996, 8-8). Yet the LeBlanc survey scrutinized the incidence of cancer while ignoring the incidence of these cardiovascular conditions. The investigators may have omitted heart diseases and strokes from their study because they expected the impending *Nova Scotia Health Survey* to address these concerns, which it did, but even their presentation of cancer statistics was troubling. The 1993 report indicated that women most commonly suffered from breast, colorectal, lung, and uterine cancers as well as lymphomas. Similarly, cancer deaths in women were most often attributable to lesions originating in the breast, lung, colon and rectum, ovaries, or pancreas, or to lymphomas (ibid., 8-13, 8-14). Despite these patterns of cancer morbidity and mortality, the IWK-Grace and Dalhousie University research team focused mainly on tracking cancers specific to women: breast, cervical, ovarian, and uterine. With the exception of lung cancer, the researchers ignored cancers that threatened both women's and men's health, such as colon and pancreatic cancer or lymphomas (ibid., 4-9 to 4-13). Not only was the context of women's health missing from this report, but women's health status was itself subject to misrepresentation.

Although the health surveys of the 1990s demonstrated a limited appreciation of the need to integrate women's issues into health care and health care reform, they were each hampered by conceptual or organizational weaknesses that limited their usefulness and impact. Some did not deal at all or deal well with the social and economic influences on women's health; some did not compare women's health with men's health. Most important, while the government sponsored two of the surveys and was certainly aware of the third, none of these reports received more than a passing mention in any of the major government documents on health care reform released in the 1990s. Women's health and health care concerns were largely absent from the restructuring process envisioned by the Gallant Commission (Gurevich 1999).

Just as women's health has been marginal to the reform agenda, so women themselves have often been marginalized in health care planning and policy development. Nova Scotia's minister of health has always been male and men have typically predominated in reform agencies and circles. The Gallant Commission, for example, had five members, only one of whom was female (NS Royal Commission 1989, iii). Ten years later, the Minister's Task Force on Regionalized Health Care in Nova Scotia had five female and nine male members (NS Dept. of Health 1999, Appendix 11). Other government reform bodies, such as the Blueprint Committee, have paid closer attention to their membership, carefully balancing the numbers of men and women. But they have invariably been chaired by men (NS Dept. of Health 1994, 68). Similarly, the original Regional Health Boards established in 1996 had equal numbers of men and women, but all four CEOs were male (NS Dept. of Health News Release 15 August 1996). Five years later, the restructuring of regional health care has not resulted in a complete transformation of gender representation. Although woman more frequently fill working positions on the new District Health Authorities, including that of the chair, eight of the nine CEOs appointed by the Minister of Health are men (see, for example, NS Dept. of Health News Release 26 September 2000).

We must evaluate this pattern of health care governance with due caution. The absence of women in positions of authority does not necessarily signal a disregard for women's issues, any more than the presence of women on governing agencies secures a voice for gender issues or analysis. Not all women are attuned to women's health care concerns; not all men are oblivious of them. Indeed, it is more important to attend to the opinions and actions, rather than the sex, of reformers in evaluating their commitment to or awareness of gender issues in health and health care. For example, while governments in the 1990s invited more women to participate in health care reform, gender issues remained virtually invisible in reform reports and on the reform agenda. More research is needed on health care governance in Nova Scotia – especially at the community level – to judge accurately the impact of regionalization on women's opportunities and women's health. But at this stage, the evidence suggests that the government has accepted the need to include women in reform and restructuring without embracing or perhaps even recognizing the importance of a gender analysis of health care.

WOMEN, HEALTH CARE AND PRIVATIZATION

While women and gender issues have typically been relegated to the wings in matters of health care policy and planning, they occupy centre stage in the delivery and consumption of health care in Nova Scotia. Women represent the majority of health care providers and support staff in the province, and women utilize health services more frequently than men. As a result, health care reform has had a significant impact on the lives of women providing professional and informal health care, and on the quality and accessibility of health care services for women.

As we have seen, doctors in Nova Scotia have enjoyed an exceedingly cordial relationship with provincial administrations. In 1997, for example, when departments and services in rural hospitals across the province were being cut, the government drummed up $8 million to "stabilize physician services" in those same hospitals (NS Dept. of Health News Release 16 April 1997). Although the privileged position of doctors has worked to the advantage of both female and male practitioners, the benefits of professional status have more often accrued to male than to female providers simply because the vast majority of physicians in Nova Scotia – 70 per cent – are men (Thorne 2000). By comparison, female care providers have often borne the brunt of restructuring and retrenchment. The plight of nurses during the reform era provides a useful counterpoint to the experiences of physicians. The largest group of health care professionals in Canada – and 98 per cent female in Nova Scotia – nurses have experienced steady erosion of their career opportunities, incomes, job security, and work schedules and conditions (Keddy 2000, 4; NS Dept. of Health 2001,1).

According to Boase and Bickerton, the relationship between governments and nurses in Nova Scotia "verges on the adversarial"(Boase 1994,102; Bickerton 1999, 167). Through the 1980s, militant lobbying by nursing associations and unions did not alter the government's predilection to support doctors at the expense of other providers and services (Boase 1994, 110; Bickerton 1999, 167). Moreover, reform strategies employed in the 1990s generally bypassed the medical profession to settle on nurses and support staff. In 1992, for example, the government legislated a five-year extension to the collective agreements governing unionized nurses in the province (Health Canada 1998-99, 28). In a position to negotiate for better wages and working conditions, nurses found themselves barred from the bargaining table until 1997. Privatization strategies likewise undermined the position of Nova Scotia's nurses. Hospital restructuring resulted in significant losses of nursing jobs and, together with private management of nursing personnel, reduced career opportunities, incomes and job security. Between 1993 and 1998, for example, "the number of registered nurses employed full time fell by nearly 800" (NS Dept. of Health 2001, 2). Nurses without permanent positions were forced to accept low-paying jobs or even to work several jobs on a casual basis to make ends meet while nurses with stable jobs and incomes found themselves working long hours of overtime to compensate for their employers' unwillingness or inability to hire additional staff. In the process, the personal and professional lives of both groups of nurses were seriously disrupted. Overworked and underpaid nurses found it difficult to provide quality care to their patients and to spend quality time with their families (Keddy 2000, 7-8, 11-12). As Barbara Keddy notes, "health care cutbacks have perpetuated unemployment for some nurses, forced overtime for others, encouraged outsourcing, and the negation of skilled, sophisticated nursing care, which ultimately undermines nurses' work"(ibid., 6).

The experiences of nurses in Nova Scotia were not unique. Health care reform posed similar challenges to nurses elsewhere in country and many experienced comparable deteriorations in their work opportunities and work environments (ibid., 8). But certain aspects of the Nova Scotia health care system created special challenges for nurses. Limited investment in alternative health care delivery programs, such as home or chronic care, led to an acute shortage of nursing positions. As hospitals eliminated nursing jobs, other institutions or programs that typically need nurses did not emerge or multiply. As a result, nurses were forced not only to accept poorly paid, casual work, but to compete with other nurses and with unskilled workers for the same limited pool of jobs. Some nurses even accepted volunteer work, simply to "keep up their hours for registration purposes" (ibid., 12). In other provinces, such as British Columbia, a stronger economy and greater investment in health care alternatives created more and better opportunities for at least some nurses (ibid.).

At the same time, divisions among nurses in Nova Scotia seriously constrained the profession's ability to resist privatization or reform strategies. Casual nurses were not admitted to the Nova Scotia Nurses' Union until 1998, long after they had come to represent a significant proportion of professional nurses in the province. Meanwhile, thousands of nurses joined other unions, such as the Nova Scotia Government Employees' Union, or chose not to join a union at all (Keddy 2000, 10). Fragmentation made it difficult for nurses to agree on professional priorities and to mobilize in defence of their interests. It also made it easier for the government to pit groups of nurses against one another. Again, by comparison, nurses in British Columbia have had greater success in articulating and defending their priorities because they all belong to a single union (ibid.).

Recently, the government has taken steps to address the concerns of Nova Scotia's nurses and the dangers posed by an increasing shortage of nurses. In 1999, the premier promised 650 new positions for nurses in Nova Scotia. But, as in the past, fiscal realities have made it difficult for the government to follow through on pledges, with the result that only 20 per cent of these jobs have materialized (ibid., 8). Moreover, dilemmas created by the reform strategies of the 1990s continue to plague the nursing profession. According to a 2001 government report, the majority of nurses are not able to find permanent full-time positions upon graduation (NS Dept. of Health 2001,1). Consequently, they must work in casual jobs that often do not afford adequate opportunities to transform academic into clinical excellence. Moreover, many nurses report ongoing dissatisfaction with their professional lives, including issues related to workloads, career development and wages. In April 2001, the government committed $5 million to develop "a coordinated, comprehensive strategy to address nursing concerns" (ibid., 8). Rather than simply creating more full-time jobs, the government plans to mount new educational opportunities for student and practicing nurses, and deploy new incentives to recruit or retain nurses. Although these programs address some of the professional concerns of nurses, other aspects of the "nursing strategy" are infused with the language and goals of privatization. New graduates will not enjoy more manageable workloads: instead they themselves will be managed in such as way that they are "more proficient and better able to handle heavier workloads." At the same time, "the Department of Health will benefit through reduced orientation costs and an increased likelihood that new graduates will remain in the province" (ibid., 5). Although this initiative represents an innovative approach to restructuring, the bottom line of the new proposal is still cost containment and efficiency. As the report concludes, the nursing strategy "moves us closer to our goal of achieving and maintaining the optimal number, mix, and distribution of nurses to meet the health needs of Nova Scotians, at a cost the province is able to afford" (ibid., 8).

Health care professionals have not been the only casualties of privatization. Cutbacks in services, shorter hospital stays and limited investment in health care alternatives have in many cases shifted the burden of patient care onto the shoulders of families, friends and communities. Because long-term care is not an insured service in Nova Scotia, relatives must choose between paying for services or providing care themselves. Many families simply cannot afford the costs of nursing homes, seniors' homes or other chronic care facilities, which in 1997 charged $69 to $135 a day (Health Canada 1998-99, 14). Even when relatives are prepared to pay for care, even when provincial subsidies help to offset the expense, there are often long delays in arranging admission to an appropriate care facility. Beds and services are simply not available because "the shift in responsibility for long-term care has not been accompanied by a commensurate transfer of resources" (Campbell 1998, 9). As a result, a significant proportion of long term care is provided by family members and, like nurses, most of these unpaid caregivers are women (ibid., 3).

Privatization of health care delivery has placed onerous demands on women caregivers. The majority – 80 per cent – are on duty 24 hours a day, seven days a week, with little or no relief. Some women provide care for only a few months while others do so for years, and a small proportion of caregivers are responsible for the care of more than one person (ibid., 16-17). At the same time, the services provided by women differ from those provided by male caregivers. The 1995 *Nova Scotia Health Survey* revealed that women were more likely to help with personal care, such as grooming and bathing, and domestic chores, including grocery shopping, meal preparation and housework, while men "helped more often with transportation, home maintenance, snow shoveling, and money management" (NS Dept. of Health 1995, 11). In other words, the responsibilities of female caregivers tend to be intense – deeply personal and constant – while the duties of male providers are generally less intimate and more intermittent. Not surprisingly, many woman caregivers feel overburdened. Although the 1995 health survey maintained that 83 per cent of caregivers feel able to cope most or all of the time, a study of rural women in Nova Scotia revealed a wide variety of strains (ibid., 12). Most could not turn easily to friends and neighbours for help, and community supports were often inadequate. Fifty per cent had left paid employment or taken part-time work, sometimes sacrificing careers and compounding the economic pressures associated with caring for a sick relative, including the costs of medications, special foods, medical and personal supplies, and transportation. Fifteen per cent of these women reported that they routinely ran out of money to purchase groceries (Campbell 1998, 16). In addition to financial worries, many caregivers experienced significant physical and emotional strains as a direct result of their home care responsibilities. "As caregivers," reported one woman, "you are living constantly with stress and ongoing stress can make you ill; and no pill can fix that. If caregiving becomes all consuming one can lose their identity. Emotions can build causing anger and frustration; family breakdown can even occur"(ibid., 20).

In 1994, the Blueprint Committee openly acknowledged both the deficiencies of home care in Nova Scotia and the crucial economic contribution made by unpaid caregivers (NS Dept. of Health 1994, 24). In order to alleviate some of the pressure on family and friends, the Committee proposed the creation of new programs to help Nova Scotians who were ineligible for home care services, such as those with terminal illnesses or those recovering from accidental injuries (NS Dept. of Health April 1995, 12). The Blueprint Committee further recommended coordination of services to ensure swifter access and more "appropriate" use of new and existing programs. While the expansion of home care undoubtedly increased the number of Nova Scotians eligible for and receiving financial aid, it is clear that many patients and caregivers continue to fall through the cracks because programs have developed slowly or not at all. By 1999, only two of the seven planned programs, acute and chronic care, had taken shape (Health Canada 1998-99, 15). Other reforms appear both salutary and solicitous, but do not address either the plight of unpaid caregivers or government dependence on their unpaid work. For example, the 2001 increase in respite services from 32 to 40 hours a month is a negligible improvement for caregivers who work all day, every day. It does not allow them to take even one weekend off a month while a week-long vacation once a year requires them to "save their hours," forfeiting all relief for more than four months (NS Dept. of Health News Release 14 February 2001). Respite services are even more inadequate for rural caregivers because a single visit to the doctor might "exceed an entire week's respite allocation, leaving no time for a rest from responsibilities" (Campbell 1998, 22). Exploitation on this scale would not be tolerated in the work place, but unpaid caregivers have no legislation and few organizations to defend their interests. Consequently, repeated demands for compensation, ranging from tax credits and pension benefits to wages, have fallen on deaf ears (ibid., 5, 19-20). As one Nova Scotia woman observed, "Caregivers are the unsung heroes of the homecare system and our government doesn't give a RIP!"(ibid., 23).

Although the members of the Blueprint Committee cautiously admitted that unpaid caregivers are "usually – but not always – women," their recommendations ignored the gender dimensions of home care. None of the policies or programs targeted women; no effort was made to evaluate the different needs, skills and experiences of male and female caregivers. Moreover, beyond promoting consultation through regionalization, a strategy of uncertain value, governments in Nova Scotia have made no effort to include informal caregivers in planning and delivery of services. As one group of researchers concluded, privatization rather than consultation has been the main aim of the government: "It seems clear that involvement of and support to caregivers has been subordinated to the pursuit of other program goals: cost reduction through substitution of services; maintaining clients in less costly locations, i.e., home environments; and prevention and monitoring services"(ibid., 10).

Privatization of health care delivery has implications for women not only as caregivers, but as recipients of health care. The impact of health care reform on women's health is perhaps most obvious with respect to seniors. Because women typically live longer than men, they are more likely than men to experience health complications associated with aging. In 1995, for example, 66 per cent of women over the age of 65 reported one or more chronic health conditions, compared with 47 per cent of men in the same age group (NS Dept. of Health 1996, 47). At the same time, female seniors more often live in poverty than do their male counterparts. Statistics for 1997 reveal that 16 per cent of elderly females in the province had low incomes whereas only 9 per cent of elderly males fell into this category (NS Provincial Health Council 2000). Deficiencies in Nova Scotia's health care programs not only affect more women than men, they affect women more profoundly than men. In the case of home care and long-term care, older women may be doubly disadvantaged because, as a group, they are more likely to need these services and to be acting as caregivers for others (Campbell 1998, 9).

The negative effects of privatization are equally evident in the reform of the Pharmacare program, Nova Scotia's prescription drug plan for seniors. Established in 1974, Pharmacare benefits were freely available to seniors throughout the province for more than two decades. But rising drug costs, an aging population and budgetary cutbacks encouraged the government to make significant changes to the program. Beginning in April 1995, seniors were charged an annual premium of $215 to cover 80 per cent of the costs of prescription drugs. The remaining 20 per cent was paid by seniors out-of-pocket, to an annual maximum of $200 (NS Dept. of Health News Release 9 January 1996). Although low-income seniors were eligible for a $300 tax credit, this benefit did not entirely offset the costs of premiums or co-payments, and seniors had to provide proof of their income to be approved for tax relief. Cost sharing and cost recovery had replaced the principle of entitlement in the Pharmacare program (Health Canada 1998-99, 20). Once again, older women suffer most as a result of these reforms because they represent the majority of older, low-income Nova Scotians. Subsequent changes to the program only aggravated the situation. In 1996, for example, the government improved access to tax credits for low-income married seniors, but not for low-income single seniors – most of whom were women (NS Dept. of Health News Release 13 March 1996). More recently, financial conditions forced the provincial government to renege on a 1998 pledge to eliminate Pharmacare premiums while the current administration, elected in 1999, has been all but silent on the future of Nova Scotia's drug benefit program.

Although health care reform has created new and serious challenges for seniors, older females are not the only women suffering the effects of privatization. Indeed, younger women face some of the same problems as older women in the province. In 1997, for example, children living in single-parent households headed by women comprised 70 per cent of low-income Nova Scotians (NS Provincial Health Council 2000). Cutbacks to health care services have dire implications for these women and children, especially when their health is compromised by poverty. At the same time, rural women in Nova Scotia, young and old alike, feel the effects of reform most keenly because health care cuts have been deepest in smaller communities (Campbell 1998, 11-12; Keddy 1999, 8). But some health care services, particularly those related to reproduction, are specific to younger women and privatization has affected their quality and availability.

According to the 1993 survey of women's health, pregnancy was the leading cause of hospitalization, and episiotomy the most common surgical procedure for women in the province (NS Dept. of Health 1993, 29). In 1995, approximately one half of hospitals births took place at the IWK-Grace Health Centre in Halifax, "the only tertiary-level maternity centre with a full range of services in Nova Scotia" (NS Dept. of Health 1997, 22). Undoubtedly some of these births followed complicated pregnancies and labours that could be managed most effectively at the Halifax hospital, but the decline of maternity services elsewhere in the province probably accounted for at least some of the births. Between 1988 and 1995, budgetary constraints led 12 community hospitals in Nova Scotia to eliminate maternity and newborn services (NS Dept. of Health 1997, 22). Loss of hospital maternity care, in turn, "prompted some family physicians to stop offering maternity care altogether," both in community and regional hospitals (ibid., 27-29). As a result, expectant mothers in these communities have been forced to travel to larger centres for prenatal care and hospital delivery, incurring significant expenses in the process. Many complain about the added costs of childcare, travel, food and accommodation, and long distance calls as well as lost income. One woman estimated that she had paid $1,800 in out-of-pocket expenses to have her baby (ibid., 39). As regionalization and rationalization of health care delivery have proceeded across the province, maternity and obstetrical services continue to be sacrificed to the goal of balanced budgets. In July 2000, for instance, Digby General Hospital suspended obstetrical services, making it necessary for women to travel more than an hour, to Yarmouth or Kentville, to deliver in hospital. The CEO of the District Health Authority assured the press that good prenatal care would reduce the likelihood of women giving birth en route. But his comments ignored the unpredictability of birth, which could proceed swiftly or necessitate prompt intervention. It also ignored the impact of restructuring on women experiencing complications, who might have to move into a city in the latter stages of pregnancy to get access to essential services (Canadian Press Newswire 12 July 2000).

Conclusion

An examination of health care reform in Nova Scotia through the lens of privatization offers a glimpse of the ways in which women's health care concerns have been subordinated to the goal of fiscal restraint. Although cuts to staff and services have affected all Nova Scotians, women have felt the effects most keenly because their needs and expectations are often invisible or incidental in the reform process. But much more information about women's health is needed to flesh out this preliminary review. Above all, we need a systematic and comprehensive comparison of women's and men's experiences in order to evaluate the impact of gender on health and health care. None of the existing surveys of health or studies of health care in Nova Scotia provide the necessary breadth of information or the depth of analysis. At the same time, some of the most glaring gaps in our knowledge of health care have to do with the experiences of diverse groups of women in the province: Aboriginal and black women; lesbians and bisexual women; francophone and rural women; immigrant women and women with disabilities. How has reform in general and privatization in particular affected the quality of their health and health care? Do Aboriginal women share more in common with Aboriginal men or with non-Aboriginal women when it comes to health care? Do all rural women have similar complaints about access to health services or do levels of satisfaction correlate more closely with class and ethnicity? Do rural men hold different opinions of health care delivery than rural women? Although we cannot yet provide definitive answers to these questions, even existing reports and studies contain subtle warnings about the dangers of ignoring or privileging gender as an explanation for differences in health status and in access and attitudes to health care. One woman, frustrated with cuts to health care services in rural Nova Scotia, explicitly contrasted her experiences with urban women. "How much does it cost a woman in Dartmouth to have her baby?" she asked. "Nothing, I bet" (NS Dept. of Health 1997, 39). Gender analysis is crucial for recognizing the fault lines among Nova Scotians and the extent to which divided loyalties and converging identities may complicate the process of negotiating meaningful and sustainable health care reform. In the end, competition for services arising from cuts to services may represent one of the most pernicious effects of privatization.

References

Bickerton, James. 1999. "Reforming Health Care Governance: The Case of Nova Scotia." *Journal of Canadian Studies*. 34 (2): 159-90.
Boase, Joan Price. 1994. *Shifting Sands: Group-Government Relationships in the Health Care Sector*. Montreal and Kingston: McGill-Queen's University Press.
Campbell, Joan, Gail Bruhm and Susan Lilley. 1998. "Caregivers' Support Needs: Insights From the Experiences of Women Providing Care in Rural Nova Scotia." Halifax, NS: Maritime Centre of Excellence for Women's Health. November.
Canadian HR Reporter. "Halifax Hospital Outsources Nurses: Private Firms Will Hire, Train and Administer 600 Casual Employees." 1996. 4 November, 9 (19): 1-2.
Canadian Institute for Health Information (CIHI). 1998. *National Health Expenditure Trends, 1975-1998*. Ottawa: Canadian Institute for Health Information.
Canadian Institute for Health Information (CIHI). 2000. *National Health Expenditures Trends, 1975-2000*. www.cihi.ca/facts/nhex/nhex2000/table_B.2.2.shtml.
Canadian Press Newswire. 20 May 1996. "Health Care Reform Worries NS Doctors."
Canadian Press Newswire. 25 July 1996. "QE II Hospital Cuts Hundreds of Jobs and Beds."
Canadian Press Newswire. 27 July 1996. "Nova Scotians Think Health Care Quality Declined: Poll."
Canadian Press Newswire. 16 September 1996. "Nurses Fear Impact of Health-Care Cut: Survey."
Canadian Press Newswire. 16 October 1996. "VON Uneasy About Privatization of Home Care."
Canadian Press Newswire. 7 June 2000. "Muir Evades Questions About Rumoured NS Hospital Cuts."
Canadian Press Newswire. 12 July 2000. "Budget Cuts Force NS Hospitals to Cut Obstetrical Services."
Chin-Yee, Fiona. 1997. "Shifting the Goal Posts and Changing the Rules: The Privatization of the Canadian Health Care System." Unpublished MA Thesis. Wolfville, NS: Acadia University.
The Community Health Planning and Evaluation Working Group. 1998. *From the Ground Up: Community Health Board Development in Nova Scotia, 1994-1997*. Halifax, NS: The Community Health Planning and Evaluation Working Group. January.
Government of Nova Scotia. Health Authorities Act. 2000. Halifax, NS: Government of Nova Scotia. www.gov.ns.ca./legi/legc/ bills/58th_1st/3rd_read/b034.htm .
Gurevich, Maria. 1999. "Privatization in Health Reform from Women's Perspectives: Research, Policy and Responses." Halifax, NS: Maritime Centre of Excellence for Women's Health. March.
Halifax Chronicle-Herald. 1996. "Talk of Privatization Worries VON Nurses." 17 October, A4.
Halifax Chronicle-Herald. 1998. "Checking up on Home Care: As Health-care Budgets Are Trimmed, Hospital Stays Are Getting Shorter. Is Home Care Saving Scarce Resources or Putting Patients at Risk?" 24 January, B5.
Halifax Chronicle-Herald. 2000. "Board Cuts 19 Beds, 57 Jobs: Union 'Ready to Fight' Move by Northern Health Body." 19 July, 4.
Health Canada. 1998-99. Health Reform Database: Overview by Province: Nova Scotia. Ottawa: Health Canada.

Keddy, Barbara. 2000. "Health Care Reform and Impact on Nurses in Nova Scotia and British Columbia: Market-Dependence and the Exploitation of Nurses' Work." Halifax, NS: Maritime Centre of Excellence for Women's Health. 3 March.

LeBlanc, John C. 1996. *Women's and Children's Health in Nova Scotia.* Halifax, NS: IWK-Grace Health Centre, Departments of Community Health and Epidemiology, Pediatrics, Population Health Research, Dalhousie University. 20 March.

Moulton, Donalee. 1999. "NS Tories holding Firm on Dismantling Regional Health Promise." *Medical Post* 35 (32) (28 September), 6.

Nova Scotia Department of Health Website. www.gov.ns.ca/health.

Nova Scotia Department of Health. 1993. *The Health Status of Women in Nova Scotia.* Halifax, NS: Nova Scotia Department of Health.

Nova Scotia Department of Health. 1994. *Home Care Nova Scotia: A Plan for Implementation.* Halifax, NS: Nova Scotia Department of Health.

Nova Scotia Department of Health. 1995. *From Blueprint to Building: Renovating Nova Scotia's Health System.* Halifax, NS: Nova Scotia Department of Health. April.

Nova Scotia Department of Health. 1996. *The Nova Scotia Health Survey, 1995.* Halifax, NS: Nova Scotia Department of Health.

Nova Scotia Department of Health. 1998. *Health Care Update: Regionalization.* Halifax, NS: Nova Scotia Department of Health. February.

Nova Scotia Department of Health. 1999. "Strengthening Primary Care in Nova Scotia Communities: An Evaluative Initiative – Background Document. Halifax, NS: Nova Scotia Department of Health." April. www.gov.ns.ca/health/primary-care/backgroun01.htm.

Nova Scotia Department of Health. 1999. *Future Direction of the Health Care System: Establishing District Authorities.* Halifax, NS: Nova Scotia Department of Health. 1 November.

Nova Scotia Department of Health. 2001. Nova Scotia's Nursing Strategy. Halifax, NS: Nova Scotia Department of Health. April.

Nova Scotia Department of Health. News Release. 23 November 1995. "QEII Health Sciences Centre Act Introduced." Halifax, NS: Nova Scotia Department of Health.

Nova Scotia Department of Health. News Release. 17 May 1996. "Act to Establish the IWK-Grace." Halifax, NS: Nova Scotia Department of Health.

Nova Scotia Department of Health. News Release. 15 August 1996. "Minister Outlines Renewal Plans." Halifax, NS: Nova Scotia Department of Health.

Nova Scotia Department of Health. News Release. 16 April 1997. "$8 Million Plan to Stabilize Physician Services." Halifax, NS: Nova Scotia Department of Health.

Nova Scotia Department of Health. News Release. 7 July 1997. "Public Health Awards of Nova Scotia Presented Today." Halifax, NS: Nova Scotia Department of Health.

Nova Scotia Department of Health. News Release. 3 February 1998. "Pharmacare Premium and Co-payment to Remain the Same." Halifax, NS: Nova Scotia Department of Health.

Nova Scotia Department of Health. News Release. 22 June 1998. "IWK Grace Physicians Enter Alternative Funding Agreement." Halifax, NS: Nova Scotia Department of Health.

Nova Scotia Department of Health. News Release. 26 June 1998. "Government Intends to Eliminate Pharmacare Premium." Halifax, NS: Nova Scotia Department of Health.

Nova Scotia Department of Health. News Release. 22 March 1999. "Nova Scotians Now Have Direct Access to Physiotherapists." Halifax, NS: Nova Scotia Department of Health.

Nova Scotia Department of Health. News Release. 25 June 1999. "Nova Scotia Moving Closer to Regulating Midwifery." Halifax, NS: Nova Scotia Department of Health.

Nova Scotia Department of Health. News Release. 26 September 2000. "District Health Authority Appointments for Antigonish, Guysborough and Richmond Counties." Halifax, NS: Nova Scotia Department of Health.

Nova Scotia Department of Health. News Release. 22 January 2001. "New Policy for Nursing-Home Admissions Puts Care Needs First." Halifax, NS: Nova Scotia Department of Health.

Nova Scotia Department of Health. News Release. 1 February 2001. "Business Planning Process with District Health Authorities Underway." Halifax, NS: Nova Scotia Department of Health.

Nova Scotia Department of Health. News Release. 14 February 2001. "Increase in Respite Services." Halifax, NS: Nova Scotia Department of Health.

Nova Scotia Provincial Health Council. 2000. *Health for Nova Scotians: The Results of a Public Consultation Process*. Halifax, NS: Provincial Health Council.

Nova Scotia. Department of Health. 1990a. *Health Strategy for the Nineties: Managing Better Health*. Halifax: Nova Scotia Department of Health.

Nova Scotia. Department of Health. 1990b. *Health Strategy for the Nineties: Managing Better Health, Summary*. Halifax: Nova Scotia Department of Health.

Nova Scotia. Royal Commission on Health Care. 1989. *Report of The Nova Scotia Royal Commission on Health Care: Towards a New Strategy, Summary*. Halifax, NS: Nova Scotia Department of Health.

Nova Scotia. The Minister's Action Committee on Health System Reform. 1994. *Nova Scotia's Blueprint for Health System Reform*. Halifax, NS: Nova Scotia Department of Health.

Nova Scotia. The Minister's Task Force on Regionalized Health Care in Nova Scotia. (1999) *Final Report and Recommendations*. Halifax, NS: Nova Scotia Department of Health.

Thorne, Bruce. Communications Officer, College of Physicians and Surgeons of Nova Scotia. 2 April 2001. Personal Communication.

Thorne, Stephen. 1997. "Government to Spend on Health Care." Canadian Press Newswire, 20 November.

Walker, Ann Graham. 2000. "$30m to be Chopped from NS Health Care: Normally Quiet MDs Sound off about Threats to Patient Care." *Medical Post*. 36 (31)(19 September): 57.

What Price Have Women Paid for Health Care Reform? The Situation in Quebec

Jocelyne Bernier and Marlène Dallaire

INTRODUCTION

The health and social services system in Quebec has undergone major transformations since the early 1990s. This chapter examines the consequences that this reform has had on women, considering the differing roles that women and men play in society.[1] It also considers the effects that these measures have had on the status and health of women from differing socioeconomic environments.

Some differences have already been well established in surveys of public health (Potvin and Frohlich 1998). More women than men report being in poor health or only fair health, and women report making more use of health care services, even when services surrounding pregnancy and childbirth are excluded (Guyon 1996). Three-quarters of the workers in the health and social services system and the vast majority of workers in community health and social services agencies are women (Conseil du statut de la femme 1996a). Moreover, the central element in recent health care reform – the shift of many services from institutions into the community – has significantly altered relationships among the government, the public health care system, private health care providers, community organizations and the "domestic" economy (Standing 1999). It has particularly affected the informal care that is provided chiefly by women in family settings.

Because of the scope and complexity of the reform in Quebec, this chapter focuses on an issue that lies at the heart of the current debate on the future of Quebec's health care system: the trend toward privatization. Our analysis is based on a review of Quebec government documents on health care policy, funding and organization, as well as on studies of the long-term evolution of the health care system.

The privatization process has been analyzed from various perspectives, including how services should be organized and delivered through the system, how it should be managed, how it should be funded and how its activities should be governed and regulated so that they serve the public interest and meet socially acceptable quality standards.[2] In the first part of this chapter, we analyze the issues raised by the current reforms by addressing a number of questions: Are the changes being made in the organization of services promoting the transfer of services to the private sector? What factors influence the relative proportions of public and private funding for health care services? Can the development of partnerships with the private health care industry improve access to and quality of health care services? Can the public health care system benefit from adopting management methods developed in the competitive marketplace?

The second part of the chapter deals with the particular impacts of health care reform on women in Quebec. It looks at four major ways that women are involved in the health care system: as users of health care services, as workers in the health and social services system, as caregivers to family members and as participants in various capacities in community organizations. It also reviews findings from various studies of women's experience in the field and from research on the impact of these sweeping changes (Association féminine d'éducation et d'action sociale *et al.* 1998; Bourbonnais *et al.* 1998). It brings out the need for more comprehensive studies and analyses designed to properly reflect gender differences.

HEALTH CARE REFORM

Background

There is nothing new about private institutions delivering health and social services in Quebec. Before 1960, the government had almost no role in funding or delivering such services, and the cost of health care was one of the main reasons that families went into debt. Hospital and social services were provided by private corporations,[3] often associated with religious institutions, and doctors worked in private practice. It was not until the advent of government hospitalization insurance in 1961 and government medical insurance in 1970 that the state began to finance most health care services, through the budgets that it allocated to public institutions and the public health insurance system that it used to compensate medical service providers.

In the early 1970s, with the adoption of the *Act respecting health services and social services,* the Quebec government began to put a public system of health and social services in place. This law, inspired by the report of the Castonguay-Nepveu Commission (1966-71), created 12 regional health and social services councils, which were given an advisory role, and hospital centres (CHs), whose administrative management was separated from their medical management. The mandate to deliver social services was given to local community services centres (CLSCs) in community settings and to social services centres (SSCs) in institutional settings, but access to government-funded social services still remained more limited than access to government-funded health care services (Ouellet and Roy 1994). The organization of Quebec's health and social services system was thus characterized by the integration of health and social services and the creation of the Ministère des affaires sociales [Department of Social Affairs], with broad authority to rationalize the system's operations and to ensure free, universal access to its services (Bergeron and Gagnon 1994).

During the 1980s, various pressures on the health care system began to build up. Technological advances brought new treatments and new tools that were increasingly expensive. Demographic changes such as increased life expectancy resulted in new needs, including an increase in the incidence of chronic illness compared with acute health problems. At the same time, changing social values transformed Quebecers' vision of sickness and health, with a new emphasis on de-institutionalizing frail individuals and helping them live in their communities. The growing ethnic and cultural diversity of Quebec society, due to immigration, necessitated adjustments in services. The increased availability of information altered the relationship between health care professionals and some of their patients, who now demanded the right to participate in decisions about their treatment, or to seek alternative therapies.

All of these changes made managing the costs of the health care system more complex. In the mid-1980s, questions began to be raised about the proportion of public expenditures that should go to the health care system. This was in part because increases in health care costs were not necessarily accompanied by improvements in public health and because our health care system consumes a larger share of the national wealth than in other developed countries (Crémieux *et al.* 1997; Rheault 1994; Contandriopoulos 1991).

In 1985, the Quebec government established a commission of inquiry on health and social services, known as the Rochon Commission, and gave it the mandate to conduct an in-depth review of Quebec's health and social services system. In its 1988 report, the Rochon Commission concluded that efforts to democratize decision-making in the health care system had failed, and that the system had become a hostage to corporate interests. The Commission proposed strengthening public participation in decision-making processes at the regional level.

Following the Rochon Commission's report, the Quebec government began restructuring the province's health care system in the early 1990s. Various analysts see this reform as pursuing the same general policy directions, while attempting to resolve tensions that had marked the development of the system over the preceding 20 years (Bergeron and Gagnon 1994; Turgeon and Anctil 1994).

Quebec Liberal Minister Marc-Yvan Côté initiated the first phase of the restructuring with the publication of a policy paper entitled *Une réforme axée sur le citoyen* [Citizen-Focussed Reform] (MSSS 1990). This paper was followed in 1991 by the passage of Bill 120, which amended the *Act respecting health services and social services*, and by the publication of a document on the funding of health care services, *Un financement équitable à la mesure de nos moyens* [Equitable Funding That is Within Our Means] (MSSS 1991). Paradoxically, it was not until 1992 that the policy objectives of improving the public's health and welfare were made public, in a paper entitled *La politique de la santé et du bien-être* [Health and Welfare Policy] (MSSS 1992).

Quebec's health and social services reform of the 1990s was carried out against a backdrop of budget cuts, which had been the order of the day in the public system since the mid-1980s, regardless of which political parties were in power in Quebec City and in Ottawa. Starting in the 1993-94 fiscal year, the cuts in the health and social services system became more severe, as the Quebec government launched a campaign to realign public spending and public administration in order to balance its budget after major cutbacks in federal transfers for health and social services. At the Ministère de la Santé et des Services Sociaux [MSSS; Department of Health and Social Services], this campaign got underway with a document entitled *Défi Qualité-Performance* [The Quality/Performance Challenge] (MSSS 1994), which proposed some $750 million in budget cuts over three years.

The election of a Parti Québécois government in 1994 did not lead to a change in policy. After the October 1995 referendum campaign and after holding an economic summit in March 1996, the Quebec government adopted a policy aimed at achieving a zero deficit in four years. All government spending and social programs – including the health and social services system, which accounted for nearly one third of Quebec government spending – were affected by successive initiatives to restore public finances. The new Minister, Jean Rochon (who had chaired the Rochon Commission from 1985 to 1988), argued more strongly than his predecessors for major reallocations of financial resources, designed to replace costly services provided in institutions with less costly services provided in the community. This was in a context where it was not always easy to determine which changes in the health and social services system reflected budget cuts and which reflected restructuring.

The regional health and social services boards, established in 1991 to replace the regional councils, were given the mandate to meet the budget targets set by the Department of Health and Social Services and to prepare the restructuring plans for the 1995-98 period. However, the major financial directions continued to be defined at the highest political levels; only administrative decisions were transferred to the regions. On the one hand, this regionalization policy, which the Quebec government was pursuing in a number of other areas as well, brought management of the health and social services system closer to the actual needs of Quebecers in the various administrative regions.[5] On the other hand, even though the government retained substantial powers over policy development and deregulation, decentralization helped to draw attention and opposition away from the government itself. Thus these two trends, budget cuts and regionalization, characterized the backdrop against which health and social services reform took place in Quebec in the 1990s.

These same trends were evident elsewhere in Canada, as Pat Armstrong's chapter in this volume makes clear. The federal government, which had provided a large proportion of health care funding since the 1960s, began unilaterally reducing its transfer payments as early as 1982. In its 1995 budget speech, the Liberal government in Ottawa announced a series of measures to cut public spending and reduce Canada's deficit. Many social programs were affected by these cutbacks, and particularly by a major reduction in federal transfer payments, which drastically reduced funding for health, education and social services in every province of Canada.

Despite having substantially reduced its contribution to the health care budget, the federal government strongly reasserted its intention to make the provinces comply with the standards of the *Canada Health Act* of 1984. It focused particularly on the requirements for health insurance plans to be publicly administered and universal, to provide comprehensive coverage for all "medically necessary" services, to provide access to treatment at no additional charge and to make benefits portable from one province to another. But because the Act applies only to medical and hospital services, it has become increasingly limited – with the advent of new kinds of services delivered outside of hospitals, new kinds of treatments delivered by other types of health care professionals and new kinds of medications that cost more and more to buy (Maioni 1999) .

Various health care services, especially ones delivered outside of hospitals, can be offered commercially. This opportunity has attracted the interest of private businesses, which are submitting more and more proposals for partnerships with the public health and social services system. The major cutbacks taking place in public institutions only make the prospects for these proposals brighter. NAFTA has created still more opportunities; major US corporations are now trying to penetrate the Canadian health care market, particularly in the areas of home care and high-tech medicine (Métivier 1999; Fuller 1998; Centrale de l'enseignement du Québec (CSQ) 1996).

Reform in the Organization and Delivery of Services

The reform begun in 1990 has overturned traditional ways of delivering health care. The goal of this reform has been to promote integration and complementarity of services and cooperation among institutions, with the underlying objective of improving the efficiency of the system as a whole (MSSS 1998b; Angus 1997). The reform has also contributed to a change in the relative proportions of health care services delivered by the public and private sectors.

The Public Health Care System

The major thrust of the changes in the ways that services are delivered has been the shift toward ambulatory care, which has been accelerating since the mid-1990s. The shift was effected very quickly, in response to the government's desire to achieve a zero deficit, and particularly altered the way that care was provided in hospital centres. The average length of hospitals stays decreased from 8 days in 1993-94 to 6.8 days in 1997-98, and the proportion of day surgeries increased by nearly 20 per cent. Yet more than 5,000 beds were closed in hospitals throughout the province and nine hospitals in the Montreal region were either shut down or converted into other types of institutions (MSSS statistical analysis service and Med-Echo).

In addition, as budget constraints led to limitations on access to diagnostic services, specialized treatment equipment and operating rooms, waiting lists grew so long that the Quebec government injected $28 million to health care in the summer of 1998 to try to shorten the wait for certain kinds of surgery.[6] In 1999, the Department of Health and Social Services began sending cancer patients to the United States to receive treatment within a reasonable time, even though this cost more than providing them with the same treatment in Quebec. According to the Montreal regional health authorities, deterioration in the accessibility of services poses the risk of creating a two-tier health care system (Régie régionale de Montréal-Centre 1997, 12).

The changes in the way hospital services are delivered have had repercussions throughout the health and social services system, especially in the CLSCs. Not enough money was reinvested in CLSC home care services to let the growing number of people being discharged earlier from hospital obtain the home care services they needed. The share of public health care spending in Quebec that went to home care rose from 1.7 per cent in 1990-91 to 2.4 per cent in 1997-98, but the province falls significantly below the Canadian average, which rose from 3.3 per cent to 4 per cent over the same period (Health Canada, Health System and Policy Division, 1998).[7]

Although total funding for CLSCs has risen, from $686 million in 1993-94 to $870 million in 1997-98, this is only 8 per cent of the total budget for the public health care and social services system. One consequence of making the CLSCs meet the increasing demand for post-hospitalization home care, without giving them enough extra funds to cope with it, is that they have had to neglect the preventive health care activities that are also part of their mandate, and part of the government's official health and welfare policy. For example, some CLSCs have withdrawn nurses from schools where they were delivering preventive programs, and reassigned them to home care services. Health care workers used to make home visits to frail seniors, for the purpose of preventing their health from deteriorating. These visits have become increasingly rare and visits to provide disabled people with basic services such as personal hygiene have had to be more widely spaced. Some agencies argue that the mandate of the CLSCs has been shelved and they have become "traffic cops" and health care providers at the expense of their other role, as providers of social services (ROC 03 1997,16).

A major goal of this health care reform was to provide easy access to frontline health and social services while limiting the use of the most expensive services, such as visits to emergency rooms and doctors' offices. This was the reason for introducing the Info-Santé CLSC services, through which the public can consult nurses by telephone 24 hours per day, 7 days per week. These services were extended to all CLSCs since 1995. Women constitute the vast majority of users of these services – 89.4 per cent (Hagan, Morin and Lépine 1998). This is consistent with other data showing that women make more frequent use of health care services in general and are more closely involved in caring for dependent persons within their families.[8]

Many CLSCs, especially in the major urban centres, do not have enough physicians to offer the full range of frontline health care services or to extend their service hours (e.g., to stay open evenings and weekends).[9] The Department of Health and Social Services favours the creation of regional general medicine departments (DRMGs), under the auspices of the regional health and social services boards, to foster cooperation[10] between CLSCs and doctors' private practices, where more than 80 per cent of all frontline medical care is delivered, especially in urban areas. Yet at present, these doctors can make more money in their private practices than they can by providing services to CLSCs. Moreover, the fee-for-service system does not encourage doctors to form group practices that take a "whole-patient" approach. In contrast, the CLSCs' services are based on an interdisciplinary approach involving several different kinds of health care and social service professionals (e.g., nurses, nutritionists, psychologists, social workers) (Turgeon and Anctil 1994).

Efforts to coordinate the work of institutions with that of the various organizations delivering services in the community were organized through regional service organization plans (PROS), which were developed in the early 1990s. These plans require every institution and community organizations to see itself as a link in a chain, with specific responsibilities in a continuum of services. A 1997 study of de-institutionalization and the regional service organization plans reported uneven results, varying according to the population concerned.[11]

With the increasingly severe budget cutbacks of the second half of the 1990s, implementation of regional service organization plans have often been set aside (MSSS 1997). The responsibility for supporting people suffering from mental illness or various disabilities has generally fallen back on their families and on community and alternative resources. As a result, an especially heavy burden has been placed on women, who traditionally assume the responsibility of caring for the frail and dependent. Many people with severe, chronic mental illness have swollen the ranks of the homeless (chiefly in major urban centres), because they lacked adequate outside assistance when their families could no longer shoulder the burden of caring for them and providing them with psychological and social support (Harnois 1996, Therrien 1989).

As the trend toward supporting people in the home has grown, the severity of the health problems of people who still live in residential and long-term care centres has increased. In the space of a few years, the percentage of residents with cognitive deficits has increased by 10 per cent, though it varies from one centre to the next, and the average age of residents is now 85 years. Most of these residents are women, because women have a longer life expectancy than men and spend more years of their life with some kind of disability.[12]

In many of these centres, neither the staff nor the facilities were ready for this sudden change, and the additional resources needed to raise the level of services were not forthcoming. On the contrary, according to the Association des CLSC et des CHSLD du Québec [Quebec Association of Local Community Services Centres and Residential and Long-Term Care Centres], financing for the 137 public residential centres in the province fell from $1.5 to $1.2 billion between 1995 and 1998, so that the average rate of care in response to residents' needs fell from 74.4 per cent to 68.3 per cent between 1991-92 and 1997-98; more than half of the residential centres fell below this provincial average (Association des CLSC et des CHSLD du Québec, quoted in Bégin 1999c, A-8).

The public network has gone through a major restructuring, with some formerly separate institutions being grouped under one board of directors, and many other institutions being merged. In some outlying regions, many public institutions with very different mandates (hospital centres, CLSCs, and residential and long-term care centres) have been combined into single administrative units. In the larger urban centres, institutions have generally been merged with others in the same or similar categories – for example, residential facilities with other residential facilities, rehabilitation centres with social services centres, and hospital centres with other hospital centres. This last type of merger has resulted in the consolidation of university hospital centres that offer highly specialized services and also perform teaching and research functions. The initial assessments of these combinations and mergers indicate that they have not met expectations, either in terms of economizing on resources or in terms of providing continuity of service to the public. In the view of David Levine, a well-known administrator in the health care system, "[translation] The mistake is that the mergers were carried out during a period of belt-tightening, because of financial constraints, without any funds being set aside to make the necessary investments in the transition" (Bégin 1999b, A-15).

These numerous organizational upheavals have also complicated implementation of the various protocols for referrals and follow-up among institutions, especially when patients are discharged from hospital early because of the shift toward ambulatory care. The quality and continuity of patient services have deteriorated. Communications between institutions are delayed, information on required treatment goes missing, home-support services fail to take over as soon as they should. Often it is the patients' relatives – mainly women – who have to make up for the shortcomings in the public system and sometimes even take charge of coordinating the services that patients need.

Recently, some steps have been taken to try to solve these problems of integrated management and coordination of services. For example, a single window for home-support services has been introduced in Montreal, and some experimental programs are underway to provide integrated services to frail seniors. However, there are still many discontinuities, especially in medical services, and the growing number of private service providers in the system may only aggravate these problems.

Private Health Care Providers
The changes in the network of public institutions have created opportunities for private health care services to begin operations or expand them into new areas.[13] For-profit private corporations are setting themselves up in competition with public institutions in areas where the public system can no longer meet the demand – such as long-term residential facilities, convalescence and rehabilitation centres, private physiotherapy and radiology clinics, and medical clinics providing state-of-the-art diagnostic services.

Private firms specializing in home care and home-support products and services (e.g., nursing services, remote diagnostic and monitoring equipment, and technical aids) are growing rapidly. One example is the Medisys Health Group, which has 450 permanent staff and employs nearly 2,000 contract workers, mainly nurses.

The number of unlicenced private residences for seniors in Quebec rose by 500 per cent between 1989 and 1996! A study by the Université de Sherbrooke's Geriatrics Institute Research Centre showed that 32 per cent of the managers of these institutions have no specialized training and 59 per cent have no experience in working with the elderly. The proportion of residents receiving inadequate care was found to be highest – over 20 per cent – in licenced and unlicenced small residences (with 9 or fewer beds) and unlicenced medium-sized residences (with 10-39 beds) (Bravo et al. 1999). According to this study, these residences are not closely supervised by the regional boards and CLSCs, which, with their limited resources, must give priority to monitoring the care provided to seniors who are living alone.

Private firms have also made proposals to take advantage of new developments in medical technology or of facilities that are being underutilized because of public funding cuts (Métivier 1999). For example, the Quebec Ministère du développement de la métropole [Department for Development of the Greater Montreal Area] and the City of Montreal have established a health committee that includes the directors of the Montreal-Centre regional health and social services board, several Montreal hospitals and a number of private firms, including Merck-Frosst, Hoechts-Marion-Roussel, Medisys and Bell Canada. A 1997 report by this committee contains a number of proposals, including "[translation] arranging technology transfers among university, hospital, government and industry research centres," "facilitating export of Quebec medical expertise – for example, through telemedicine," and "developing the market of foreign clients for Quebec medical services, where the system has excess capacity" (quoted in Patenaude and Lambert 1998, 83). This partnership with the health care industry is encouraged in the 1998-2002 plan of the Montreal-Centre regional health and social services board, which wants to strengthen the industry's position as one of the economic pillars of the Montreal region (Régie régionale de Montréal-Centre 1998, 105 ss.)

This strategy has received further impetus from the report of a task force commissioned by Quebec former health minister Jean Rochon to examine the complementarity of the private sector in pursuing the fundamental objectives of the public health care system in Quebec (Groupe de travail sur la complémentarité du secteur privé 1999a). The report of this task force, known as the Arpin Report, proposes letting hospitals negotiate partnership agreements under which "affiliated" private clinics could provide certain services that do not require hospitalization. The clinics would be compensated by the Quebec health insurance plan and compensation would include the costs of specialized equipment that the clinics use (ibid.). The wisdom of this approach is questionable, given that hospitals are currently being forced to curtail the use of their own equipment for lack of funding.

The prevailing discourse gives more and more prominence to private sector delivery of health care and social services in Quebec, with the risk of whittling away at public institutions until they are left with the responsibility to care for only those clients who require the most resources.

Community Organizations

The reorganization of the public system has also affected the network of community organizations active in the health and social services field. Many of these groups were established in the 1960s and 1970s to respond to emerging needs or to implement new practices in areas where the public network was not taking action. Examples include women's health centres, shelters for battered women, alternative mental health facilities, drug addiction treatment centres, and programs that work with the homeless. Some of these organizations have inspired new initiatives in the public system – for example, community health clinics and health centres served as the original models for the government-run CLSCs (Dumais 1999).

After exerting much pressure, these organizations gained official recognition in the 1991 *Act respecting health services and social services*. Many of them received funding increases and formed new partnerships with the public system. The budget for community organizations rose from $86 million in 1989-90 to $171 million in 1997-98 (MSSS 1998c). But according to representatives of these groups,

> [translation] Not all community agencies have received funding increases. In fact, most new funding is being channelled to organizations that are useful to the government, in sectors that enable the government to achieve its own priorities. Thus, in the field of health and social services, the community agencies that receive the most funding are those that 'participate' in the shift to ambulatory care (for example, by providing assistance in the home or running support groups for psychiatric patients) or that accept government contracts (for example, to run half-way houses). (Greason 1999, B-3)

According to the Montreal-Centre regional health and social services board, the number of people who made use of Montreal community agencies more than doubled from 1995 to 1997. The Regroupement Intersectoriel des Organismes Communautaires de Montréal (RIOCM; Inter-sectoral Coalition of Montreal Community Organizations) notes that the increase in demand often exceeds the additional funding provided to cope with it (RIOCM 1998, 43). Moreover, the problems of the people who seek help from community agencies are becoming more complex. In these organizations, which consist mostly of women, staff working conditions are deteriorating and volunteers are assuming more responsibilities for a population that is more and more distressed. Some agencies feel that they are becoming a catch basin for the overflow that the public system can no longer absorb.

Under these circumstances, relations between community organizations and government institutions have produced many tensions. According to the RIOCM (1998, 83), "[Such relations,] when they exist, are more often than not, hierarchical, even if words like 'partnership', 'concerted action', and 'dialogue' are promoted." A number of community groups perceive official recognition as a two-edged sword:

> [translation] Today, more lip-service is being paid to the value of community-based agencies, but what the government mainly wants to do is offload its former obligations onto private organizations that will provide the services for free. This amounts to contracting out ... In the current context, unfortunately, community agencies are being recognized not for the alternatives they provide, but for their ability to compensate for gaps in the public system. (Doré 1991: 4)

While some community organizations have been negatively affected by the offloading of demand from the overburdened public system, others have initiated "social economy enterprises" projects designed to achieve two goals at once. These projects are intended both to create jobs that will help people re-enter the workforce and to provide services to meet unmet needs that have emerged as the result of de-institutionalization and the shift to ambulatory care. These projects have also introduced fees for services that the CLSCs can no longer provide.[14]

In its 1995 March Against Poverty, the Quebec women's movement demanded public investment not simply to produce government goods and services but to produce "social infrastructure" – socially useful goods and services. Social economy enterprises that provide home-support services are one way that this idea has been put into practice. But some authors say that these enterprises end up shifting women from well-paid jobs in the public sector to insecure jobs in the "social economy" (Boivin and Fortier 1999; Conseil du statut de la femme 1996b). Other authors use the term "*communautarisation*" ["communitization"] to make a distinction between the shifting of services to community organizations and the commercialization of services by for-profit businesses (Vaillancourt and Jetté 1997). They think that the social economy strategy should be encouraged, not only to keep the private, for-profit sector from taking over all of the services formerly provided by the state, but to motivate the public sector to innovate.

Regional social economy committees are being established, and social economy enterprises that provide home services are being included in the restructuring plans of certain regional health and social services boards. These developments have triggered debates in the community sector regarding its role in the rationing of public services and the transfer of certain responsibilities to for-profit and non-profit private organizations.

The transfer of responsibilities for health and social services to private organizations is not simply the result of changes in service delivery methods. It also reflects the ascendancy of a logic of competition that emphasizes efficiency and performance in the management of the health and social services system.

Reform in the Management of the Health and Social Services System

Various strategies have been applied to reduce the costs of services in public institutions. Efficiency has become the watchword. Some directors of public institutions hope to improve their management methods by adopting practices developed in the competitive market (Demers *et al.* 1999). The influence of the US health care system, dominated by large private corporations focused on competition and the profit motive, is being felt. This corporate culture is also seen in the increased use of private consulting firms.

Management performance has often become a more important criterion than service quality and health outcomes in the administration of health care institutions. Beds are closed for budgetary reasons. Budget and staffing cutbacks are making waiting lists for treatment longer, causing patients to turn to the private sector to obtain certain services. Sometimes, public institutions redirect their own patients to private services. For example, to cope with the excess demand for post-hospital home nursing services, some CLSCs have encouraged patients with private insurance to obtain their care through private agencies.[15] Other CLSCs purchase services, at lower cost, from private agencies or social economy enterprises that offer their mainly female workers less advantageous working conditions than in the public sector. In February 1999, when the crowding of Quebec hospital emergency rooms reached crisis proportions, the private nursing agencies said they were so overwhelmed that they had trouble meeting requests from hospital centres and CLSCs to handle the overflow of patients requiring post-hospitalization home care (Desjardins 1999, A-3).

Because nearly 80 per cent of all public health care expenditures goes to pay wages and salaries for all categories of staff,[16] spending reductions in the sector have been achieved by slashing payrolls. The measures used to achieve payroll cutbacks have included increased use of casual labour, a wide-scale early retirement program and mass transfers of staff in connection with restructuring of the network.

Women, who in 1991 accounted for 74.7 per cent of all workers in the health and social services system, have been hit hard by these measures. With the shift toward ambulatory care, the number of patients in the acute treatment phase is increasing, placing growing pressure on a smaller, less experienced staff. The substantially heavier workload and other adjustment problems associated with these measures are realities that some managers in the public system openly acknowledge (Bégin 1998, A-25).

Hospital support services have also been targeted by the Quebec Department of Health and Social Services in the effort to reduce costs (MSSS 1996, 24). The Montreal-Centre regional health and social services board targeted cleaning, laundry, facilities maintenance and general administration as support services on which a 10 per cent spending reduction could be achieved. This board has also announced plans to have a private management firm analyze its situation and make recommendations for improving its return on investment (Régie régionale de Montréal-Centre 1997, 145).

Subcontracting to the private sector is being considered as a way of reducing the costs of producing services, as if this were a sector independent of public health care services. In one region, public health care institutions purchase laundry services from private and prison laundries, through a regional laundry service that acts as a broker. But studies have shown that buying from the private sector does not guarantee lower costs. The Chair of Socio-Economic Studies at the Université du Québec à Montréal compared five privatized food services with 23 comparably sized food services managed by public institutions. The study showed that the cost of a meal served by a privatized food service was 10.5 per cent higher than the same meal served by a government-run service (Patenaude and Lambert 1998). The Association des hôpitaux du Québec [Quebec Hospital Association], in its January 1998 report, also stressed certain dangers of privatization, stating that "[translation] a comparative analysis of health care systems indicates that the more developed the private sector, the harder it becomes to control costs and quality."

Some hospitals that no longer have sufficient budgets to run their equipment and their staff at full capacity have proposed obtaining additional private funding by offering specialized treatments to American clients who can afford to pay for it. Other institutions have achieved notable revenue increases by charging for "ancillary" services (e.g., making residents in long-term facilities pay higher housing fees, charging hospital patients extra for private rooms, charging for ambulance services, raising parking fees). According to the Quebec Department of Health and Social Services, "[translation] The revenues generated from billable services totalled close to $1 billion in 1994-1995, or the equivalent of 7.5% of government spending in this sector" (MSSS, 1996: 35).

Various authors (Contandriopoulos *et al.* 1989, 1999; Contandriopoulos 1991; Rheault 1995) have reported on the ways that methods of obtaining funding and paying for resources affect access to services, equity in health care treatment, efficiency and control of public costs and total costs of health and social services.[17]

Proposals have been made to stimulate "internal competition" among public institutions in order to contain cost increases for health and social services, even as the need to increase the complementarity and continuity of these services is being felt. Based on the observation that funding and payment methods do not provide health care institutions or professionals with any incentive to assume responsibility for specific populations, some authors have proposed a 180-degree turn in resource allocation methods. Jérôme-Forget and Forget (1998, 13) write: "[translation] At present, our hospitals receive global budgets, and our doctors are paid on a fee-for-service basis. Instead, we propose a capitation payment method, in which doctors receive a budget based on the number of patients who are signed up with them, and the hospitals obtain their funding from the flat fees that doctors pay them for their services." This proposal is inspired by the experience with HMOs in the United States and with GP (general practitioner) fundholders in the United Kingdom.[18] It raises some complex issues for the future of the public health and social services system. Both the capitation model and the GP fundholders model of resource allocation need to be analyzed in depth to determine their effects on public health, because they pose the risk of selecting clients who have higher incomes and better health, while screening out sicker clients with fewer resources, a majority of whom are women.

In December 2000, the Commission d'étude sur les services de santé et les services sociaux [Commission on Health and Social Services], also known as the Clair Commission, proposed setting up groups of practitioners in family medicine, involving mixed forms of payment, including the capitation method (2000). This type of organization cannot make services more accessible as long as management of the system remains focused on the production of services by categories of institutions, rather than on service usage patterns and continuity among the various providers.

In reviewing methods of managing the health care system, we must ask a number of questions. How much should the public system rely on the private sector? Can management methods developed in the competitive market benefit the health care system, where the relationship between users and providers is so radically different from that between consumers and suppliers in market transactions? Before we transpose private-sector management methods into such a sensitive setting as health care, we must evaluate their impact on accessibility and quality of health care services.

Changes in Public and Private Funding of the Health Care System

The Quebec government's budget for health and social services fell from $13.17 billion in 1994-95 to $12.61 billion in 1997-98 (MSSS 1998c).[19] This means that public spending per person per year on these services fell from $1,692 to $1,608 over this period. This is lower than in any of the other provinces, and represents a significant deviation (-11.7%) from the Canadian mean, which was estimated at $1,821 per capita for 1997-98 (MSSS, Canadian Institute for Health Information, cited in Groupe de travail sur la complémentarité du secteur privé 1999b, 46). The proportion of public funding in the Quebec system fell from 81.5 per cent in 1980 to 69.1 per cent in 1998. Quebec can thus boast the sorry record of having gone from being the Canadian province with the highest percentage of public funding in 1980 to being one of two provinces with the lowest percentages in 1998.[20] It should be pointed out that the federal contribution to the funding of total health care expenditures in Quebec also fell, from 42 per cent in 1986 to 30.4 per cent in 1997, thus becoming approximately even with the proportion of funding from private sources (30.9 per cent).

Since the mid-1980s, the percentage of private spending has risen continuously, though this growth slowed with the economic downturn of the early 1990s.[21] Private health care spending as a proportion of total health care spending increased from 25 per cent in 1989 to 30.9 per cent in 1998.[22] The majority of private funding – 55 per cent – comes from direct outlays by individuals, and only 35 per cent from private insurance (Métivier 1999).

The Conseil de la santé et du bien-être (CSBE; Quebec Health and Welfare Council) attributes the increase in private spending to four major factors: the growth in spending on items not covered by the public system, the de-listing of services previously covered by the public system, the emergence of new kinds of services that are not well supported by the public system, and government-imposed increases in user contributions (CSBE 1997). The Arpin Report, however, states that not all of the growth in private expenditures can be regarded as a substitution effect of the reduction in public funding.[23]

Indeed, the increase in private spending has come in areas not covered by the *Canada Health Act*, such as consultation of professionals other than medical doctors, purchases of prescription drugs and care at non-hospital institutions. In 1994, the proportion of private spending was especially high for services by professionals other than medical doctors (89.3%) and for prescription drugs (68.7%). There has also been a rise in direct outlays by individuals for services and expenses associated with participation in private insurance plans. This trend raises the fear that ability to pay may become a factor that limits access to certain essential services, particularly for women, who see health care professionals more than men do and whose average personal income is only 58 per cent that of men (Guyon 1996, 30).[24]

Since the early 1990s, certain cost transfers have also been achieved through active de-listing measures, such as limiting the services covered by Quebec's public health insurance plan or excluding certain categories of clients who were previously covered for dentists' or optometrists' services. In 1992, with the de-listing of therapeutic dental services for children over the age of 10, the number of eligible children fell from 1.5 million to 1 million in a single year – half a million children lost their benefits under the plan. The decrease in the total number of children's dental treatments paid for by the Quebec health insurance plan is even more striking. From 1981 to 1996, it fell from 9.6 million to 1.6 million, a drop of about 83 per cent. The trend for optometry services is similar. In 1992, people aged 18-40 stopped being covered for such services. In 1993, people aged 41-64 were excluded as well. The number of insured treatments in optometry fell by 57 per cent from 1991 to 1996 (Patenaude and Lambert 1998).

As the government has withdrawn from these areas, private insurance companies have taken over, offering supplementary coverage to people who qualify for group insurance plans. The result has been an increase in costs. A brochure from one of these companies, SSQ-Vie, states that since 1992, dental insurance premiums have risen by 10 per cent. Private insurers also offer to defray the costs of using private services to bridge the gaps and avoid the waiting lists encountered in the public sector. SSQ-Vie reports that total reimbursements for visits to private physiotherapy clinics rose from about $1 million in 1990 to over $4 million in 1996. The private insurance sector is growing rapidly. For example, in 1987, health insurance premiums represented only 13.6 per cent of the total premiums collected by the Sun Life Assurance Company. By 1996, they represented 19.8 per cent – a 45.6 per cent increase over the figure one decade ago (ibid.).

Another phenomenon has been a kind of passive de-listing of health and social services. For example, the Quebec government's budget for 1999-2000 introduced a refundable tax credit for persons aged 70 and over who are no longer wholly self-sufficient but wish to continue living at home. The tax credit allows seniors to claim 23 per cent of the eligible expenses they incur for the home-support services they need. The ceiling on eligible expenses is $12,000 per year and any difference has to be made up entirely by the seniors themselves. Eligible expenses are for home-support services such as meal preparation, supervision and support, and assistance in daily activities such as eating, dressing and personal hygiene. These are the kinds of services that are normally provided for free by family and social assistants from the CLSCs. But in this case these services paid with "service employment paycheques" may be provided by private agencies, or by social economy enterprises, or by independent workers, typically women, who act in a sense as subcontractors of the CLSCs. The CSF [Quebec Council for the Status of Women] rightly criticizes these arrangements as representing a drift toward privatization of home services (CSF 1999a, 104).

Another part of the passive de-listing trend is that as more and more treatments are provided at home after patients are discharged from hospital, part of the costs of drugs and medical supplies that hospitals used to provide for free must now be borne by patients and their families. And because these "ambulatory" patients may have to visit their doctors frequently, they incur additional expenses for transportation and for people to accompany them. Those who are fortunate enough to have private medical insurance may be offered new kinds of coverage for the costs that they incur while convalescing at home. Thus people with private insurance have different access to treatment and services than people who depend solely on services provided free by the public system or covered by the Quebec health insurance plan. A substantial portion of the people who cannot afford private insurance are low-income women and women in casual employment.

The Quebec Prescription Drug Insurance Plan

The Quebec government introduced a public drug insurance plan in 1997.[25] It did so with several objectives: to provide drug coverage for more than 1.2 million people not insured by private plans; to use various funding mechanisms (including premiums, deductibles, and co-insurance) so that the government itself would not have to make any outlays; and to preserve the private sector's predominance in the insurance industry (St-Pierre 1999, 74). Another objective that we might cite would be the desire to maintain the advantages that drug companies enjoy in Quebec, such as 10-year patent protection for their new products. The government yielded to pressure from these companies by not requiring drug insurance reimbursements to be limited to the cost of equivalent generic drugs.[26]

The Quebec Prescription Drug Insurance Plan, which is administered by Quebec's provincial health insurance plan (the RAMQ) is available only to people who do not already have access to private group insurance either directly or through their spouse.[27] The public drug insurance plan thus supplements the coverage provided by private insurers. This is a far cry from how Quebec's provincial medical insurance works. Though the Quebec Prescription Drug Insurance Plan is an improvement for people who would otherwise have no coverage, it still leaves a large part of all such coverage in the hands of private companies. It also includes deductibles and co-insurance requirements that make insured persons pay part of the costs themselves when they purchase their drugs. The plan has also put an end to full drug coverage for the poorest members of society, which again means mostly women, namely elderly and welfare recipients.

Between fiscal years 1997-98 and 1998-99, spending by the public drug insurance plan rose by $156 million, or 15 per cent of the total cost of the plan, which exceeds $1 billion. This increase can be attributed to two causes: more people than expected have joined the plan, and the cost of prescription drugs has risen steadily. The plan's projected deficit for 1999 is $210 million. To deal with it, Quebec former Health and Social Services Minister Pauline Marois doubled the premiums for the year 2000.

As some analysts have pointed out, "[translation] The funding mechanism for Quebec's public drug insurance plan is the least redistributive of Quebec's three major health-related public insurance plans, because unlike its public hospital and medical insurance plans, it is not financed through personal income tax" (Reinharz, Rousseau, and Rheault 1999, 163). Thus, even though drugs play an ever-growing role in medical treatment, the law does not regard them as "medically necessary" services and hence excludes them from the basket of services that are fully covered by public funds, even when they are prescribed by doctors. In other words, medications are being treated simply as consumer goods that are marketed by major pharmaceutical companies.

Reform and Governance of the Health Care System

The reform of Quebec's health and social services system has been accompanied by a process of decentralization. The Quebec government has given the regional health and social services boards a mandate to consult the population of the regions they serve about how services should be organized in these regions, and to develop cooperative efforts among the various players in the health and social services system. It is through these regional boards that health and social services institutions receive close to three-quarters of their health care budgets each year. Many reasons for pursuing decentralization have been cited: political reasons, such as ensuring more citizen control; economic arguments, presenting regionalization as a way to meet public needs more efficiently and effectively; and administrative reasons, such as better integration and coordination of services (Turgeon and Lemieux 1999, 181-82).

In practice, the decentralization achieved by creating the regional boards has been primarily administrative. These boards are chiefly responsible for implementing decisions of the provincial Department of Health and Social Services and serving as its go-between with the various players in the health and social services system. This does not really represent a decentralization of power from the province to the regions, because the boards operate within tight parameters established by the Quebec Government. One indication that the real authority still rests with the Department was the abolition in 1996 of annual meetings where representatives of the health care system, community organizations and other stakeholders (municipalities, school boards, etc.) in each region would receive a report on the regional board's activities. Abolishing these annual assemblies has reduced the accountability of the regional boards and removed one forum for public debate about the way the system is managed.[28]

The absence of any real room for decision-making may help explain why few citizens vote in the elections for health care boards and why some members of boards of directors are so disillusioned. In the fall 1996 elections, scarcely 2.5 per cent of the people eligible to vote bothered to do so. Citizens do not feel that they exercise any real power when they sit on a board of directors. According to the chairman of the board of directors of the Saint-Laurent CLSC-CHSLD [Local Community Service Centre/Residential and Long-Term Care Centre] in Montreal: "[translation] Getting elected is one thing, but then there's the question of real power. The real power lies more with the regional boards, the Department, and the civil servants." He says the volunteers who sit on boards are literally "stifled" by the laws, regulations and directives coming down from higher levels of the health care system (quoted in Bégin, 1999a, A-6). This sense of disappointment has also been expressed by the representatives of women's groups (see L'R des centres de femmes, 1997). This raises the question, what should the logical organizing principle be for the governance of the health care system?

The rationale for reforming the health and social services system was to "place citizens at the heart of the system," in their roles as users, payers and decision-makers. This implied a democratic approach to governance, whereby the public participated in defining needs and solutions for the health care system, as well as in administering it. But such an approach never really had a chance to become established, in the face of a technocratic logic that bases decision-making on a rational planning process.

Some analysts believe that under the prevailing model of central regulation with administrative decentralization, the government's withdrawal from health care funding will result in a gradual transfer of health spending from the public to the private sector (Bélanger, G. 1994; Bergeron and Gagnon 1994; Angus 1997; Contandriopoulos 1998; Deber 1999). Weakening the mechanisms for public consultations and public participation in decision-making encourages assertion of an economic logic that focuses on efficiency and promotes deregulation to facilitate the "free play of supply and demand" within a framework of "internal competition," thus reinforcing the process of privatization.

THE PRICE OF HEALTH CARE REFORM FOR WOMEN IN QUEBEC

The reform of Quebec's health and social services system is being carried out with no consideration for the way that the two sexes relate within the family. In Western countries over the past 30 years, the realities of family life have undergone significant changes. Fertility rates have fallen. Families have become more diverse and now include single-parent families, "blended" families, homosexual couples and immigrant families with different cultural norms. Life expectancy has increased, and relations between the generations have changed. Emotional ties with family members remain a significant factor in individual well-being, and society still values the support that family members give each other. But the interactions among family members are increasingly subject to negotiation and do not have the same meaning as they did in past generations. The family network is becoming smaller, and women – more and more of whom work outside the home – must cope with multiple tasks, sometimes having to take care of their children and their aging parents at the same time.[29] These changes affect families' ability and willingness to care for relatives who are sick or who can no longer take care of themselves. Meanwhile, the Quebec government is developing conflicting policies in this regard – instituting a $5-a-day day care system to help parents with pre-school age children while at the same time thrusting back onto families much of the responsibility of caring for their aging members.

Reform is also having repercussions that may affect women in each of their roles as health care workers, health care users, family caregivers and participants in community organizations. For example, because of budget cutbacks, the size of the workforce in Quebec's public health and social services system has been reduced. In July 1997, 17,678 unionized workers and 1,051 managers took advantage of the government's early-retirement program. According to Quebec's Commission administrative des régimes de retraite et d'assurance du secteur public (CARRA; Commission for Administering Public Sector Retirement and Insurance Plans), these retirements represent a 10 per cent decline in the size of the total workforce (Bégin 1998). Staff reductions have consequences for the way that work is organized in health care institutions, and hence for the women who work in the public system. They include growing workloads, increased stress and the need to adapt to new service delivery methods. All of this affects the quality of care and therefore affects women as users of health care services. Women are also affected when they are increasingly called upon to compensate for the system's deficiencies by providing care in their own homes or by working in community organizations.

All of these effects are linked to the trend toward privatization described in the preceding sections. The literature reveals a certain consensus that the shift toward ambulatory care would not have the same effects on women if sufficient resources were made available in their communities to provide pre- and post-hospital care and if the drugs and equipment that patients needed in their homes after being discharged from hospital were provided automatically and free of charge (AFÉAS *et al.* 1998; Coalition féministe pour une transformation du système de santé et des services sociaux 1998; RIOCM 1998).

Some consequences of health care reform affect both women and men, while others are specific to or more pronounced among women. Other consequences differ according to women's living conditions and personal traits. For example, problems of accessibility of health and social services are more pronounced or even different in nature for women who have low incomes or live in remote regions, where doctors are scarce and costs of travel for treatment are higher. The deteriorating quality of health care has an especially strong impact on elderly and women with disabilities who live at home or in residential centres. Ethnic and cultural diversity must also be considered in analyzing the effects of health care reform in terms of accessibility and suitability of services and differing dynamics surrounding the care of family members.

Women as Users of Health Care Services

Women are the primary users of Quebec's health care system. As Guyon (1996, 67) states, "[translation] The Quebec health insurance plan's statistics on hospitalization and medical consultations reveal a greater general use of health care services among women aged 15 to 64." It is reasonable to assume that these women are more affected by the consequences of reform, including poorer service quality, longer waiting times, de-listing of certain formerly insured services, and the downloading of costs, as well as confusion caused by mergers of health care institutions and changes in their missions.

The deterioration in the quality of health care is especially apparent in hospital emergency rooms, according to the Collège des médecins du Québec [Quebec College of Physicians] itself:

> [translation] The staff exhaustion and long delays caused by chronic overcrowding in emergency rooms are affecting the quality of care... Too many patients spend too much time lying on stretchers in packed hallways while waiting for the overworked doctors and nurses to have the time to give them care or treatment, or simply to deal with them at all. (Collège des médecins 1999, 1)

The College even describes an "emergency room syndrome" in which patients need treatment but delay going to hospital because of bad experiences in emergency rooms.

A wide-ranging survey of over 2,000 nurses in various institutions in the Quebec City area revealed that many nurses think that physical care is being given at the expense of other needs (Bourbonnais, Comeau and CSPQ 1998). The cuts in nursing staff are also affecting hospital patients' health. According to Valerie Shannon, Director of Nursing at the McGill University Health Centre,

> [translation] Studies confirm that the results of medical interventions are affected by the number of nurses and their skills. These two important variables are closely correlated with patient mortality... Other studies show that patients treated in short-staffed units experience more complications (such as bed sores and urinary infections) than comparable patients treated in 'adequately' staffed units. (Shannon 1999, B-3)

The shortage of resources also affects the quality of care received by seniors living in institutions, the great majority of whom are women. According to the Association des CLSC et des CHSLD du Québec [Quebec Association of Local Community Services Centres and Residential and Long-Term Care Centres], only two-thirds of residents' care needs are being met (Begin 1999c). The Fédération des infirmières et infirmiers du Québec (FIIQ; Quebec Nurses' Federation) and the Ordre des infirmières et infirmiers du Québec (OIIQ; Quebec Order of Nurses) report that in some residential and long-term care centres, there is no nurse on duty at night or in the evening, which increases the use of physical and chemical restraints and the incidence of falls and bed sores among residents. As these two nursing organizations also state,

> [translation] Nurses are in a position to observe the increase in complications that could have been avoided and that cause patients to come back to emergency rooms, or even to be readmitted to hospital. (FIIQ and OIIQ 1997, 2)

In hospitals, the pressure to free up beds is so intense that hospital stays are being cut short.[30] There do not seem to be any strictly applied professional standards for determining when a patient is "cured":

> [translation] Only a minimal, approximate assessment of the patient's physical condition is done when the decision is being made whether to

discharge them. Sometimes all it seems to cover is whether the patient can get up and walk, even though the patient may still be dizzy or in a generally weakened state. (AFÉAS *et al.* 1998, 23)

A survey conducted for the Quebec City regional health and social services board found that "[translation] Between 20% and 40% of respondents who had had inpatient surgery and 24% of respondents who had had outpatient surgery would have preferred to stay in hospital longer" (Régie régionale de Québec 1997, 29). The reduction in the length of hospital stays and early postpartum discharge from hospital[31] sometimes create hardships for new mothers, especially when they have little support at home. This is a source of increased anxiety, particularly for young mothers and mothers living on modest incomes.

With bed closures and staff shortages, waiting times are growing longer (Jérôme-Forget and Forget 1998). To see a psychiatrist on an outpatient basis, patients can expect to wait several months (RIOCM 1998). And one delay often leads to another (Ramsay and Walker 1998). In the breast cancer prevention program, for example, screening examinations are provided for free in private x-ray clinics. But if further investigation is necessary, a woman will wait about four months to get an ultrasound at a hospital, unless she wants to pay the fee to obtain this service in the private sector. She will encounter further delays if she needs treatment, and many women are then referred to the United States.

In 1993, "[translation] Quebec was the province where patients waited the least time to see a specialist – 2.9 weeks. As of 1997, Quebec patients were enduring waits of 5.4 weeks, or 2.5 weeks longer" (Léger 1998, A 5).[32] The long delays increase patients' distress and anxiety and can even affect their health:

In this regard there is no persuasive evidence that mortality rates in Canada are increasing significantly owing to a failure to provide medical services. If however, one regards the elimination of pain and suffering as the objective of medical care, then any additional pain suffered by patients because of delays is medical treatment denied. (Ramsay and Walker 1998, 5)

Access to abortion services in public institutions is also limited and subject to long waits, which encourages women to go to private clinics where they must pay for the services themselves. What becomes of the principle of free, universal, accessible health care that is supposed to be the foundation of the public system?

After discharge from hospital, continuity of care is not ensured. The complaints commissioner of the Quebec Department of Health and Social Services reports a 15 per cent increase in complaints in 1997-98 compared with the preceding year, particularly complaints regarding accessibility and continuity of care (Commissaire aux plaintes en santé et services sociaux 1999).

Ground has also been lost in delivery of preventive programs. For example, some CLSCs now offer prenatal courses and postnatal follow-up only to women who have a certain number of risk factors in their pregnancies (AFÉAS *et al.* 1998). However, some of the preventive programs that have received priority from the Department of Health and Social Services and various regional boards deal with matters of concern to women, such as curbing domestic violence, reducing deaths from breast cancer and improving infant health and welfare by working with mothers during pregnancy. This represents progress, but it remains fragile, because the resources allocated for these objectives are not always adequate, and the efforts at coordination with other sectors – particularly the community network – have had uneven success in the various regions of the province.

Another way that health care reform affects women as users of health care services is the downloading of costs from the public system to users, which takes various guises. With the shift toward ambulatory care and outpatient surgery, pre-operative and post-discharge nursing care must be provided in the home. The CLSCs are designated to provide this care, but their resources are clearly insufficient to meet the demand. When a request for home services is received at some CLSCs, they first check whether the person has private insurance that covers such services, and if they do, the CLSC directs them to a private agency (Coalition féministe 1998). Some people with disabilities who used to receive many home-support services for free must now defray the costs themselves.

Women users of health services assume an increasingly large share of the costs of drugs and supplies. The shortening of hospital stays has also shortened the time during which the hospital provides these supplies for free. The Quebec Prescription Drug Insurance Plan does not cover all prescribed drugs, nor all the costs of purchasing drugs. Co-insurance fees – premiums that must be paid by the insured – put a major dent in the incomes of senior citizens and welfare recipients. The Quebec Ombudsman has intervened with the government on different occasions to demand a fairer system. Community organizations observe that the drug insurance plan destabilizes the poorest members of society,

> [translation] first, by its impact on their budget, but also in some cases by its impact on their health, either by preventing them from purchasing a prescription drug or by forcing them to go without food or to delay paying their rent or their phone or electrical bills in order to purchase the drug. (ROC 03 1997, 20)

A study by researchers at McGill University (Tamblyn *et al.* 1999) found that the introduction of the Quebec Prescription Drug Insurance Plan caused use of medications to drop by an average of 9 per cent among seniors and by an average of 14 per cent among welfare recipients. The decline in use of essential drugs had negative effects on the health of the most vulnerable groups and increased their use of other health services (e.g., doctors' visits, emergency room visits, hospital admissions). These negative effects were greater among welfare recipients than among seniors, and greatest among welfare recipients who suffered from serious, persistent mental illness. On the other hand, the decrease in the use of less essential drugs reduced the number of doctors' visits among seniors who took these kinds of drugs regularly. However,

> [translation] the most recent changes in the drug insurance plan [designed to restore free access to medication for people suffering from chronic mental illness] have not been extended to seniors. One reason cited was that seniors have higher incomes than welfare recipients do. This is true if no distinction is made between men's incomes and women's. But if you look at the situation more closely, the incomes of many older women who live alone place them below the poverty line. (Conseil du statut de la femme 1999b, 45)

The Coalition sur l'assurance-médicaments [Coalition on Drug Insurance], whose members include several Quebec rights groups, has pointed out other problems associated with the drug insurance plan:

> [translation]: the inequalities that it creates among citizens who have the same incomes but have to contribute different amounts when purchasing prescription drugs; the obligation that it imposes on thousands of workers to cover their spouse and their children under their private plans, which drastically increases their premiums; the disparities between the public plan and private plans; and the lack of confidentiality, since claims for reimbursement must sometimes be submitted through people's employers. (Guay 1999, A-7)

Women as Health and Social Services Workers

Women represent three out of every four employees in the public health and social services sector. They have been hit hard by the reform that it has undergone. The changes that have had the greatest impact on women's working conditions in the public system are closures and mergers of institutions, redefinitions of jobs, large-scale transfers of personnel and massive departures.

The large number of staff transfers has required a great deal of flexibility and adaptability on the part of thousands of female health and social services workers. For example, a nurse who is transferred from a specialized unit in a hospital to a CLSC where she has to perform a much wider range of tasks may feel unqualified for her new job, especially if she did not receive any refresher training to prepare her. Transfers have also dismantled teams of workers with years of experience in their workplace, sending them off to work in new environments with different organizational cultures, which can be a major source of stress. Temporary workers have suffered as well; when they see new full-time staff with job security transferred in from other institutions, it makes them feel less secure in their own jobs. These many sources of tension, combined with a heavier workload, pose a risk of exhaustion for workers in the system.

In all types of institutions, working conditions are harder. There is too much work, the pace is faster, the nature of jobs is being transformed, and the risk of errors is increasing (AFÉAS *et al.* 1998). In hospitals, there are fewer staff to take care of patients who are sicker and need more care.

In a survey of nurses (both male and female) in the Quebec City region, the workload for nursing staff was reported to have increased by 85 per cent, and 74 per cent of respondents said that they did not have enough time to do their jobs (Bourbonnais *et al.* 1998). In the same survey, the nursing staff reported much higher levels of psychological stress than in 1994 (41% compared with 29%), the year before the shift to ambulatory care and the wave of budget cutbacks began. This high level of psychological stress (which was even higher – 56% – among women with no job security) makes nurses a group at risk of developing health problems (Conseil du statut de la femme 1999a, 70).

In emergency rooms, working conditions have deteriorated badly. At the Hôpital du Sacré-Coeur de Montréal, for example, nurses have refused on more than one occasion to show up for work, because they deemed the working conditions at their jobs to be hazardous. And the Commission de la santé et de la sécurité du travail (the Quebec Occupational Health and Safety Commission) has found in their favour. Doctors too perceive an increase in their workload, in all areas of practice (Leclerc 1998).

Heavier workloads are also very common for the CLSC workers who provide home care. The number of home visits that a CLSC nurse must make each day has increased by about 50 per cent. The CLSCs' family and social assistants also must work faster, and their risk of work accidents is growing, especially when they work alone and have to move people with limited mobility from one place to another in their homes. "[translation] The data for 1993-96 show that assistants suffer 48% of all work injuries, even though they constitute only 13% of the work force" (Conseil du statut de la femme 1999a, 71). The number and kinds of clients for home services are increasing continuously, so women who provide such services face increased risks of harassment and verbal aggression, and sometimes even physical aggression.

Changes in professional practices, together with workforce reductions, raise questions about professional roles and the ways employees' skills are used (Dussault 1994). One concern is that poorer working conditions, decreased job security and the growing proportion of casual and part-time jobs may lead to a loss of technical competence. Another concern is that cutting staff and redefining jobs will create role conflicts between, for example, registered nurses and nurses' aides. The traditional division of labour between these groups has been overturned by hospital restructuring and staff reductions. Some occupational groups look as if they will eventually disappear, with all the risks that this entails for the organization of work within the health care system. Members of all occupational groups worry about being replaced with "cheaper" workers.

As discussed in the section on community organizations, private agencies and social economy enterprises providing home care have proliferated, in part because of contracting out by overwhelmed CLSCs. In 1994-95, CLSCs in the Montréal-Centre health and social services region purchased over $8 million worth of services from private agencies, at an average hourly rate of $9.94, while the average hourly wage of CLSC family assistants was $16 to $18 (Corbin 1996). The data from an initial assessment of social economy enterprises (prepared for the Quebec Department of Health and Social Services) indicate that close to 9 out of 10 of their employees are women and that 40 per cent of them were receiving income security benefits before being hired. Though there are some notable variations among these enterprises, the hourly wage of their employees who provide direct services ranges from $6.80 to $8.30, and close to half of these employees work only part-time (Bélanger 1998). A comparison with working conditions in the public system suggests that the government is reducing the costs of health care services by creating "second-tier" jobs for the women who constitute the vast majority of health care workers. There is no denying that on the whole, the gains realized by women in this female-dominated sector of employment have been rendered more fragile by the reform of the health care system.

Women as Caregivers

Current reforms have also produced a new division of responsibilities between families and the state. As far as home-support for elderly persons is concerned, families have become the main, if not the only, source of help. A review of the Canadian, Quebec and United States literature on support for the aged (Garant and Bolduc 1990) indicates that beginning in the 1990s, 70 per cent to 80 per cent of personal care and services for the aged were provided by family members. The combined contribution of community organizations and government agencies was only 10 per cent. More recent research has confirmed that families still provide 70 per cent of nursing care and assistance for frail seniors who live at home and receive some services from the public health and social services system. For seniors who do not receive any help from the public system, this figure is even higher – 80 per cent (Hébert et al. 1997).

With the shift to ambulatory care, however, there has been a paradigm shift as well. Home care is now being provided to people of all ages, including many seniors who are discharged early from hospital after surgery or medical treatment. These seniors do not always need long-term care, but their conditions do mean that they need family members to be available, often at very short notice. The home has become an officially recognized site for providing health care, and women who help their family members are more and more becoming health care providers. These changes increase the pressure on families, and especially on women.

Women are being expected to provide increasingly complex kinds of care, but are not being adequately prepared for their more extensive responsibilities. This is an additional source of stress, especially for older women

(Ducharme 1998). Moreover, the kind of care that one family member provides to another is very different from the kind of care provided by professionals who are subject to ongoing assessment and professional standards. The inextricable emotional component in any family relationship makes it more difficult for caregivers to have their own personal limitations recognized.

Women bear most of the responsibility for providing care and support to family members. A survey conducted for the Rochon Commission of a representative sample of people providing care to frail seniors, showed that 67 per cent of caregivers were women (Jutras and Veilleux 1989). In a report on new trends in informal health care, prepared for Health Canada, Nancy Guberman writes:

> Research has documented that in most families it is not the family unit, be it extended or nuclear, but one family member who assumes the primary responsibility for care, and this member is usually a woman. (1999, 25)

A survey for Santé Quebec has also shown that among female and male caregivers who live with the person to whom they are providing care, 80 per cent of the females are primary caregivers, while only 46 per cent of the males fulfil that role (Lavoie, Lévesque and Jutras 1995). Various studies show that if the caregiver is a man, different use is made of formal and informal supports, reflecting the pressure exerted by the social roles that women are expected to play (Vezina and Pelletier, 1998).[33]

Family dynamics often contribute to a sense of guilt among female caregivers, even when the relative in question is being cared for in a residential facility. This plays a role in families' reluctance to make use of formal services:

> [translation] Men seem less reticent than women to ask for support... Men in general are more 'vulnerable' when placed in a caregiving situation, because they feel at a loss to handle tasks that they traditionally have not performed. (Paquet 1999,117)

The kinds of tasks and responsibilities that caregivers assume also vary with their sex. Female caregivers provide more personal and domestic care than males and spend more hours per week giving care. Men are more likely to provide transportation and do administrative chores. Male caregivers also experience less conflict between their caregiving tasks and their regular jobs (Guberman *et al.* 1991).

Despite the massive influx of women into the workforce in the past few decades, the division of domestic labour has not changed significantly. The increased responsibilities of caregiving thus make it even harder for women to reconcile the demands of home with those of their paid jobs. More than a third of female caregivers in Canada are employed, and one third of this latter group report that their caregiving responsibilities interfere with their work (Canadian Study in Health and Aging 1994; Guberman, Maheu and Maillé

1993). In this regard, a survey has revealed that 9 per cent of caregivers, mostly women, have curtailed their hours of work, 5 per cent have turned down professional responsibilities and 6 per cent have stopped working (Jutras and Veilleux 1989). These figures, which are undoubtedly much higher more than a decade later, indicate the major price being paid by women who take care of family members with acute or chronic health problems.

A number of articles have reported the impact of the caregiving role on women's living conditions and quality of life, as well as on their health (stress, anxiety, physical and emotional exhaustion);[34] on their personal, family and spousal relationships (where role conflicts create many tensions); and on their ability to engage in other social activities at their jobs, on their own time or as volunteers in various organizations. When caregivers have to continue providing care for extended periods, the effects on their living conditions and their health are substantial (Lauzon and al. 1998; Gottlieb 1998).

Despite these well-known facts, an analysis of home-service policies and programs in Quebec reveals a lack of interest in the health of female caregivers (Lavoie 1998). The policy documents not only of the Department of Health and Social Services, but also of the regional health and social services boards and the CLSCs (with a few exceptions) place little emphasis on the situation of caregivers. These institutions' lack of understanding of this issue is apparent in the assessment tools that they use and in the way they regard caregivers as largely a means to an end. To the extent that they talk about the situation of caregivers at all, policies and programs focus mainly on the need to support them so that they do not become exhausted.

The assessments that have been made of various caregiver-support programs to determine their most important elements and impacts have not always been conclusive (Gottlieb 1998). Combinations of various support strategies should therefore be tried, including community initiatives (e.g., self-help groups and support and respite services for caregivers), government initiatives (e.g., tax deductions for taking care of dependent persons at home), and private sector initiatives (e.g., flexible work hours and family leave) (Guberman 1999, Lessard 2000).

The contribution that women make to the care of people who are sick or incapacitated represents a major human, social and economic cost. A study by the Quebec Department of Health and Social Services

> [translation] confirms the significant value of the work done by family members to support dependent seniors who live at home. This contribution represents more than half of the total costs of such support, averaging from $37 to $60 per day, depending on the value (public sector cost or private sector cost) imputed to them ... The burden of this work affects caregivers own health and interferes with their own functioning, so it also generates significant indirect social costs. (Hébert et al. 1997, 260)

Some economic analyses of the restructuring of health and social services evaluate only the short-term improvements in the efficiency of public institutions, without analyzing the cost effectiveness of restructuring from the standpoint of the longer-term health of both the recipients and the providers of home care (MSSS 1991, 1994, 1996; Angus *et al.* 1995). And yet, some perverse effects of this restructuring are emerging, and they could generate extra costs in the long run – for example, the costs of providing health care to the caregivers themselves, or of re-institutionalizing the sick and disabled because their home caregivers had suffered burnout. Analyses of the efficiency of public health care spending must be placed in the context of total health care costs, including the money that families have to spend privately because public services have been restructured.

More and more analyses are taking a penetrating look at the consequences of health care reform for caregivers. Some studies indicate that people who receive care from their family network use fewer government and community services. But on the whole these studies indicate the need for a change in policies (Lessard 2000; RAANM 1999; Guberman 1999; Paquet, 1999; Lavoie *et al.* 1998; Ducharme 1998; Vézina and Pelletier 1998; Guberman, Maheu and Maillé 1991, 1993; Saillant 1992).

Women Involved in Community Organizations

Whether as workers, as activists or as volunteers, women play a vibrant role in community health and social services organizations and constitute the majority of their membership. Increasingly, it is to such organizations that public institutions are sending people when they need support (AFÉAS *et al.* 1998; RIOCM 1998; ROC 03 1997; Parent 1997). Under this new pressure, community groups tend to lose sight of their mission and alter their practices. The service provider mentality infiltrates community organizations at the expense of their work of educating the public, increasing public awareness and mobilizing public action. People get used to requesting services from community groups without seeing any need to get involved themselves. One woman representative of a rights group comments: "In the beginning... the people in the groups were activists. Then we had members. Now, we have users of services" (RIOCM 1998,120).

According to a survey that the RIOCM [Inter-Sectoral Coalition of Montreal Community Organizations] conducted among its member organizations, many groups have increased the services that they provide without creating any new positions. A representative of a community agency that works with families reports:

> The workload is heavier, and because of that there is more pressure on the work team. We no longer succeed in managing all the priorities; everything is a priority now. Our work schedules expand in virtually unlimited fashion. We have to be versatile, we have to be able to do a bit of everything as well as assuming the uncertainty of our own financial situation. (RIOCM 1998, 126)

Some people fear that the overload will cause relations among their workers and the quality of their work to deteriorate.

> [translation] Volunteers' motivation is decreasing steadily, because the new demands are perverting the whole concept of volunteerism, which is based on making a gift of one's own time of one's own accord. Some of these demands are perceived as abusive – for example, volunteers are being asked to look after people who have just had serious operations, or to provide respite care overnight and on weekends. (Coalition féministe 1998, 30)

There have been few systematic studies of the consequences of health care reform for community organizations and the women involved in them. The public health and social services system often refers to these organizations as if they were simply extensions of the system, without really understanding how reform is affecting the women who work for these groups, either in paid jobs or as volunteers.

Participation of Quebec Women's Groups in Public Decision-making Bodies

In Quebec, the Conseil du statut de la femme [Quebec Council for the Status of Women] and women's groups around the province are raising questions about the ways that women participate in the various decision-making and advisory bodies established to help implement health care reform. Representatives of the women's groups would like to act as partners in the regionalization of the health care system, but they experience culture shock when their community orientation comes up against the culture of the regional decision-making and advisory bodies (Tremblay 1999; L'R des centres de femmes du Québec 1997). In these bodies, technocratic discourse predominates. Questions about women's health and the impact of reform on their health and living conditions generate little interest and are rarely the subject of discussion. A study by the Conseil du statut de la femme (1995) has shown that from 1980 to 1995, these bodies neglected the entire issue of women's living conditions.

Some concerns raised by the women's movement have been addressed in new policies and programs, such as the Department of Health and Social Services' action plan on the status of women,[35] or the recognition of midwives as health care practitioners. But many women who have participated in decision-making bodies within the health and social services system feel that they lost their bearings in an approach that emphasizes "clients," "programs" and management through a "continuum of services."[36]

The privatization of the funding and delivery of services augurs badly for women's participation in decisions about the health and social services system. Moreover, citizen involvement, which was supposed to facilitate reform by democratizing regional bodies and decision-making processes, has been frustrated by some of the effects of the reform itself. Women from community organizations are overburdened. They are being called on to provide care and services in both their professional and their private lives, at the same time as they are being hit by cuts in social programs and growing poverty.

CONCLUSION

To understand the consequences of health care reform that affect women specifically, it is important to recognize the social roles that condition women's experience in the family, in the workforce, in the health care system itself, and in women's public role, particularly in community organizations and decision-making bodies within the health and social services system. Women have always played a fundamental role in caring for people, both in their families and in health care institutions, but their contribution has not always been recognized. The government's talk about making families more responsible for caring for their members (so that the state can stop doing so) belies the reality that families already provide far more care to their sick and disabled members than the public system does. And despite the increasingly complex kinds of health care that must be provided in the home, women still play a major role in providing health care to their families. The development and professionalization of the public health and social services system may disguise the special contribution that women make to the well-being of our society. For years the women's movement has been demanding that the various stages of life be "demedicalized" and that women have control over their own bodies. These demands have contributed to a change in values concerning health and the use of health care services. To reflect these facts, a comparative analysis of the two sexes is essential. This approach must be fully and genuinely integrated into any analysis of the consequences of health care reform and of the best ways of transforming the health and social services system.

Many studies have shown that investing more resources in the health and social services system does not necessarily improve public health, at least not in industrialized countries. But this does not mean that the current sweeping changes and budget cutbacks in this system have no effect on the health of the public in general, or of women in particular, because the health care system interacts with other determinants of health. Some effects of health care reform are direct. For example, budgets for long-term residential facilities are cut back, but the need for their services keeps increasing; more and more services must be provided at home, even though insufficient resources are reallocated for the purpose. The constantly decreasing quality of health care services has an impact on the health status of women, many of them elderly. When reforms reduce access to public health services, waiting lines for health care grow longer, increasing stress and affecting the health of the people who are waiting for care.

Other effects of health system reform are less direct, occurring in combination with other health determinants. For example, reforms are shifting the burden of providing increasingly complex forms of care to families, and mainly to the women in these families, without providing adequate support for this purpose. This new responsibility creates multiple tensions in women's immediate social surroundings. It also makes it harder for women who work outside the home to reconcile their domestic chores with the requirements of their jobs. The heavier workload and numerous structural upheavals in health and social services institutions have had significant effects on the health of workers in this environment, most of whom are women. The job cuts and increased use of casual labour both in public and in private health care organizations have been a significant step backward for their mainly female work force, with ripple effects on women in the workforce as a whole.

Changes in the health care system interact with the other determinants of health in such a way that the reforms affect women differently according to factors such as their age, their physical disabilities, their support network, their social and economic status, their ethnic and cultural background and whether they live in a rural or an urban area. Older women are especially affected in their role as users of health care services and as caregivers. In rural areas, which many young people have left, there is more pressure on women to provide support to people who need it in their communities, so that some authors regard these women as having become "career caregivers" (Guberman 1999; Therrien 1989).

Women who live on modest incomes – especially older women who live alone and women who are heads of single-parent families – must absorb downloaded costs that represent a greater burden for them than for women with higher incomes or access to private insurance. For women from various ethnic and cultural communities, differing values and family dynamics colour the way they make use of services and their ability to adapt to rapid structural changes in the organizations that provide them. These are just some examples of the variety of situations that women experience. They illustrate the need to pursue more systematic research to identify the many consequences of health system reform on the living conditions and health of women from various backgrounds, and to propose remedies based on meaningful data.

This chapter shows that the effects of health care reform on women's health are related to the trend toward privatization, which is accentuating the current changes. This raises the questions: Are there any options for the future of the health and social services system besides privatization? Is replacing public services with unpaid labour by women in the family setting, or by private services that pay women low wages, the only way to achieve de-institutionalization? Wouldn't it be better to provide significant support to families (in particular to women who agree to care for their relatives at home) and to develop some alternative ways of caring for people in the community?

Another assumption of health care reform seems to be that the way to manage health and social services more effectively and efficiently is to foster "internal competition," contract work out, and place a heavier workload on a predominantly female workforce. Perhaps instead we should promote the development of integrated, inter-institutional service networks and build stronger multidisciplinary teams that improve services by drawing on the varied skills of these women, including both professional and non-professional staff.

Similarly, perhaps the best way to allocate resources so as to ensure equality and equity in accessing health care services is not to rely more heavily on private spending. Perhaps it is to go back to funding health care mainly through fiscal mechanisms – especially since increasing the proportion of private spending does not reduce the total cost of health care, while it does put more of a burden on women, who as a group still live on much lower incomes than men.

Health care reform cannot be adequately analyzed from a narrow perspective that seeks to increase efficiency and reduce public spending in the short term while ignoring negative effects that could increase health and social services costs in the long run. A broader perspective that includes a specific analysis of differences between women and men can make a special contribution. It can provide a more nuanced understanding of the processes involved in organizing and funding health care services. This perspective will shed vital light on the options being considered for renewing health care practices and reorganizing health and social services. Any attempt to find solutions to the challenges faced by the health and social services system must recognize and seek to reduce the considerable price that women are being forced to pay for the recent sweeping changes in this system.

Notes

1. In Quebec, the Coalition féministe pour une transformation du système de santé [Feminist Coalition for Transforming the Health Care System], the Conseil du statut de la femme [Council on the Status of Women] and other coalitions of community organizations and labour unions have sounded the alarm about the specific effects that health care reform has had on women. See in particular Coalition féministe pour une transformation du système de santé et de services sociaux 1998 and Conseil du statut de la femme 1999.
2. See in particular Conseil du statut de la femme 1999a; Métivier 1999; Contandriopoulos 1999; Patenaude and Lambert 1998; Conseil de la santé et du bien-être du Québec 1997, 1995; Vaillancourt and Jetté 1997; Armstrong and Armstrong 1996; National Forum on Health 1995, 1997; Gouvernement du Québec, MSSS 1991; Janssen and Van der Made 1990; Soderstrom 1987; Vaillancourt et al. 1987; Stoddart and Labelle 1983.
3. Many private corporations still own the buildings in which public hospital centres are located and have a reserved seat on their boards of directors.
4. This summit brought together government, business, union and community representatives to discuss government priorities, including ways to revitalize the economy and employment and to balance public finances.
5. There are currently 16 regional boards, and a health and social services council operates in the First Nations territories of northern Quebec.
6. Despite these additional resources, the total number of people in the Montreal region waiting for all types of surgery rose from 35,109 in September 1998 to 39,318 in September 1999, an increase of 12 per cent (Bégin 1999d).
7. In 1999-2000, Quebec still had the lowest per capita spending for home care services: $65 compared to $129 in Manitoba, $108 in New Brunswick and $92 in Ontario (MSSS 2000).

8. According to Hagan, Morin and Lépine (1998), most of the women using these telephone services are well educated and middle-aged and they report being satisfied with the advice they received. The Centre of Excellence for Women's Health is conducting a study on how well these CLSC-based health information services are meeting the needs of immigrant women. It would also be worthwhile to examine ways to ensure that other women's diverse learning styles are taken into account.
9. [Translation] "The Fédération des CLSC [now the Association des CLSC et CHSLD]... is calling for financial incentives to attract more than 250 new general practitioners, whose services are essential if the CLSCs are to play their role properly." (Gagnon 1999, A-21)
10. Such cooperation should include sharing of "off-hours" duties between doctors in private clinics and doctors in CLSCs. Some observers have noted that one of the reasons hospital emergency rooms become so overcrowded during holidays is that private medical clinics and CLSCs are closed then.
11. Vaillancourt and Jetté (1997) gives differing assessments of de-institutionalization for the mentally ill and for the intellectually handicapped, though in the latter case, families also assume a significant portion of the burden of taking care of people who are often vulnerable and unable to care for themselves.
12. This trend will probably grow more pronounced in the coming years, even though the gap between men's and women's life expectancy is starting to close. According to Guyon (1996, 34). "Females born in Quebec in 1992-1993 can expect to spend 12.3 years, or 15% of their lives, with some form of disability, whereas their male counterparts, who will die younger, will spend 11% of their lives in this condition."
13. According to Senator Monique Bégin, "la décision prise par certaines administrations gouvernementales de ne pas investir dans les soins à domicile ne reflète pas simplement une attitude de laisser faire, mais s'inscrit dans une stratégie délibérée visant à permettre au secteur privé de prendre le relais comme il le juge bon" (Bégin 1999, 104-105)
14. In social economy enterprises, clients who receive home-support services must pay fees, but the fees are adjusted to the client's ability to pay.
15. The number of nurses in private practice who are registered with the Ordre des infirmières et infirmiers du Québec also increased by 11% from 1996 to 1997. This number is still small – it represents only 1% of nurses registered with the Order – but the trend is accelerating with the shift toward ambulatory care.
16. This figure includes payments made to physicians, dentists and optometrists through Quebec's provincial health insurance plan.
17. Contandriopoulos (1991) finds that the more a health care system is funded through budget allocations determined in advance, on the basis of the populations to be served (e.g., by capitation), the more equitable it tends to be. In contrast, he finds the more that resources are paid for after the fact, on the basis of the services provided, the more potential there is for the system to contain inequities. Contandriopoulos therefore believes that a health care system will have a greater chance of being equitable if it includes mechanisms for gathering, analyzing and disseminating information on the health outcomes and effectiveness of the services it provides.
18. Health Maintenance Organizations (HMOs) in the United States were established by private corporations and insurance companies. Their clients sign up with them and, in exchange for a premium, are assured of receiving the services that the organization deems appropriate, based on the recommendations of health care professionals. There are many criticisms of the HMO model, in particular that it has a selection bias that tends to exclude people with chronic health problems, and that it tends to ration services for financial reasons. In the GP fundholders arrangements in the UK, GPs receive public funds according to the number of patients they have, and they can negotiate service contracts for more specialized treatment with hospitals and other health care establishments.
19. The two major items included in these figures are the budgets for public health care institutions and for the Régie de l'assurance-maladie du Québec (RAMQ – Quebec Health Insurance Plan), which pays for doctors' services and a few complementary services.
20. Based on data from the Canadian Institute for Health Information (CIHI) and the MSSS statistical analysis service. Only in Ontario does public funding account for a lower proportion of total health care spending: 66.9%.

21. The growth rate for private spending fell from 9.5% per year for the period 1989 to 1991 to 5% per year for the period 1991 to 1998, while the growth rate for public spending dropped more radically, from 9.4% for the former period to 0.7% for the latter.
22. According to the Arpin Report, the figure of 30.9% for private spending as a proportion of total health care spending is based on more recent CIHI data and on adjustments made by the Quebec Department of Health and Social Services (Groupe de travail sur la complémentatité du secteur privé 1999a, 1999b). Another source of private funding is foundations, which contribute in ways such as purchasing high-tech medical equipment for hospitals.
23. But here is how the Arpin Report explains the 5.9 percentage point increase in private spending – "by a gross increase of 12.5 percentage points, due solely to the slowdown in public health care spending starting in 1991, from which 5 percentage points must be subtracted to account for changes in the price of services (due partly to the decline in employee wages) and a few more percentage points attributable to a slight slowdown in the use of private spending and the interaction of various factors" (Groupe de travail sur la complémentarité du secteur privé 1999b, 17). This argument seems like camouflage!
24. This data includes all sources of income: "[translation] Most differences between the sexes can be explained by the poverty rate of three types of families: Women under 65 living alone (38% poor), women 65 and over living alone (47% poor) and single mothers with children under 18 (60% poor)" (Conseil national du bien-être social, cited by Guyon 1996, 20).
25. This plan was made available somewhat earlier for senior citizens and welfare recipients, in summer 1996.
26. Dr. Jean Cusson, chair of the Quebec government's Conseil consultatif de pharmacologie [Pharmacology Advisory Board], denounced the extensive political pressure exerted by the drug companies to get their products included on the list of drugs covered by the provincial drug insurance plan. According to Dr. Cusson "[translation] The weaker their case is scientifically, the more pressure they exert." (See Hachey 2000, A-6).
27. Many complaints have arisen from the requirement to take out all the coverage available for spouses and dependents under private plans, which involves costly premiums.
28. In the spring of 2001, Health and Social Services Minister Rémi Trudel presented a Bill requiring board members of all Regional Health and Social Services Authorities to be nominated by the Minister rather than being elected through a regional process. If put in place, this Bill could be part of a re-centralization process.
29. A paper published by the Conference Board of Canada, *Caring About Caregiving: The Eldercare Responsibilities of Canadian Workers and the Impact on Employers*, 1999, refers to workers who are in this position as the "sandwich generation." Such workers are now estimated to represent 15% of the work force, compared with 9.5% just a few years ago. (See Church 1999).
30. "[Translation] Whether it is cutting the number or length of hospital stays, what is striking is the highly quantitative objectives that are driving the shift toward ambulatory care." says the Conseil du statut de la femme (1999a, 34). The pressure on institutions to achieve better performance as measured against such benchmarks is very strong. The Bas-Saint-Laurent regional health and social services board received a letter of reprimand from the Minister when it failed to engage in such a measurement exercise (Letter included in the 1995-1998 three-year plan for this regional board) (CSF 1999a, 35).
31. As a result of the shift toward ambulatory care, the average length of a woman's hospital stay after a vaginal delivery without complications has fallen from 3.5 days in 1992-93 to 2.5 days in 1996-97. The average length of the stay after a delivery by caesarian section has fallen from 6 days to 4.8 days. (MSSS, *Bilan ponctuel sur les programmes de congé précoce en périnatalité au Québec*, cited in Conseil du statut de la femme 1999a, 88).
32. However, a report conducted by three research teams and sponsored by Health Canada, *Waiting lists and waiting times for health care in Canada: more management! more money?* (Macdonald et al. 1998), concludes that there are no reliable data on waiting lists and waiting times to obtain health care services in Canada. The report adds that the harmful effects of these delays on health and on recourse to private services have not been demonstrated either.
33. "[Translation] Male primary caregivers receive more help from other family members than female primary caregivers do (Walker 1991). When a man takes care of his wife because she cannot care

for herself, he gets help from his daughters. This does not happen so often when a women is taking care of her husband (Roy *et al*. 1992). In the few cases where a son is caring for an elderly parent, his wife – the daughter-in-law – very often takes on major responsibilities for the parent's care. According to Matthews and Rosner (1998), a daughter who cannot or does not want to take care of an elderly parent feels guilty and has to offer some good excuses. For a son, not helping seems more normal." (Vézina and Pelletier 1998, 8).
34. The data from the most recent survey by Santé Québec showed that 35% of women who were "natural caregivers" showed high levels of psychological stress.
35. See MSSS 1998a. The plan proposes that differential analysis by sex be used in planning policies for the Quebec Department of Health and Social Services, and that an assessment be done of the impact of health care system reforms on caregivers and workers in this sytem, most of whom are women.
36. The regional boards' transformation plans are generally based on "continuums of services" in physical health, mental health, services for seniors, services for the physically challenged, services for the intellectually challenged, and social adjustment services.

References

Angus, Douglas *et al*. 1995. *Sustainable Health Care for Canada*. Queen's and University of Ottawa Economic Projects. Ottawa: University of Ottawa.

Angus, Douglas E. 1997 . "Le système de santé public de demain: l'équité sacrifiée au profit de l'efficience?" *Ruptures* 4 (2): 206-18. Montreal: Groupe de recherche interdisciplinaire en santé, Faculté de médecine, Université de Montréal.

Armstrong, Pat, and Armstrong, Hugh. 1996. *Wasting Away. The Undermining of Canadian Health Care*. Toronto: Oxford University Press.

Association féminine d'éducation et d'action sociale (AFEAS) *et al*. 1998. *Who Will Be Responsible for Providing Care? The Impact of the Shift to Ambulatory Care and of Social Economy Policies on Quebec Women*. Ottawa: Status of Women Canada.

Bégin, Jean-François. 1998. "Un réseau vidé de son savoir." *La Presse*, 14 novembre, A 25.

—. 1999a. "Doit-on abolir les élections dans le réseau de la santé?" *La Presse*, 18 octobre, A-6.

—. 1999b. "Fusions d'hôpitaux: il manque des conditions gagnantes." La Presse, 4 novembre, A-15.

—. 1999c. "Les centres d'hébergement de longue durée réclament 357 millions à Québec." *La Presse*, 24 novembre, A-8.

—. 1999d. "Les listes d'attente en chirurgie continuent de grimper à Montréal." *La Presse*, 26 novembre, A-15.

Bégin, Monique. 1999. "Redefining Entitlement to Health Care." In Margaret A. Somerville *et al*., eds., *Do We Care?Renewing Canada's Commitment to Health: Proceedings of the First Directions for Canadian Health Care Conference*, 95-98. Montreal: McGill-Queen's University Press.

Bélanger, Gérard. 1994. "Le financement centralisé et la décentralisation des décisions: une incompatibilité." In Vincent Lemieux *et al*., eds., *Le système de santé au Québec: Organisations, acteurs et enjeux*. Quebec : Les Presses de l'Université Laval.

Bélanger, Lucie. 1998. *Les entreprises d'économie sociale en aide domestique: un premier bilan*. Quebec : MSSS (direction de la recherche et de l'évaluation).

Bergeron, Pierre and France Gagnon. 1994. "La prise en charge étatique de la santé au Québec." In Vincent Lemieux, Pierre Bergeron, Clermont Bégin and Gérard Bélanger, eds., *Le système de santé*

au Québec: Organisations, acteurs et enjeux. Quebec: Les Presses de l'Université Laval.
Boivin, Louise and M. Fortier. 1998. *L'économie sociale: l'avenir d'une illusion.* Montreal: Fides.
Bourbonnais, Renée, Monique Comeau and Centre de santé publique de Québec (CSPQ). 1998. *La transformation du réseau de la santé: mesure des caractéristiques du travail et de la santé des infirmières de l'agglomération de Québec.* Beauport: Direction de la santé publique de Québec.
Bravo, Gina *et al.* 1999. "Quality of Care in Unlicensed Homes for the Aged in the Eastern Township of Quebec."*Canadian Medical Association Journal* 160(19).
Centrale de l'enseignement du Québec. 1996. *Puzzle sur le virage ambulatoire et la reconfiguration du réseau de services de santé et de services sociaux.* Montreal: CEQ.
Church, E. 1999. "Number of workers who care for elderly and children rising." *Globe and Mail,* 11 November 1999, B-12.
Coalition féministe pour une transformation du système de santé et des services sociaux. 1998. *Pour des services sociaux et de santé adaptés aux attentes des femmes. Cahier de revendications.* Montreal: La Coalition.
Collège des médecins du Québec. 1999. *Le collège des médecins du Québec s'inquiète de la qualité des soins dans les salles d'urgence.* Press Release, 25 février.
Commissaire aux plaintes en santé et services sociaux (CPSSS). 1999. *Rapport sur l'application de la procédure d'examen des plaintes 1997-1998.* Montreal: MSSS.
Commission d'étude sur les services de santé et les services sociaux. 1999. *Les solutions émergentes. Rapport et recommandations.* Quebec: MSSS.
Conseil de la santé et du bien-être (CSBE). 1995.*Un juste prix pour les services de santé.* Quebec : CSBE.
—. 1997. *Évolution des rapports public-privé dans les services de santé et les services sociaux. Rapport remis au ministre de la santé et des services sociaux.* Quebec: CSBE.
Conseil du statut de la femme (CSF). 1995. *État de situation sur le mandat de condition de vie des femmes au sein des régies régionales de la santé et des services sociaux* (researched and edited by Hélène Latérière). Quebec : CSF
—. 1996a. *Virage ambulatoire: notes exploratoires* (researched and edited by Mariangela Di Domenico). Quebec: CSF.
—. 1996b. *L'économie sociale et les femmes: garder l'oeil ouvert* (researched and edited by Chantal Martel). Quebec : CSF.
—. 1999a. *Virage ambulatoire: le prix caché pour les femmes* (researched and edited by Marie Moisan). Quebec: CSF.
—. 1999b. *Des nouvelles d'elles. Les femmes âgées du Québec* (edited by Diane Guilbault). Quebec : CSF.
Contandriopoulos, André-Pierre. 1991. *Coûts et équité des systèmes de santé.* Montreal: Département d'administration de la santé and Groupe de recherche interdisciplinaire en santé (GRIS), Université de Montréal.
—. 1998. *La régulation d'un système de soins sans murs.* Montreal: Département d'administration de la santé and Groupe de recherche interdisciplinaire en santé (GRIS), Université de Montréal.
—. 1999. "Pourra-t-on encore, demain, compter sur un système de santé universel, accessible à tous et de qualité?" in *Patrimoine.* Montreal: Université de Montréal.
Contandriopoulos, André-Pierre *et al.* 1989. *Modalités de financement et contrôle des coûts du système de soins: l'exemple du Québec.* Montreal: Département d'administration de la santé and Groupe de recherche interdisciplinaire en santé (GRIS), Université de Montréal.
—. 1999. "Les mesures incitatives et le paiement des ressources." In Clermont Bégin *et al.,* eds., *Le système de santé québécois: un modèle en transformation.* Quebec: Les Presses de l'Université Laval.
Corbin, Lise. 1996. *L'aide domestique dans le cadre des services d'aide à domicile. Rapport d'étape.* Montreal: Régie régionale de la santé et des services sociaux de Montréal-Centre.
Crémieux, Pierre-Yves, Pierre Ouellette and Caroline Pilon. 1997. *Public and Private Health Care Spending as a Determinant of Health Outcomes.* Montreal: Département d'économique, Université du Québec à Montréal.

Deber, Raisa. 1999. "The Use and Misuse of Economics." In Margaret A. Somerville *et al.*, eds., *Do We Care? Renewing Canada's Commitment to Health: Proceedings of the First Directions for Canadian Health Care Conference.* Montreal: McGill-Queen's University Press.

Demers, Louis, Albert Dumas and Clermont Bégin. 1999. "La gestion des établissements de santé au Québec." In Clermont Bégin *et al.*, eds., *Le système de santé québécois: un modèle en transformation.* Quebec: Les Presses de l'Université Laval.

Desjardins, Christiane. 1999. "Après les urgences, les agences débordent." *La Presse,* 15 février, A-3.

Doré, Gérald. 1991. "Les relations réseau -communautaire: vers la coopération conflictuelle." In *Circuit socio-communautaire* 3 (1).

Ducharme, Francine. 1998. "Femmes âgées et virage ambulatoire: quelques résultats." *Sans préjudice...pour la santé des femmes* 16 (Fall 1998), 8-10.

Dumais, Monique. 1999. "La dynamique du communautaire dans les services de santé et les services sociaux au Québec." In Pierre Fortin, ed., *La réforme de la santé au Québec.* Montreal: Fides.

Dussault, Gilles. 1994. "Les producteurs de services sociosanitaires." In Vincent Lemieux *et al.*, eds., *Le système de santé au Québec: Organisations, acteurs et enjeux.* Quebec: Les Presses de l'Université Laval.

FIIQ and OIIQ. 1997. *"La FIIQ et l'OIIQ, ensemble contre la dégradation des soins."* Press Release, 12 février.

Fuller, Colleen. 1998. *Caring for Profit: How Corporations Are Taking Over Canada's Health Care System.* Vancouver: New Star Books and Canadian Centre for Policy Alternatives.

Gagnon, Katia. 1999. "Médecins: les CLSC refusent d'abandonner." *La Presse,* 6 mars, A-21.

Garant, Louise and Mario Bolduc. 1990. *L'aide par les proches: mythes et réalités.* Quebec: MSSS (direction de la planification et de l'évaluation).

Gottlieb, B. H. 1998. "Promouvoir et protéger le bien-être des aidants naturels." *Les déterminants de la santé: Le cadre et les enjeux.* Vol. 3. Sainte-Foy: Edition MultiMondes (Studies commissioned by the National Forum on Health).

Gouvernement du Québec, *An Act respecting health services and social services,* R.S.Q., c. S-4.2, 8th edition, annotated, 1993-94. Montreal: Wilson et Lafleur, Ltd.

Greason, Vincent. 1999. "Le communautaire est-il à vendre?" *La Presse,* 6 octobre, B-3.

Groupe de travail sur la complémentarité du secteur privé dans la poursuite des objectifs fondamentaux du système public de santé au Québec. 1999a. *La complémentarité du secteur privé dans la poursuite des objectifs fondamentaux du système public de santé au Québec: Rapport du groupe de travail.* Quebec: MSSS.

—. 1999b. *La présence du privé dans la santé au Québec: État détaillé de la situation.* Quebec: MSSS.

Guay, Lorraine. 1999. "Assurance-médicaments: après la guignolée...la gratuité." *Le Devoir,* 12 janvier, A 7.

Guberman, Nancy. 1999. "Caregivers and Caregiving: New Trends and Their Implications for Policy." Final Report Prepared for Health Canada.

Guberman, Nancy, Pierre Maheu and Chantal Maillé. 1991. *Et si l'amour ne suffisait pas...Femmes, familles et adultes dépendants.* Montreal: Éditions du remue-ménage.

—. 1993. *Travail et soins aux proches dépendants.* Montreal: Éditions du remue-ménage.

Guyon, Louise. 1996. *Derrière les apparences. Santé et conditions de vie des femmes.* Quebec City: MSSS.

Hachey, Isabelle. 2000. "Les compagnies pharmaceutiques font pression sur le gouvernement: Le Dr Jean Cusson dénonce leurs stratagèmes pour allonger la liste des médicaments remboursés par l'État." *La Presse,* 28 janvier, A-6.

Hagan, Louise, Diane Morin and Rachel Lépine. 1998. *Évaluation provinciale des services Info-Santé CLSC. Perception des utilisateurs.* Sainte-Foy: Université Laval.

Harnois, Gaston. 1996. "Un virage ambulatoire, mais pour qui?" in *Santé mentale au Québec,* Vol. XXI, No.1, pp. 22-26.

Health Canada. 1998. *Dépenses publiques de soins à domicile au Canada, 1975-1976 à 1997-1998.* Health System and Policy Division. http://www.hc-sc.ga.ca/datapcb/datahesa/homecare/Fhome.htm

Hébert, Réjean et al. 1997. *Services requis par les personnes âgées en perte d?autonomie; évaluation clinique et estimation des coûts selon le milieu de vie.* Quebec: MSSS.

Janssen, Richard and Jan Van der Made. 1990. "Privatization in Health Care: Concepts, Motives and Policies." *Health Policy* (14 May): 191-201.

Jérôme-Forget, Monique and Claude E. Forget. 1998. *Qui est maître à bord? Projet de réforme du système de santé canadien.* Montreal: Institut de recherche en politique publique.

Jutras, Sylvie and France Veilleux. 1989. *Des partenaires méconnus: les aidants des personnes âgées en perte d?autonomie.* Montreal, Groupe de recherche sur les aspects sociaux de la prévention, Université de Montréal.

Lavoie, Jean-Pierre et al. 1998. *Les modèles de relations entre les services formels et les aidantes naturelles. Une analyse des politiques de soutien à domicile au Québec.* Montreal: Régie régionale de la santé et des services sociaux de Montréal-Centre.

Lavoie, Jean-Pierre, Louise Lévesque and Sylvie Jutras. 1995. "Les aidants familiaux." In *Aspects sociaux reliés à la santé. Rapport de l'enquête sociale et de santé 1992-1993*, Vol. 2, Santé Québec, 45-71.

Lauzon, Sylvie et al. 1998. *Bilan critique des études menées sur les expériences des aidantes naturelles à partir d'une perspective émique - Rapport final.* Montreal: Centre d'excellence pour la santé des femmes.

Leclerc, Bernard-Simon. 1998. *Enquête auprès des médecins de la région de Lanaudière au regard des impacts du virage ambulatoire et de la réorganisation des services de santé sur la pratique médicale et la qualité des soins.* Régie régionale de la santé et des services sociaux de Lanaudière.

Léger, Marie-France. 1998. "La palme de l'inflation des listes d'attente." *La Presse,* 12 août, A-5.

Lessard, Diane, L. Barylak and D. Côté. 2000. *Aidantes "naturelles" et services de soutien, acquérir du pouvoir sur sa situation.* Montreal: CLSC René-Cassin/Institut universitaire de gérontologie sociale du Québec.

Lévesque, Lia. 2000. "Marois met la table pour le débat sur le financement de la santé."

La Presse, 21 janvier.

L'R des centres de femmes du Québec. 1997. *Femmes, santé et régionalisation: visionnaires et partenaires. Cahier-synthèse des séminaires.* Montreal: L'R des centres de femmes du Québec.

Macdonald, Paul et al. 1998. *Waiting lists and waiting times for health care in Canada: more management! more money?* Summary Report. Ottawa: Health Canada.

Maioni, Antonia. 1999. "Les normes centrales et les politiques de santé." In Clermont Bégin et al., eds., *Le système de santé québécois: un modèle en transformation.* Quebec : Les Presses de l'Université Laval.

Métivier, Céline. 1999. *La production de biens et services destinés au marché québécois de la santé face à la privatisation. Rapport final.* Montreal: Groupe de recherche sur la reconversion industrielle, Université du Québec à Montréal.

Ministère de la Santé et des Services sociaux (MSSS).1990. *Une réforme axée sur le citoyen.* Quebec: MSSS.

—. 1991. *Un financement équitable à la mesure de nos moyens.* Quebec: MSSS.

—. 1992. *La politique de la santé et du bien-être.* Quebec: MSSS.

—. 1994. *Défi Qualité-performance : stratégie triennale d'intervention 1994-1997.* Quebec: MSSS.

—. 1996. *La santé et les services sociaux: Enjeux et orientations stratégiques d'un système en transformation.* Quebec: MSSS.

—. 1997. *Plan de transformation des services en santé mentale.* Quebec: MSSS.

—. 1998a. *Plan d'action 1997-2000: santé, bien-être et conditions de vie des femmes.* Quebec: MSSS.

—. 1998b. *Le virage ambulatoire en santé physique. Enjeux et perspectives.* Quebec: MSSS.

—. 1998c. *Portrait de la transformation du système de santé et de services sociaux du Québec. À mi-chemin du parcours (1995-1998).* Quebec: MSSS.

—. 1999. *Évaluation du régime général d'assurance-médicaments.* Quebec: MSSS.

—. 2000. *Pour une politique de soutien à domicile des personnes ayant des incapacités et de soutien aux proches*. Rapport du Comité pour la révision du cadre de référence sur les services à domicile. Direction générale de la planification stratégique et de l'évaluation.

National Forum on Health. 1995. *The Public and Private Financing of Canada's Health System*. Ottawa: Department of Public Works and Government Services.

—. 1997. *Canada Health Action: Building on the Legacy: Striking a Balance Working Group Synthesis Report*. Ottawa: Department of Public Works and Government Services.

Ouellet, Hector, and Jacques Roy. 1994. "L'accessibilité aux services sociaux." In Fernand Dumont et al., eds., *Traité des problèmes sociaux*. Quebec: Institut québécois de recherche sur la culture.

Paquet, Mario. 1999. *Logique familiale de soutien auprès des personnes âgées dépendantes. Une étude exploratoire sur le recours aux services*. St-Charles-Boromée: Régie régionale de la santé et des services sociaux de Lanaudière, Direction de la santé publique.

Parent, Claudia. 1997. *Les répercussions du virage ambulatoire sur les ressources communautaires et la population itinérante*. Montreal: Réseau d'aide aux personnes seules et itinérantes de Montréal.

Patenaude, François and Gino Lambert. 1998. "Premier cas: la santé." In C. Poirier, ed., *À qui profite le démantèlement de l'État?* Montreal: Chaire d'études socio-économiques de l'UQAM.

Poirier, C., ed. 1998. *À qui profite le démantèlement de l'État?* Montreal: Chaire d'études socio-économiques de l'UQAM.

Potvin, Louise and Katherine Frohlich. 1998. "L'utilité de la notion de genre pour comprendre les inégalités de santé entre les hommes et les femmes." *Ruptures* 5 (2):142-52.

Ramsay, Cynthia and Michael Walker. 1998. *Waiting Your Turn - Hospital Waiting Lists in Canada*. 8th ed. Vancouver: Fraser Institute.

Régie régionale de la santé et des services sociaux de Montréal-Centre (RRSSSM-C). 1997. *Le défi de l'accès. Choisir des solutions d'avenir pour améliorer nos services*. (Supporting document for consultations). Montreal: RRSSSM-C.

—. 1998. *Plan d'amélioration des services de santé et des services sociaux 1998-2002: Le défi de l'accès*. Montreal: RRSSSM-C.

Régie régionale de la santé et des services sociaux de Québec. 1997. *Suivi des répercussions de la transformation des services de santé et des services sociaux sur l'utilisation des services et la santé de la population*. Quebec : RRSSSQ.

Regroupement des aidantes et aidants naturel(le)s de Montréal. 1999. *Au coeur de l'aide, au coeur du changement. Journée de réflexion des personnes aidantes*. Montreal: RAANM.

Regroupement des organismes communautaires de la région 03 (ROC 03). 1997. *Le pelletage des établissements publics...les communautés et les organismes communautaires en ont plein le dos!* Quebec: ROC 03.

Regroupement Intersectoriel des Organismes Communautaires de Montréal. 1998. *Their Balance Leaves Us Off-Balance. Fact-Finding Report on the Impact of the Transformation of the Health and Social Services System*. Montreal: RIOCM.

Reinharz, Daniel, Louise Rousseau and Sylvie Rheault. 1999. "La place du médicament dans le système de santé du Québec." In Clermont Bégin et al., eds., *Le système de santé québécois: un modèle en transformation*. Quebec: Les Presses de l'Université Laval.

Rheault, Sylvie. 1994. "L'évolution du financement des dépenses québécoises en services de santé." In Vincent Lemieux et al., eds., *Le système de santé au Québec: Organisations, acteurs et enjeux*. Quebec : Les Presses de l'Université Laval.

—. 1995. *Évaluation des modalités de financement et de paiement dans le domaine sociosanitaire*. Quebec: Gouvernement du Québec, MSSS.

Saillant, Francine. 1992. "La part des femmes dans les soins de santé." *International Review of Community Development* 28 (68)(Fall): 95-106.

St-Pierre, Nathalie. 1999. "Who Bears the Burden of Quebec's Universal Drug Plan?" In Margaret A. Somerville et al., eds., *Do We Care?: Renewing Canada's Commitment to Health: Proceedings of the First Directions for Canadian Health Care Conference*. Montreal: McGill-Queen's University Press.

Shannon, Valérie. 1999. "La valeur des soins infirmiers." *La Presse,* 13 juillet, B-3.

Soderstrom, Lee. 1987. *Privatization: Adopt or Adapt.* Commission d'enquête sur les services de santé et les services sociaux, synthèse critique No. 36. Quebec: Les publications du Québec.

Standing Hillary. 1999. *Framework for Understanding Gender Inequalities and Health Sector Reform: An Analysis and Review of Policy Issues.* Paper prepared under the Global Health Equity Initiative Project on "Gender and Health Equity." Boston: Harvard Center for Population and Development Studies.

Stoddart, Greg and Roberta Labelle. 1985. *Privatization in the Canadian Health Care System: Assertions, Evidence, Ideology and Options.* Ottawa: Health and Welfare Canada.

Tamblyn, Robyn *et al.* 1999. *Évaluation de l'impact du régime général d'assurance-médicaments.* Montreal: McGill University, Université de Montréal, McMaster University (CHEPA) USAGE.

Therrien, Rita. 1989. "La responsabilité des familles et des femmes dans le maintien à domicile des personnes âgées: une politique de désengagement ou de soutien de l'État." *Santé mentale au Québec* XIV(1): 152-64.

Tremblay, Mireille. 1999. "Une démocratie en santé: Utopie ou réalité?" In Pierre Fortin, ed., *La réforme de la santé au Québec.* Montreal: Fides.

Turgeon, Jean and Hervé Anctil. 1994. "Le ministère et le réseau public." In Vincent Lemieux *et al.*, eds., *Le système de santé au Québec: Organisations, acteurs et enjeux.* Quebec: Les Presses de l'Université Laval.

Turgeon, Jean and Vincent Lemieux. 1999. "La décentralisation: panacée ou boîte de Pandore?" In Clermont Bégin *et al.*, eds., *Le système de santé québécois: un modèle en transformation.* Quebec: Les Presses de l'Université Laval.

Vaillancourt, Yves, Denis Bourque, Françoise David and E. Ouellet. 1987. *La privatisation des services sociaux.* Commission d'enquête sur les services de santé et les services sociaux, synthèse critique No.37. Quebec: Les publications du Québec.

Vaillancourt, Yves and C. Jetté. 1997. *Vers un nouveau partage des responsabilités dans les services sociaux de santé: Rôles de l'État, du marché, de l'économie sociale et du secteur informel.* Montreal: Cahiers du Laboratoire de recherche sur les pratiques et les politiques sociales, Université du Québec à Montréal.

Vézina, Aline and Daniel Pelletier. 1998. *Une même famille, deux univers: aidants principaux, fonctionnement familial et soutien à domicile des personnes âgées.* Quebec: Centre de recherche sur les services communautaires, Université Laval.

Women, Privatization and Health Care Reform: The Ontario Case

Pat Armstrong and Hugh Armstrong

INTRODUCTION

Privatization of public health care did not begin in 1995 when the Conservatives won a majority government in Ontario. The previous Liberal and New Democratic governments had already begun to de-list some services and promote the contracting out of others. However, the government of Mike Harris increased dramatically both the pace and the extent of change. Titling their program *The Common Sense Revolution,* the Conservatives promised to "provide the people of Ontario with *better* for *less,"* while guaranteeing "full funding for health care," "without touching a penny" of the money for health services. These promises were to be kept through a reinvestment of savings achieved "by cutting overhead or by bringing in the best management techniques and thinking," and by "rooting out waste, abuse, health card fraud, mis-management and duplication," with "no new user fees." Although the document talked about children, single parents, middle-class families, workers, youth, the less fortunate and disadvantaged, it did not talk about women (Ontario Conservative Party 1993, 2, 3, 6 and 7).

Later, in the weeks preceding the 1999 election call, the Conservative government produced a series of television advertisements and pamphlets for Ontario citizens. Their basic claim was that the government had kept its promises – funding was not only maintained but increased and services expanded, especially in relation to mammograms, cardiac care and long-term care beds. And although there was acknowledgment of some painful restructuring, the government asserted that the emerging system was stronger and better.

It is difficult to assess these assertions, especially in relation to women (Lindgren 1999). The limited figures provided cannot easily be evaluated, in part because they lump together under health spending budget items previously found under other ministries, in part because they include the costs of laying off workers and closing services, and in part because there are few alternative sources for the information offered. Some of the figures add together multi-year funding and some include money that has not been or cannot be spent. What is clear is that real per capita spending has declined by $115 since 1994-95 (Bezanson and Noce 1999, table 1).

Our enquiries about privatization, made to research and professional organizations, to unions and to government employees, produced a common response. We were told that change is so rapid and short-term that it is difficult to track what is happening, let alone what the consequences are for women. In addition, as the editor of the leading hospital trade journal in Ontario put it in 1996, "I am finding the current regime at the Ontario Ministry of Health decidedly uncooperative" (Woods 1996, 3). Research on the extent or impact of privatization, if it is being undertaken, is not publicly available. This paucity of information reflects a downloading of responsibility combined with a centralization of decision-making (Harden 1999).

Public health nursing provides just one example. In 1998, Bill 152, which is literally titled *An Act to Improve Services, Increase Efficiency, and Benefit Taxpayers by Eliminating Duplication and Reallocating Responsibilities Between Provincial and Municipal Governments in Various Areas and to Implement Other Aspects of the Government's "Who Does What" Agenda*, gave funding responsibility for public health to municipalities while the province continued to mandate services. According to the Registered Nurses Association of Ontario (RNAO), the resulting changes took place "most often without evidence for or against the effectiveness of specific programs and typically with limited or no input from nurses or clients." Even the data on the reductions in the number of public health nurses are difficult to obtain because no one body is systematically tracking the change.

The downloading contradicted recommendations from the government's own committees instructed to investigate these issues (CHNIG and RNAO 1998, 4, 5). In January 1999, Ontario reinstated cost sharing for public health, offering to pay half the specified expenditures. The reversal reinforced the claim that the policy was not based on evidence, and provided yet one more example of sudden announcements and reversals that make tracking impossible.

Of necessity, then, this chapter focuses more on Ontario health care reform and privatization than it does on the consequences for women and for different groups of women. It is also more about what we do not know than it is about what we have evidence to support.

HOSPITALS

Why Hospitals?

For several reasons, hospitals have been a primary focus for both health care reform and privatization in the 1990s. First, they comprise the single largest item in the provincial health care budget, accounting for 45.3 per cent of public health spending in the province in 1990 (CIHI 1998, table D.3.6.2). Labour costs account for most hospital spending. In 1990, 70 per cent of Ontario hospital budgets went to salaries, wages and benefits (Statistics Canada 1993, table 21). Although the female-dominated workforce once did much of the labour as unpaid trainees or as very low-paid employees, the unionization of almost all the women employed in hospitals has significantly improved both pay and conditions of work (Akyeampong 1997, 4; Gunderson and Hyatt 1996, 8). In addition, the 1987 pay equity legislation both revealed the gender bias in hospital pay practices and resulted in wage gains for those working in female-dominated jobs. Not surprisingly, then, various Ontario governments bent on reducing costs looked to hospitals and their labour force.

Second, hospitals are explicitly covered by the *Canada Health Act*. Setting out the conditions for federal funding, the *Act* lists a wide range of services, tests, technologies, drugs and care work that is to be provided without fees within hospitals. As long as patients stay in the hospital, they are not individually responsible for the costs of necessary care. For its part, the current Ontario *Health Insurance Act* makes it clear that services are insured services "only if they are provided in or by designated hospitals or health facilities" and guarantees medically necessary care there "under such conditions and limitations as may be prescribed" (*Health Insurance Act* 1990, sec. 11.2(1) and (3)). Private insurance is prohibited for insured care, but private insurers may cover costs not paid by the Plan (ibid., sec. 14). The Act also allows the Lieutenant Governor in Council to make a broad range of regulations, including the establishment of co-payments and the determination of which services or parts of services are insured (ibid., sec. 44).

In order to lower the level of public expenditures, reformers have thus sought to limit admission to and reduce the time spent in hospital. They have also developed much more stringent definitions of hospitals and of the necessary care provided within them. These definitions are important not only in terms of determining who stays in a hospital but also whether patients pay fees when they do stay there. Under Ontario regulations, a charge to the patient for accommodation is allowed if, in the opinion of the attending physician, the patient requires chronic care and is more or less permanently resident in the institution (*Health Insurance Act*, Reg. 552, sec. 10(1)).[1] The *Public Hospitals Act* further requires municipalities to pay a daily rate for indigent people admitted to hospitals who are declared by the attending physical "not to require continued medical and skilled nursing care in a hospital" but to require only custodial care, and allows hospitals to refuse admission to "any person who merely requires custodial care" (*Public Hospitals Act* 1990, sec. 21 and 22).

The third reason for the focus on hospitals is that new technologies, drugs and techniques have created conditions for the transformation of hospital care. Some of this technology, such as magnetic resonance imaging (MRI), is expensive to purchase and operate, increasing costs and making it beyond the reach of many hospitals. Some aspects, such as microscopic surgery, make it possible to reduce recovery time. Some, such as portable dialysis machines, mean that services previously provided in-hospital can be transferred to the home. Combined with the pressure to cut overall public expenditures, these new approaches have contributed to shortened patient stays and the move to day surgery and outpatient services. They have also helped justify the centralization of hospital services.

Fourth, hospitals appear to the reformers to be quite similar to large, private sector corporations. Strategies developed for large corporations therefore seem to offer appropriate models for hospital reform, especially when such models seem to increase efficiency and effectiveness defined in monetary terms (see, for example, Hassen 1993).[2] Coinciding with calls for health care reform are revolutionary strategies for transforming the private sector, strategies that promise more for less (see, for example, Hammer and Champy 1993).

Guiding Philosophies

Hospital reform is not simply driven by costs; it is also guided by various assumptions and critiques. The title of a report prepared for the federal/provincial/territorial deputy ministers of health summed up a central theme, "When Less is Better" (WGHSU 1994). It is a theme echoed in the Ontario Conservative party's 1995 election program. The deputy ministers' report argued that hospitals were often dangerous and uncomfortable places that should be avoided as much as possible in the interests of health. This approach fits well with the move to shorten patient stays, de-institutionalize, downsize and bring care closer to home. It also fits well with feminist critiques of an illness system that is focused on treatment and on the institutionalization of life processes such as birthing. Feminists, too, have often supported a move to community and home, resisting the medicalization associated with hospital stays and the medical control they implied. Women's groups, government planners and various research organizations maintain that much of the care currently provided is ineffective in promoting health.

Another important principle in hospital reform is the emphasis on evidence and science. This evidence comes in at least three forms. One form is related to medical interventions and their effectiveness. The *Practice Atlases* produced by Ontario's Institute for Clinical Evaluative Sciences (ICES) document the considerable variations in, for example, caesarian rates from hospital to hospital. Such evidence supports claims from various women's groups about the unscientific nature of medical practice at the same time as it supports efforts to develop more stringent guidelines for doctors and to implement cutbacks to health services. A second form of evidence concerns measures such as length of patient stays that are assumed to indicate efficiency. Evidence related to workloads and task allocation constitutes a third form, one also linked to efficiency. Hospitals throughout Ontario have introduced measures intended to calculate and control the work of the mainly female health labour force. Performance indicators of various kinds have been introduced and justified as measures ensuring accountability.

This emphasis on evidence is understood to be compatible with an emphasis on management. With the problem defined as one of inefficiency leading to cost increases and ineffectiveness leading to care expenses, reformers have turned to management science for direction. Increasingly, management looks to measurement made possible by computers. "If you can't measure it, you can't manage it," is a central principle in current managerial philosophies (WGHSU 1994, 16, quoting a vice-president of the United Health Care Corporation in the United States). And it is assumed that the market necessarily makes private sector management efficient and effective (Ontario Ministry of Health 1998d, 2).

Finally, health care reform has increasingly been built on the assumption that we cannot afford the demands created by an aging population. Undoubtedly the senior population is increasing and the majority of the elderly are women. In 1998, "57% of all people aged 65 and over, and 70% aged 85 and older, were female" (Lindsay 1999, 24). However, most of these seniors – 93 per cent of them in 1996 – lived in their own homes, even though more than a third of the elderly women lived alone. These seniors are mainly looking after themselves, often with assistance from their female relatives, although a significant proportion also help others (ibid., 24-25; Chappell 1992). Equally important, the research available indicates that the rising costs related to the growing number of senior women are at least as much a result of medicalization as they are of ill health (Chappell 1997; Barer, Evans and Herztman 1995, 218).

Hospitals have been targeted not only because they provide expensive, guaranteed public services provided primarily by women. They also appear amenable to new strategies taken from the private sector, and have been criticized by a wide range of groups, including those taking women's perspectives. Hospital restructuring reflects all these influences – but privatization in the form of management practices taken from the for-profit sector is at the centre of the reforms.

Hospital Restructuring

Early in its mandate, the NDP government asked the District Health Councils (DHCs) in major cities to examine hospitals with a view to merging or closing services. These councils, composed of members appointed by the government, have seldom been very powerful and never had much influence over hospitals. Unlike all other provinces, Ontario has not decentralized any substantive decision-making authority to district or regional bodies. However, especially in major centres such as Toronto, Ottawa and Windsor, the DHCs took their advisory task seriously. They appointed special committees to recommend hospital restructuring plans, but the NDP government had barely begun to act on these recommendations when its mandate ended in 1995. Only one hospital, in Burks Falls, was actually closed during the NDP's term in office; it was turned into a community health centre. This decision was later reversed by the Conservative government, and the ten-bed hospital was reopened. It was located in the constituency of the new finance minister.

When the Conservatives took over, they appointed a group to determine the future of hospital services in the province. Established in April 1996, the Health Services Restructuring Commission (HSRC) was mandated "to make decisions about hospital restructuring, and to recommend changes to other aspects of the health care system" (HSRC 1997, 5). Although the commission included a physician and a woman with experience in both federal health care policy and women's health, the 11-member body was dominated by the business sector – including the deputy chair of an insurance company; a former executive of General Motors; two lawyers, one of whom is a former president of the Ontario Chamber of Commerce; a senior executive in a private broadcasting corporation; and the executive director of an organization representing for-profit nursing homes (Landsberg 1997, A2).

The commission was given the power to order hospital closures and mergers, even though the hospitals were not owned by the province. The process was "quick and imposed with almost no public consultation" (Bezanson and Noce 1999, 3). The government justified these extraordinary powers on the basis of the expertise of the members and the need for action that was both swift and systematic. It did, nonetheless, intervene part way through the commission's mandate to exclude northern and rural hospitals from its mandate (*Toronto Star* 1997, F2). The justification for this intrusion was that these areas have special needs, which should be addressed in a framework developed by a panel of medical and nursing experts (Ontario Ministry of Health 1997). Meanwhile, the government went to great pains to argue that it was taking the politics out of the tough decisions, leaving these decisions on hospital closures to experts.

In the end, 35 hospitals – about one in six across the province – were ordered closed. The mergers and closures have had major consequences for services such as home care and long-term care. Although the commission's orders were based on the assumption that these other services would be in place, it lacked the power to ensure they would be available before the hospitals disappeared.

There is little evidence to suggest that women's issues and concerns were taken into account, or even that evidence on such issues was gathered. The commission made it clear that there were "three imperatives driving change in the health care system": financial constraints, the changing role of hospitals and hospital reform (HSRC 1996, 1). But none of these led the commission to a gender-based analysis.

In three instances at least, however, hospital closures were resisted on the grounds that they would be harmful to women. In the case of Pembroke Civic Hospital, a Charter challenge argued that the closure of the hospital would leave only a Catholic hospital to serve the area and, as a consequence, access to health services involving sexuality and reproduction, particularly abortion, would be restricted. The court rejected this claim. The judge maintained that one physician gave evidence that he had never experienced interference in carrying out his medical responsibilities related to sexuality and that abortion had not been provided in either hospital for the last 14 years. The judge concluded that the "closure of the Civic will have no impact on the current access of Pembroke residents to abortion services and that other claims around reproductive health issues were generally unsubstantiated" (*Pembroke Civic Hospital and Lowe v. Health Services Restructuring Commission* 1997, 11).

In the commission report that ordered the closure, women are not even mentioned in the section on demographics or in the one on health status profiles. So, for example, while there are references to the number of single-parent families and the number of elderly living alone, there is no indication that the majority in both groups is female. Women's issues are not listed as a category, and only under the discussion of Case Mix Groups is there a breakdown of the data by gender. Equally important, when the commission ordered the Pembroke General Hospital to develop a plan to ensure representation on the governing board, it included the "cultural, linguistic, religious and socio-economic makeup of the community" but not gender. (HSRC 1996, 51).

In the case of Wellesley in Toronto, the hospital launched a court appeal against the order closing the hospital and transferring its services to St. Michael's. Located in the city core, the hospital had served many of the most marginalized women in the community. It had also been one of the pioneers in de-emphasizing the medical model in normal births and in welcoming midwives with admitting privileges. The Charter challenge to its closure argued that the rights of patients, particularly homosexuals and women seeking birth control, would be violated by having to obtain treatment at a Catholic hospital. The hospital was not successful in the challenge and the services were transferred. St. Michael's "moved swiftly to halt all abortions and vasectomies and restrict other birth control procedures at the former Wellesley hospital site" (Daly 1998b, A1).

The protests were more successful in the case of Women's College Hospital in Toronto. The commission ordered Women's College closed and the services transferred to the Sunnybrook Health Sciences Centre, a hospital originally established to serve war veterans and located in the northeast area of the city. The Friends of Women's College, a group representing providers and patients, fought a long battle to defend the Women's College control of its services. According to the hospital's submission to the commission, the concerns related to three main areas:

> the loss of governance and its likely impact on a dedicated focus on women's health; the need for experienced leadership in province-wide initiatives, namely the Women's Health Council; and the preservation of academic women's health programming in the downtown core. (Women's College Hospital 1997, 1)

The long battle was to some extent at least resolved by a private member's bill that kept Women's College's downtown site open as an ambulatory centre, with its own governing board. Inpatient services have been merged into the new megahospital called the Sunnybrook and Women's College

Health Sciences Centre. Women's College was guaranteed seven members on the 26-member board.

Another Toronto hospital, Doctors, disappeared with much less public outcry. This inner-city hospital was particularly used by the homeless and members of the Aboriginal and immigrant communities, many of whom are of course women. Easily accessible by public transit (which is disproportionately used by women), and staffed in ways that broadly reflected the populations it served, Doctors Hospital had neither sufficiently strong community leadership nor sufficiently close links with decision-makers. After closure, the site became a temporary hostel for the homeless, and has now been demolished.

Protests were also partially successful in the case of two Toronto chronic care hospitals. Both Runnymede and Riverdale were slated for closure. These hospitals served people with severe and long-term disabilities – such as Huntington's disease, brain injuries and multiple sclerosis – which require intensive care. A campaign by community groups allied through the Toronto Health Coalition led to the announcement, just before the 1999 election, that both hospitals, along with two similar chronic care hospitals in other parts of the province, would remain open. The victory was limited by the terms of the announcement, which transformed these hospitals into long-term care facilities.

This has important implications for the providers and the patients, the majority of whom are women. First, as the RNAO made clear, the change will mean patients requiring 24-hour a day care will be in facilities with almost no registered nurses. When a similar conversion resulted from a commission order at the Perley-Rideau Veteran's Health Centre in Ottawa, staff nurses saw their workload double from a ratio of one nurse for every 20 patients to one to 40, and to one to 80 in the year 2000. This is not surprising, given that funding per patient is much lower in long-term care than in chronic care. The second implication is that the facilities are no longer protected under the *Canada Health Act*. The government is free to charge fees on at least part of the care and to hand over the entire operation to a for-profit concern.

Hospital closures are only part of the story. In all, the government maintains that more than a billion dollars will have been cut from hospital budgets as a result of commission orders. According to research conducted for the Caledon Institute:

> Forty-five hospital sites in Ontario have been closed or will be closing, almost all before the end of 2000, and dozens more have been amalgamated. Thirty-three public hospitals are closing (two already have shut down and 31 more are slated to close). Six psychiatric hospitals and six private hospitals will close their doors...Thirty emergency departments are being affected by changes in hospital organization: six have already closed and two have changed hours or roles; most of the rest will close soon. (Bezanson and Noce 1999, 6)

For the most part, these closures and mergers were based on assumptions rather than on evidence, and very little attention was paid to the consequences for women as patients, providers or decision-makers. Indeed, Markham and Lomas argue that there is no empirical evidence to demonstrate economic, quality or human resource gains with multi-hospital arrangements, and some evidence that costs may increase, flexibility and responsiveness to individual patient needs decline and relationships with employees deteriorate (Markham and Lomas 1995). Research from the United States indicated that complex interventions were best done at hospitals where the procedures were performed frequently. And management consulting firms did provide data to the district health councils, data which were in turn examined by the commission before the orders were made. But many of the orders were based on the twin assumptions that such strategies worked to reduce cost and increase efficiency in the private sector, and that what worked in the private sector would work in hospitals.

There is a growing body of evidence from the private sector indicating that both worker morale and innovation suffer with downsizing, mergers and constant change, while money may not be saved in the long run (see, for example, Greenglass and Burke 1997; Armstrong et al., 1997b). The limited information available on the cost impact of hospital mergers in Ontario does not show a clear financial gain, especially when the costs to those for whom services are made less accessible are taken into account. Equally important, the case can be made that health care should not be treated as a business like the rest (Mintzberg 1989, esp. ch. 10). Competitive market principles simply do not apply. Hospitals need to be large, which means that outside large cities they operate as monopolies. The urgency of many health care decisions and the state of the patients when the decisions have to be made mean that they cannot exercise informed consumer choice. The complexity of the decisions is often beyond the capacity of even well-informed lay persons (these points are made in Woolhandler and Himmelstein 1999, 445-46). It is for this reason, after all, that we justify granting special privileges and responsibilities to those we term professionals.

Differences between health care and other organizations are particularly evident when we look more closely at the employees. The women who work in health care feel a responsibility for their patients that makes these employees different from those in other sectors. Jerry White's research, for example, showed how female hospital employees surprised both their union and their employers when they were willing to strike over the quality of patient care (White 1990). The public support shown for the nurses on strike in Quebec and several other provinces during 1999 suggests that the public as well holds health care work and workers in special, high regard.

One of the most obvious consequences of restructuring is the loss of nursing jobs. According to data prepared by the RNAO, the number of RNs and RPNs employed in Ontario hospitals declined from 74,007 in 1991 to 60,446 in 1998. This 13,561 reduction has been only partially overcome by the creation of new jobs in the community. There were nearly 2,500 fewer nurses employed in 1998 than in 1991, and many more of those with paid work had only part-time or casual employment. The number employed on a casual basis increased by 4,778 during this period while the number employed full-time declined by 9,000. Many of those with casual employment work in for-profit firms providing community services.

Almost all of these nurses are women. Many of those experiencing job loss are from immigrant and visible minority groups. The Conservative government ordered the destruction of the data that had been collected for employment equity purposes, making it difficult to determine the distribution precisely. Although research indicated that equity-seeking groups are present in health care work in numbers that match their proportion of the total labour force (see Statistics Canada 1995; Das Gupta 1996),[3] the Ontario Nurses Association has argued that women from these groups are disproportionately located in areas of the hospital system where nurses are most likely to be replaced by unregulated care providers (cited in Lum and Williams 2000).

The loss of jobs in the hospital sector also often means a loss of pay and benefits, even for full-time employees. "Hourly rates for RNs providing home nursing services range from approximately $16 to $23, versus a range of approximately $19 to $28 per hour in hospital settings" (Nursing Task Force 1999, 8). Moreover, Bill 136, the *Public Sector Labour Relations and Transition Act, 1997*, prevents unions and employers from using the Labour Relations Board to decide issues such as successor rights. Instead, a new commission will decide all successor rights and the basis on which it will make these decisions remains unclear, as do the consequences for the mainly female labour force. What is clear is that the new commission's members are to be selected by the government, rather than agreed to by employers and unions.

In addition, the *Regulated Health Professions Act* of 1994 made it easier for employers to assign care tasks to providers with the least training and the lowest pay. This legislation severely limits the monopolies traditionally held by various health professionals. It grants nurses, for example, the right to perform three "controlled acts." However, it goes on to allow the delegation of these controlled acts to unregulated care providers and, in exceptional circumstances, these acts can be carried out by unregulated providers without delegation. With this deregulation, nurses can be more easily replaced by lowest cost care providers.

The negative impact is obvious not only to nurses but also to patients. Pressure from both groups led the Ontario government to appoint a task force to investigate the situation. The Nursing Task Force confirmed that:

> There are fewer permanent and full-time nursing positions available, and many nurses are working several casual jobs to make ends meet – often without benefits that a permanent position offers. Nursing enrollments and graduations have decreased and nurses are leaving Ontario to go to other jurisdictions or to jobs outside health care. (Nursing Task Force 1999, 2)

The task force recommended that "a comprehensive investment in the nursing sector be made across the spectrum of the health care delivery system," at a cost of $375 million to create 7,700 RN and 2,541 RPN positions (ibid.). The Ministry of Health promised to implement and even exceed the recommendations by 2000-2001, although an RNAO analysis indicates the creation of only 5,576 new positions and 3,300 previously announced ones (RNAO 1999). The task force notes that most nurses are women and that women traditionally care for families, often leading to increases in absenteeism and stress leave. But there is no additional analysis of the implications of this female domination for the providers, patients or employers.

The loss of other health care jobs for women has been less visible to the public, perhaps because laundry, cleaning, dietary and clerical workers are not as obviously connected to patient care. Callers to a phone hotline set up by the Ontario Council of Hospital Unions in the mid-1990s did complain bitterly about deteriorating conditions (Armstrong et al. 1997c, 74).

Undoubtedly it is mainly women's jobs that are disappearing. In 1991, 96 per cent of housekeepers and 74 per cent of those preparing food in health care were women (Statistics Canada 1992, table 1). In Pembroke, for example, savings from laboratories were estimated as 25 per cent, from dietary as 30 per cent and from materials management as 45 per cent (HSRC 1996, 46). The Nursing Task Force shows that "housekeeping, patient transportation, and food service support declined" between 1994 and 1996 (Nursing Task Force 1999, 45), and such jobs are disproportionately performed by women from equity-seeking groups. There has not, however, been a task force set up to address this loss. Indeed, the government eliminated the Health Sector Training and Adjustment Program (HSTAP), which was established to provide training and assistance for those facing layoffs as a result of health care reform.

Another consequence is a reduction in the access to care. Since 1990, the number of hospital beds has declined by 29 per cent and the average length of stay decreased from 8.2 to 6.4 days (ibid., 9). By 1992-93, Ontario already had the lowest hospital patient days to population ratio in the country, over 20 per cent lower than that of British Columbia, the next lowest jurisdiction (HSUTF 1994, 52). Between 1995 and 1998, 7,371 beds disappeared (Bezanson and Noce 1999, table 3). How many of these were lost to women is difficult to say, although in 1991 women were much more likely than men to be in hospitals and to stay there longer (Ontario Ministry of Health [1993]).[4] So it seems likely that more women than men are being denied entry to hospitals as a result of restructuring. Women being shipped around the province in search of neonatal beds or to the United States for breast cancer treatments are just two examples.

Emergency room reductions were particularly obvious to an increasingly concerned public. In response, and as it had done in the case of similar outcries over access to kidney dialysis services and MRIs, the government announced an infusion of special funding. But hospitals experienced difficulty gaining access to the announced funds.

The $225 million for emergency rooms is a good example. Although announced in April 1998, no money actually flowed to hospitals until October 1998, when the funding was reannounced. The funding is to be spread over two years and is one-time only. Other promised funding, such as the money to operate MRIs, did not cover full costs (some MRIs were approved with only 15 percent of operating expenses covered) (Bezanson and Noce 1999, 8).

A study conducted for the Caledon Institute of Social Policy found that "decreasing accessibility and shrinking universality have eroded the quality of health care in Ontario" (ibid., 2). Evidence for this conclusion is found in a study on the increasingly common practice of sending babies and their mothers home from hospital less than 48 hours after birth. Of over 7,000 babies born without complications in Scarborough General Hospital between 1993 and 1997, 11.7 per cent of those sent home in less than two days had to be readmitted within the first month, as opposed to 6.7 per cent of those kept in hospital longer (Abraham 1999, A1-A2). When infants are returned to hospital, they cannot re-enter the maternity ward. In general they are admitted to children's wards, where they are exposed to new sources of infection.

The conclusion about declining quality is also corroborated by a 1999 CIHI study that reported that a third of Ontario's chronic care patients are restrained daily, typically by being tied to wheelchairs or placed in chairs so deep that they cannot climb out. Excessive use of restraints can result in pressure ulcers, bone and muscle loss, constipation and incontinence, as well as increased agitation and falls. Ontario's use of restraints is double that of the United States (Priest 1999, A2).

Even before the dramatic cutbacks, research was demonstrating a decline in quality. One woman who phoned the OCHU hotline in 1994 summed up the situation by observing, "Nobody had time to look or pay attention" (quoted in Armstrong *et al.* 1977c, 76). Within the hospitals themselves, much of the care has been privatized. As a hotline caller explained with reference to her father-in-law, "It's lucky that my 73-year-old mother-in-law was with him every day and was able to sponge him. She had to provide all the other care as well" (ibid., 78).

As important as access is the question of response to specific needs. The Caledon study maintains that the new generic hospital, designed for the average patient, "cannot meet the needs of a diverse population" (Bezanson and Noce 1999, 11). Continuity of care is disrupted by mergers and closures, although there seems to be little research done on what this means in terms of support and safety for women.

Hospital restructuring since 1995 has also altered women's opportunities to participate in decisions about the future of health care. Information on change is difficult to obtain. Many changes appear without any prior warning and some are reversed without warning. The sweeping powers of the commission, combined with the speed of decision-making and the absence of appeal procedures, have all made it difficult for women to influence decisions. Decisions of crucial importance are made and remade, and the multitude of sweeping changes constantly appearing provide another obstacle for those who would like time to investigate and respond appropriately.

Changes Within Hospitals

The same forces that motivated overall hospital restructuring are behind reorganization within hospitals. Pushed by financial cutbacks, aided by new technologies and techniques, and assisted by managerial strategies taken from the private sector, hospitals have reorganized work, contracted out services, shortened patient stays, and moved to day surgery and out-patient services.

In the 1990s, hospital reform began to be defined primarily as a management issue. Some hospitals hired management consultants to manage or to advise on management, while others purchased software and other aids from the private sector to provide the basis for new managerial approaches. What they have in common is a reliance on people trained more as managers than as providers (Armstrong and Armstrong 1996, ch. 4), people who are often trained for management in the private sector and use techniques developed in that sector (Armstrong *et al.* 1997b; Hassen 1993; Cybulski *et al.* 1997, 9).

Flattened Hierarchies

The new managers have fundamentally reorganized hospital work. Hierarchies have been flattened, leading to a significant decrease in management positions held by RNs, one of the few areas with a high proportion of female managers (Baumgart 1997). Some providers initially supported this move, assuming there would be more participation in decision-making. Experience has led, however, to concerns that flattened hierarchies do the reverse. The Nursing Task Force noted that, as a result, "the ability of nurses to be fully integrated into the decision-making process on matters that affect health care consumers have been diminished" (Nursing Task Force 1999; see also Armstrong *et al.* 2000, 113-19). The mainly female non-nursing staff also have found that the promise of participation was never fulfilled. Instead, their choices were increasingly restricted by the new processes (Armstrong *et al.* 1997b).

Care Measurement Systems

The lack of choice is linked to new management systems designed to measure, redistribute and regulate work within the hospital in the same ways it had been done at Motorola or other private sector workplaces. Many health care workers initially welcomed the introduction of patient classification schemes, clinical care pathways and other workload and work process measures (Choiniere 1993). These measurement techniques seemed to offer the possibility for greater independence, for relief from tasks inappropriate to training and for demonstrating the actual work done each day. Instead, they have tended to result in increased workloads, reduced individual control over work, and both deskilling and multi-tasking (Armstrong *et al.* 1997b; Armstrong *et al.* 1997c).

The central management idea is to reduce waste by carefully measuring tasks and needs. The method involves the development of formulas for care. The problem with the formulas, though, is that they become prescriptions for care that ignore the individual needs of women as patients and the individual skills of providers in assessing and meeting these needs.

Contracting Out

In addition to reorganizing work within hospitals, new managers have also contracted out services to the private sector or organized shared services with the private sector. Ontario moved to promote this strategy when it abolished successor rights that bound partnerships or contractors to previous union agreements. Ontario is now the only major jurisdiction that does not protect these rights.[5] The private sector firms are therefore often able to pay lower wages and provide fewer benefits while offering less job security. This is especially the case because the government has also frozen the minimum wage and changed the Wage Protection Program, threatening severance or termination pay for laid-off workers.

Services in such areas as food, cleaning, clerical and laboratory have been contracted out or reorganized as partnerships with for-profit firms. Despite the determinants of health literature that demonstrates the importance of such services, they have been redefined as "hotel services." This term distances them from health care and relocates them as private sector concerns. The contracting-out strategy has been adopted without supporting evidence to indicate that costs will be lower in the long run or that quality will be maintained. The unions have argued that patients, providers and costs all suffer.

> Meal quality has deteriorated dramatically since cook-chill was introduced. There is a set meal and patients no longer have choices between menu items. All patients are served cold breakfasts. Not even toast is served.

> The new rethermalizing technology is proving problematic in Toronto. The high tech cleaning function on the $15,000 carts has turned out to be useless. The carts have to be scrubbed down by hand, creating a great deal of extra work. The excessive packaging has created headaches for the workers and tremendous physical waste, e.g., all slices of bread are individually wrapped. Since switching from conventional to cook-chill and shared food production, Toronto Hospital has had its first ever deficit in its dietary budget. (CUPE 1998, 8)

Unions have raised similar issues in relation to laboratories. In one Ontario study, cost per test in a private lab was 34 per cent higher than in a public hospital one. Private labs also provide less comprehensive service and are less accessible in terms of hours (NUPGE 1997). There seems to be little research beyond these union studies on the impact of privatization, and these do not focus on women. Yet women, especially women who are from visible minority or immigrant groups, are the dominant workforce in the sectors undergoing privatization.

Cost and Care Privatization

Along with work reorganization has come a sharp decline in the number of hospital beds available, a dramatic drop in length of hospital stays combined with an increase in day surgery and outpatient services. To some extent, these changes reflect new techniques and procedures. Long waits in the emergency room for a bed suggest, however, that the reductions have not simply reflected different ways of doing the work. Many of these changes are about cost and care shifting; in other words, they are about privatization.

Take drugs, for example. The new regulations on outpatient services explicitly exclude proprietary medicines, and a growing number of medications used are proprietary (*Health Insurance Act,* Reg. 552, 1998, sec. 8 (1) 5). Under specified conditions, 12 drugs are provided to outpatients for use at home (ibid., sec. 8). Other medications patients take home are not covered even though the outpatient services are often made possible by drugs that can be taken at home. At the same time, Bill 26 introduced user fees and deductibles on drugs for seniors and welfare recipients. Those with annual incomes under $16,000 now must pay $2 per prescription. If seniors' individual incomes are above this, or if their family income is over $24,000, they are required to pay a $100 deductible each year as well as the $2 dispensing fee. This cutback not only transfers costs, it also sets up a bureaucratic structure that facilitates the future privatization of the service.

Bill 26 also deregulated drug prices. The cost of prescription drugs has risen 35 per cent since 1994, accounting for a significant share of the increased health spending that so concerns the government (Daly and Hudson 1999, A7). Women, who constitute the majority of the seniors, the welfare recipients and the outpatients, are thus forced to cover more of their drug costs. Many may go without, given that women are more likely than men to be poor, especially in old age, and that many have not been eligible for insurance coverage through their places of employment. An Institute for Clinical Evaluative Sciences (ICES) study found that, as a result, "many seniors turned to over-the-counter drugs" (ibid.) As co-payments and de-listings have increased individual costs, private insurance premiums have risen (Bezanson and Noce 1999, 29-30) and a growing number of women have casual or part-time employment with no drug or other supplementary health coverage.

Even when the care takes place in the hospital, patients may find that they have to pay for some services. Under the Conservative government, 22 services or procedures have been deemed not medically necessary and thus not covered by the public insurance scheme (Ontario, Ministry of Health and the Ontario Medical Association 1998). With limited, mainly low income-based exemptions, co-payments are now required of all hospital patients designated as needing chronic care, even if they remain in acute hospital beds. These are patients with long-term illnesses or disabilities who cannot be treated at home. Beginning 1 August 1999, the co-payment rate was increased to $1,277.95 a month (Ontario, Ministry of Health 1999).

In doctors' offices, a maximum of two pap smears are covered each year, and pregnant women can have only one ultrasound covered by the Ontario Health Insurance Plan (OHIP). As a result, physicians are denied the use of their judgement about individual patient needs in ordering these tests, unless the women concerned can pay the $30 for a pap smear or the $128 for an ultrasound. Eye examinations are limited to one every two years between the ages of 20 and 64, a restriction that ignores the many eye problems women experience with menopause. Pre-departure preventive medicine services for those travelling outside Canada are never covered.

Ambulance services usually cost at least $45, and are not covered if the use is not found to be medically necessary. The cost of a land ambulance assessed as being medically unnecessary is $240. The cost of an air ambulance in this case is much higher (Ontario Ministry of Health 1993a). At the same time, ambulance services (but not the related dispatch services) are being downloaded to municipalities and are being further privatized, with a very few, large for-profit firms active in the bidding. We could not find documentation indicating what the specific impact is on women, or on women from different groups.

LONG-TERM CARE IN THE COMMUNITY
Why Long-term Care?

Long-term care in the so-called community has become an issue for a number of reasons. First, the new definitions of hospitals and of necessary care mean that fewer people are eligible for hospital admission and, as a result, must rely on other forms of care. Second, new practices in hospital care mean people spend more time at home preparing for care and recovering from care. Third, only insured services are protected by the *Canada Health Act*, making it easier to shift responsibility for both the care and the costs of long-term care to individuals through user fees and care denial. Fourth, long-term care has become an important site for profit-making, and large corporations, with powerful lobbyists representing them, have become active in the field. Fifth, a wide spectrum of groups, among them many representing women, support notions of community care and are opposed to the medicalization of health that institutions represent. Sixth, the existing system has often failed to provide coordinated care across a spectrum of needs, and demands for integration have grown along with greater reliance on such care. Seventh, there was a widespread assumption that a shift to long-term care in various forms would be both care- and cost-effective (though there is little evidence to support this).

The 1998 Provincial Auditor's Report maintained that "Comparing the costs of long-term care community services with institutional care requires good information about the actual costs of these services. At the time of our audit, the Ministry did not have systems in place to provide this information" (Ontario Office of the Provincial Auditor 1998, 107). Equally important, the costs to individual women of this massive change have not been calculated.

The Legal and Administrative Structure
Ontario began the decade with a complex array of arrangements for long-term institutional care and home care (Deber and Williams 1995). Responsibility for such services was mainly with the Ministry of Community and Social Services. There was no single regional authority responsible for this care, nor was there a history of direct government provision for most services, except for case managers, therapists and social workers. The province mainly purchased the services through Placement Coordination Services and regional home care programs, negotiating a visit fee and the volume of service with the same providers year after year (Bezanson and Noce 1999, 18). Residential care for the aged was dominated by the private sector, with 63 per cent of the facilities proprietary and accounting for over half of all available beds (Statistics Canada 1993, table 2).

Home care services were purchased mainly from four non-profit organizations: the Victorian Order of Nurses (VON), St. Elizabeth Health Care, the Red Cross and the Visiting Homemakers Association. The overwhelming majority of the providers working for these organizations are women. Eighty per cent of the organizations have less than a quarter of their workers in unions, although half the VON nurses are unionized and SEIU in particular is actively organizing in this sector. Nurses in these agencies are covered by pay equity legislation and in general, are more likely to have benefits than those in the for-profit sector (Daly 1998a, F1). For-profit agencies have long provided some homemaking services, mainly on a fee basis to clients.

In an attempt to bring greater coherence to these services, the NDP government introduced the *Long-Term Care Act* in 1994. The legislation provided for multi-service agencies that would directly provide care, set out what was meant by community support, homemaking, personal support and professional services, and established a process for reviewing complaints. It also set out a patient's bill of rights (*Long-Term Care Act* 1994, ch 26, November 1998). This Act was proclaimed but no regulations had been passed by the time the NDP lost the 1995 election (Ontario Office of the Provincial Auditor 1998, 104). Only after the 1999 election did the Conservative government quietly pass the regulations. They impose strict limits on the amount of home care individuals can receive, for example 80 hours of homemaking service in the first 30 days and 60 hours in each subsequent 30-day period (Boyle 1999, A8; Coutts 1999b, A7). Because there were no regulations prior to this, according to the Caledon study, eligibility was not addressed, inspections of long-term care community service agencies did not take place, quality management and monitoring systems had not been established and complaints from service recipients were not subject to formal review (Bezanson and Noce 1999, 19).

Community Care Access Centres
The Conservative government established Community Care Access Centres (CCACs) and transferred responsibility for long-term care to the Ministry of Health. In 1996, 43 CCACs replaced the 36 Placement Coordination Services

and the 38 Home Care Programs. These non-profit corporations are responsible for providing information on public services and programs, conducting assessments, determining eligibility, planning a program of care and ensuring services are delivered. What this means in practice is that CCACs arrange for homemaking and professional services for eligible people in their communities. They also organize admissions to long-term care facilities and referral to five kinds of support services: Meals on Wheels, transportation, home maintenance and repair, friendly visits and security checks. And they determine who provides care.

CCACs are prohibited from directly providing services, except for case management. They are being required to divest themselves of the therapists and social workers they inherited when they took over the Placement Coordination Services and the Home Care Programs. These health care professionals must now be employed by agencies that are awarded CCAC contracts, with all the instability this change entails for these predominantly female professionals and the predominantly female citizens they serve. District Health Councils, fewer in number and with boundaries that do not necessarily coincide with those of the CCACs, continue to exist strictly as advisory regional planning organizations.

Initially, the CCACs were governed by government-appointed boards, but each year four appointed members are being replaced by elected ones. Any resident of the designated area can, for a small fee, become a voting member of the local CCAC and vote in its annual elections. We were unable to find research on who these appointed and elected members are, or on what the impact of board membership is on women as providers, patients and decision-makers.

The authority of and standards for the CCACs are not set out firmly in all areas and frequently change or remain unstated. It is unclear, for instance, whether they are covered by the *Freedom of Information and Protection of Privacy Act*. As is the case in other areas, the CCACs are a contradictory mix of central control under fluctuating orders, and local responsibility with little standardization.

In-home Services: Managed Competition

The government has made it clear that CCACs must use a competitive Request for Proposals (RFP) process for contracting home care services and that both for-profit and not-for-profit organizations are eligible to bid on service provision. The details of this bidding process have been closely specified. The shift to a market mechanism was phased in, with current providers made to compete for 10 per cent of their existing home care services in 1996-97, for 20 per cent in the second year and 30 per cent in the third. After that, there is no protection and there is no extra money allocated to help providers inexperienced in such competitive processes to prepare their bids. CCACs are required to ensure that there is a "mix" of service providers involved in each activity (home nursing visits, shift nursing, and homemaking services). Any service provider is eligible to compete for unprotected volume, including for-profit and foreign-owned firms (Ontario Ministry of Health 1996, 3-4).

All proposals are confidential, although bidders have a right to request the name of the successful bidder, the services they promise to provide and the price of those services (ibid., 13) The members of the CCAC boards and the women and men who use the services do not seem entitled to know the details of any particular decision-making process or of any contractor's bid. As a result, it is difficult to assess whether the contracts go to the most appropriate provider or if the contractors are fulfilling their promises.

Although the minimum number of bidders is usually two, it is possible for several organizations to combine bids in a way that covers most of the field, and there is no requirement to divide the work equally among bidders (ibid., 22). The effect, especially in the long run, may be to eliminate the competition that is supposed to ensure efficiency and effectiveness. In other words, it would be possible for virtually the entire home care service contract to go to a single, foreign-owned operation.

Maude Barlow (1999, A18) points to another risk created by this process as a result of the North American Free Trade Agreement (NAFTA).

> If a government dedicated to public health were to replace the Tories in a future election and tried to bring home care into the public sphere, Canada would be forced to pay billions of dollars to these US companies exercising their NAFTA rights to compensation for the resulting "expropriation of their future profits."

Dimensions of quality and quality expectations are briefly set out by the Ministry, but attention to women's needs is not part of the list. Evaluation processes are required but their particular form is not specified except to say they should include the "standard tools" of satisfaction surveys and client incident reports (Ontario Ministry of Health 1996, 15). Performance reviews and continuous quality improvement strategies of the sort found in many businesses are outlined. At the same time, there no specification of the skill mix required of caregivers. Instead, bidders are to set out how they intend to maintain quality control and the determination of skills is left to the contracted agency.

Although the guidelines contain quality indicators, they are not being used in practice. The Provincial Auditor concludes that the Ministry needs to "measure and report on the relevant performance indicators" and to "develop appropriate procedures and timelines for the inspection of long-term care community service agencies." Indeed, he maintains that the Ministry should "establish adequate procedures for verifying that services paid for were actually provided" (Ontario Office of the Provincial Auditor 1998, 106). This fear seems justified, given that at least one of the companies granted contracts in Ontario has been charged with fraud for not delivering promised care under United States medicare and for delivering shoddy care when it does fulfill the contract (Lindgren and Den Tandt 1998, A6; Walkom 1998, 31).

New bids are required frequently, even annually, making it difficult to ensure continuity and creating both extra work and insecurity for service providers. Each year, there may be new agencies and new practices for the skill mix of providers. CCAC boards are given the responsibility for the bidding process within overall budgets established by the province. Their budgets and business plan must be approved each year (Ontario Ministry of Health 1998f). Ministry decisions on budget allocations seem to be based on population utilization data which, according to a wide range of nurses' organizations, often ignore or under-represent the needs of certain populations and "produce findings that are on the side of smaller service capacity" (College of Nurses *et al*. 1997, 4). A joint submission from nurses' associations to the HSRC argued forcefully that the commission's methodology for assessing needs was based on "partial and unrepresentative populations."

> For the home care sector, the Commission's estimates were based on hospital discharge cases only, and failed to consider home care services associated with referrals from the community or the portion of home care services used to prevent admissions to the hospital. (ibid., 4)

Managed competition, especially when combined with such methodologies for calculating need, creates a host of problems for the mainly female providers and patients. In their submission to the Nursing Task Force, the Community Health Nurses Interest Group raised several concerns related to both costs and control.

> Some home care experts have expressed the view that the private companies are deliberately driving down the cost per visit in order to squeeze out as many players as possible at which point they will be in a position to raise the price per visit. Another criticism of the managed competition system is that it creates costly duplication and overlap of services by utilizing case managers to plan client care and monitor and evaluate the work and outcomes of the providers performing the care – activities the visit nurse already does on each and every visit. Visiting and other nurses are obliged to give detailed and time consuming reports about their care plans and outcomes to the case managers, and to obtain approval for their planned interventions as well as for the visit frequency and duration. Accordingly, the system severely restricts the autonomy of the visiting nurse's role, creating a dominant role not for the physician, but for the case manager who is most often (although not always) another nurse. (CHNIG and RNAO 1998, 18)

The submission from St. Elizabeth Health Care echoes these concerns. In addition, this non-profit organization points out that as a result of the bidding process, rates for nursing visits have dropped on average by 3-13 per cent. At the same time, nurses are pressured to "see more patients in less time" and "there is less 'paid' support for orientation, team time, on-going education and certification and preceptoring students." Part-time work has increased and "the nursing workforce experiences significant upheaval in the transition, as providers are unsuccessful and new providers enter the market." While these changes are happening, it is difficult to assess the impact on the quality of care because "Common quality indicators and performance measurements that identify best practice in the community are absent" (St. Elizabeth Health Care 1998, 2).

Although the home care employers' association supports the bidding process, it too has some criticisms about quality control, continuity and management. The organization recommends that quality, not price, be the major determining factor in assigning contracts and that "existing internal standards of providers and associations should be explicitly acknowledged" in weighing quality (OHHCPA 1999, 8). There is, however, no clear indication of how quality is to be measured. The paper calls for province-wide consistency in evaluation and greater transparency in the process. Perhaps most significantly, the paper acknowledges that here and abroad the bidding process has created instability and adversarial relationships. The solution offered, however, is not a return to a non-market model but more control of the market through long-term relationships such as multi-year contracts. Yet multi-year contracts could eliminate the very competition that is supposed to make the process effective and efficient. Non-profit and small organizations cannot wait around for years until they get a contract and thus may be put out of the running by longer term relationships.

Women's groups and other community organizations have been more critical of managed competition and the care available through CCACs. A joint statement from the Older Women's Network and the RNAO points out that "some of the for-profit agencies are better able to survive a temporary low bid by promoting additional, for-profit service once in the home" (OWN and RNAO n.d., 2). At the same time, the low budgets offered by the ministry are pushing all CCACs, regardless of their commitment to quality, to take the lowest bid (ibid.). This is combined with what then Long-Term Care Minister Cam Jackson called "horizontal equity," a formula intended to ensure each Ontarian needing services receives the same amount (Walkom 1998, 31). The result is both too little care for everyone and a failure to take individual needs of women into account.

Recipients of Care and Providers of Care

Home care is care for and by women. "Two-thirds of home care recipients are women" and while most are elderly, a significant number of them are young (Wilkins and Park 1998, 31-32). In 1994-95, more than half of those who needed help with personal care received no formal care and the percentage was even greater for those who needed help with the instrumental activities of daily living (ibid., 35). Although these data are for Canada, there is every reason to believe that similar patterns can be found within Ontario. And these data cover a period before the dramatic reforms shifted much more care to the home.

As the Ontario Health Coalition puts it, the "underfunding of in-home services is forcing providers to ration the services for which no fee is charged"

(OHC 1999, 2). Even though they reported a $34 million deficit in 1997-98, the CCACs were following government guidelines setting "a maximum of 4 nursing visits per day and 80 hours of homemaking per month, for the first month, and 60 hours of homemaking per month thereafter" (Canadian Home Care Association cited in ibid.). The 1998 government guidelines also state that to be eligible for public services, people must have first exhausted the caregiving and support capacities of their friends, relatives and other community services (Ontario, Ministry of Health 1998b, 6). In the Brant CCAC, for example, "Individuals who have a capable caregiver are not eligible for home support services. This includes caregivers who work outside the home" (OHC 1999, 2). Needless to say, women are the most likely to be classified as capable caregivers.

Meanwhile, the government is rationing other parts of home care services. There are stricter criteria for home oxygen, for example. In one year, the number of patients eligible for this service was cut by 2,000 (NUPGE 1998, 17). Assistive devices have also been increasingly rationed.

To some extent, other criteria for eligibility are set by each CCAC, in the context that it must stay within its budget. These criteria are not readily available to the women who need or provide care, making it difficult to determine whether the criteria are fair or fairly applied. According to research conducted by the Ontario Hospital Association,

> [I]t is the CCAC, not the professional caregiver who dictates the terms and conditions of service (including the number and nature of visits, level of care provider, reporting requirements, and response time). Many of these decisions are made without seeing the patient. It is subsequently very difficult for staff who are in the home and with the patient to make changes (particularly where a more costly level of caregiver, or an increase in care is judged to be needed). (OHA 1998, 5)

Within the area covered by CCACs, the new practices can mean not only that very limited care is provided but that the capacity of caregivers to use their skills in responding to individual needs is undermined. At the same time, the local control over some criteria creates enormous inequality among regions. Meanwhile, these practices leave women recipients with uniformly inadequate care.

While little research has been done on them, privatized services appear to be filling the care gap. Both for-profit and not-for-profit agencies are charging for services no longer provided by the public agencies, although the latter are more likely to have a sliding scale that takes income into account.

> Too often, their rates are prohibitive for low-income women. Despite the popularity of the well-to-do "snow birds" myth, an alarming 49 per cent of senior women living on their own are existing on the Guaranteed Income Supplement, which is slightly more than $11,000 per year, well below Statistics Canada's Low Income Cut Off. It is out of the question for these individuals to pay $15 an hour if they need to supplement or

substitute for the care they should be receiving from the CCAC. (OWN and RNAO n.d., 2-3)

It is reported that one 81-year-old woman who hurt her back was given 24-hour care for five days and then cut to two hours a day. In the end, she spent nearly $5,000 for four weeks of private care (Daly 1998a, F1).

Nor is there much research on the quality of care recipients receive. Care Watch Toronto, a network of organizations and individuals concerned about the quality of life for those receiving care in their homes, has established a phoneline project. Care Watch identified five problem areas on the basis of what it heard over the phone. First, more of the callers "talked about hours and costs than any other category of concerns", complaining both that there were "not enough hours of care" and that they could not afford the cost of services needed to supplement those provided through the CCAC (Care Watch Toronto 1999, ii).

Second, callers raised questions about the competence, dependability and attitude of some providers. "We know that some provider agencies are paying sub-standard wages and insisting on casual status for their workers, the better to control their own costs and their own profits" (ibid., 10). Like the callers to Care Watch, the Ontario Provincial Auditor has noted that the government needs to "ensure that individuals providing personal services are properly trained" (Ontario Office of the Provincial Auditor 1998, 106). The Nursing Task Force also identified a problem with "fragmented care as unregulated workers take on more nursing responsibilities" (Nursing Task Force 1999, 8). In addition, the rush to remove waste and promote profit eliminates the time to learn and teach. In the previous systems, the non-profit organizations used surplus time or money to train staff (Lindgren and Den Tandt 1998, A6).

The third issue identified from the phone calls was "the lack of adequate public education about the home care system" (Care Watch Toronto 1999, ii). Without information, women cannot appropriately access services. The fourth problem was one CCACs were designed to address: continuity, organization and promptness. According to the callers, "No system is in place to guarantee that one CCAC co-ordinator will know the time and post-discharge needs of every patient and, therefore, the promptness of initiating services may be compromised" (ibid., iii). Both the Nursing Task Force and the Ontario Hospital Association expressed similar concerns. The community health nurses pointed out that a smaller volume of clients for each organization has an additional problem related to continuity. With fewer visits to people with similar problems, "certified staff must either carry a mixed caseload or work on a referral basis – options which make it difficult to attract and retain certified staff, and for such staff to make sufficient visits to maintain a high level of clinical competence" (CHNIG and RNAO 1998, 19).

Some provider agencies hire only on a casual basis and organize assignments in a manner that limits the likelihood of continuity. Comcare, for example, does not offer full-time or permanent part-time jobs. Nurses working for Comcare receive no benefits or overtime pay, another practice that is likely to discourage loyalty and continuity. Nurses won the right to a first contract with one Comcare franchise after a three-month dispute, but most for-profit companies are not unionized (Landsberg 1998, F1; Daly 1998a, F1). This helps explain why they can produce a bid lower than the traditional provider organizations and still make a profit (Walkom 1999, A2).

Finally, callers told of problems traveling to visit partners sent to far-away nursing homes, to have their own care needs met and to get respite care. "Some of the most disturbing stories we hear are from family caregivers, struggling to keep their loved ones as comfortable as possible, but struggling under the load because they are unable to access adequate respite" (Care Watch Toronto 1999, iii). Women are necessarily conscripted into caregiving, creating problems for both the providers and the recipients of care.

The Care Watch Toronto report concludes by recommending that the *Long-Term Care Act* be made operational and that an independent complaints office be established. Sub-acute beds (previously recommended by the Health Services Restructuring Commission), increased funding for the CCACs in order to accommodate the frail elderly, adequate training for providers, and the expansion of respite care are all required, according to Care Watch Toronto. So too are diligent efforts to monitor the quality of care provided by the contracting agencies. The report does not offer a gender analysis of the responses it received but, given what we know about who the patients and their providers are, most of those who called were doubtless women. Whether or not the responses from women differed from those of men cannot, however, be learned from the report.

In Ontario, then, virtually every aspect of home care has become more privatized. Overall management is now based on private sector principles and practices, with government policy presented as a Business Plan rather than as an Annual Report to citizens. More of the publicly paid for care is delivered by for-profit firms. More of the care is paid for by individual women. More of this private care is required, because reforms have dramatically reduced the care provided in institutions. More of the care is provided by women unpaid and untrained for the task. The government has certainly carried out its promise to make health an individual responsibility.

The impact on nurses has been documented and, to a small extent, addressed, but other women paid to provide care have received less attention and these women are disproportionately from visible minority and immigrant groups. Although newspapers have covered the transfer of responsibility to unpaid female providers, and although women's groups have expressed concern, there has been little published research on these groups in Ontario. The impact on women with disabilities and on frail elderly women is the subject of some research. It is known that women with disabilities are increasingly forced into workfare programs, and that the spending on assistive devices has been significantly reduced (Health Canada 1998, 28). What is happening to women from other groups, though, is anybody's guess and, it appears, not much of a concern to government.

Long-term Residential Care
Providers and Payers
Long-term care facilities fall into two basic categories. Homes for the aged, owned and operated either by municipalities or by charitable foundations, are non-profit and account for about 43 per cent of the total beds. The rest are nursing homes, which are privately owned and operated. An estimated 90 per cent of nursing homes, including all but some of the smallest are for-profit (Ontario Ministry of Health 1998c, 9), and they are often organized into national or international chains. Legislation requires that all municipalities establish homes for the aged, and nursing homes require provincial licences that specify the number of beds each can operate. Unionization rates are high in these residential care facilities, although wages are usually lower than in the hospital sector (Gunderson and Hyatt 1996, 20).

Both types of facility receive provincial operating funds according to the same formula. Residents are charged fees for the accommodation portion of their costs, with the province subsidizing those who have passed a means test. Extra fees are charged for private rooms, with the rates established by the province. Fees can also be charged for other services such as hairdressing, mending, non-prescription drugs and uninsured health care services such as specialized foot care. It is with the fees charged individual residents that corporations make much of their profit, especially as more drugs and services are de-listed. Experience in the United States suggests that some may also make profits by reducing care and lowering the skill requirements for providers.

The funding formula is based on a case mix measure that is calculated to allocate existing funds in relation to average provincial levels of acuity. However, as the Older Women's Network and the RNAO point out, "If levels of care increase in all facilities, the funding may well not reflect this rise" (OWN and RNAO n.d., 3). There is, moreover, an inevitable lag between rising acuity levels and the point in time at which residents are classified by case mix criteria.

For-profit and not-for-profit homes get the same subsidies for nursing and personal care, program and support services and accommodation. However, the nursing homes receive some additional revenues from the government. These include 33 cents per resident day to nursing homes accredited by the Canadian Council on Service Accreditation, 91 cents per resident day to nursing homes that comply with the ministry's structural standards, and reimbursement for a limited share of debt retirement costs. Both nursing homes and charitable homes are also reimbursed for 90 per cent of their municipal tax assessments. The new government money available for renovation to facilities "selected because of their cramped size and lack of wheelchair accessibility" (Hudson 1998b, A8) is also likely to go mainly to the private sector. Perhaps more importantly, the government has invited tenders for the new 20,000 beds, opening the bidding to the for-profit sector. The fact that 84 per cent of the new long-term beds in Ottawa-Carleton went to large, for-profit firms suggests that this will be the case.

Why not have long-term care provided by the for-profit sector? The simple answer was offered to Cabinet by the Conservative health minister in 1969: "They are concerned about one thing only, making as much money as possible and giving as little as possible in return to the patients...the sooner this is gotten into on a public basis, the sooner we will be able to provide good quality health care for this segment of the population" (quoted in Struthers 1998, 181). He came to this conclusion after the government had tried setting standards and developing other forms of regulation. In 1990, Vera Ingrid Tarman came to a similar conclusion after comparing the for-profit and not-for-profit homes. Although she recognized that the not-for-profits were far from perfect, she found that they "have provided care that better meets the criteria of access, accountability and quality of care" (Tarman 1990, 92). By contrast, "the ambition to provide efficient services and incorporate a profit has been at the expense of providing reasonable level of health care" (ibid., 97).

It is also at the expense of the mainly female work force. With reported illness and injury rates that are higher than those in the construction industry, long-term care facilities are dangerous places to work. An Ontario survey found that private nursing homes are particularly hazardous, with more private sector workers reporting musculoskeletal disability, pain or discomfort in the last 12 months and in the last seven days, more cases needing medical attention and more time off work due to musculoskeletal troubles, as well as more fear of job repercussions for reporting a work-related injury/ accident. Ninety-four per cent of those responding to the survey were female (OHCOWI 1998).

For-profit homes are unreliable not only in terms of quality but also in terms of continuity. Tarman warned that these homes had no compunction about closing if profits disappeared. This is what happened in Cobden, Ontario in 1997, when the nursing home closed without providing for placement of the 53 residents (Egan 1997, D6). Such closures will be more likely if the firm is foreign-owned. In addition, Tarman found that for-profit firms are less accountable to the public than either public facilities or charitable ones serving the needs of particular communities. Here, too, foreign-owned companies are even less responsive than Canadian ones. Providers in long-term care facilities drawing on management consultants sent in from the foreign head office found they did not know Canadian labour laws or even our statutory holidays (Armstrong and Jansen interviews 1999).

Access to Quality Care and to Satisfactory Work

CCACs determine eligibility for admission to nursing homes and homes for the aged, and coordinate the placement of residents in these homes. As hospitals are increasingly restricted to the provision of acute care, now defined to mean "care or treatment for illness or injury requiring concentrated attention by health care workers, usually for a short period of time" (HSRC 1997, 137), these homes have come under intensified pressure. The announced closure of 3,506 chronic care beds can only increase the pressure (Bezanson and Noce 1999, 21). The government announced in 1998 that over the next eight years (since reduced to five years), it would increase the overall number of long-term care beds by 20,000 (Ontario Ministry of Health 1998e). However, nearly 5,000 beds are needed by those being moved out of chronic and acute care hospitals, and in 1998 there were an additional 18,000 people living in the community while on waiting lists for entry to long-term care facilities (Bezanson and Noce 1999, 21-22). In other words, 23,000 beds are needed right now, and the demand can only increase. Between 1998 and 2003, the Ontario population aged 80 and over is projected to grow by 85,427 or 27.5 per cent (calculated from Statistics Canada 1999, tables 1.10 and 5.1). Even using its minimalist formula, the HSRC estimated that "41,600 additional long-term care places will be required to equitably address the need for care in 2003" (HSRC 1997, 40).

Pressure within these homes has also risen as a result of rising acuity levels. In 1996, Ministry of Health figures indicated that almost 4,000 more residents required the most acute level of care, while the numbers at the least acute levels had dropped significantly (OWN and RNAO n.d., 3). In the same year, the government revised the *Nursing Home Act* to remove the requirements that an RN be on duty and that institutions employ sufficient staff to provide a minimum of 2.5 hours of nursing care per resident per day. This policy change cannot have been based on research into its consequences, given that "no staffing statistics were available for the time frame 1993 to 1997 in the long-term care (LTC) sector" by the time the Nursing Task Force met (O'Brien-Pallas, Baumann and Lochhass-Gerlach 1998, 52).

"Long-term care facilities now have to deal with a patient population of whom 60 per cent require heavy care, estimated to be 3.5 hours per day or more" (OWN and RNAO n.d., 3) and this is before the transfer of all the patients forced out of chronic care and acute care hospitals. Most of this population is female. Indeed, it could be said that long-term care is care for women by women. In 1997, almost three-quarters of the residents in long-term care facilities were widowed women between the ages of 80 and 89. Most had multiple health problems, with 60 per cent suffering from mental disorders and the same proportion from incontinence. Close to half had circulatory diseases and 46 per cent had musculoskeletal disabilities. The majority required "considerable supervision and assistance with activities of everyday living." They took on average four or more medications each day and nearly a third required special treatments ordered by their physicians and provided by nursing staff, ranging from catheters to ostomies to oxygen (Ontario Ministry of Health 1998c, 8).

In the future, even more severe illnesses may be treated in long-term care and more women from other age groups may be there as well. According to the HSRC's plans, "In the restructured system, long-term care facilities will provide almost all institutional long-term care" (HSRC 1997, 23). Yet the current formula for determining the number of beds required seems to be based only on the number of people over 75, without taking into account their sex, their illnesses or the decline in other services. It also seems to ignore the research, cited by the nurses in their submission, indicating that "clients in Long-term Care (LTC) units required at least as much nursing care as those in medical/surgical units" and that those with cognitive problems needed significant care time (College of Nurses *et al.* 1997, 10-11).

The nurses go on to point out that quality is a major concern in long-term care, especially in for-profit organizations. A survey of 2,780 long-term care providers found that 94 per cent had seen a significant decline in care quality in recent years, a decline that harms both themselves and the residents they serve. Eighty per cent said they did not have enough time to do their jobs and that they had less time to talk to residents. A majority said they no longer had time to carry out care plans or even to adequately bathe residents. The rush to care, respondents said, is leading to an increase in errors, accidents and injuries to both residents and providers. Illness among providers is rising at the same time (Armstrong *et al.* 1997a).

Gaps in care are made up by staff as best they can, at great expense to themselves. Even if care loads had remained the same, caregivers would be working harder to the handle the increase in individual care needs. Those interviewed for research funded by the National Network on Environments and Women's Health (NNEWH) report that new formulas and management techniques fail to take this increase into account. Staff say they are not being trained for the new demands, especially those resulting from the transfer of difficult psychiatric cases with the closure of mental health facilities. Nor are the equipment and facilities appropriate for these new conditions. Violence towards other residents and providers is on the rise, and those interviewed felt they had neither the skills nor the support to handle this escalation. Many of the new staff, they say, have come out of workfare programs, often with minimal training. Because they have not freely chosen the job, the workfare women frequently find it difficult to cope, especially under the increasingly stressful conditions (Armstrong and Jansen interviews 1999).

As the nurses point out, one of the main reasons the HSRC thinks long-term care will save money is that they have assumed lower-cost care providers with less training. The nurses are concerned that unregulated and untrained providers will be employed, in spite of the evidence indicating the need for a skill mix that includes highly trained staff (College of Nurses *et al.* 1997, 8). The new for-profit organizations moving into long-term care may be particularly prone to this strategy, and better able to carry it out because more of them may face non-union staff. The results would not only be more gaps in care but poor care.

Families, especially women in families, make up the gaps by paying others to do the work or by giving up paid work or their own health to provide the care themselves. According to the Older Women's Network and the Registered Nurses Association of Ontario,

> Families who can afford it are now hiring private attendants to care for their loved ones within facilities. It is also not surprising that many low-income women who cannot afford this "luxury" are extremely

frightened about having to enter a long-term care facility. (OWN and RNAO n.d., 4)

Extra payments for nursing care are in addition to the "more than $2,000 a month some families are already paying for [the accommodation portion of] nursing home care" (Daly and Hudson 1999, A7). Costs may be even higher in the many for-profit independent facilities that people access when they cannot get into the publicly subsidized centres or when the centres assigned by the CCAC do not meet their needs. The channeling of care through a single CCAC often means that patients are located far from home, making it difficult or impossible for elderly women to visit, let alone assist in caregiving (OWN and RNAO n.d., 4).

Some of the gaps are being filled by volunteers, both within hospitals and within the community. Although men perform a great deal of volunteer work, it is mainly women who volunteer as care providers (Denton *et al*. 1998). Once chiefly the preserve of older, white, middle-class women, volunteer care work is now increasingly performed by the young, who come from a range of backgrounds and are often in search of experience that will help in the pursuit of education and employment opportunities. Research by Elizabeth Esteves indicates that this work too is being transformed as management consultants and hospital administrators assume more control over volunteers and treat them more like paid employees (Esteves 2000). At the same time, more women who have lost their paid employment in health care are returning to the work as volunteers. In the process, women who volunteer have fewer choices and fewer rewards.

Jane Aronson and Sheila Neysmith succinctly identify "the reality that the costs of LTC are being redistributed to the private sphere" and thus to women. Their summary applies equally to home care and to long-term care facilities, to paid and unpaid female providers.

> By providing inadequate or meagre responses to their needs, the costs of frailty are effectively transferred to their shoulders to be endured or dealt with privately or alone. Some of the costs also shift to family members, our second group of concern, who typically step in to provide needed care. And, thirdly, costs are shifted to paid home care providers who are, for the most part, cheaper, less well-organized, and more isolated than their institutional counterparts and, thus, more open to exploitation. (Aronson and Neysmith 1997, 42)

In terms of institutional care, women in need of care face the problem of getting in, of severe limitations on choice, of payment and of care quality. Paid providers face work intensification, the frustration of not being able to do the job and often not being trained for the job, of poor skill mixes and of insecure or casual employment. More women from equity-seeking groups work here rather than in hospitals, but we could find no research on what difference this makes. Unpaid providers increasingly face long treks to the designated location, lack of training and no time for the job.

Primary Care
Why Primary Care?
Primary care refers to "the contact most people have with the health care system." Primary care providers include family doctors and pediatricians, nurses and nurse practitioners, midwives and other health professionals and people involved in various aspects of health promotion (Provincial Coordinating Committee on Community and Academic Health Science Centre Relations 1996, 1, 3). Throughout the research and policy literatures, primary care is identified as the key element in health care reform, both in terms of cost savings and in terms of improving care. It is the gateway to the system, and thus its control centre as well. A 1994 review of the research prepared for the Ontario Ministry of Health identified several common themes in primary care reform. Basically, these include a shift away from institutional care towards a more integrated system that increasingly emphasizes prevention and accountability to both governments and the people served (Abelson and Hutchison 1994, 1). This review does not offer a gender-based analysis. It does however note that, "With the exception of the nurse-practitioner literature, there is a paucity of research that rigorously evaluated nurse-centred delivery models. The relative scarcity of these models in jurisdictions around the world may be an important explanation for these findings" (ibid., 11). The review concludes both that there is a paucity of rigorous research in the entire area of primary care and, to the extent that the research demonstrates anything, that there is no single, most suitable model for primary care (ibid., 47).

Primary Care Models
The lack of a gender-based analysis in the review is surprising, given that the most common primary care model is one centred on the family or general practitioner and that "64% of women physicians were general or family practitioners" in 1994. Women accounted for 40 per cent of family and general physicians aged 30 to 34, and are expected to increase their shares with each subsequent graduating class (Woodward *et al.* 1996, 1). A 1996 study of gender differences among family physicians who are in the early stages of their careers

> documents that while many similarities exist between women and men in family medicine, important differences exist, even with a relatively homogeneous cohort of new family physicians. These differences suggest that women make different choices than their male colleagues in several key areas and that the increasing entry of women into medicine, therefore, does generate a potential for change, not just in the demographic face of medicine but in the organization of physicians' practices, in the doctor-patient relationship, and in the profession's response to government health policy. (ibid., 50-51)

Female patients, the study showed, prefer female physicians. The study observed that as the number of women increase and provide different role models, "they are likely to influence the attitudes and behaviour of male physicians as well, many of whom, our data suggest, welcome alternatives to traditional male role models" (ibid.).

The researchers warned that changes proposed by the new provincial government "may force women into a traditionally male model of practice, reducing their effectiveness as agents of change in relation to their male colleagues and overwhelming the evolutionary changes they might have generated within the profession" (ibid., 51).

Among the changes identified are new limits on the number of admissions to medical schools and on the mix of available residency positions, and restrictions on practising in what are deemed over-serviced locations. Although these changes may help increase women's access to services in northern and rural areas of the province, they may also reduce the choices available to female doctors, and in particular those with partners working in large cities.[6]

The government's suggestion that it may negotiate directly with groups of physicians over methods of payment is another policy that may have a particular impact on women. The impact of these changes taken together is already evident in physician numbers. According to the Ministry's *Business Plan 1998-99*, it "helped 501 new physicians establish practice in Ontario" (Ontario Ministry of Health 1998e). At the same time, the research conducted for its Nursing Task Force shows a significant decline in the ratio of physicians to population, and the government continues to restrict the number of places in the province's medical schools below levels set a decade ago (Nursing Task Force 1999, 40). This is taking place just as women become a major proportion of the physician workforce.

After initially proposing in its omnibus Bill 26 to introduce further controls on fee-for-service payments to doctors, the government has actually lifted some restrictions. Pressure from organized medicine was clearly responsible for this reversal. The government has set up five pilot projects designed to change the relationship between patients and physicians. In introducing clinics staffed by physicians joining on a voluntary basis, the government has followed the advice of a Ministry-appointed committee and the Ontario Medical Association's (OMA) Subcommittee on Primary Health Care (Boyle 1998, A7). These pilot projects will last for three years and will be continually evaluated. Patients were to sign up, in what is often referred to as a rostering system. Doctors meanwhile are to choose among three payment schemes.

> Some will operate under a revised version of the fee-for-service model, with the number of patients on the roster factored in. Others will be paid extra for services related to preventative medicine, home care, and palliative care. Still others with older patients will be paid strictly on the basis of the roster, with older patients earning more than younger ones. (Ibbitson 1998, A3)

When the program was announced, the plan was to provide the choices of payment scheme to doctors but not to patients. Patients would be allowed to select their clinic of choice but, once in, would have to pay extra for seeking care outside that clinic. This provision reflected the OMA's belief that "patients drive up the costs of health care by flitting from doctor to doctor for the same ailment." Rostering would, they assumed, prevent "doctor shopping" (Hudson 1998a, A8).

Women, especially lesbians, those from immigrant groups and those in their teens, have often found their symptoms dismissed or transformed by particular practitioners. Equally important, medicine is as much an art as a science, and even the scientific part is known only partially by any specific physician. What the OMA calls "doctor shopping" could also be termed seeking an essential "second opinion." The restriction on seeking care outside the pilot project clinics was abandoned in part because of a fear that it would violate the *Canada Health Act* and in part because it was "not publicly palatable to the politicians," according to Dr Wendy Graham, a physician who helped negotiate for the clinics on behalf of the OMA (quoted in Ibbitson 1998, A3). What role, if any, women's protests or concerns played in this reversal is not clear from either research or media reports.

The fee-for-service payment system for physicians is unlikely to save taxpayer dollars, to reduce mistreatment or to increase the emphasis on health promotion (CUPE 1995). At the same time, the proposed alternative payment schemes "could lead to the biggest problem of the capitation systems – that doctors may avoid treating patients with complex problems," and many of those with complex problems are elderly women (Coutts 1997, A3). It should be noted that Ontario has had a number of community health centres in place for 20 years or more, primarily located in areas serving disadvantaged populations. These 55 not-for-profit, multi-service agencies pay doctors and other providers on a salaried basis. According to one doctor, this system "encourages its doctors to get to know their patients, rather than churning them out like links in a sausage factory" (Thow 1998, A17). Also of long standing in the province are 27 Health Service Organizations (HSOs), consisting essentially of partnerships of family physicians who are paid on a capitation basis. No official explanation has been forthcoming as to why these CHCs and HSOs are not the pilot projects for reformed primary care.

Benefits and Risks

The new pilot project clinics may well improve women's access to health care. They are intended to be open for extended hours in the evening and to offer telephone triage lines overnight. They may well focus more on health promotion. There are, however, risks associated with these clinics.

The first risk is related to the announced introduction of "new information privacy laws that would make it easier for doctors to share patient data with other practitioners" (Chamberlain 1997, A8). With research demonstrating that doctors all too often inappropriately diagnose women's problems as being "all in their heads", this information sharing may well have gender consequences. We have not, however, found any references to this problem in the Ontario research.

On a related point, the government appears keen to protect the privacy of clinic owners. Of 186 private clinics (out of the total of about 1,000) inspected by the College of Physicians and Surgeons on behalf of the Ministry of Health in 1999, 10 per cent revealed problems so serious that inspectors recommended that their licences be suspended, and another 10 per cent warranted recommendations for improvement. Yet the Ministry refused to divulge the names of the deficient clinics, citing the *Freedom of Information and Protection of Privacy Act.* Even the *Ottawa Citizen* (1999, B4), a Southam newspaper, was moved to editorialize that the job of government officials is to look after the public interest, not commercial interests, and that agencies delivering health care should be "subject to the simplest tests of public accountability" by having reports on their inspections made public.

The second pilot project risk is that of privatization. These new clinics are very similar to the managed care clinics operating in the United States. The majority there are for-profit operations, and the establishment of similar clinics here may make it easier for private, for-profit operators of United States or Canadian corporations to move in. This has already happened with walk-in clinics (which, unlike CHCs and the new pilot project clinics, are not based on providing ongoing service to a stable population) and with a newly developed doctors' house call business in Ontario (*Globe and Mail* 1998, A6).

Another type of private clinic may be particularly harmful for women. Private clinics offering a range of cosmetic and other plastic surgeries are increasingly common in Ontario, although it is difficult to tell how many there are or who uses them. There are several reasons for this paucity of information. First, private health facilities are unregulated and are therefore not required to submit reports to the Ministry or to open their premises for inspection. Unlike hospitals, which must conform to all kinds of regulation, these clinics perform surgery outside public scrutiny unless subject to specific complaints.

A second reason for the lack of information can be found in the classification of most cosmetic surgery as falling beyond the coverage of OHIP. When these surgeons bill their patients rather than OHIP, there is no reporting on their procedures to a public agency. The College of Physicians and Surgeons, the profession's regulatory body, responds only to complaints of malpractice; it does not pro-actively monitor doctors or their practices. Moreover, there is no specific training in cosmetic surgery in the province, and no regulation of physician practices in this field (Harvey 1998b, A1). The onus is thus on the patient to check both the surgeon and the facility. Checking the surgeon may not be enough, however, as they are allowed to delegate many procedures to other practitioners. This delegation of controlled acts has proven problematic in several Ontario clinics where cosmetic surgery is performed (Harvey 1998a, A25).

A third reason for the limited information on these clinics can be found in the nature of the service. Many of those who undergo cosmetic surgery do not wish this to become public knowledge, and may be hesitant to acknowledge that the service has been provided. According to malpractice lawyer Jerry Leviton, "People, primarily women, are being exposed to tremendous health risks" as a result (quoted in Harvey 1998b, A1).

In response to a request for information on private clinics, the Canadian Health Services Research Foundation (CHSRF) posted an appeal for such information on its website. According to a senior member of the CHSRF staff, there have been no replies. It seems that very little research is being conducted on this burgeoning and lucrative development, one that may well be having profound consequences for women's health.

Both as patients and as providers, women have benefited from another primary care initiative, one that expands the public sector, at least as far as one category of nurses and those they serve are concerned. The government has introduced new legislation on nurse practitioners. While nurse practitioners are not new to Ontario, in 1999 the government announced new funding for primary care by them in under-serviced areas. This should benefit the female patients in these areas, a significant proportion of whom are Aboriginal. Government figures indicate that 80 new nurse practitioner positions are to be created in under-serviced areas, and another 20 positions in nursing homes. This target falls short of providing employment for the estimated 300 nurse practitioners currently available in the province, however (RNAO 1999, 1). Part of the problem is that they are to be paid salaries primarily through community health centres, but are needed in many areas of the province that are without CHCs. Another part is that the RFP process for funding the new positions has yet to appear (Coutts 1999a, A5).

In sum, the current government has moved to expand public primary care through the introduction of the five new pilot project clinics and with the new money for nurse practitioners. At the same time, however, it has allowed OHIP billings by doctors to rise appreciably, and has used this increase in expenditures to justify cuts in other areas. Undoubtedly, some women will benefit from expanded clinic and nurse practitioner services, and these women may well be from the most vulnerable groups. We could find no research on this question, however.

Midwifery

Midwives buck the trend towards privatization. Women organizing for midwifery fought a long, continuous and ultimately successful battle for public support. As a 1988 article by one of the battle's leaders explained:

> In seeking to change the conditions of childbirth for women in Ontario, midwives and their supporters have focused on gaining recognition and government support for midwifery services. They have asserted their demands in a variety of ways – from holding demonstrations to proposing detailed models for legislation, and mobilizing community support and international attention. The strategy of the midwifery movement has been to create a highly visible practice outside of the health system while pressuring for legislation, autonomy, government funding and access for all women. (Van Wagner 1988, 115)

The initial result of this long struggle – a struggle that took place both within the midwifery movement and between it and others in the larger society – was the creation of the Midwifery Task Force of Ontario in 1985. After extensive consultation within and outside Canada, the task force recommended that midwifery be established as an independent, self-regulating profession with its own regulatory college (Eberts *et al.* 1987). In 1989, the Liberal government appointed the Interim Regulatory Council on Midwifery to carry out the task force report. Like the task force itself, the council was chaired by Mary Eberts. The council was concerned both with ensuring that the principles of midwifery – including an emphasis on continuous, woman-centred care – be put into practice, and with recognizing the diversity of midwifery practices. A four-year baccalaureate program was established at three university sites as the main entry route to the profession, and special provisions were made for traditional Aboriginal midwives. Also established was a procedure for the prior learning assessment and recognition of midwives trained in other countries or who had already been practising in Canada when midwifery was brought under provincial regulation (Bourgeault and Fynes 1997, 7; Armstrong *et al.* 1993).

Midwifery became legal in Ontario in 1991, but did not officially become a self-regulating profession until December 1993. By this time, an NDP government was in office.

> As defined in the Midwifery Act, the midwives' scope of practice is "the assessment and monitoring of women during pregnancy, labour and the post-partum period and of their newborn babies, the provision of care during normal pregnancy, labour and post-partum period and the conducting of normal, spontaneous, vaginal deliveries." (Ontario Ministry of Health 1993b, 1)

Accompanying legalization was the negotiation by the government and the midwives' association of a salary structure that reflected their professional status. At the same time, and in response to a community lobby, the government invited proposals from community groups for the establishment of three stand-alone birthing centres to be staffed primarily by midwives. By 1994, 71 midwives were registered in the province, and since 1997 the numbers have grown by between 40 and 70 each year (Association of Ontario Midwives 1998).

There is a considerable body of research both on the development of legislation for midwifery and on its impact on women. The legislation has undoubtedly improved the conditions of work for the women who have been accepted as midwives, although there is still debate about who was excluded from the original licencing process, about who is excluded by the demands of a four-year university program and about whether there should have been state regulation at all. Midwifery does seem to mean less medical intervention. Surveys of midwifery practices indicate that women with midwives are significantly less likely to deliver by caesarian (6% vs. 20% with physicians), to have episiotomies (8% vs. 50%), or to receive epidural anesthetics for pain relief (5% vs. 30%). About 40 per cent of midwifer deliveries take place at home, and women with midwives are much more likely than other women to leave hospital the same day they deliver, both because they have midwives to help at home and because they experience less intervention while in hospital (Association of Ontario Midwives n.d.)

The transformation of midwifery into a public service has also increased access for women because the service is no longer limited to those who can afford to pay out of their own pockets and to those who are prepared to take the risk that their delivery will be normal. One of the first acts of the new Conservative government was, however, to eliminate funding for free-standing birthing clinics (Health Canada n.d. [1998], 7). Although we have not found systematic data on changes in the characteristics of the women using midwifery services, there are discussions of how to respond to the high and growing demand for these services and of how to ensure equal access for commonly under-served populations such as Aboriginal women, teen mothers, lesbians and immigrant women (Katherine 1995, 21).

MENTAL HEALTH

As a consequence of restructuring, two psychiatric hospitals have been closed, and a third has been transformed into a forensic psychiatric hospital. Many of those with severe mental difficulties are being removed from chronic care hospitals. There are no readily accessible data on how many of those currently being served by these hospitals are women. We do know, however, that a majority of psychiatric patients are women and that they are a minority among those classified as forensic psychiatric cases.

Patients removed from psychiatric hospitals may end up in long-term care facilities. However, the reallocation formulas used by the HSRC ignored psychiatric patients under the age of 14 and underestimated the needs of the rest (College of Nurses et al. 1997, 4). What does not seem to have been considered by the HSRC is how well these patients would be served by long-term care institutions, which have traditionally provided care only for the very old. Long-term care providers often lack the training to care for those with severe mental health problems. Nor do the institutions have the appropriate facilities. Young patients with mental health problems are being mixed with frail, elderly, immobile women. As noted in the section on long-term residential care, violence against elderly residents and staff is increasingly frequent, and the providers feel ill-equipped to handle it (Armstrong and Jansen interviews 1999).

Those who do not fit the eligibility requirements for admission to long-term care facilities are being sent home, to be cared for by mothers or other relatives. One study of mothers caring for their mentally ill adult children revealed how often they face violence, and how poorly equipped they are for responsibilities that they shoulder with decreasing support from public agencies (Vatri Boydell 1996). There is little evidence of any new support services for these family care providers.

Those who do not have homes to go to or whose homes cannot handle their care often end up on the streets. Already ill-served by the old system, the vulnerable mental health population is increasingly finding that it has no service at all. Although it is not possible to determine how many of the homeless are mentally ill women, it has been estimated that from 30 to 40 per cent of the homeless suffer from mental illness and that a growing proportion of the homeless are women (Queen Street Mental Health Centre Medical Staff Association 1998, 11). Private, fee-charging agencies may well spring up to help fill the gap, but they will be beyond the financial reach of most women.

REHABILITATION SERVICES

It is difficult to tell what has been happening in terms of rehabilitation services and privatization, especially in relation to women. The purchase of services from private, for-profit providers is common, and has been since before 1990. There are severe restrictions on public payments to chiropractors, and massage therapists have never been part of the public health insurance plan. Traditionally, however, much of rehab care was provided at public expense in hospitals, and by nurses, occupational therapists and physiotherapists who were almost all women. As the role of hospitals has been more narrowly defined to concentrate on acute care, some rehab services have been pushed out or made more difficult to access in a hospital setting.

A 1995 study by the Institute for Work and Health did not find a significant trend towards decreased full-time employment among the occupational groups usually associated with rehabilitation (Holyoke and Elkin 1995, 53). Cautioning, however, that its data may not capture what many of the authors' respondents believe is a move away from public provision, the report noted that the hospital data used for the study were unaudited and not current. In addition, many commentators hold that the 1994 changes to automobile insurance "have caused a shift from the public to the private sector" (ibid.). The introduction of no-fault insurance opened the door to private companies, as did changes to the Workers' Compensation Board's (WCB) strategy to promote a "migration of direct service providers from the public to the private sector" (ibid.).

As the Institute's report was being prepared, the Liberty Mutual Insurance group, the largest provider of workers' compensation services in the United States, purchased a chain of private rehab clinics in Ontario. It was also engaged both in the controversial purchase from the Ontario Hospital Association of the then not-for-profit Ontario Blue Cross supplementary insurance enterprise and in a multi-million dollar set of studies of workers' compensation in Ontario and other Canadian jurisdictions. In describing the purposes, assumptions and objectives for its studies, Liberty International Canada (sic) stated that "significant increases in administrative costs and concerns about the efficiency and financial stability of some provinces' WCB systems have opened a debate about the effectiveness of state monopoly systems" (Anastakis and Rachlis n.d., 13). Not surprisingly, the option favoured by this firm for

Ontario was that "the government permit other organizations capable of providing quality services in the sector to enter into competition with the public WCB" (Liberty Canada 1996, 18).

It would of course also allow the largest private sector firm in workers' compensation an enormous foothold in the province from which not only to manage and provide workers' compensation services but to influence the entire health care system. Although competing workers' compensation providers have not to date been introduced to Ontario, workers' compensation may be the most significant trojan horse at the gates of the Canadian system of public health care. With Liberty Canada (Liberty Mutual, Liberty International Canada, Liberty Health – it goes by different names) at the lead, private sector firms seek to take over the management and delivery of care for work-related injuries and illnesses, thus undermining the "single-payer" feature of the current system, by which firms are prohibited from insuring medically necessary care. The Liberty Canada studies of workers' compensation contain no gender-based data, analyses or arguments.

Since the Institute of Work and Health report was released, whole sections of the WCB and its services have been privatized, and hospitals have severely curtailed the number of available rehab beds. It seems likely, then, that the Institute's findings on the limited extent of rehab privatization are out of date.

The most obvious example of privatized, for-profit provision is the King's Health Centre in downtown Toronto. According to Colleen Fuller,

> King's did offer some publicly funded health-care services, but its main source of revenue was "third-party payers" – private insurers or employers who paid directly for services to get employees back to work sooner and off disability payments. It offered "new methods of disability management,"...and planned to set up satellite clinics for injured workers in cities where high injury rates promised to increase business. (Fuller 1998, 243)

Funds for the King's Health Centre came mainly from the public purse, but a portion of them ended up as corporate profits. There is reason for concern that care is determined according to bottom-line criteria rather than on the basis of need. The King's Health Centre featured the services of a golf swing clinic that busy executives could purchase.[7]

The removal of most rehabilitation services from a hospital system more strictly devoted to acute care means that more individuals are now either paying privately for rehab services or are using for-profit clinics for OHIP-covered services. "In the Greater Toronto area, half of the private physio clinics are now owned by third-party business operators who have no affiliation with the physiotherapy profession" (Daly and Hudson 1999, A7). For example, "Columbia Health Care Inc., a subsidiary of a US company, has 28 physiotherapy clinics in Canada," a number of them in Ontario (Medline 1997, A1).

Women have not been the majority of those with recognized claims under workers' compensation or private long-term disability. With increasing injury rates among health care workers in particular, however, these changes in rehabilitation are likely to have a particular impact on women.[8] And the primarily female rehab providers will see their jobs transformed as more care is provided privately. We could not, however, find any Ontario research on this issue.

TARGETED PROGRAMS FOR WOMEN
Women's Health Council

In January 1998, the government announced the establishment of a Women's Health Council. It is headed by Jane Pepino, a Conservative lawyer, former member of the Canadian Advisory Council on the Status of Women and current chair of the Women's College Hospital Board, which has engaged in protracted negotiations first to resist being absorbed by Sunnybrook Health Sciences Centre and then to merge with it while maintaining some independence. The rest of this appointed council, which was not announced until December 1998, consists of five physicians, three researchers with nursing backgrounds, a university administrator, a pharmacist, the president of General Motors Canada, a *Toronto Sun* journalist who covers health issues, and an activist for women's support groups. All but one are women and, according to their press release biographical sketches, several have experience with gender-based analysis (Government of Ontario Press Releases 1998a).

> The Council is mandated to review and provide advice about women's immediate health priorities, covering three key areas. The first group of issues concerns the major stages in women's lives, for example health promotion targeting teens on smoking and eating disorders, maternal and newborn care and mid-life and older women. The second relates to prevention and treatment issues, focusing on cardiovascular disease and the fact that women traditionally have a larger caregiving role than men. The third looks at new approaches in education about disease prevention and health promotion (Government of Ontario Press Releases 1998b).

Although the December 1998 press release promised that it would "work to create proactive partnerships with government, educators, business, researchers, health care organizations and other community groups" (Government of Ontario Press Releases 1998a), there has been little public information on the council's activities. It commissioned the Centre for Research in Women's Health at the Sunnybrook and Women's College Health Sciences Centre to examine women's health research in relation to demographic shifts, policy differences at different levels and environmental factors that determine decision-making in women's health care policy. The report was scheduled for submission to the Women's Health Council in October 1999 (Maher personal communication 1999; Maher conducted the study along with Heather Maclean). Perhaps the lack of news is a consequence of the fact that the council's mandate is to advise the Ministry of Health and not the public. There is no mention in the press releases of the possibility of, much less the requirement for, public disclosure of any of its deliberations or advice.

Other Programs Identified by the Government

The government has also announced several funding allocations targeted at women's health. Two of these concern medical interventions related to women's reproductive systems, namely the expansion of the breast and cervical screening programs. At the same time, however, the government has set strict guidelines concerning the frequency of these tests and the requirement that women pay individually for any additional tests beyond the established number. In terms of women and cardiac care, the government counts all the funding for expanded cardiac services without indicating whether or not these services will take into account the quite different symptoms and diagnoses women face. Instead, the press release promises "greater emphasis on addressing women in heart health promotion programs" (Government of Ontario Press Releases 1998b). Similarly, it is unclear how much of an announced $16.5 million "reinvestment" in cancer care services represents new funding, how much of it will go to services for women, and to what extent the services will be based on a gender-sensitive analysis. Reinvestment in long-term care is also listed among the programs targeted for women, but with no indication of how women's particular issues will be addressed in the restructuring process.

Four of the initiatives listed by the government to improve health services for women – Healthy Babies, Healthy Children; Better Beginnings, Better Futures; the Kids Foundation; and Pre-school Speech and Language Services – are mainly about children. At least one of them focuses on women's parenting skills, with the potential for reinforcing the notion that individual women are to blame for their children's problems, and more generally for reinforcing the privatization of responsibility to individuals. These initiatives are from the same government that cut the $37 monthly nutrition supplement for pregnant women on social assistance on the grounds that they would only spend the extra money on beer, and that reintroduced and made more punitive "spouse in the house" rules against lone mothers on social assistance (Orwen and Monsebraaten 1998, A2).

Three research funding initiatives were also listed in January 1998 as being among the targeted programs for women: $350,000 for the Nursing Task Force, an unstated amount for an abortion access study to be conducted by the Institute of Clinical Evaluative Sciences, and $1.03 million for unspecified research on women's health (Government of Ontario Press Releases 1998b). Given the size of the province's total health budget – over $18 billion – and the major health issues faced by women, these amounts are very small. With such low levels of public funding, women will have to rely more on private sources of research support, support that often comes with strings attached. Even the limited public funds that are available are increasingly tied to partnerships with the private sector.

Finally, the government included two programs that may well entail public responsibility for what are often considered private concerns. The first is the expansion of eating disorder programs in four regions. The second is Agenda for Action, a program designed to reduce violence against women. Early in its first mandate, the Conservative government was criticized for its approach to violence issues, and in particular for its cancellation of funding for second-stage women's shelters. This initiative is said to "help community-based organizations offer abused and assaulted women a seamless range of services and programs in our communities" (Ontario Women's Directorate 1999b).

Several of these initiatives are targeted at specific groups of women. For example, there is a new French language services plan. Information for Toronto distribution has been produced in nine languages, and there is special funding for the Sioux Lookout Zone, an area with a significant Aboriginal population. "Through the availability of new funding for medical equipment, all 27 Sexual Assault Treatment Centres in Ontario can now provide better examinations and treatments to women with physical disabilities" (Ontario Women's Directorate 1999c). There is now special training for staff working with women who have disabilities, and eight domestic violence courts. Between 1997 and 1999, 90 community-based violence prevention projects have been funded, with a particular emphasis on "northern communities, immigrant and refugee women, and women with disabilities" (Ontario Women's Directorate 1999a). These small, one-time grants tend to support programs that stress education and skills that in turn encourage individual women to become economically independent (Ontario Women's Directorate 1999d).

We have not been able to locate any analyses of these initiatives. The available information suggests however that their focus is on the individual and on private responsibility. It is also unclear how much in these initiatives is new, given the government's tendency to announce and re-announce the same programs, at times without spending some or all of the announced funds.

HEALTH INFORMATION TECHNOLOGY

Information is at the core of both health care reform and health decision-making. New technologies have expanded enormously the capacity for recording, storing, retrieving and manipulating data on patients, providers, procedures, work times, finances and other health management concerns. Along with this expansion has come a greatly increased capacity for manipulating and controlling care.

Health information is not simply a technical matter involving objective data. At every step in the process of collecting, analyzing and using information, value-laden decisions are made. These decisions have profound consequences for women. In spite of the exploding potential for public involvement in health decision-making opened up by new technologies, the control of health information is increasingly in private, for-profit and often foreign hands.

Hospitals in Ontario, for example, are purchasing clinical care pathway software systems from US firms, without much regard to the very different context for care here. Similarly, patient classification systems that are used to enhance managerial control over both patients and providers are in place throughout the province. Other classification and organizational software systems are also being introduced enthusiastically (see, for example, Choiniere 1993). At the same time, there are few safeguards in place to ensure that information on patients and providers remains confidential in terms of what is recorded, how it is recorded, who has access to what is recorded, and how it is analyzed and used.

In Ontario, the privatization of information has received scant attention, and there is little research on its impact on women. Only in the case of individual health cards has there been much public controversy. In requiring the production of these cards at every visit to a doctor or a hospital, the government has emphasized fraud, presumably by non-resident and illegally resident patients. An effect, however, has been to jeopardize access to care by the homeless in particular.

Conclusion

Ontario has privatized health care more extensively and rapidly than has any other province. The data on private expenditure provide a stark but partial picture of this privatization. While 72.9 per cent of health expenditures in Ontario were public in 1990, by 1998 the province's public share had dropped to 66.9 per cent. The province next in line was Alberta at 69.4 per cent (CIHI 1998, table B.3.3). During the same period, total health expenditures continued to climb, suggesting that the decline in public spending did not mean that health spending in general was under control or that reforms have served to promote health instead of medicine. Private spending grew in all areas, including in the areas traditionally covered by public health insurance. The largest increase, however, was for drugs (ibid., table D.2.6.1). This growth is in part a consequence of several provincial initiatives: the deregulation of drugs, the introduction of fees for seniors and welfare recipients, and de-institutionalization.

This shift to private payment happened despite the government's promises to maintain public spending and counter to its claims that this promise has been fulfilled. A host of surveys and research have demonstrated that citizens strongly oppose this privatization and that women are even more likely than men to support public care (see, for example, Environics Research Group 1999; Greenspon and Windsor 1998, A1, A8). These citizens pay for care, one way or another, but they are not happy with how their money is being spent. Patients are dissatisfied with both access to care and the quality of care they receive when they do gain access (Ontario Hospital Association and the University of Toronto 1998). And research on the paid and unpaid providers shows that the overwhelming majority of them do not have time to provide necessary care. They are trying to do so to the point where it has threatened their own health.

The shift in costs is not the only form of privatization. Privatization is also taking place in less visible and less consistently documented ways. One of these ways is the massive shift to a business philosophy and to approaches taken from the for-profit sector. The government has adopted business practices and required the entire health system to do the same. The transformation of the Ministry's Annual Report into a Business Plan is a clear sign of the transformation. So too is its *Health Report to Taxpayers* (see volume 1, Winter 1999), rather than to citizens.

Another form of privatization is the contracting out of services to for-profit concerns, both in the community, following specific requirements set out for managed competition and within institutions, as a result of funding cutbacks combined with a new business philosophy. Care work has also been privatized. Increasingly, the responsibility has shifted mainly to women who provide the care without pay not only in the home but within the institutions as well.

In many ways, these developments are consistent with the government's "commitment to move to a greater community responsibility for health and health services" (Ontario Ministry of Health 1998d, 2). They are certainly consistent with the government's conviction that "each individual has responsibility for his or her own health" (ibid., 10). Both community and individual responsibility may be supported by some groups representing women. Yet this privatization has often been combined with a centralization of power through the use of Ministry orders and approvals, according to guidelines that are difficult to determine and with dramatic reversals that deny community, or even individual, control. This is especially the case given that adequate resources have not been transferred along with responsibility. The available research suggests that many of these developments may be hazardous to the health of women as patients and providers while limiting their right to make decisions about their lives and work. It also suggests that the impact varies among women, but we found even less research on differences among women in relation to health care reform.

Women as Decision-makers

Women have little say in how, where and when reform happens, in spite of the fact that they are the majority of both care recipients and care providers. The current government does little to conduct research, inform or consult on change. Information that is as timely, appropriate and accurate as possible is fundamental to decision-making and choice. However, it is difficult to find such information, especially information that is about actual practice rather than about promises. One example comes from long-term care. A municipal councillor reports that the "Ministry of Health is refusing to release records of complaints and investigations of two of the companies that have recently been allocated nursing home beds in Ottawa-Carleton" (Munter 1999). Both are for-profit firms. Increasingly investigators are turning to their freedom of information rights but this too is often difficult. A study of access to information in Ontario found that "Ontario is now one of the most expensive provinces for freedom of information requests" (Mallan 1999, A6).

Not only do women have difficulty accessing information on such things as the eligibility criteria for home care, they face problems in having their complaints investigated or their appeals heard. Although government documents say there are procedures for appeals and complaints, the Provincial Auditor's report makes clear this is not happening as promised in long-term care.[9] Combined with formulas for funding that fail to take differences into account, with the reduction in services available, with new fees, and with new rules about eligibility, women's choices about care are increasingly restricted.

Women's choices are restricted as well by new business practices. Formulas for care time and care treatment, along with more centralized control, are increasingly limiting providers' ability to respond to individual needs, circumstances and preferences on the basis of their skilled judgement. This is the case both within institutions and within the community; and these developments have a greater impact on the frail elderly and those with disabilities than they do on those with fewer chronic health problems and more capacity to resist. They also have a greater impact on poor women who cannot afford the cost of supplementing care and do not have the resources to successfully demand appropriate care. Women's choices are also being fundamentally altered by their conscription into work as unpaid care providers in the home and the lack of public support for, or respite from, this work. Tellingly, these limits on women's choices are happening just as they are increasingly being described as consumers rather than as patients or care recipients.

When the government does bring women to the table for consultation, the women tend to be experts in medical or nursing practices. This is less the case with seniors. The government has created a Seniors' Secretariat with its own business plan, but we could find no research to demonstrate that this has resulted in meaningful consultation or an analysis of the particular nature of women's needs. The consultation may be meaningful in the case of Aboriginal women. The Ontario Native Women's Association is represented on the Aboriginal Management Committee that makes recommendations to Health Canada on projects intended to meet community needs. There is little evidence that the provincial government consults with other groups or care providers, although its strained relationship with unions representing health care workers may be easing. Meanwhile, the increasing use of confidential bidding processes and business practices leave women with only very limited "consumer" choices rather than with meaningful consultation (Aronson 1993).

Women as Care Recipients

Under current reforms less money for public provision usually means less care, in spite of claims that less is better. Business practices often mean both less time for care and less attention to individual needs, in spite of claims about consumer preferences. The result, too frequently, is decreasing access and poor care for women, according to the community groups, employer organizations and unions that have done mainly qualitative research. More official and quantitative assessments of quality, to the extent they exist, tend to emphasize such measures as length of stay, financial costs to governments, variations in intervention rates and patient satisfaction. According to the

Provincial Auditor, at least in the case of long-term care, there are no adequate means for assuring that the amount or the quality care is delivered as promised.

There has been a dramatic reduction in the number of hospital and chronic care beds available without adequate provision for appropriate care in other places. The shift has assumed a reduction in the need for skilled care, although unions and community groups have pointed to research denying this assumption's validity. Most of those moved out of chronic care beds are women, and therefore most of those waiting for, or denied access to, long-term care are women. And they are, for the most part, women who cannot afford to pay for supplementary care. Although the government lists long-term care as a program targeted at women, we could find no evidence that women's particular concerns or differences among women are being taken into account. This is the case despite research demonstrating dramatic differences in, for example, heart disease, lung cancer and breast cancer not only between women and men but also among women from different ethnic backgrounds (Talaga 1999, A3; see also O'Loughlin 1999, 152-53). Nor could we find current evidence on how for-profit providers compare to not-for-profit ones, although earlier research and research conducted in the United States suggests that for-profit care tends to be shoddier and less frequently delivered as promised than not-for- profit care. It is also more expensive, at least where for-profit concerns dominate. Where for-profit and not-for profit concerns compete, the not-for-profits may be forced to adopt the more expensive practices of the for-profits (Woolhandler and Himmelstein 1999, 445). This is worrisome, given that the for-profit companies dominate long-term care in the province and seem to be increasing their share. Meanwhile, home care has become crisis intervention, often leaving the frail elderly and the disabled without care, and new research indicates that immigrant and refugee women face particular barriers to care as a result of the reforms (Guruge, Morrison and Donner 2000).

Women have organized, or joined, a variety of community organizations to work for better access and quality care. These organizations have worked to counter the official claims, to expose the deterioration and to demand improvements. The Older Women's Network is an example of a group that has successfully put senior women's issues on the agenda.

Women as Providers

Health care is women's work, whether it is paid or unpaid. There has been significant job loss for those who have been paid to do the work and significant work increases for the unpaid. The work for those who are still paid has been transformed. Business practices applied in both the for-profit and not-for-profit sectors are making women work harder, with fewer benefits, less satisfaction, fewer recognized skills, less job security and fewer choices about how to provide care and what care to provide.

Little, if any, data are available on the current skill mix of providers, but research from various caregiver organizations reveals a shift to the lowest trained and lowest paid women (Sky 1995). The shift to community is frequently a shift away from a unionized and skilled workforce, and from the protection of pay equity or such other employment standards that remain. Without successor rights, women find it difficult to maintain even the lower wages and benefits that they have won in the community sector.

The women who work in the health sector have been resisting these trends. The nurses have been particularly successful in being heard, although the support promised them falls short of their demands. Midwives and nurse practitioners have also gained a place, countering the more general move to privatization. Other workers have been less successful, especially those who work in home care. However, the Ontario Nurses Association (ONA) has won a first contract with a for-profit home care firm and the Service Employees International Union (SEIU) has just organized a large group of home care workers, a significant proportion of whom are women of colour and immigrant women. Several unions are actively organizing in this field.

The SEIU also successfully challenged the government's repeal of proxy regulations that had extended pay equity benefits to many women working in community health care. The provision allowed these women to make significant wage gains, a victory that meant some of the most vulnerable women saw their wages rise to a more appropriate level, at least for the time being (Armstrong 1996). The increases are currently paid by the government and cannot be factored into service contracts in long-term care. However, it is not clear how the government takes these payments into account when approving CCAC contracts.

Unpaid caregivers have been less organized but have become increasingly vocal. The requirement that their services be exhausted before home care is publicly provided may well provoke further resistance from these already heavily burdened providers.

There seems to be very little research on the health of health care providers, paid or unpaid, other than the musculoskeletal study and the Armstrong and Jansen project now underway (OHCOWI 1998; Armstrong and Jansen interviews 1999). Although the research on home care does link women in the household to the formal health care system, we could not find research linking the changes in paid work to women's domestic lives. Preliminary analysis of the Armstrong and Jansen interviews with long-term care providers suggests that the consequences are profound. Asked what differences reforms make to their domestic relations, the prompt response has been "No sex life" (Armstrong and Jansen interviews 1999).

Research

Primarily because the government appointed a Nursing Task Force, there is a considerable amount of information on nurses. There is, however, much less information on other workers, and what is available comes more from unions and community groups than it does from the government or universities.

The joint McMaster and University of Toronto nursing research unit produces a variety of research data and analysis. The University of Toronto's Home Care Evaluation and Research Centre investigates many aspects of home care and the Institute for Clinical Evaluative Sciences tracks a wide range of clinical interventions. Their focuses, however, are neither on women's health nor on female health workers.

A number of university centres concentrate on women's health issues. The Centre for Research in Women's Health, a joint project of Sunnybrook and Women's College Health Sciences Centre and the University of Toronto is one example, and the Institute of Gerontology and the McMaster Research Centre for the Promotion of Women's Health at McMaster University are other examples of research units that are sensitive to women's concerns. But, as far as we could discover, only NNEWH has identified health care reform and work in this sector as women's issues. Some differences among women, such as age, have been considered but there is not extensive research on differences among women as these relate to health care reform.

Privatization is a major problem for researchers. It is difficult both to monitor and to assess, particularly in terms of the impact on different groups of women. Change is so rapid that it is virtually impossible to keep track of what is happening, let alone to assess the results. Combined with government secrecy, reversals in policy, programs announced but never delivered, the failure to produce or publish much data on women and limited research funding, much of which is tied to partnerships with the private sector, the issue is a researcher's nightmare. It is also a researcher's dream, because it leaves plenty of scope for new and innovative work on women from different groups.

Notes

1. Like many of the other major changes in Ontario, these rules are set out in regulations rather than legislation, making them both less democratic and less visible.
2. For the contrary view, see for example Henry Mintzberg (1989), *Mintzberg on Management* (New York: Free Press), esp. chap. 10. He recently observed that we now have the cult of measurable efficiency in health care. "We're starting to find out what we lost, but it took years to find out. They knew what they were saving instantly." Quoted in Jamie Swift, "Saving the Corporate Soul," *Canadian Forum* (June 1999): 19.
3. This is not to imply that discrimination and exclusion are absent from health care. Indeed, there is evidence that both are present.
4. Separation rates per 1,000 population were 81.8 for women and 48.8 for men. Days of care of separations, rate per 1,000 population, were 537.6 for women and 403.4 for men.
5. Bill 26, known as the Omnibus Bill, was introduced in late 1995 and passed in 1996. At 221 pages, it amended 44 statutes, created three new Acts and repealed two others. The changes were organized into 17 schedules, and came with a compendium of about 2,225 pages consisting largely of excerpts from the 44 Acts slated for amendment.
6. The Government reports that in 1997-98 it recruited 69 physicians to positions in under-serviced areas, although it is unclear how this figure relates to need or to the number leaving under-serviced areas. (See Ontario Ministry of Health (1998e), *Business Plan 1998-1999*, Key Achievements section.)

7. The King's Health Centre is no more, having been forced out of business when its co-owners fled the country amidst charges of fraud. They have since returned to Canada to face criminal charges.
8. According to the Service Employees International Union, a study conducted by the technical staff at the Occupational Health Clinics for Ontario Workers shows that nursing home work is three times more dangerous than construction work, and that nursing assistants, aides and orderlies experience an average of three times as many lost-time injuries due to sprains and strains as do other occupations. See Network News (19 July 1999), an email newsletter produced by the SEIU Canadian office; Occupational Health for Ontario Workers Inc. (Toronto) (July 1998), "Musculoskeletal Complaints in the Private and Public Nursing Homes: Results of a Questionnaire Survey."
9. The right to appeal long-term care decisions has apparently been instituted as part of the regulation adopted in July 1999, placing CCACs under the *Long-Term Care Act*.

References

Abelson, Julian, and Brian Hutchison. 1994. "Primary Health Care Delivery Models: What Can Ontario Learn from Other Jurisdictions "A Review of the Literature." Submitted to the Ontario Ministry of Health.

Abraham, Carolyn. 1999. "Early Release of Newborns Linked to Health Problems." *Globe and Mail*, 10 August, A1-A2.

Akyeampong, Ernest. 1997. "A Statistical Portrait of the Trade Union Movement." *Perspectives on Labour and Income* 9 (Winter).

Anastakis, Catherine, and Chuck Rachlis. n.d. "Options and Choices for Workers' Compensation in Canada." Markham, ON: Liberty International Canada.

Armstrong, Pat. 1996. Affidavit, Service Employees International Union and Ontario, Ontario Court of Justice, General Division.

Armstrong, Pat, and Hugh Armstrong. 1996. *Wasting Away: The Undermining of Canadian Health Care*. Toronto: Oxford University Press.

Armstrong, Pat, and Irene Jansen with Erin Connell and Mavis Sones. 1999. Interviews for "Assessing the Impact of Restructuring and Work Reorganization in Long-Term Care: Workers Issues: Available from nnewh@yorku.ca."

Armstrong, Pat *et al*. 1993. "Report on Prior Learning Assessment for the Transitional Council, College of Midwives of Ontario." Toronto.

—. 1997a. "The Consequences of Government Policy Changes in Long-Term Care in Ontario: A Survey of Care Providers." A report prepared for the Canadian Union of Public Employees and the Service Employees International Union.

—. 1997b. "The Promise and the Price: New Work Organizations in Ontario Hospitals." In Pat Armstrong *et al., Medical Alert: New Work Organizations in Health Care*, 31-68. Toronto: Garamond.

—. 1997c. "When Patients Don't Matter." In Pat Armstrong *et al., Medical Alert: New Work Organizations in Health Care*, 69-129. Toronto: Garamond.

—. 2000. "Heal Thyself": Managing Health Care Reform. Toronto: Garamond.

Aronson, Jane. 1993. "Giving Consumers a Say in Policy Development: Influencing Policy or Just Being Heard." *Canadian Public Policy* 19.

Aronson, Jane and Sheila Neysmith. 1997. "The Retreat of the State and Long-Term Provision: Implications for Frail Elderly People, Unpaid Family Carers and Paid Home Care Workers." *Studies in Political Economy* 53 (Summer): 37-66.

Association of Ontario Midwives. 1998. "Fact Sheet. Midwifery in Ontario: An Overview." Toronto: AOM.

—. n.d. "Fact Sheet. Cost-Effectiveness of Midwifery Care." Toronto: AOM.

Barer, Morris L., Robert Evans and Clyde Hertzman. 1995. "Avalanche or Glacier? Health Care and the Demographic Rhetoric. "*Canadian Journal on Aging* 14 (2).

Barlow, Maude. 1999. "Start of the End of Medicare." *National Post*, 4 February, A18.

Baumgart, Alice. 1997. "Hospital Reform and Nursing Labour Market Trends Across Canada." *Medical Care* 35 (10). Supplement.

Bezanson, Kate and Louise Noce. 1999. *Costs, Closures and Confusion: People in Ontario Talk About Health Care.* Toronto: Caledon Institute of Social Policy.

Bourgeault, Ivy Lynn and Mary Fynes. 1997. "Integrating Lay and Nurse-Midwifery into the US and Canadian Health Care Systems." *Social Science and Medicine* 44 (7).

Boyle, Theresa. 1998. "Ontario Prescribes New Patient Care System." *Toronto Star*, 27 May, A7.

—. 1999. "Province Limiting Home Care to Two Hours a Day: Hampton." *Toronto Star*, 23 July, A8.

Canadian Institute for Health Information (CIHI). 1998. *National Health Expenditure Trends, 1975-1998.* Ottawa: CIHI.

Canadian Union of Public Employees (CUPE). 1995. *Primary Health Care Reform: Alternatives to Fee-for-Service Medicine.* Ottawa: CUPE.

—. 1998. "Cooking Up a Storm: Part II." Ottawa: CUPE.

Care Watch Toronto. 1999. "Behind Closed Doors: Home Care Stories from the Community." Toronto: CWT.

Chamberlain, Art. 1997. "Radical Changes, Coming Soon, to Patient Care." *Toronto Star*, 4 December, A8.

Chappell, Neena. 1992. *Social Support and Aging.* Toronto: Butterworths.

—. 1997. "Health Care Reform: Implications for Seniors." *Journal of Aging Studies* 11:171-75.

Choiniere, Jacqueline A. 1993. "A Case Study Examination of Nurses and Patient Information Technology." In Pat Armstrong, Jacqueline Choiniere and Elaine Day, *Vital Signs: Nursing in Transition*, 59-87. Toronto: Garamond.

College of Nurses *et al.* 1997. "Preserving the Culture of Care in Ontario's Health System." Submission to the HSRC on its July 1997 Discussion Paper, "Rebuilding Ontario's Health System: Interim Planning Guidelines and Implementation Strategies." Toronto.

Community Health Nurses Interest Group (CHNIG) and Registered Nurses Association of Ontario (RNAO). 1998. Submission to the Nursing Task Force, Toronto, 4 November.

Coutts, Jane. 1997. "OMA Boots MD from Board." *Globe and Mail*, 13 December, A3.

—. 1999a. "Doctors' Aides Ready, Willing but Unable: A Possible Solution to Ontario's Chronic MD Shortage, Qualified Nurse Practitioners Are Hobbled by a Lack of Funds." *Globe and Mail*, 3 August, A5.

—. 1999b. "Home-Care Limits Concealed During Vote: Coalition." *Globe and Mail*, 11 August, A7.

Cybulski, Nancy *et al.* 1997. *Reinventing Hospitals: On Target for the 21st Century.* Toronto: McLeod.

Daly, Rita. 1998a. "Home Sweet Profit." *Toronto Star*, 22 March, F1.

—. 1998b. "Abortions Banned in Wellesley Takeover." *Toronto Star*, 10 April, A1.

Daly, Rita, and Kellie Hudson. 1999. "Reform Brings Healthy Profits." *Toronto Star*, 29 March, A7.

Das Gupta, Tania. 1996. "Anti-Black Racism in Nursing in Ontario." *Studies in Political Economy* 51 (Fall): 97-116.

Deber, Raisa and Paul Williams. 1995. "Policy, Payment and Participation: Long Term Care Reform in Ontario." *Canadian Journal on Aging* 14 (2): 294-318.

Denton, Margaret *et al.* 1998. "Healthy Work Environments in Community-Based Health and Social Service Agencies." Stage Two Report: Volunteer Questionnaire Findings. Hamilton: McMaster Research Centre for the Promotion of Women's Health, McMaster University.

Eberts, Mary et al. 1987. *Report of the Task Force on the Implementation of Midwifery in Ontario,* Toronto: Queen's Printer for Ontario.

Egan, Kelly. 1997. "Cobden Nursing Home to Close." *Ottawa Citizen*, 10 July, D6.

Environics Research Group. 1999. "Government Spending and Preferences and Perceived Quality of Hospital Care." Toronto: ERG.

Esteves, Elizabeth. 2000. "The New Wageless Worker: Volunteering and Market-Guided Health Care Reform." In Diana L. Gustafson, ed., *Care and Consequences: The Impact of Health Care Reform on Canadian Women*, 154-76. Halifax: Fernwood.

Fuller, Colleen. 1998. *Caring for Profit*. Vancouver: New Star.

Globe and Mail. 1998. "Doctors' House Calls Make a Controversial Comeback." 20 March, A6.

Greenglass Esther R., and Ronald J. Burke. 1997. "Hospital Restructuring, Anger and Hostility in Nurses." Paper presented at the 11th Conference of the European Health Psychology Society, Bordeaux, France.

Greenspon, Edward, and Hugh Windsor. 1997. "Spending Increases Favoured, Poll Finds." *Globe and Mail*, 23 January, A1 and A8.

Gunderson, Morley, and Douglas Hyatt. 1996. "Health Sector Human Resources in Ontario: Results from the HSTAP's Survey." Toronto, 17 June.

Guruge, Sepali, Lynn Morrison and Gail Donner. 2000. "Canadian Health Reform and the Impact on Recent Immigrant and Refugee Women." In Diana L. Gustafson, ed., *Care and Consequences: The Impact of Health Care Reform on Canadian Women*, 222-42. Halifax: Fernwood.

Hammer, Michael, and James Champy. 1993. *Re-engineering the Corporation: A Manifesto for Business Revolution*. New York: Harper.

Harden, Joel Davidson. 1999. "The Rhetoric of Community Control in a Neo-Liberal Era." In Daniel Drache and Terry Sullivan, eds., *Health Reform: Public Success, Private Failure*. London: Routledge.

Harvey, Robin. 1998a."Clinic Hit by Arrest and Complaints." *Toronto Star*, 13 June, A25.

—. 1998b."Why Cosmetic Surgery Rules Need a Facelift." *Toronto Star*, 14 June, A1.

Hassen, Philip. 1993. *Rx for Hospitals: New Hope for Medicare in the Nineties*. Toronto: Stoddart.

Health Canada. n.d. [1998]."Health System Reform in Ontario." Ottawa: Health Canada.

Health Insurance Act, Regulation 552, Amended to O. Reg. 378/98, section 10 (1).

Health Insurance Act. Revised Statute of Ontario 1990 as amended to 1997, 28 July 1998.

Health Services Restructuring Commission (HSRC). 1996. *Pembroke Health Services Restructuring Report*. December.

—. 1997. "Rebuilding Ontario's Health System: Interim Planning Guidelines and Implementation Strategy. Home Care, Long Term Care, Mental Health, Rehabilitation and Sub-Acute Care. A Discussion Paper." Toronto: HSRC.

Holyoke, Paul, and Lyn Elkin. 1995."Rehabilitation Services Inventory and Quality Project: Phase One Report." Toronto: Institute for Work and Health.

Hudson, Kellie. 1998a."Health Care Revamp to be Tested in 5 Towns." *Toronto Star*, 23 April, A8.

—. 1998b."Ontario Nursing Homes Get Facelift." *Toronto Star*, 11 June, A8.

Ibbitson, John. 1998."New-Style Health Care Has Test Run." *Ottawa Citizen*, 5 March, A3.

Katherine, Wendy. 1995."A Report on the Ethics of Client Selection Workshop." *Association of Ontario Midwives Journal* 1 (2).

Landsberg, Michele.1997. "Patients to Pay Painful Price for Restructuring Plans." *Toronto Star*, 27 April, A2.

—. 1998."Home Care Privatization Squeezes Sick to Ensure Profits." *Toronto Star*, January 31, F1.

Liberty Canada. 1996. "New Approaches to Workers' Safety and Compensation in Ontario."Markham, ON: Liberty Canada.

Lindgren, April. 1999."Ontario Health Ads Tell Selective Truths." *Ottawa Citizen*, May.

Lindgren, April, and Michael Den Tandt. 1998."Home Care: Sold to the Highest Bidder." *Ottawa Citizen*, 1 June, A6.

Lindsay, Colin. 1999."Seniors: A Diverse Group Aging Well." *Canadian Social Trends* 52 (Spring).

Long-Term Care Act, 1994, Chapter 26, November 1998.

Lum, Janet M. and A. Paul Williams. 2000."Professional Fault Lines: Nursing in Ontario after the Regulated Health Professions Act," in Diana L. Gustafson, ed., *Care and Consequences: The Impact of Health Care Reform on Canadian Women*, 49-71. Halifax: Fernwood.

Maher, Janet. 1999. Personal communication to authors, 13 August.

Mallan, Caroline. 1999."Hefty Price for the 'Right to Know.'" *Toronto Star*, 22 July, A6.

Markham, Barbara and Jonathan Lomas. 1995."Review of the Multi-Hospital Arrangements Literature: Benefits, Disadvantages and Lessons for Implementation." *Health Care Management Forum* 8 (Fall).

Medline, Elaine. 1997."You Get Better, Others Get Richer." *Ottawa Citizen*, 10 February, A1.

Mintzberg, Henry. 1989. *Mintzberg on Management*. New York: Free Press.

Munter, Alex. 1999. Memo to Paul Brent/John Ruttle, CJOH.

National Union of Provincial and General Employees (NUPGE). 1997."Medical Lab Services: Private vs. Public Delivery Systems." Nepean, ON: NUPGE.

—. 1998. "Health Restructuring Update: A Province by Province Review. "Nepean, ON: NUPGE.

Nursing Task Force. 1999. Report. *Good Nursing, Good Health: An Investment in the 21st Century*. Toronto: Ontario Ministry of Health.

O'Brien-Pallas, Linda, Andrea Baumann and Jacqueline Lochhass-Gerlach. 1998."Health Human Resources: A Preliminary Analysis of Nursing Personnel in Ontario." Toronto: Nursing Effectiveness, Utilization and Outcomes Research Unit, University of Toronto.

O'Brien-Pallas, Linda et al. 1995. "The Nursing and Personal Care Provider Study: Final Report." Toronto:

O'Loughlin, Jennifer. 1999."Understanding the role of ethnicity in chronic disease: a challenge for the new millenium." *Canadian Medical Association Journal* 161 (2).

Occupational Health Clinics for Ontario Workers Inc. (Toronto). (OHCOWI). 1998."Musculoskeletal Complaints in the Private and Public Nursing Homes: Results of a Questionnaire Survey."

Older Women's Network (OWN) and the Registered Nurses Association of Ontario (RNAO). n.d. Joint Statement,"The Impact of Health-Care Restructuring on Older Women." Toronto.

Ontario Conservative Party. 1993. *The Common Sense Revolution*. Toronto: Ontario Conservative Party.

Ontario Health Coalition (OHC). 1999. Fact Sheet #8. Toronto: OHC.

Ontario Home Health Care Providers' Association (OHHCPA). 1999."The Competitive Process in Contracting For Home Health and Social Care Provision." Hamilton: OHHCPA.

Ontario Hospital Association (OHA). 1998."The Hospital-Home Care Interface: Current State and Future Opportunities." Toronto: OHA.

Ontario Hospital Association and The University of Toronto (G. Ross, principal investigator). 1998. *The Hospital Report '98: A System-Wide Review of Ontario's Hospitals*. Toronto: OHA.

Ontario. Government of Ontario Press Releases. 1998a."Government Names Membership of Women's Health Council." *Canada NewsWire*. <http://www.newswire.ca/government/...releases/December 1998/08/c2902.html>. 8 December.

—. Government of Ontario Press Releases. 1998b."Minister Witmer Launches Women's Health Council." *Canada NewsWire*. <http://www.newswire.ca.government/...releases/January 1998/23/c5369.html>. 23 January.

Ontario. Ministry of Health. [1993]. *Hospital Statistics 1991/92*. Toronto: Ministry of Health.

—. 1993a."Ambulance Services." Toronto: Queen's Printer for Ontario.

—. 1993b."Midwifery Questions and Answers: General, Out-of-Hospital Birthing Centres, Funding, Midwives in Hospitals, Education." Mimeograph.

—. 1996. Long Term Care Division."Provincial Requirements for the Request for Proposal Process for the Provision of In-Home Services, Supplies and Equipment." Toronto: Queen's Printer of Ontario.

—. 1997."Access to Quality Health Care in Rural and Northern Ontario: The Rural and Northern Ontario Health Care Framework." Toronto: Ministry of Health.

—. 1998a. "Long-Term Care Community Based Services Activity." Toronto: Queen's Printer for Ontario.

—. 1998b."Long Term Care, Central Region: Suggestions for Priorization and Eligibility Criteria for CCAC's." Toronto: Queen's Printer for Ontario.
—. 1998c."Request for Proposals to Develop 420 Long-Term Care Facility Beds in the Regional Municipality of York." Toronto: Queen's Printer for Ontario.
—. 1998d. "Business Plan 1998-1999. Minister's Message." *Government of Ontario.* <www.gov.on.ca/english/pub/ministry/bplan98.html#report>.
—. 1998e. *Business Plan 1998-1999.* "Key Strategies and Commitments." Toronto: Queen's Printer for Ontario.
—. 1998f. Standard Agreement Between the Minister of Health and the CCAC.
—. 1999. *"Chronic Care Co-payment."* Toronto: Queen's Printer for Ontario.
Ontario. Ministry of Health and the Ontario Medical Association. 1998. Schedule of Benefits Working Group."Summary of 1998 Updates and Definitions for the OHIP Schedule of Benefits." Toronto: Ministry of Health and OMA.
Ontario. Office of the Provincial Auditor. 1998. *1998 Annual Report.* Chap. 3, "Ministry of Health, Long-Term Care Community Based Service Activity." Toronto: Queen's Printer for Ontario.
Ontario Women's Directorate. 1999a."Welcome Page, Prevention." *Government of Ontario.* <http://www.gov.on.ca/owd/news/May99/prevention.htm>.
Ontario Women's Directorate 1999b. Minister Responsible for Women's Issues. "A Message from Diane Cunningham." *Government of Ontario.* <http://www.gov.on.ca/owd/news/may99...ual_assult_prev.month_message>.
Ontario Women's Directorate. 1999c. Minister Responsible for Women's Issues. "The Prevention of Violence against Women: An Agenda for Action Progress Report - Safety." *Government of Ontario.* <http://www.gov.on.ca/owd/news/May99/safety.htm>.
Ontario Women's Directorate. 1999d. Untitled. *Government of Ontario.* <http://www.gov.on.ca/owd/news/june98/99-grants/recipients.htm>.
Orwen, Patricia, and Laurie Monsebraaten. 1998."Pregnant Women Lose Benefit." *Toronto Star,* 16 April, A2.
Ottawa Citizen. 1999."This Secrecy Is Unhealthy." 10 August, B4.
Pembroke Civic Hospital and Lowe v. Health Services Restructuring Commission, (1997). 394/97.
Priest, Lisa. 1999."Restraints Used Often on Chronic-Care Patients: Study." *Toronto Star,* 6 August, A2.
Provincial Coordinating Committee on Community and Academic Health Science Centre Relations. 1996. Subcommittee on Primary Health Care,"New Directions in Primary Health Care." Toronto.
Public Hospitals Act. Revised statutes of Ontario, 1990, Chapter P.40, as amended to 1997, 30 September 1998.
Queen Street Mental Health Centre Medical Staff Association. 1997."Submission to the HSRC in Response to the Metro Toronto HSR Report, March 1977."
Registered Nurses Association of Ontario. (RNAO). 1999. "RNAO's Report Card: Initial Response." 30 March.
Saint Elizabeth Health Care. 1998. Submission to the Nursing Task Force, Markham, Ontario.
Sky, Laura. 1995. "Lean and Mean: The Creation of the Generic Worker and the Deregulation of Health Care," Working Paper 95-3, Health Research Project, Ontario Federation of Labour.
Statistics Canada. 1992. *1991 Census: Employment Income by Occupation.* Ottawa: Ministry of Industry, Science and Technology.
—. 1993. *Hospital Annual Statistics 1989-90, Part 5.* Ottawa: Ministry of Industry, Science and Technology.
—. 1995. *Women in Canada. A Statistical Report,* 3rd ed. Ottawa: Ministry of Industry.
—. 1999. *Annual Demographic Statistics, 1998.* Ottawa: Ministry of Industry. Cat. No. 91-213.
Struthers, James. 1997. "Reluctant Partners: State Regulation of Private Nursing Homes in Ontario, 1941-72." In Raymond Blake, Penny Bryden and Frank Strain, eds., *The Welfare State in Canada: Past, Present and Future,* 171-92. Concord: Irwin.
Swift, Jamie. 1999. "Saving the Corporate Soul." *Canadian Forum* (June).

Talaga, Tanya. 1999."Ethnic Death Rates Studied." *Toronto Star*, 27 July, A3, reporting on Tej Sheth *et al.* 1999."Cardiovascular and Cancer Mortality Among Canadians of European, South Asian and Chinese Origin from 1979 to 1993: An Analysis of 1.2 Million Deaths." *Canadian Medical Association Journal* 161(2): 132-38.

Tarman, Vera Ingrid. 1990. *Privatization and Health Care: The Case of Ontario Nursing Homes*, Toronto: Garamond.

Thow, Dr David. 1998."Is There a Doctor in the House?" *Globe and Mail*, 2 July, A17.

Toronto Star. 1997. "Health Commission Loses Independence.", 29 June, F2.

Van Wagner, Vicki. 1988."Women Organizing for Midwifery in Ontario." *Resources for Feminist Research* 17 (3).

Vatri Boydell, Katherine. 1996."Mothering Adult Children with Schizophrenia: Hidden Realities of Caring," PhD dissertation, Department of Sociology, York University, Toronto.

Walkom, Thomas. 1998."Hard Labor of Love." *Toronto Star*, 31 October, 31.

—. 1999."Money Woes Leave Home Care in Sad Shape." *Toronto Star,* 27 April, A2.

White, Jerry. 1990. *Hospital Strike: Women, Unions and Public Sector Conflict*. Toronto: Thompson.

Wilkins, Kathryn and Evelyn Park. 1998. "Home Care in Canada." *Health Reports* 10 (1).

Women's College Hospital. 1997. Submission to the Health Services Restructuring Commission, Maintaining Women's Health Values in the Context of Change. 9 May.

Woods, Cindy. 1996."Editorial: Health Ministry Not Forthcoming with Information." *Hospital News* 9 (August).

Woodward, C.A. *et al.* 1996."A Profile of Ontario Family Physicians Early in Their Careers: Gender Differences and Policy Implications." Mimeograph.

Woolhandler, Steffie and David U. Himmelstein. 1999."When Money Is the Mission — The High Cost of Investor-Owned Care." *New England Journal of Medicine* 341(6).

Working Group on Health Services Utilization (WGHSU). 1994. *When Less Is Better: Using Canada's Hospitals Efficiently*. Report for the Federal/Provincial/Territorial Deputy Ministers of Health. Ottawa: WGHSU.

Missing Links: The Effects of Health Care Privatization on Women in Manitoba and Saskatchewan

Kay Willson and Jennifer Howard

INTRODUCTION

Prairie Women and the Changing Health System

Prairie women's organizations played an important role in the historical development of a publicly funded and administered health care system in Canada. Saskatchewan is the birthplace of medicare. While former Saskatchewan Premier Tommy Douglas is often credited as one of the "fathers of medicare," prairie women like Violet McNaughton, Sophia Dixon and Louise Lucas could well be called the "mothers of medicare." Years before the introduction of medicare, organizations of rural women campaigned for a publicly funded, locally controlled system that would ensure medical assistance to all. They raised public awareness and built alliances that encouraged prairie farm organizations, the Canadian Commonwealth Federation (CCF) and eventually the Saskatchewan New Democratic Party (NDP) government to develop a publicly funded, universal health insurance program – allocating health care services on the basis of need rather than the ability to pay. Recognizing the effects of poverty and inequality on the well-being of people and communities, many also campaigned for a radical redistribution of wealth and a greater voice in decision-making (Taylor 1998).

In 1947, the CCF introduced a public program of universal hospitalization insurance for residents of Saskatchewan. Manitoba brought in its first universal hospital insurance on 1 July 1958, with the support of the federal government. In 1962, the Saskatchewan NDP introduced *The Medical Care Insurance Act,* providing universal public health insurance for physicians' services. In 1969, Manitoba joined the federal government and other provinces in adopting medicare.

During the past fifteen years, the governments of Manitoba and Saskatchewan, like those in other provinces, have introduced major changes to the health care system. Several of these reforms can be understood as a renegotiation of the boundaries between public and private responsibility for health care. Privatization in the health care system has significant impacts on women as users of health services, as health care workers, as unpaid care providers and as citizens engaged in shaping the future of the health care system. This chapter provides an overview of health care privatization in Manitoba and Saskatchewan and identifies some of its impacts on various groups of women in the two provinces.

Health Reform in Manitoba and Saskatchewan

From 1988 to 1999, Manitoba was governed by the Progressive Conservative Party, led by Premier Gary Filmon. In the early 1990s, the Manitoba Minister of Health committed to achieving the goals of health reform without introducing user fees or compromising "the fundamental concept of Medicare" (Manitoba Health 1992, v). There was no reference to privatization in any of the health care reform documents authored by Manitoba Health. However, Manitoba health care reforms included several large-scale attempts to turn over parts of the public health care system to private for-profit corporations. The Conservative government was not ideologically opposed to privatization, as can be seen by attempts to privatize parts of the Home Care Program, contract out food services at Winnipeg hospitals and enter into a contract with Electronic Data Systems (EDS) and the Royal Bank of Canada to construct a Provincial Health Information Network. In 1999, the NDP was elected to a majority government and Gary Doer became Premier. Health care was a major – perhaps deciding – issue in this election.

During the 1980s, the Progressive Conservative government in Saskatchewan, led by Premier Grant Devine, privatized some parts of the health care system by eliminating the publicly funded, publicly delivered school dental program, reducing coverage for prescription drugs, and cutting public funding for health and social programs. In 1991, Saskatchewan elected an NDP government led by Premier Roy Romanow. During the 1990s, health care reforms in Saskatchewan placed limits on some forms of health care privatization while allowing other forms of privatization to expand. For example, there were no premiums charged for the provincial health insurance plan and the burden of private payment for health care was not as high as in some other provinces. In 1996, the government, concerned about the potential expansion of private health facilities, introduced *The Health Facilities Licensing Act*, which placed restrictions on private health facilities by requiring them to secure a license from the province, and prohibiting them from charging patients extra fees. On the other hand, private expenditures for health care in Saskatchewan have risen, hospitals have been closed, care has been shifted from institutions to private households, long-term care in private personal care homes has increased, and some health sector services have been contracted out to private, for-profit corporations. In both provinces there is evidence of privatization creeping into the health care system. More health care costs have been transferred to the individual as a result of the shift from institutional to "community"[1] care. This trend has also transferred carework to private households. While many rely on public home care services or the unpaid carework of family and friends, others with the financial resources have utilized private health services to meet some of their needs.

In the 1990s, both Manitoba and Saskatchewan embarked on programs of major health policy changes in response to escalating provincial health expenditures and decreasing federal contributions for health care and social services. Although these processes occurred under ideologically different governments, they had very similar goals and components:

- a shift to population health frameworks with an emphasis on the determinants of health, disease prevention and health promotion;

- a shift to regional governance of health services; and

- a shift from institutional care to "community" and home-based care.

These various health policy changes were made to meet the goals of effectiveness and efficiency – achieving better health outcomes for individuals at the lowest possible cost to the provinces.

Health care reform in Manitoba and Saskatchewan occurred at a time when provinces were receiving less federal funding for health care and social services. In 1995, the federal government introduced the Canadian Health and Social Transfer (CHST), which effectively abolished national standards and severely cut funding for social programs. It is estimated that this change will remove $1.1 billion from social program spending in Manitoba by 2002 (Black and Silver 1999, 13). In 1996-97, federal transfers for health to the province of Saskatchewan were reduced by $47 million (Saskatchewan 1996). Controlling public expenditures for health has been a priority and shifting to population health was seen as an opportunity to cut health care costs.

In 1992, the Saskatchewan NDP government embarked on a process of health reform outlined in *A Saskatchewan Vision for Health: A Framework for Change*. Some of the problems with the health system, according to this document, were an emphasis on disease treatment rather than on health promotion; overutilization of institutional care; fragmented service; and escalating health costs in a time of fiscal crisis. Noting that 60 per cent of the provincial health budget was allocated to hospitals and long-term care institutions, the government embarked on a strategy of "streamlining institutional delivery systems." Health reforms were designed to "encourage and enable people to take more responsibility for their own health," and "make the health system more effective and efficient" (Saskatchewan Health 1992a, 10-11).

In 1992, Manitoba Health published *Quality Health for Manitobans: The Action Plan*, which set out the goals of health reform. These goals included, among others: to provide appropriate, effective and efficient health services; to develop mechanisms to assess and monitor quality of care, utilization and cost-effectiveness; to promote reasonable public expectations of health care; and to promote delivery of alternative and less expensive services (Manitoba Health 1992, 2). To address concerns with the rising cost of health services, *The Action Plan* included plans to "restructure the hospital system" and "reform systemic cost drivers" (ibid., 19).

Population Health

Policy makers in both provinces adopted a population health philosophy, recognizing that determinants of health included income, social status, education, environmental conditions and social support, as well as biology and access to health care services. In 1994, the Saskatchewan Provincial Health Council issued a report, *Population Health Goals for Saskatchewan: A Framework for Improved Health for All*, which set forth the following health goals for the province:

- to change our thinking about health and to consider the broad determinants of health;
- to provide equal opportunity for achieving health for all Saskatchewan people and communities;
- to foster healthy social environments for individuals, families and communities;
- to preserve and promote clean, safe physical environments which support health;
- to place more emphasis on health promotion and illness avoidance; and
- to improve health and create a healthier society through the cooperation and shared responsibility of all members of society. (Saskatchewan Provincial Health Council 1994)

Both provinces identify several determinants of health: income and social status, education, employment and working conditions, personal health practices and coping skills, biology and genetic endowment, child development, social support networks, physical environment and health services (Manitoba Health 1996, 4; Saskatchewan Health 1999a, 11-12). Recognizing that the determinants of health involved policy areas beyond the delivery of health services, the Manitoba government promised a commitment to "healthy public policy" which would ensure that "every major action and policy of government will be evaluated in terms of its implications for...health" (Manitoba Health 1992, 10).

There are some indications that gender has occasionally been recognized as a determinant of health. In 1999, Manitoba Health announced the formation of a Women's Health Unit within the department, including a Director of Women's Health responsible for implementing strategies related to women's health needs. In 1999, Saskatchewan Health's *Population Health Promotion Model: A Resource Binder* was revised to include a section on gender as a health determinant (Saskatchewan Health 1999b).

Regional Governance

Health reforms included the integration of health services under the jurisdiction of new regional governance bodies, known as health districts in Saskatchewan and Regional Health Authorities (RHAs) in Manitoba.

In 1993, Saskatchewan passed *The Health Districts Act* and established 30 health districts in the southern half of the province. In 1995, most Saskatchewan Health community-based programs were transferred to the health districts and the first elections for district health boards were held. In 1996, two more health districts were established in northern Saskatchewan (Saskatchewan Health 1996-97, 45). Saskatchewan Health continues to play a role in defining the overall framework for health care in the province, but health services are now planned and delivered by the districts, each governed by a district health board of elected and appointed members. Balanced gender representation is one of the criteria considered in board appointments, and in 1999, there were 188 women (or 51%) of 367 district health board members in the province (Sherry Miller, Saskatchewan Health, personal communication November 1999).

In 1996, the Manitoba government introduced *The Regional Health Authorities and Consequential Amendments Act*, creating ten RHAs outside of Brandon and Winnipeg. One year later, the government introduced legislation to create the Brandon Regional Health Authority, as well as two health authorities in the city of Winnipeg. The Winnipeg Hospital Authority (WHA) had authority over hospitals and the Winnipeg Long Term and Community Care Authority (WCA) had responsibility for community health clinics and other community-based care, including responsibility for home care and mental health. Following its election, the NDP government took steps to merge the two Winnipeg Health Authorities as a way to cut costs and minimize bureaucracy. These authorities are governed by government-appointed boards. There is no provision for gender equality in board appointments. Recently the government changed the rules governing RHA board appointments, allowing health care workers to serve on them. Women have historically been under-represented on RHA Boards.

In both provinces, regional health bodies are given some flexibility in determining the particular combination of services to be delivered within the region in order to be more responsive to local health needs. District health boards receive funding from Saskatchewan Health largely on a population needs-based formula. The district health boards allocate funding to health service providers and facilities within the district. A district health board can, for example, decide to expand the range of home care services offered within the district, hire an advanced clinical practice nurse to provide primary health care in rural areas, or establish a community development team to work with local groups. It is also within their jurisdiction to directly provide or contract out some services – such as meal services, laundry and cleaning for health care facilities – to for-profit companies.

Both Saskatchewan health districts and Manitoba RHAs are responsible for service delivery, health needs assessment, regional health planning and evaluation. Provincial departments of health retain authority over funding allocations, legislation and policy, and maintaining standards of service (Manitoba Health 1996, 5). Regional health bodies are also responsible for ensuring that all residents have access to a set of core services; however, regional governance structures make decisions on the appropriate method, site and allocation of staff resources to deliver these services. Not all core services are offered in every geographic region or by every region or district.

The Shift to "Community" and Home-based Care

The reduction in hospital services has been seen as an important strategy for controlling public expenditures. In Manitoba and Saskatchewan, shifting care out of institutions into the "community" was a key component of health care reform.

In both provinces this shift resulted in bed closures and funding decreases for hospitals. In Manitoba, the share of provincial health expenditures allocated for hospitals decreased from 56 per cent of the health budget in 1977 to 54 per cent in 1987 to 46 per cent in 1998 (CIHI 2001). Between 1992 and 1998, 1,317 acute care hospital beds were closed in Manitoba, reducing the ratio of acute care beds from 4.8 per 1,000 persons to 3.6 per 1000 persons (Manitoba Health 1993, 1998). As part of its promise to "end hallway medicine" (a reference to the overcrowding of Winnipeg emergency rooms that led to the use of hospital hallways to house patients), in 1999 the newly elected NDP government in Manitoba announced a plan to open 138 acute care beds in the province (Manitoba Health News Release 1998).

During the 1980s, the Saskatchewan Conservative government pursued an active program of hospital and nursing home construction. While the number of institutional beds increased, operating budgets were tightened, staffing levels cut and concerns raised that the quality of care provided in institutions was being undermined. Under the NDP health reforms, 50 hospitals throughout Saskatchewan were closed or converted into community health centres. Between 1991-92 and 1994-95, 1,200 hospital beds were removed from the health system in the province. Between 1991-92 and 1996-97, funding for hospitals in Saskatchewan was reduced by $44 million, or from 37 per cent to 35 per cent of the total health budget (Saskatchewan Health 1996-97, 30). Part of the rationale for reducing hospital beds was that dollars saved could be redirected to more appropriate home and community-based care.

Women and Health Care Reform

There is little evidence of gender analysis in the framework documents that laid the foundation for health care reform. In response to our inquiry for documents pertaining to the impact of privatization and health care reform on women, we received the following reply from a former Deputy Minister of Health:

> While there is a basis for your inquiry into the impacts on women, [at] the time the decisions were taken by the government, the impacts by

gender were not a key component of the analysis... therefore one now can't readily obtain the information you need. (Duane Adams, personal communication 1999, used with permission)

Analyzing health care reform through a gender lens has been largely left up to non-government organizations (NGOs) such as the Manitoba-based Women and Health Reform Working Group, a coalition of provincial women's organizations. In its gender analysis of Manitoba health care reforms, it identified the scarcity of female appointments to RHA boards, the lack of gender-sensitive planning and the absence of information regarding the health care reform process as key concerns (Women and Health Reform Working Group 1997, 7). The Working Group argued that the shift to early discharge and community care meant that women bore an increased burden of providing care, while women in the health sector were experiencing job losses (ibid., 4). The Working Group also found that the Manitoba Core Services Agreement provided limited access to reproductive health services, such as birth control information, abortion and delivery in a woman's home community, and was lacking in woman-centred health promotion strategies (ibid., 8). It recommended that the regionalization legislation establish women's health advisory committees for each RHA. It also recommended that "gender analysis and gender-sensitive planning be incorporated into all policies and activities undertaken with respect to the health reform at the regional and provincial level, especially the Community Health Needs Assessment" (ibid., iii). These recommendations were not accepted by Manitoba Health. Community Health Needs Assessments (CHNAs) are carried out by regional health bodies in Manitoba and Saskatchewan. These form the basis for regional health plans, which are submitted to the appropriate provincial department of health for funding. In 1999, the Prairie Women's Health Centre of Excellence published a report titled *Invisible Women*, which examined health assessment and planning documents in Manitoba and Saskatchewan for evidence of gender-based analysis. Among the eight Manitoba RHAs and 17 Saskatchewan health districts participating in the study, there was little evidence of sex-disaggregated data, background information on women's health, gender analysis of health needs or gender-sensitive strategies for promoting health (Horne, Donner and Thurston 1999, 56-57).

PRIVATIZATION

Cutbacks in Public Funding for Health and Social Programs

During the late 1980s, the Saskatchewan Conservative government pursued a pro-privatization agenda, advocating cutbacks in public sector jobs, greater reliance on the market, contracting out of government services and the sale of Crown corporations. This is similar to the legislative and policy agenda forwarded by the Manitoba Conservative government in the 1990s.

In 1987, the Saskatchewan government announced a series of cutbacks in health and social programs. The Saskatchewan Public Health Association sponsored a study to examine the effects of provincial cutbacks on a wide array of health and social services. Brown (1987) provided an overview of the cutbacks, which effectively transferred costs to non-profit agencies, community groups, families and individuals. She noted the pressures placed on NGOs by rising demands for services and declining government funding. She described an increased reliance on community fundraising and the promotion of volunteerism in the provision of community services. She noted increases in user fees for persons in special care homes or receiving home care services. She argued that reductions in health care services, earlier discharge from hospitals, and declining community services for seniors were indirectly encouraging the growth of private sector nurses and caregivers. Brown reported cuts to groups engaged in advocacy for persons with disabilities, persons on social assistance and women. She concluded that funding cuts were increasing inequities in health and that natives, youth, children, the elderly, the disabled, psychiatric patients, the mentally handicapped and victims of abuse were the losers.

Privatizing the Costs of Health Care

Saskatchewan and Manitoba's health systems are funded through a combination of general tax revenues and federal transfer payments. The vast majority of health services and programs are publicly financed, without additional fees to patients. There are no health care premiums assessed to residents. However, some health services are funded by private health insurance, out-of-pocket payments, worker's compensation and public auto insurance. Many people pay privately for prescription drugs, dental care, optometry, podiatry, physiotherapy and other health services, complementary therapies, long-term care, and some home care services. In 1995, the National Forum on Health reported that approximately 72 per cent of the total health expenditures in Canada were publicly funded (National Forum on Health 1995, 3). In Saskatchewan and Manitoba, that figure was slightly higher than the national average at 74.8 per cent and 74.5 per cent, respectively (CIHI 1999, 99).

Private expenditures for health care in Saskatchewan and Manitoba indicate a steady and dramatic increase since 1990. Between 1990 and 1996, private health care expenditures increased by 43 per cent in Saskatchewan and 33 per cent in Manitoba. By 2000, private contributions had reached almost a quarter of total health care expenditures in both provinces – 24 per cent in Saskatchewan and 23 per cent in Manitoba (CIHI 2001, 73). In contrast, between 1990 and 1996, public financing of the health system increased by only 3.2 per cent in Saskatchewan and 7 per cent in Manitoba.

Increases in Deductibles and Co-payments

Changes in Provincial Prescription Drug Plans

The cost of prescription drugs is one of the fastest growing health care costs. Both Saskatchewan and Manitoba have provincial drug plans that partially cover the costs of prescription drugs for some segments of the population. Some changes to these plans have shifted responsibility for payment to individuals and private health insurance plans. As Manitoba and Saskatchewan were increasing deductibles and co-payments of provincial drug plans, federal legislation was passed that allowed pharmaceutical companies to retain patents on drugs for 20 years, delaying the introduction of cheaper, generic drugs. Between 1987 and 1996, the cost of prescription drugs in Canada rose by 93 per cent (Russell 1999, A12).

Changing Public Coverage of Health Services
Elimination of Children's Dental Health Programs

Payment for the majority of dental care in Manitoba and Saskatchewan is the responsibility of individuals and may be covered by private insurance. People receiving social assistance and Aboriginal people who are Status Indians receive insured dental care benefits. Manitoba and Saskatchewan independently introduced coverage for dental care for children as part of the publicly insured health plans. School-based dental health programs that featured strong prevention and education components were popular features of the children's dental health programs.

In 1987, the Conservative government in Saskatchewan announced the elimination of the 13-year-old school-based dental program, despite studies that indicated its effectiveness. In one of the clearest examples of privatization of health services in recent Saskatchewan history, 570 school-based dental clinics were closed. These services were delivered by public sector workers, most of whom were women employed as dental therapists and dental assistants. Under the new system, dentists in private practice became the main providers of dental services for children. Provincial coverage for children's dental services was discontinued for young people 14-17 years old.

The Manitoba Children's Dental Program operated from 1976 until 1993, providing dental treatment and prevention services to rural Manitoba children between the ages of 6 and 14. The treatment program was cancelled in 1993 and almost all clinical staff members were laid off. In 1995 the in-school fluoride rinse program was cancelled as well. Currently Manitoba Health has only one dental staff position, a Senior Dental Consultant working in the Public Health Branch. Manitoba Health does not currently support any dental treatment programs for children, adults or seniors.

Over time, financial responsibility for children's dental care has shifted to families and private dental insurance programs. Provincial governments continue to provide coverage for children on social assistance and in other low-income families. A universal, publicly funded, children's dental program has been replaced by privatized service delivery and a mixture of public and private payment.

Midwifery: Who Will Pay?

For many years, women's advocacy organizations in Manitoba and Saskatchewan have lobbied for the legalization of midwifery and the public provision of women-centred midwifery services. In the 1990s, both provinces legalized midwifery and Manitoba has made a commitment to public financing for midwifery services, including attendance at home and hospital births.

In 1994, the Saskatchewan Minister of Health established a Midwifery Advisory Committee. In 1996, the committee issued a report recommending that the province legalize midwifery, allow home births and provide public funding for midwifery care. A Midwifery Implementation Committee was established to advise on the process of integrating midwifery services into the provincial health system. In May 1999, the Saskatchewan legislature passed *The Midwifery Act*, legalizing midwifery and establishing provincial licensing and regulation of the profession.

However, the Saskatchewan government has made no commitment to provide public funding for midwives' services, although women under a midwife's care would have their hospitalization and diagnostic tests covered. Without public funding, women choosing a midwife would be required to pay privately for those services. According to the Midwives Association of Saskatchewan,

> [w]ithout government money, midwifery in the province is in danger of becoming non-existent.... When the regulation of midwifery comes into practice, midwives will have to pay for malpractice insurance, association fees, and clinical costs, all of which will force them to raise fees to about $2,000 per birth.... Increased midwifery fees and no public funding will mean a two-tiered system where only the elite will be able to choose the care of a midwife. (MacPherson 1999)

In 1997, the Manitoba government introduced and unanimously passed legislation legalizing midwifery in Manitoba. In June 2000 this legislation was proclaimed into law. Midwifery is a funded service in Manitoba, not an insured service. Manitoba Health has provided funding for 26 midwives to all Regional Health Authorities in Manitoba. Sixteen of these positions are located in Winnipeg (Manitoba Health 2000). Because midwifery is not an insured service, midwives not employed by an RHA may engage in private practice and charge fees to their clients. The availability of midwifery services in Manitoba depends on an RHA's belief about the needs for these services. Given that research has demonstrated that RHAs have not successfully included gender analysis in their health planning process in the past, a woman's access to midwifery in Manitoba may be limited by her geographic location.

Although there has been some consensus achieved on the legislation and regulation of midwifery services, home births remain an area of contention. Liability concerns and a lack of acceptance by some doctors can act as barriers to midwife provision of service in the home.

De-listing Eye Exams in Manitoba

In April 1996, regular eye examinations for people between 18 and 64 years of age were taken off the Manitoba Health insured services list. Exceptions are made for people with medical conditions that require exams by optometrists. Current fees for eye exams range from $45 to $90 and are often offered at locations that also sell eyeglasses and contact lenses. Manitoba Health saved $3 million by eliminating its responsibility to pay for 45 per cent of eye exams (ibid., 29).

Complementary Therapies

Complementary therapies such as acupuncture, naturopathy, massage, homeopathy and herbalist consultation are not covered in Manitoba or Saskatchewan. These practitioners charge their clients fees for their services.

Chiropractic care is subsidized by Manitoba Health. Manitobans are allowed 12 visits per year to a chiropractor for adjustments only and are assessed a fee for each visit. The number of visits allowed has been cut in recent years. Treatment resulting from motor vehicle accidents is covered by Manitoba Public Insurance Corporation (Manitoba Health Website 2001). In Saskatchewan, the province provides coverage for chiropractic services, but chiropractors may charge patients additional fees. Full coverage is provided to persons eligible for supplemental health benefits (Health Canada 1998-99, 27).

Private Surgical Clinics

In some provinces, doctors practising at private surgical clinics have been allowed to bill governments a fee-for-service for insured services while patients are charged additional facility fees. Access to these services is restricted to those who can afford to pay. In 1996, the Saskatchewan government introduced legislation specifically designed to prevent the development of a two-tier health system. Under *The Health Facilities Licensing Act*, all private health facilities are required to obtain a licence from the provincial government and are prohibited from charging additional fees for services covered by medicare.

In 1997, there were approximately 130 private clinics offering surgical procedures in Manitoba. These clinics offered insured and non-insured procedures such as endoscopy, abortion, eye surgery, plastic surgery and oral surgery. Physicians at these clinics would receive a fee-for-service from Manitoba Health for insured services, and charged an additional "facility fee" to the patient. Health Canada viewed this as a violation of the *Canada Health Act* and penalized Manitoba $49,000 per month for allowing the practice of extra-billing (Health Canada 1997, 28).

In 1999, the provincial Conservative government in Manitoba passed legislation that banned the charging of facility fees to patients and required private surgical clinics to enter into contracts with the provincial government if they wished to receive facility fee payments from the provincial government on behalf of patients. These contracts specified the type and volume of surgical procedures to be performed. Contracts were signed with three private, for-profit surgical clinics. Procedures offered at these clinics included cataract and minor orthopedic day surgeries. The NDP government has continued these contracts, but has also indicated a policy shift away from for-profit surgical clinics.

In 2001, the Manitoba government announced plans to purchase the privately owned Pan-Am Clinic and integrate it into the operations of the Winnipeg Regional Health Authority. The Pan-Am Clinic has operated for more than 20 years and has a reputation for offering high-quality orthopedic day surgeries, as well as rehabilitation services. Also in 2001, the Manitoba government introduced Bill 25, the *Health Services Insurance Amendment Act*. This legislation will restrict surgical clinics – both private and public – from offering overnight stays. It will also forbid health care providers from charging a patient's friend or family member for services on their behalf. This practice, sometimes known as "third-party billing," has occurred in British Columbia and is seen as a way to "get around" the *Canada Health Act*'s restrictions on user fees. The Manitoba government portrays Bill 25 as a way to stem the growth of for-profit health care and close the door on private hospitals.

Privatizing the Delivery of Health Care Services

Privatization of the delivery of health services in Manitoba and Saskatchewan has occurred in a piecemeal fashion by shifting control of components of the health care system to for-profit, private corporations. In Manitoba, there have been three main attempts at this: the creation of the Urban Shared Services Corporation (USSC) and the development of a centralized food production facility, managed by a private corporation, to supply the major Winnipeg hospitals and long-term care facilities; the SmartHealth initiative by Royal Bank and later Electronic Data Systems (EDS) to administer an electronic health and drug information network; and the transfer of a significant portion of home care clients to a private, US-based corporation, Olsten Health Services. The provincial government publicly stated that these initiatives would deliver services more effectively and reduce expenditures in the health care system. However, none of these large-scale privatization initiatives achieved this goal. The privatization of parts of the home care system was abandoned after it was found that none of the private corporations who bid on the contract could deliver the volume of services at or below the expenditure level provided by the public system. The SmartHealth initiative ended in 1998 after costing an estimated $34 million without achieving the main goals of the project. The USSC Food Services operation was investigated by Manitoba's Provincial Auditor who found that the project was not able to meet its cost or performance goals.

The lack of provincial legislation strengthening public delivery and provision of services, such as legislation introduced in British Columbia,[2] has allowed some RHAs and health districts in Manitoba and Saskatchewan to contract out non-medical services such as food preparation and cleaning services to for-profit suppliers. These services are the less visible parts of health care facilities, although providing nutritious, appetizing food and a clean physical environment are key in the recovery and long-term health of patients. Administrators and the public may view the privatization of these services as less threatening to a universal and high-quality health care system than the privatization of medical services. In fact, a press release announcing the formation of a non-profit corporation to allow Winnipeg hospital and long-term care facilities to share certain non-medical services described these services as "areas behind the scenes, not in direct contact with patients and their families" (Manitoba Government News Release 1994).

Most of the privatization of health care services in Manitoba and Saskatchewan has not occurred in bold transfers to for-profit corporations. Privatization has occurred in a less obvious way by moving the delivery of services out of traditionally defined hospitals, and therefore beyond the umbrella of coverage by the *Canada Health Act*.

Shifting from Institutional to Home and Community-based Care

In terms of health care privatization, there is perhaps no better example of shifting the cost and delivery of health care services to the individual than the trend of shifting care from institutional settings to home and community-based settings. It transfers the costs of prescription drugs and medical supplies to the individual. It also opens the door to private, for-profit provision of home health care services and private ownership and operation of long-term care facilities. Provision of care is privatized as more of the caring work becomes invisible, transferred to women in the home.

The costs of hospitalization account for a major portion of provincial health budgets. As governments of all political stripes have focused on reducing deficits, the reduction in hospital services has been seen as an important strategy for controlling public expenditures. Between 1991 and 1995, 1,200 hospital beds were removed from the health system in Saskatchewan. Over 50 hospitals throughout the province were closed or converted into community health centres. Part of the rationale for reducing hospital beds was the argument that dollars saved could be redirected to more appropriate home and community-based care. Between 1992 and 1998, 1,317 acute care hospital beds were closed in Manitoba, reducing the ratio of acute care beds from 4.8:1,000 persons to 3.6:1,000 persons (Manitoba Health 1993, 1998).

Home Care

Both Manitoba and Saskatchewan offer some form of publicly funded home care program. In both provinces, home care is delivered regionally and funded by the provincial government. In Saskatchewan residents are charged user fees for home care services. According to the Canadian Home Care Association, user fees for chargeable home care services in Saskatchewan total approximately $6 million per year (Canadian Home Care Association 1998, 2).

Home care services have increased in both provinces and the types of services provided within homes has changed. Long-term care in home and community settings, early discharge, outpatient surgery, and post-operative care in the home are all considered more cost-effective than utilization of acute care beds in hospitals. Care and treatment outside of institutional settings may cost the health care system less because of savings in terms of labour and facility costs, but it is also true that savings are realized because individuals bear a greater responsibility for health care costs and care provision.

A key principle of health reform in Saskatchewan is to provide health services in the community wherever possible. The provincial government and district health boards have encouraged this shift to community care by more than doubling spending on home-based services since 1991, to $67 million. At the same time, spending on acute care has dropped 14 per cent, to $585 million. Today, patients are staying in hospital one day less than they did in 1991. One in four home care clients now receives home treatment which might otherwise have been provided in hospital, up from one in 10 in 1991. (HSURC 1998, 1)

The Shift to For-profit Providers and Unpaid Caregivers

For the most part, health care reforms in Saskatchewan have not directly transferred publicly delivered health services to for-profit or non-profit service providers. However, by shifting more responsibility for caregiving to families, they may have indirectly created a market for private health care and home support services. The expansion of privately delivered home care services may be an unintended consequence of policies designed to keep people out of institutions, while failing to provide sufficient public home care services to meet their needs.

It is difficult to track the changes in home care service delivery and actual patterns of private expenditures on home care, as they vary across health districts, and there does not appear to be a provincial data base that gathers this information for the whole province. Some sources indicate that user fees for home care services have declined, while others suggest that personal support and homemaking services are more costly and less accessible than in the past. Some districts have shifted home care resources to acute care and nursing while cutting back on homemaking and personal support services that help people maintain their health and independence. There is variation within and between health districts, with rural residents having access to fewer home care support services than their urban counterparts.

In April 1996, the Manitoba government announced its intention to privatize 25 per cent of personal care services provided by the Manitoba Home Care Program. Estimates of cost savings from this initiative ranged as high as $10 million. This move resulted in a five-week strike by home care workers belonging to the Manitoba Government Employees Union (MGEU). The contract that ended the strike assured employees that there would be no layoffs for the duration of the contract; that the private contract would be confined to 20 per cent of personal services; and that the privatization initiative would be evaluated in two years.

In March 1997, the Manitoba government announced that Olsten Health Services, a US-based corporation, would provide nursing, home attendant and home support services to all new long-term care clients in certain areas of Winnipeg. This amounted to 10 per cent of the workforce, rather than the government's maximum of 20 per cent. Analysts concluded that no private bids could provide the volume of service initially slated for privatization (Shapiro 1997, 1-13).

In December 1997, the government announced that the contract with Olsten would not be renewed. This announcement coincided with the release of a Canadian Centre for Policy Alternatives paper that reported FBI investigations of Olsten for improper medicare billing in the US. The paper also described Olsten as "a US based multinational corporation...[that is] largely non-unionized...[and] has been charged by the State of Washington for allegedly failing to carry out physicians' instructions" (Silver 1997, 2).

Several concerns were expressed by critics of the province's plan to privatize elements of the home care system. Although the plan was not successful in Manitoba, these concerns can provide a framework for analyzing other privatization initiatives:

- privatization would result in lower wages for care providers, failing to attract and retain qualified service deliverers;

- privatization would lead to loss of control over standards, planning and administration, leaving the system open to over-billing;

- clients would be pressured to purchase additional costly and un-prescribed health systems by private care providers; and

- a private home care system would not include an appeals process. (Silver 1997, 2)

Health care reforms have been founded upon certain assumptions about the caregiving responsibilities of families. These assumptions and the values they reflect need to be examined more closely. As public support for "personal" care has declined, public resources for home care may be increasingly focused on medical procedures and nursing care. The provision of social, emotional and practical support, while recognized as an important determinant of health, continues to be defined as a private responsibility.

While publicly funded, publicly provided home care services have clearly increased, most home health care is provided by informal caregivers within the family. To support unpaid caregivers, Saskatchewan Health reports that respite beds have increased 44 per cent and respite days in nursing homes have increased 54 per cent between 1991-92 and 1996-97 (Saskatchewan Health 1996, 3-5).

In 1995, the Seniors Education Centre at the University of Regina conducted in-depth community consultations with caregivers and service providers. The resulting video and discussion guide portray the experiences and insights of several unpaid caregivers and present the following information:

- every day in Saskatchewan more than 80,000 unpaid caregivers provide assistance and support to chronically ill, disabled or elderly adult family members. Some fulfill this role while also maintaining full-time jobs, while raising children of their own, or while growing more elderly and in need of care themselves;

- three out of four caregivers are women, between 50 and 65 years of age;

- 10 per cent of female caregivers are over the age of 75;
- almost half of all seniors age 65 to 74 live with some form of disability;
- the actual cost to the health care system of maintaining a person in a long-term care facility is approximately $3,000 per month. Clients and their families typically pay about one third of that cost. Thus, by keeping family members at home, unpaid caregivers save the health care system more than $2,000 per month or $24,000 per year. (*Living for Others* 1995, 1)

The Transfer of Costs to Individuals

One result of early discharge from hospital of surgical and medical patients has been the transfer of costs for medical supplies to the individual. While patients are in hospital, the cost of prescription drugs and medical supplies and equipment are insured. In the home setting, individuals bear these costs. Although Manitoba and Saskatchewan have created programs to help cover these costs, more and more responsibility for paying for the materials of health care fall to individuals.

Long-term Care

Part of the shift to less expensive care settings included moving long-term care patients out of acute care beds into a variety of facilities and settings, such as nursing homes and personal care homes. Both Saskatchewan and Manitoba experienced a significant loss of acute care beds as a result of health care reform measures. One of the arguments for closing these beds was that many of the patients in acute care beds could be adequately served in long-term care facilities. In Manitoba, 436 new personal care home beds were opened between 1992 and 1998, at the same time as more than 1,200 acute care beds were closed (Manitoba Health 1992-98). In Saskatchewan, the number of people living in special care homes has decreased as many seniors with lower care needs now reside in privately operated personal care homes or private family homes. As a result, more long-term care has been privatized. In Manitoba, costs of long-term care continue to be transferred to the individual, even when that care is received in a hospital setting.

Saskatchewan continues to have the highest proportion of persons over 75 living in nursing homes, though their numbers have declined. In 1992, the Saskatchewan government stopped direct funding to long-term care facilities for persons requiring light care (Level 1 and Level 2). Between 1985 and 1994, 94 per cent of the Level 1 beds and 69 per cent of the Level 2 beds were removed from the health system (Canadian College of Health Service Executives 1997). Between 1992 and 1998, the number of Saskatchewan people living in special care homes dropped by more than 10 per cent, from 10,141 residents to 9,111 (Saskatchewan Health 1997-98, 21). Between 1991 and 1997, Saskatchewan's nursing home bed ratio dropped from 158 beds per 1,000 people over 75 years of age to 143 beds per 1,000 people over 75 years of age, getting closer to the national average of 129 per 1,000 people over 75 years of age (Saskatchewan Health 1996, 3-5). Many of the people requiring light levels of care have remained in their own homes or moved into privately run personal care homes, where they pay resident fees.

In Manitoba, long-term institutional care is mostly provided in personal care homes. As of March 31, 2000, there were 124 personal care homes in Manitoba licensed with a total of 9,385 beds. Fifteen per cent of Manitoba's personal care homes are privately owned and operated for profit. The remaining personal care homes are operated by non-profit bodies, including religious or charitable organizations (Manitoba Health 2000, 62-63).

Mental Health Services

In Manitoba, mental health services have gone through extensive changes. One of the most substantial has been moving clients from institutions into community-based care settings that include group homes and supported independent living sites. Non-profit, non-government agencies, such as the Canadian Mental Health Association and the Salvation Army, have been partners in many of these initiatives, receiving funding to provide services. The Brandon Mental Health Centre was formally closed on March 31, 1998 (Manitoba Health 1997-98). Other mental health institutions continue to operate in Manitoba.

The delivery of services by faith-based agencies, such as the Salvation Army, raises concerns for some clients, especially gays and lesbians. If faith-based agencies support a traditional and patriarchal family model, women who are lesbian, survivors of childhood sexual abuse and/or family violence, may be less likely to receive the services they need.

In July 1997, Manitoba Health announced that long-term psychiatric patients receiving care in a psychiatric facility would be charged income-based per diem rates. A long-term stay was defined as being over 180 days. These fees are not applied to patients who are admitted involuntarily (Health Canada 1997, 27). Anti-poverty activists raised concerns that these fees would be unmanageable for a population that relies on a fixed low income and would result in patients leaving facilities before their treatment was complete because they could no longer afford per diem rates.

THE IMPACT OF PRIVATIZATION ON WOMEN

In 1987, women's organizations in Saskatchewan protested against the Conservative government's cutbacks to health and social services. In a journal published by the Saskatchewan Action Committee on the Status of Women, Susan Dusel argued that reductions in state support for health care services would have particularly adverse effects on women as health care providers, as health service users and as unpaid care providers.

> When the health care system is cutback women get hit with a triple whammy. First, women tend to be the health care workers who are losing their jobs or are being run off their feet because of understaffing. Second, women and their children tend to be the heaviest users of the health care system. Finally, women have to pick up the slack when the state no longer funds health care services. (1987, 4)

Have the health care reforms of the recent past delivered a triple whammy to women? To what degree has the public health care system been cut back? In what ways has health care been privatized? How have these changes affected female health care workers, service users and unpaid care providers? Within these broad categories, which women have benefited from health reforms, and which have been harmed?

In attempting to answer these questions, we searched government documents on health care reform, as well as the health and social science literature. We found little evidence that health care reform policies in either province have been subject to a gender analysis. The various forms of health care privatization and their impacts on women have received little attention from health system planners or researchers. Yet women comprise the majority of those employed in health care, those receiving care and those providing unpaid care in the home. Given the lack of research in this area, we cannot provide a clear answer to the question, "How have the various forms of health care privatization affected women in Saskatchewan and Manitoba?" We are able to present evidence that shows how some forms of privatization have affected or may be affecting various groups of women. This evidence points to the need for further investigation of the impact of health reform on women.

Women's Employment

In Manitoba and Saskatchewan, as in the rest of the Canada, over 80 per cent of those employed in health care occupations are women (Statistics Canada 1999). The number of women employed full time in health occupations increased in both provinces between 1990 and 1998. The number of women employed part time in health occupations declined in Saskatchewan, but increased in Manitoba during the same time period. A closer examination of women's employment in health care occupations reveals a disturbing pattern of job loss and deteriorating conditions of work.

Job Loss

When the Conservative government in Saskatchewan eliminated the school-based dental program in 1987, over 400 dental workers lost their jobs (Smillie 1987-88, 27). The overwhelming majority of these workers were women. Under the program, dental services had been delivered by a largely female profession of dental therapists, working independently, in schools throughout the province, including many in rural communities. Dental therapists were unionized public sector workers represented by the Saskatchewan Government Employees Union (SGEU). When dental services were privatized, dental therapists were left to seek employment with dentists in private practice, most of whom were located in urban centres. The cancellation of the school dental program in Manitoba resulted in job loss for approximately 50 dental health practitioners, mostly women (Shauna Martin, NDP Caucus Health Researcher, personal communication March 1999).

Hospital closures and health care restructuring have led to layoffs among health care workers. According to the Canadian Union of Public Employees (CUPE) in Saskatchewan, "The failure to implement a provincial labour adjustment strategy at the beginning of health reform led to thousands of health care workers being laid off without retraining opportunities" (CUPE 1999, 3).

Reduced hospital budgets and efforts to streamline institutional care have often been made at the expense of nursing staff. The Manitoba Nurses' Union (MNU) estimates that more than 1000 nurses have been removed from the health care system since 1992 (1996, 9). The Manitoba NDP reported that 500 other health care workers were laid off during the Conservative administration (1998a). The Saskatchewan Union of Nurses (SUN) reported that "Saskatchewan nurses have lost the equivalent of 579.5 full time positions since 1990, nearly a 10 per cent decline" (1998a). In 1999, in response to nurses' demands and public concern over nursing shortages, the governments of both Manitoba and Saskatchewan made commitments to provide funding and improve conditions of work in order to recruit and retain more nurses.

When the Saskatchewan government decided to stop funding light care (Level 1 and Level 2) for residents of long-term care facilities, the gap in services was partially filled by private, for-profit personal care homes. In some cases, unionized workers who were laid off from long-term care facilities were offered jobs in the privatized personal care homes, at lower rates of pay (CUPE 1999, 3).

The consolidation and privatization of food and other services within the health system has also been associated with job loss. An analysis of the Urban Shared Services Corporation (USSC) centralized food system, which was developed to provide food to nine Winnipeg hospitals, projected the loss of between 252 and 357 jobs (Cyrenne 1999; CUPE 1998,6). Unions in both provinces have opposed the contracting out of laundry, meal and cleaning services to private, for-profit corporations.

In 1993, 53.2 per cent of women working in health care in Canada belonged to unions (CLC 1997, 13). The loss of unionized public sector jobs for women in health care occupations is sure to have an impact on women's income, economic status and conditions of work, all of which are regarded as important determinants of health. Data comparing wages, benefits and job satisfaction between public sector and private sector health care workers was not found.

Data concerning the representation of visible minority women, Aboriginal women and women with disabilities in the health care paid employment sector is also lacking. Shrinking employment opportunities or the transfer of jobs to the private sector could make it more difficult for these women to gain access to full-time, well-paid employment. According to a study of privatization commissioned by the CUPE, "[n]ot only are women as a group losing work that's full time and well-paid, immigrant, visible minority and Aboriginal women just getting a foot in the door are now fighting to keep the door from slamming shut altogether" (CUPE Website 1999). Health care job loss is also of particular concern to women living in rural and northern areas, as public sector jobs are often the best paid jobs for women in these communities.

Working Conditions

Nurses and other hospital workers in Saskatchewan and Manitoba have repeatedly raised concerns about workloads, understaffing and stressful working conditions. When SUN called a province-wide strike in April 1999, it was the latest in a series of actions designed to call attention to conditions of work. Within hours, the NDP government passed legislation ordering the nurses back to work. However, Saskatchewan nurses defied the back-to-work legislation and refused to return to work until receiving a commitment that salary and workload issues, among others, would be addressed. According to a SUN representative,

> In the last five years, Saskatchewan nurses have experienced enormous cumulative stress. RNs and RPNs have watched administrators and nurse managers toy with "mission statements" and "governance models" while nurses struggle to provide safe care with diminishing resources amidst the confusion and chaos of closures, amalgamations, and conversions. There was no orderly plan for restructuring." (LeMoal 1998,1)

Nurses' concerns have included inadequate levels of pay, job losses, understaffing, increased workloads, increased levels of stress and "the steady erosion of 'caring' as an essential service in health delivery"(LeMoal 1998, 2). According to Glenda Doerksen, staff member of the Manitoba Nurses' Union (MNU),

> Health Reform has not been a positive thing for front line direct care providers. Even though we were the largest group affected by the changes, we were allowed no input into the process.... Nurses feel devalued, frustrated and exhausted. There is no longer any time for the caring part of nursing or for patient teaching. (1999, 52)

In 1998, the MNU published a report outlining the impact of cuts to the health care system. Eighty per cent of nurses responding to a survey reported their workload had increased since September 1995. Nearly half reported that they suffered from three or more symptoms of "burn-out." The report also cited evidence that the number of RNs leaving the province exceeded the numbers of new registrants, including new Manitoba graduates (1998, 4).

With the management emphasis on cost-effectiveness, some have argued that the health care workforce is being de-skilled, with less-trained and lower-paid workers taking over tasks and reducing the number of nurses. According to the SUN,

> [s]ince 1993, 'licensed providers' including RNs, RPNs and LPNs have lost 279.5 positions, while the number of health providers in the aide category has increased by 153.5. (Within the aide category there has been a shift from nurses' aides to more special care aides and home care aides.) Registered nurses, as a percentage of these six health providers, have declined to 45.3 from 46.7 per cent. (1998b, 7)

On the other hand, some health policy analysts predict that as health care reform evolves, nurses will take on increasingly important roles in the health care system (e.g., as advanced clinical practitioners in community health centres and other community-based services).

In Manitoba, a report on nursing staffing from an American-based health care consultant recommended several changes designed to lower expenditures for nursing staff. One example is the de-skilling of nursing providers, where tasks performed by a higher skill level nurse are transferred to lower skill level, and hence lower-paid, staff. This strategy resulted in the layoffs of many LPNs in the Manitoba health care system, whose tasks were transferred to health care aides.

In 1996, the MNU analyzed 2000 Workload Staffing Reports (WSRs) filed in 1995-96. A WSR is filed when a nurse believes that "the workload/ staffing situation is such that adverse effects regarding patient/resident well-being may occur" (1996, 1). Documentation of WSRs increased by 34 per cent between 1993 and 1996. The WSRs most frequently cite inadequate care and monitoring of patients, inadequate time to provide psychological and emotional support to patients and families, and inadequate time for patient teaching as results of nursing workload and staffing problems (MNU 1996, 15). According to the report, some of the contributing factors to this increase include provincial funding cuts, bed closures, nursing layoffs, as well as the de-skilling, intensification and casualization of nursing labour.

Intensification or speeding up of nursing care is a management practice that cuts costs by increasing nursing workloads and reducing nursing staff levels. Intensification occurs as nurses are required to perform a target number of tasks, such as delivery of medications or monitoring vital signs, within a certain time frame. Bed closures and shorter hospital stays can contribute to intensification, since there is a greater number of admissions and discharges to manage, and the patients in hospitals are those who require higher levels of care. Nurses report that one of the results of intensification of their tasks is a loss of time for patient teaching and providing emotional support to patients and their families (MNU 1998, 12).

Casualization of nurses – meaning that there are more nurses hired on a casual basis and fewer full-time, permanent nursing positions – is also occurring in Manitoba. Casual nurses provide services to different wards on an intermittent basis, thereby affecting the continuity of care provided to patients.

How do private, for-profit employers and private sector management practices affect working conditions in the health sector? Are women particularly vulnerable to employer expectations that they do more with less? Health sector unions have raised concerns about health care privatization, public sector job losses, deteriorating working conditions and lower wages. Some argue that health management practices that emphasize cost-cutting are changing the pace and organization of work. Some of these changes also pose a threat to workers' health and safety. Hospital food services, for example, may come to resemble a fast-paced assembly line, thus increasing the potential for job stress or occupational injuries, such as repetitive strain disorders (CUPE 1998, 6). According to CUPE Saskatchewan,

> [f]or several years, the health care sector has had the highest rate of WCB injury rates in the province. Health care workers are working short-staffed and under incredible stress because of staffing cuts and non-replacement of workers on sick leave. (ibid.)

The shift from institutional to home care moves the locus of care work to the private household. How does this form of privatization affect health care workers? What occupational hazards are associated with care given in private households? Increased acuity of home care, the use of new medical technologies in the home and the lack of institutional supports have all been identified by home care staff as factors affecting their work and the quality of care they are able to provide.

There are many unexplored questions regarding the experiences of women in a variety of health occupations. What are the levels of pay, job security, hours of work, and conditions of work? Have part-time and casual positions increased? What differences exist between private, for-profit, and non-profit health care agencies? How do recent changes in the health system affect the health of health care providers?

The Impact on Unpaid Caregivers

Women perform most of the unpaid caregiving work in Manitoba and Saskatchewan. In 1996, 188,475 Manitoba and Saskatchewan women reported performing some hours of unpaid care to seniors. Over 30,000 women in the two provinces reported spending 10 or more hours per week on elder care (Statistics Canada 1996 Census). Wives, daughters and mothers provide the bulk of care to family members who are ill or disabled.

Home care policies in both provinces are based on the assumption that care within the home is largely a family responsibility. According to the Canadian Home Care Association,

> The purpose of home care is to help people who need acute, palliative and supportive care to remain independent at home. It is intended to supplement, but not replace, support provided by the family and the community. (1998, 1)

When government health care reforms emphasize "partnerships with the community," women are often the "partners" expected to provide care at home. Often they do so without sufficient support services, such as respite and home care services, or supportive policies, such as leave from paid employment (Women and Health Reform Working Group 1997, 8).

While some of the architects of health care reform acknowledge the potential impact on unpaid caregivers, they have made little effort to monitor it. In a 1999 study of regional health planning in Manitoba and Saskatchewan, only one of 23 regional health plans included recognition that unpaid caregivers are more likely to be women than men (Horne, Donner and Thurston 1999, 39).

In 1997, the International Centre for Unpaid Work organized three public forums on unpaid work in Saskatchewan (in LaRonge, Saskatoon and Swift Current). Participants in the forums expressed a desire for

> more recognition that the majority of health care is done by family members at home, mostly women...[and that] the health system is taking advantage of them by shifting care from paid workers without taking responsibility for understanding and protecting the conditions under which the unpaid caregivers work. (Lees 1997, 9)

Research on family caregivers has shown that caregiving can have significant negative effects on the caregiver's physical, emotional, financial and social well-being. Older caregivers have reported increased stress, high blood pressure, fatigue, exhaustion and a greater susceptibility to physical illness (National Advisory Council on Aging, cited in *Living for Others* 1995, 3). Caregivers are twice as likely to suffer from depression as non-caregivers (ibid.).While caregiving can be personally satisfying, it can also lead to feelings of anger, guilt, resentment, frustration, grief, depression, loneliness and fear (*Living for Others* 1995, 3). In one Saskatchewan study, nearly half the caregivers reported that their health had deteriorated since they had begun caregiving. They reported increased depression, exhaustion, stress headaches and back pain since assuming duties as unpaid caregivers (Blakley and Jaffe 1999). While many unpaid caregivers choose to provide care and find the experience rewarding, lack of access to institutional care or adequate support services leave some family members feeling trapped in roles as "involuntary" caregivers (Saskatchewan Health Coalition 1998). According to some observers, "[health care] reform will work only if caregivers are connected to a network of services which are accessible, flexible, affordable and responsive" (*Living for Others* 1995, 5).

The International Centre on Unpaid Work reported that caregivers in Saskatchewan were adversely affected by the rising expectations of the health care system and the lack of adequate protection and support:

> Home based caregivers are providing ever increasing amounts of care, at ever higher levels, without adequate support services, without payment, pensions, labour standards, insurance protection or workers' compensation. Unpaid workers describe heavy work loads and excessive hours of work, insecurity, isolation, exhaustion and feelings of helplessness. Pushing unpaid workers beyond their ability to cope leads to stress and depression, increases their risk of mental or physical breakdown, and reduces the quality of patient care. (Lees 1997, 9)

Unpaid caregivers often face additional costs and financial burdens, including payment of user fees for home care services, the cost of home adaptations, the purchase of equipment and supplies, fees for respite care, transportation to medical appointments, and direct medical expenses. Older women on fixed incomes and women living in poverty do not have the financial resources to access a range of support services that would reduce their burden of care. Support services are crucial to maintaining the well-being of the caregiver, but only if they are affordable and accessible. Some caregivers report that fees charged for home care services, adult day care and respite services restrict access to families with the ability to pay:

> Money, of course buys anything you need, if you have it. So if you have lots of money then it's a moot point, because you can buy any service that you want to buy. If you don't have money, you're at the mercy of whatever system you can find, negotiate and make work for you. (*Living for Others* 1995)

Many caregivers experience reductions in income as they adjust their employment in order to fulfill their caregiving responsibilities. A study of rural informal caregivers in Saskatchewan found that several women retired from paid employment because of the demands of caregiving, and several reduced their hours of paid work in order to have time for their caregiving responsibilities (Blakley and Jaffe 1999, 117-18).

A 1998 Saskatchewan study (HSURC 1998) sought to determine whether the substitution of home care for hospital care was truly cost-effective. While it included efforts to measure caregivers' burden and costs, including the value of caregivers' time and out-of-pocket expenditures, the data were not presented in ways that allowed for a gender analysis. Beyond noting that 61 per cent of the caregivers who completed interviews were female, there was no analysis of gender differences in hours of care or measures of caregivers' burden. Income information gathered was based on household rather than personal income so it is impossible to measure changes in women's individual incomes or their increased economic dependence on others. The interview results have been reduced to numerical scores used for comparing the level of burden between different groups of caregivers. They provide no adequate description of the conditions that reduce or exacerbate the burdens of caregiving.

The study found that self-reported levels of caregivers' burden were higher among caregivers who were 45 to 59 years of age, living with small children, in poorer health, caring for a parent, or caring for a person with lower physical or mental health scores. Caregivers' burden scores and levels of satisfaction with services were similar, whether the patient received post-acute care in the hospital or post-acute home care services. The study concluded that it makes sense to opt for the less expensive alternatives to hospital-based post-acute care.

Those who provide care to family members and whose first language is not English face greater risk of isolation than other caregivers. In cross-cultural situations, service providers may not be able to communicate with the clients or be aware of diverse cultural needs. Thus, caregivers are more reluctant to leave the care recipient in someone else's care. As one caregiver pointed out, "even if you get some care, extra care, nobody could look after her because of the language barriers" (*Living for Others* 1995).

Many caregivers experience a sense of accomplishment and personal growth through their role in a caregiving relationship. Some report that their lives are enriched by supportive individuals they have met within the health care system, church and community. However, some describe caregiving situations that undermine their own health and well-being, and go beyond reasonable expectations of family care. A single mother with a chronically ill child described her caregiving situation in rural Saskatchewan:

> I do daily the work of three shifts of nurses in a hospital setting: I administer 10 hours of peritoneal dialysis six day per week. I prepare charts which are reviewed by doctors. I dispense medications around the clock. I change surgical dressings. I oversee daily vomiting sessions. I attend all bathroom visits because of immobility due to renal osteoporosis. I hand feed one meal per day because of renal anorexia. I order medical supplies. I do daily the work of a hospital orderly: I lift a 46-pound child countless times. I lift her wheelchair as well as one very heavy bucket of dialysis effluent daily. I transport and lift 60 boxes per month of dialysis fluid. I have the physiotherapy exercises to oversee daily for strengthening leg muscles. I have the responsibility of a doctor, with my patient's life literally in my hands on a daily basis; one wrong gesture on my part with the dialysis tubing and she runs the risk of fatal infection. All these responsibilities are well over and above the task of responsible motherhood and I firmly believe they must be paid for....[I] am currently expected by the medical and social institutions to be "on duty" 24 hours per day with no days off, no vacations and no benefits. (Lees 1997, 4)

She described a number of consequences of the health system's expectation that she perform the duties of a skilled health care provider 24 hours per day: social isolation, loss of paid employment, poverty, dependence on social assistance, physical and emotional strain. She has argued that the expectation that she provide these services free of charge is a violation of her human rights, and has asked to be paid for the health care services she provides. Calculating her work time as 312 hours per month at an estimated value of $20 per hour, she argues that the health district should be paying her $6,240 per month. Her claim has drawn the attention of feminist academics and human rights activists at the University of Regina and the University of Saskatchewan who have helped present her claim to members of the provincial government.

While informal caregiving is often assumed to take place within the home, family caregivers also report that they provide necessary care to family and friends within institutions. The level of informal caregiving within health care institutions has not been monitored, although anecdotal evidence suggests that family members take over tasks that paid health care providers do not have time to perform.

The Impact on Women as Care Receivers

Little research in Manitoba or Saskatchewan has focused on women's experiences of health care reform as patients or users of health services. A 1999 study of community health needs assessments and health plans revealed that many regional health bodies in Manitoba and Saskatchewan did not disaggregate data by sex and were thus limited in their ability to identify the health needs of women in their regions (Horne, Donner and Thurston 1999, 33).

During the 1990s, the proportion of health care expenditures paid by individuals or private health insurance has increased. Many women may face financial barriers to accessing health services not fully covered by medicare. Women, because of their lower incomes, their greater risk of poverty and their lack of access to employment-based health insurance coverage, may be disproportionately affected by the privatization of health care costs. Many single mothers, women with disabilities, Aboriginal women and senior women live well below the poverty line. User fees for health care services would be especially damaging to low-income women who have high health care needs.

Under the pressure to contain public expenditures on health, governments have shifted some of the responsibility for payment to individual users of services. Private expenditures for some health services have increased, though targeted public programs provide coverage to some low-income people. Combined public/private payment schemes apply to prescription drugs, dental, eye care services and other supplemental health services. While programs of targeted financial coverage of health expenses reduce financial barriers and provide access for some, they are not without problems. A participatory action research project on poverty and health in Saskatoon revealed that some low-income persons felt they were subjected to second-class treatment because their health cards identified them as social assistance recipients. Low-income residents who did not qualify for drug coverage or supplemental health coverage felt that their access was restricted by their inability to pay (Personal Aspects of Poverty Group 1995, 32). In addition, targeted programs, in contrast to universal programs, run the risk of losing support from members of the public who are not eligible for benefits. Private, for-profit health service providers can be hired to provide home or in-hospital care for patients who can pay the fees. As the number of nurses has decreased in hospitals, some families are opting for this high-priced alternative to supplement care. Costs for these services can amount to $100 per day (Manitoba NDP 1998b). Women may find themselves in a variety of situations where their access to some health services is mediated by their income and their access to public or private health coverage.

We found little research related to health care privatization and women's access to reproductive health services. In both Manitoba and Saskatchewan, the recent passage of midwifery legislation could expand the range of choices in prenatal, birthing and postpartum care. However, in Saskatchewan, there has been no commitment to include midwifery services under the public health insurance program. Without public financing of midwives' services, this kind of care may be inaccessible to those unable to pay. A 1999 study of women's experiences of midwifery care found that midwifery clients valued the time midwives spent with them, the personalized care and support, and the holistic, unobtrusive, low-tech style of care. Participants in the study recommended that midwifery services be publicly funded in order to be accessible to all women regardless of economic status (Moon, Breitkreuz, Ellis and Hanson 1999).

Women in Manitoba seeking abortions may experience shorter wait times if they pay up to $550 for the procedure at the privately run Morgentaler Clinic. The Manitoba NDP government, as part of its policy shift away from for-profit clinics, has attempted to convert the Morgentaler Clinic to not-for-profit status. These negotiations have not yet been successful. The previous government passed regulations to exclude non-hospital abortions from the list of insured services. The exclusion from insured health benefits of abortions performed in clinics, while other clinic-based surgical procedures are covered by Manitoba Health, is an example of a differential impact of privatization on women.

Manitoba has consistently had waiting lists for personal care home beds. At the same time as more than 1,200 acute care beds were being closed in Manitoba, 436 new personal care home beds were created, with the intention of moving people from the more expensive acute care. If a personal care home bed has become available and an individual refuses to accept it, hospitals are able to charge the full per diem cost for a hospital bed. According to Manitoba Health Annual Reports from 1989 to 1997, home care clients in Manitoba increased by 23 per cent over that eight-year period (Manitoba Health 1990-97). Women are the majority of home care recipients.

In Saskatchewan, many older women who in the past would have received care in publicly funded long-term care facilities, are now living at home or in private personal care homes. The policy shift from institutional care toward more home and community care could be having a number of benefits for senior women who are able to maintain their independence and live at home. Home care may offer them some of the support needed to remain in familiar surroundings, close to family and friends, with access to health services provided at or near home. However, this major shift in care options for senior women should be monitored to ensure that residents of personal care homes have access to high quality care, and that women living independently receive the necessary support to remain healthy at home. Reduced access to institutional care could mean reduced access to health services, unless an adequate system of community-based support services has been developed.

The policy of reducing hospitalization through outpatient surgery and earlier discharge has increased the number of home care patients receiving post-acute care. Some health care providers have raised concerns that shifting post-acute care to delivery within private households is changing the nature of home care toward a more medicalized model. According to the MNU Survey, 79 per cent of nurses in Manitoba reported that patient teaching is neglected (1998, 13). The lack of appropriate patient education can lead to additional problems when patients are discharged soon after surgical procedures, as patients may not know how to care for wounds.

The overwhelming majority of elder care in Canada is provided by family members in the home. Many people express preference for this type of care yet some older women may not be well-served by a privatized pattern of care. Women receiving care at home may experience social isolation, increased dependence on family members, feelings of being a burden, inadequate or unskilled care, neglect or abuse.

Family care of older women occurs within a cultural context that marginalizes older women and places a high value on individuals who are independent and self-reliant. Does the high value placed on independence and the expectation of family care create barriers to senior women seeking support and care from other sources? What happens to senior women who need more care than home care services and their family members are able or willing to provide? The needs of dependent aging women may be given lower priority than competing caregivers' obligations to jobs, spouses and children. In Canadian society, older women are often culturally devalued and portrayed as a burden to their families and society at large, thus diminishing their sense of entitlement. The expectation that care is a private family responsibility may make them reluctant to make demands on public services.

The rhetoric of health care reform promised that home and community-based health services would be enhanced, but more detailed monitoring of the changes in services is required to assess how well these promises have been kept. A study of home care services should monitor whether resources have been diverted from the health maintenance and home support services that were seen as central to home care in the past. Because services are delivered on a regional basis, and may vary across regions, it is difficult to determine whether the support services needed by older women who wish to remain in their own homes have become more or less accessible.

CONCLUSION

Overview of Health Care Privatization

In Manitoba and Saskatchewan, reforms to the health care system have occurred in an environment of decreasing federal and provincial public spending on social programs. Since the early 1990s, provincial governments have tried to make the health care system more effective at improving health status and more efficient at spending resources. Provincial governments in Manitoba and Saskatchewan have allowed a creeping privatization in various parts of the health care system. Health reform policy strategies, such as regional governance and the transfer of care from institutions to the home and "community" have resulted in a shift of responsibility for the costs of health care to the individual, as well as the provision of these services to for-profit companies and unpaid caregivers. While privatization was not an explicit goal of health care reform in Manitoba and Saskatchewan, it appears to have been one of the results.

Most health services and programs in Manitoba and Saskatchewan are provided as publicly insured services, without additional fees charged to patients. However, many people pay privately for prescription drugs, dental care, optometric services, complementary medicines, treatments by non-physicians, long-term care and some home care services. Since 1990, public expenditures as a proportion of total health spending have declined and private health expenditures have risen substantially. Changes have been made to provincial prescription drug plans and provincial public health insurance plans have de-listed or excluded some important health services. The shift from institutional to community-based care has resulted in a transfer of costs to the individual, as supplies and services provided at public expense to hospitalized patients are no longer covered for outpatients. Private health insurance programs have expanded to fill the gaps in public coverage, but private insurance is not accessible to all.

In addition to the costs of health services, the delivery of health services has been privatized in a number of ways, although the patterns vary in the two provinces. Examples of privatization include the elimination of the school-based dental program; the contracting out of food and cleaning services in hospitals to private, for-profit companies; the use of private, for-profit medical laboratories; the expansion of private personal care homes; and the privatization of home care services. In the cases of abortion and physiotherapy, private options exist in part due to long wait times for public services. While some government policies and regional health decisions have opened the doors to further privatization in the health sector, other policies have attempted to place limits on the privatization of health care. The debate over the scope of public responsibility for health care continues.

There have been three major attempts at privatization involving for-profit companies in Manitoba: Home Care (Olsten Corporation); the Manitoba Health Information Network (EDS, Inc. and SmartHealth, a subsidiary of the Royal Bank of Canada); and the Urban Shared Services Corporation Food Services (Aramark). In each case, the government cited cost-effectiveness as a primary motivation, yet in each case, opponents of privatization were able to demonstrate that cost savings were negligible. In each of the attempts to shift control of large sectors of the health care system to private, for-profit corporations, American companies became involved in the deal by purchasing interests in the participating for-profit corporations.

Health care in Manitoba and Saskatchewan has also been privatized in the sense that care work has been transferred from institutions to private households. In Saskatchewan, many small rural hospitals were closed or converted to community health centres and public funding for light levels of institutional care was eliminated. Home care services have increased and the number of institutional beds in both hospitals and nursing homes has declined. Privatization has crept into many areas of the health care system, especially as more care has shifted out of institutions and into the home and community.

The Impact on Women: Missing Links

Women, to a greater extent than men, utilize the health care system to access services for themselves and other family members. Women are the majority of workers in several health care occupations, and women provide most of the unpaid, informal health care within the home. Women earn less than men, are more likely to live in poverty, and are less likely to have private health insurance. Privatization in the health care system can be expected to have significant impact on women as users of health services, as health care workers and as informal caregivers.

Health care policies and programs in Manitoba and Saskatchewan are rarely informed by a gender analysis. Few studies focus on the impact of health care privatization on women. Nevertheless, several important impacts on female health care workers were identified, including job losses, increased workloads and stressful working conditions. These pose threats to the physical and emotional health of women working in the health care system and make it difficult for them to provide high quality care.

The privatization of heath care expenditures in all likelihood has created financial barriers that affect women's access to services, yet very little is known about the impact of privatization on women as users of health services. According to health care workers, efforts to control health expenditures have created staff shortages, which have affected the quality of care, patient safety and patient education. The health system's assumption that family members are available and able to provide care also may leave some women vulnerable to inadequate or inappropriate levels of care, particularly as more complex caregiving tasks are being transferred to the home.

The shift from institutional to community and home care places new demands on unpaid caregivers. The studies of caregivers identify their feelings of isolation, unrelenting demands on their time, lack of choices, loss of employment income, reduced social participation and declining health. These studies point to the need to develop policies that promote the well-being of care providers and increase their participation in the decisions that affect them.

Women's Response to Health Reform

Women have been voicing their concerns about health care reform and some have been organizing to develop health policies more responsive to women's health needs. In 1996, the Women's Health Clinic in Winnipeg published an article entitled, "Health Care Reform and Regionalization: Can Women's Voices Be Heard?," urging women to seek opportunities arising from regional restructuring to advocate for services that would address women's needs. The Women and Health Reform Working Group was formed in Manitoba in January 1996. Members include the Manitoba Women's Institute, the Manitoba Women's Advisory Council, the UN Platform for Action Committee, the Provincial Council of Women, the Women's Health Clinic and the Prairie Women's Health Centre of Excellence. The group has organized outreach workshops to discuss regionalization and health care reform with women. It meets monthly, providing a forum for women's health researchers, advocates and policy-makers. The group has met with Manitoba Health and staff of the Winnipeg Regional Health Authority to discuss women's experiences with the health care system, in areas such as mental health, home care and health planning. In 1999, the group organized a conference on Women and Health Reform that attracted over 100 participants.

Nurses' unions in both provinces have taken action to bring nurses' perspectives on health care reform to the attention of the public and policy makers. In the spring of 1999, the Saskatchewan Union of Nurses went on strike demanding a collective agreement that would address their concerns over wages, workloads, working conditions and staffing practices. Within hours, the government of Saskatchewan introduced legislation to force the nurses back to work. The nurses refused to comply and continued the strike until some of their concerns over wages and working conditions were addressed.

Women employed in the health care system often address their work-related issues through participation in labour unions and professional organizations. Health care workers in CUPE are part of a national campaign to oppose privatization of public services. CUPE Saskatchewan brought a policy paper on privatization of health care before their annual convention in 1999. The union has since lobbied the government for expanded home care coverage under the provincial health insurance plan, prescription drug coverage for home care patients, increased public funding to address staffing levels in health care, and public funding for light levels of care in nursing homes. The union also urged the adoption of community clinic models of care with salaried physicians rather than fee for service.

Public sector unions, such as CUPE, the National Union of Public Government Employees and the Manitoba Government Employees Union have been vocal opponents of privatization because their members stand to lose well-paid jobs. In Saskatchewan, CUPE was successful in several of its efforts to oppose privatization through contracting out food, housekeeping and laboratory services.

A group of caregivers in Saskatchewan worked with the Seniors' Education Centre at the University of Regina to produce *Living for Others,* a video that documents many of the problems experienced by informal caregivers. The video and accompanying discussion guide present caregiving as a valuable and important activity that must be a shared responsibility of men and women, families, communities and government. They challenge the assumption that caregiving is solely women's work.

Directions for Future Research

Women are disproportionately affected by changes in health policy because women comprise the majority of paid workers, care recipients and unpaid workers in the health care system. Without gender-sensitive research, the effects of changes in health care policy cannot be adequately measured. Researchers have given little attention to the impact of health care privatization or health care reform on women. A thorough assessment of the impact of health care privatization on women is needed.

Given the lack of systematic research on the impact of health reform on women's lives, it is important that research in this area be supported. There are a number of unanswered questions about privatization, its various aspects and their effects on women in diverse social locations. While analyzing sex-disaggregated data is part of the solution, it is important to know which data to gather, and to place it within a conceptual framework that captures the social conditions that play a major role in determining women's health. Research studies must be designed to let us hear women's voices describing their experiences, naming the barriers they encounter, and defining the solutions that will meet their needs. Qualitative and quantitative studies are needed to define the broad patterns of women's experiences so that policies can address the needs of those groups of women whose health is most at risk.

Studies of the impact of health care reform on women must pay attention to the broad social context and the major policy directions influencing government and institutional decisions. When the social environmental context is included in studies of caregivers, it is sometimes limited to the immediate household environment. What is left out of the picture are the social, economic and health care systems that structure the circumstances and conditions within which caregivers find themselves. Links need to be made between the problems encountered by individual women and the broader political economic forces shaping their experiences.

It is also important to locate studies of women and health care reform within a cultural or ideological landscape that defines the scope of public and private responsibility for health care and often equates caregiving with "women's work" or a "labour of love." Only by articulating those underlying cultural assumptions can we examine their consequences and consider alternatives.

Earlier this century, women on the Prairies organized campaigns for public policies that would address their needs for access to health care services. Women were involved in the political and social movements which led to public funding for hospitals, public medical insurance for physician's services, public programs of support for other health care needs, and the recognition that health care is a public responsibility and a basic human right. Today, women as citizens, care providers and users of health services are seeking ways to make the health system more responsive to their needs and concerns. Health policies must be analyzed for differential impact among women, and between women and men. Women must be involved in the processes of policy evaluation and policy development. Women need the opportunity to participate democratically in decision-making which will set the course for health care in the coming years. Just as it was important for women earlier this century to communicate the conditions of their daily lives, their health concerns and their visions to citizen organizations, political parties and policy-makers, so too are women's voices needed today in the current debates over health care and health care reform.

Notes

We would like to express our sincere appreciation to Valda Dohlen, our former colleague at the Prairie Women's Health Centre of Excellence, whose earlier research and work on privatization in Saskatchewan was an important source of information for this report. We also thank Pat Armstrong and all the members of the National Coordinating Group on Women and Health Care Reform for providing a stimulating collaborative environment in which we could explore these issues together. We appreciate the assistance and helpful advice provided to us by our colleagues at the Prairie Women's Health Centre of Excellence, particularly Linda DuBick and Sharon Jeanson. Finally, we would like to thank the Women's Health Bureau, Health Canada, for providing information, encouragement and financial support.

1. The term "community" is used throughout health care reform documents in Manitoba and Saskatchewan, usually in the context of shifting the responsibility for caring for sick people from institutions to home and neighbourhood-based options. The term is misleading, since it is often women, in low-paid and unpaid positions, who carry the load.
2. Section 3.3 of the British Columbia *Health Authorities Act* (Provincial Standards) states that "The minister must ensure that... health services in British Columbia continue to be provided on a predominantly not for profit basis."

References

Armstrong, Pat. 1994."Closer to Home: More Work for Women." In Pat Armstrong *et al.*, eds., *Take Care: Warning Signals for Canada's Health System*. Toronto: Garamond Press.

Armstrong, Pat and Hugh Armstrong. 1996. *Wasting Away: The Undermining of Canadian Health Care*. Toronto: Oxford University Press.

Aronson, Jane. 1998. "Women's Perspectives on Informal Care of the Elderly: Public Ideology and Personal Experience of Giving and Receiving Care. " In David Coburn, Carl D'Arcy and George Torrance, eds., *Health and Canadian Society: Sociological Perspectives* 3rd ed. Toronto: University of Toronto Press.

Biggs, Lesley. 1991. "Building Binges and Budget Cuts: Health Care in Saskatchewan, 1982-1990." In Lesley Biggs and Mark Stobbe, eds., *Devine Rule in Saskatchewan*. Saskatoon: Fifth House.

Black, Errol, and Jim Silver. 1999. *A Flawed Economic Experiment: The New Political Economy of Manitoba*. Winnipeg: Canadian Centre for Policy Alternatives.

Blakley, Bonnie, and JoAnn Jaffe. 1999. "Coping as a Rural Caregiver: The Impact of Health Care Reforms on Rural Women Informal Caregivers." Winnipeg: Prairie Women's Health Centre of Excellence.

Brown, Carol. 1987. *Profile of Reductions in Health Care in Saskatchewan*. Saskatchewan Public Health Association.

Brownwell, Marni, Noralou Roos and Charles Burchill. 1999. *Monitoring the Winnipeg Hospital System 1990/91-1996/97*. Winnipeg: Centre for Health Policy and Evaluation.

Canadian Healthcare Association. 1996. *Canada's Health System under Challenge: Comprehensiveness and Core Insured Benefits in the Canadian Health System*. Ottawa: Canadian Healthcare Association.

Canadian Home Care Association in collaboration with l'Association des CLSC et des CHSLD du Québec. 1998. "Portrait of Canada: An Overview of Public Home Care Programs."

Canadian Institute for Health Information (CIHI). 1998. *National Health Expenditure Trends, 1975-1998*. Ottawa: CIHI.

—. 2000. http://www.cihi.ca/facts/nhex/provnhex/tableC.7.2.shtml
—. 2001. *Health Care in Canada*. Ottawa: CIHI.
Canadian Labour Congress. 1997. *Women's Work: A Report*. Ottawa: CLC.
Canadian Union of Public Employees (CUPE). 1998. *Cooking Up a Storm: Part II*. Ottawa: CUPE.
—. 1999. "Protecting Public Health Care. "CUPE Saskatchewan Policy Paper." Saskatchewan: CUPE.
Carrière, K.C. DeCoster, Sandra Peterson, Randy Walld and Leonard MacWilliam. 1998. "Summary by R.J Currie, Surgical Waiting Times in Manitoba." Winnipeg: Manitoba Centre for Health Policy and Evaluation.
Chin-Yee, Fiona. 1997. "Shifting the Goal Posts and Changing the Rules: The Privatization of the Canadian Health Care System." Master's thesis, Acadia University.
Cyrenne, Philippe. 1999. *Analysing Shared Service Contracts: The Case of Food Services for Winnipeg Hospitals*. Winnipeg: Canadian Centre for Policy Alternatives.
Doerksen, Glenda. 1999. "Providing Care." In Paula Kierstead and Gail Finkel, eds., "Health Reform and Women: Opportunities for Change." Proceedings of the 1999 Provincial Forum, Winnipeg, March.
Dusel, Susan. 1987. "Government Puts the Brakes on Women's Movement." *Network of Saskatchewan Women* 4 (7).
Fuller, Colleen. 1998. *Caring for Profit*. Vancouver: New Star Books.
Gardner, Ellen. 1998. "The Gathering Storm." *Briarpatch* (November): 12-14.
Harrison, Lesley Graff, Noralou P. Roos and Marni Brownell. 1995. Summary by R.J. Currie, "Discharging Patients Earlier From Hospital: Does it Adversely Affect Quality of Care?" Winnipeg: Manitoba Centre for Health Policy and Evaluation. <www.umanitoba.ca/centres/mchpe/readmit.htm.>
Health Canada. 1997. *Provincial Health System Reform in Canada - Manitoba Version 3* Ottawa: Health Canada.
—. 1999. "Health System Reform in Saskatchewan." In *Health Reform Database, Overview by Province, 1998-99*. Ottawa: Health Canada.
Health Services Utilization and Research Commission (HSURC). 1994. "Long-Term Care in Saskatchewan: Final Report." Saskatoon: HSURC.
—. 1996. "Measuring the Effectiveness of Home Care. HSURC Background Paper No. 1." Saskatoon: HSURC.
—. 1998. "Hospital and Home Care Study. Summary Report No. 10." Saskatoon: HSURC.
Horne, Tammy, Lissa Donner, and Wilfreda E. Thurston. 1999. *Invisible Women: Gender and Health Planning in Manitoba and Saskatchewan and Models for Progress*. Winnipeg: Prairie Women's Health Centre of Excellence.
Kierstead, Paula and Gail Finkel, eds. 1999. "Health Reform and Women: Opportunities for Change." Proceedings of the 1999 Provincial Forum, Winnipeg, March.
Lees, Carol. 1997. Public Forums on Unpaid Work in Saskatchewan. Saskatoon: International Centre on Unpaid Work.
LeMoal, Larry. 1998. "Nursing: In sickness or in health?" *Spectrum* (January).
Living for Others: The Life Stories of Older Women in Saskatchewan. 1995. University of Regina Seniors Education Centre. Discussion Guide and Video.
MacPherson, Jillian. 1999. "Midwifery Threatened by Lack of Government Support." *Saskatoon Star Phoenix*, 26 October.
Manitoba Advisory Committee to the Continuing Care Program. 1996. *Home Care Reform: Challenge and Opportunity*. Winnipeg: Manitoba Health.
Manitoba Centre for Health Policy and Evaluation. 1999. "Bed Closures in Winnipeg: Problem or Progress?" <www.umanitoba.ca/centres/mchpe/bedclz3.htm>. (June 2001).
Manitoba Health. *Annual Reports 1992/93-1997/98*. <www.gov.mb.ca/health/ann/199798/4abcdefg.html>.
—. 1992. *Quality Health for Manitobans: The Action Plan*. Winnipeg: Manitoba Queen's Printer.
—. 1996. *A Planning Framework to Promote, Preserve and Protect the Health of Manitobans*. Winnipeg: Manitoba Queen's Printer.

—. 1997. *Core Health Services in Manitoba.*
—. 1998. "Manitoba Health to Pay Facility Fees for All Medically Insured Services." *News Release* (December 30).
—. 1999. "Five Point Plan Announced to End Hallway Medicine." *News Release.* (November 22).
—. 2001. Website.<www.gov.mb.ca/health/ib/oipb.html>.
Manitoba NDP. 1997. "Privatization continues under new minister." *News Release* (January 27).
—. 1998a. "Filmon's Layoffs Coming Back to Haunt Him." *News Release* (February 9).
—. 1998b. "Two-Tier Health System Evident in Westman." *News Release* (March 17).
Manitoba Nurses' Union (MNU). 1996. *Documenting Nursing Workload: Workload and Staffing Report 1995/96.* Winnipeg: Manitoba Nurses' Union.
—. 1998. *Health Care in Manitoba: A Report from the Front Lines.* Winnipeg: Manitoba Nurses' Union.
Moon, Meaghan, Lorna Breitkreuz, Cathy Ellis, Cindy Hanson. 1999. *Midwifery Care: Women's Experiences, Hopes and Reflections.* Winnipeg: Prairie Women's Health Centre of Excellence.
National Council of Welfare. *1995. The 1995 Budget and Block Funding.* Ottawa: National Council of Welfare.
National Forum on Health. 1995. *The Public and Private Financing of Canada's Health System.* Ottawa: National Forum on Health.
Personal Aspects of Poverty Group. 1995. *Poverty, People, Participation.* Saskatoon: PAPG.
Russell, Frances. 1999. "Profit Drives Up Health Costs." *Winnipeg Free Press*, 8 December, A12.
Saskatchewan. 1996. Budget Address, Minister of Finance.
Saskatchewan Commission on Directions in Health Care. 1990. *Future Directions for Health Care in Saskatchewan.* Regina: Government of Saskatchewan.
Saskatchewan Health. *Annual Reports 1991/92-1997/98.*
—. 1992. *A Saskatchewan Vision for Health: A Framework for Change. Regina*: Government of Saskatchewan.
—. 1993. *A Guide to Core Services for Saskatchewan Health Districts. Regina*: Government of Saskatchewan.
—. 1996. *Health Renewal is Working: Progress Report.* Regina: Government of Saskatchewan.
—. 1997. *Drug Plan and Extended Benefits Branch. Annual Statistical Report 1996-97.*
—. 1999a. *A Population Health Promotion Framework for Saskatchewan Health Districts.* Regina: Government of Saskatchewan.
—. 1999b. Population Health Promotion Model: A Resource Binder, Regina, 1999 revisions.
Saskatchewan Provincial Health Council. 1994. *Population Health Goals for Saskatchewan.* Regina: SPHC.
Saskatchewan Union of Nurses (SUN).1998a. "Health Reform Offering Constraints and Opportunities." *Spectrum* (January).
—. 1998b. "How Rationalization of Health Services is Effecting Nursing in Saskatchewan." *Spectrum* (January).
Schmitz, Jan. 1998. "Women and Caregiving." University of Saskatchewan, Women's Studies Research Unit Newsletter, 11 (2) (June).
Shapiro, Evelyn. 1997. *The Cost of Privatization: A Case Study of Home Care in Manitoba.* Winnipeg: Canadian Centre for Policy Alternatives.
Silver, Jim. 1997. *The Cost of Privatization: Olsten Corporation and the Crisis in American For-Profit Home Care.* Winnipeg: Canadian Centre for Policy Alternatives.
—. 1999. "Privatization by Stealth: The Growth of Private, For-Profit Health Care in Manitoba." *Quarterly Review* 1 (1). Winnipeg: Canadian Centre for Policy Alternatives.
Smillie, Adele. 1998. "Home Sick Home: A Study of Home Care in Saskatchewan." *Briarpatch* (March).
Smillie, Elizabeth. 1994. "A Deal in the Making." *Briarpatch* (April).
—. 1987-88. "Dental Plan in Decay." *Network of Saskatchewan Women* 4 (10).
Statistics Canada. 1996. "Population 15 Years and Over in Private Households by Census Family Status, Presence of Children, Labour Force Activity and Sex, Showing Hours of Unpaid Care

to Seniors, for Canada, Provinces and Territories." 1996 Census. <www.statcan.ca/english/census96/mar17/house/table11/t11p46a.htm.> [date of download?]
—. 1999. *Labour Force Historical Review.*
Taylor, Georgina. 1998. "Mothers of Medicare." Lecture. Women's History Month, Saskatoon Public Library, Saskatoon, October.
Thompson, Loraine. 1998. *Caregiving: Exploring the Options.* University of Regina, Seniors Education Centre.
Women's Health Clinic. 1996. *Womanly Times* (Spring).
Women and Health Reform Working Group. 1997. *Health Reform - Making it Work for Women.* Winnipeg: Women's Health Clinic.

The Differential Impact of Health Care Privatization on Women in Alberta

C. M. Scott, T. Horne and W.E. Thurston

INTRODUCTION

This chapter explores the extent to which health care privatization is taking place in Alberta, and considers the impact of health care privatization on women. While it does not attempt to provide a complete review of all policy related to health care privatization, it provides an overview of policies and initiatives that exemplify the Alberta government's policy platform.

Horne, Donner and Thurston (1999) reviewed tools for applying gender-based analysis within the health sector, developed a framework and applied it to policy documents in Manitoba and Saskatchewan. They recommended that both processes and policy or program content be assessed for gender sensitivity, citing the following as key issues in each category.

Processes

- representation of women in policy decision-making and in leadership roles within the health sector (e.g., employees, board members);
- inclusion of men as well as women in redressing inequities and promoting women's health and equality;
- availability of training in women's health and gender issues (in both practice and research) for both decision-makers and staff;
- use of inclusive public participation processes that take differential barriers to participation into account (e.g., child care, language, disability);
- links to women's organizations and other sources of expertise in gender analysis, as well as other equity-seeking organizations (e.g., Aboriginal); and

- inclusion of women in research, both as participants and as decision-makers.

Content

- recognition of the differential impact of social context on health (i.e., social and economic factors);
- assessing whether the focus on women's health is inclusive (e.g., reproduction, role as mothers, conditions specific to women);
- gender sensitivity in all programs, not just those specifically intended for women;
- the focus of outcomes on equality rather than sameness of activities or treatment and inclusiveness of indicators of success (i.e., an equity approach);
- equitable distribution of resources, access and quality of services;
- disaggregation of data by sex and other demographics; and
- the impacts of health policies on family members through unpaid caregiving and out-of-pocket expenses.

We use this framework to guide our analysis of provincial policies and explore the socio-political context and how it has defined the discussion of health care reform in Alberta. We also conduct a detailed gender analysis of the privatization of health care in Alberta and discuss the implications of this analysis.

GENDER-BASED ANALYSIS IN ALBERTA

This section reviews the current level of gender-based health policy analysis supported by the Alberta Government.

Linda Trimble examined the Alberta Legislative debates between 1972 and 1994 to determine whether a critical mass of women made a difference in having women's concerns addressed within the parliamentary system. Trimble's systematic analysis of the Alberta *Hansard* index demonstrated that "under certain circumstances, female legislators can make a difference" (Trimble 1997, 151). In particular, she noted the impact of female MLAs raising issues and educating colleagues from all parties:

Before 1986, six governing-party women had little effect, while Opposition men (and one Tory backbencher) occasionally raised gender-equality issues. The 1986 election brought four Opposition women to the legislature, and they had a significant impact on the tone and direction of debate. They introduced feminist analysis of a wide range of issues, analysis that was adopted by their male colleagues in the Opposition ranks (Trimble 1997, 151-52). Between 1986 and 1993, female MLAs cooperated across party lines to bring women's issues to the table. Since 1993, however, this level of cross-party cooperation has all but disappeared. Although the ruling Conservative caucus included several women, they publicly supported their party's economic and social policy agendas (Trimble 1997). The government position was that deficit reduction measures were gender-neutral "despite evidence to the contrary" (151), and consistently resisted taking gender into account as part of policy formulation. Having several women in caucus was not sufficient to make gender-based analysis a reality, but we have no way of knowing if or how they moderated the decisions and the potential impacts on women and children. We do know that the environment became more anti-feminist in the last decade. Although the current provincial government has had a number of high-profile female ministers since1993, including the former Minister of Health and the Minister without Portfolio, who co-chaired the Health Planning Secretariat, these women have tended not to take a feminist perspective, and in some cases, have been overtly anti-feminist.

A major barrier to incorporating gender-based analysis into the discourse on health care privatization in Alberta, therefore, is the provincial government's history of anti-feminism and the pejorative labelling of women's organizations and others critical of government policy as "special interest groups," or more recently, as "left-wing nuts." Dacks, Green and Trimble (1995) note that some members of Caucus have been publicly aligned with the Alberta Federation of Women United for Families, a group that supports traditional patriarchal family roles for men and women, and is opposed to any policy that questions those traditions (e.g., child care programs, pay and employment equity).

Further evidence of the government's lack of interest in hearing about gender analysis is the dismantling of the Alberta Advisory Council on Women's Issues (AACWI), which was in existence from 1986 to 1996. Intended to be arm's length from government, AACWI's main roles were to conduct research, to make recommendations to government, and to consult with and provide feedback to the public. The Council commissioned 13 research reports and discussion papers, but of the 86 recommendations put forward to the government, only seven were accepted (AACWI 1996a).

Academics, women's health organizations, regional health authorities, unions and others have also conducted gender-based analyses despite the government's lack of interest. Dacks, Green and Tremble (1995) pointed out that Alberta's deficit reduction initiatives – cutting health, education and social services – have hurt women most. Women benefit from the welfare state both as service recipients and as employees, and public sector employment has contributed to many women's economic independence. The authors cite public sector union statistics indicating that more women than men suffered job losses in 1993 and 1994, as more of the employees were female. They note that job losses by women in the public sector have two effects: women are forced to look for work in the private sector (usually for lower pay, security and benefits); and they compensate for loss of public services by providing unpaid labour to take up the slack (e.g., more caregiving as hospitals admit fewer patients and release patients sooner).

A study for the Edmonton Women's Health Network (EWHN) of the impact of health reform on women in the Capital Region found that women had five major concerns, pertaining to the provision of services and working conditions for women in the health care system:

- money is not allocated to appropriate areas of the health care system (including health promotion and home care);
- financial barriers interfere with women's ability to care for themselves and their families (in particular for services such as physiotherapy and midwifery);
- minority Canadians have difficulty accessing the health care system (e.g., because of language and cultural barriers);
- women sense a lack of trust, understanding and support from health professionals (e.g., regarding choice of treatment and caregiving responsibilities); and
- health care reform has had a negative impact on women's ability to care for themselves and their families (e.g., early discharge, stress on health professionals). (Bubel and Spitzer 1996)

In 1997, Thurston, Scott and Crow examined the published literature and held focus groups with women who represented women's organizations in rural and urban Alberta to discuss two policy initiatives, health care reform and funding for women's organizations. The authors concluded that while substantial work had been done by policy-makers on gender-based analysis of social issues, such analysis was "inconsistent and often weak unless the document is specifically about women, and the implications of the analysis cannot often be found in the policy recommendations that follow" (p. 11). The predominant focus of policy documents that do demonstrate a gender-based analysis is on the health needs of women and men identified by epidemiological research rather than on the role of gender in the production of these health needs, or the access to and utilization of services.

Thurston, Crow and Scott (1998) surveyed nine of the 17 Regional Health Authorities in Alberta to determine how women's health was treated in administrative policies and programs once regionalization occurred. Overall, urban centres had more comprehensive approaches, and a specific focus on women's health was more evident than in the rural areas. The survey showed, however, that woman-centred programming was narrowly (and medically) defined in most.

Thurston, Crow and Scott (1998) noted that it is chiefly through women's organizations that women have participated in the public policy process, and cutbacks to organizations that serve disadvantaged women have coincided with cutbacks in health services. These cutbacks have resulted in a shift in roles of women's organizations away from advocacy and lobbying so that direct service demands can be addressed. Thus, mechanisms for participation in policy development are being eroded at the same time that women are being required to assume increased burdens both as formal and informal caregivers. Despite this, women have organized and been effective on many fronts, most often at the local level (e.g., providing and sustaining services to abused women, affecting municipal policies and Regional Health Authority programs).

THE EVOLUTION OF ALBERTA HEALTH AND SOCIAL POLICY

The history of commitment to universal health care policies has ebbed and flowed with provincial political and economic tides. Although Alberta has been ruled by various conservatively oriented political parties for over 75 years, there have been variations in their health policy.

Ralph Klein's Progressive Conservative Party has been in power in Alberta since 1992, and it was preceded by two Conservative governments (1971-1985 and 1985-1992). Alberta is one of the wealthiest provinces in Canada. It has no provincial sales tax and one of the lowest rates of personal income tax. Alberta's wealth is largely dependent on the oil and gas industry, and although economic diversification has occurred, this industry continues to hold enormous political influence. The energy sector is a male-dominated employment sector strongly in favour of a market-oriented economy and small government. The energy sector and its Alberta political supporters have a history of anti-federalist sentiment, support globalization and have the resources to influence policy that few civil society organizations could imagine.

The market-oriented approach to health care is historical in Alberta. When the economic depression of the 1930s forced Canadians to re-evaluate the country's social organization, the Social Credit Party of Alberta advanced an entrepreneurial-philanthropic approach to social programs (Crichton, Hsu and Tsang 1990). The approach was based on individual enterprise and responsibility and was associated with the proliferation of voluntary social service agencies and charity hospitals. Municipal assistance programs frequently supported the philanthropic enterprises and in some instances, where the economic base for charity did not exist, smaller municipalities became the social assistance authority. We continue to see individual enterprise and responsibility in today's discourse.

In Alberta, the lack of ideological support for social welfare programs meant that as the economy improved during the 1950s and 1960s, support for an entrepreneurial system began to re-emerge as a dominant theme. Medical care prepayment schemes and fee-for-service options regained viability in more economically prosperous times. The *Medical Care Insurance Act* was passed in Canada in 1966 despite opposition from the governments of Alberta and Quebec. These provinces expressed the concern that the Act would interfere with provincial priorities (Wilson 1995). The Act promised 50/50 federal-provincial cost-sharing of hospital and physician services if provincial plans met four health care principles (comprehensiveness, universality, public administration and portability). The 1984 *Canada Health Act* added a fifth principle – accessibility – thus prohibiting extra-billing and user fees.

Enforcement of the *Canada Health Act* took the form of financial penalties levied on those provinces that failed to comply with the Act. Since 1984, the federal government has continued to cut back the block transfers to the provinces. Bills C-69 (1990) and C-70 (1991) effectively froze transfer payments for five years. In 1995, the *Canada Health and Social Transfer Act* (Bill C-76) combined federal-provincial health and social transfers into one block payment (Wilson 1995). This Act continued the trend toward reduced levels of federal expenditures on health care while giving the provinces even greater flexibility in implementing health and social programs. The Alberta Government's response to Bill C-76 has been to implement a series of policy initiatives that reflect a return to an emphasis on individual enterprise and individual and private responsibility.

In 1994, Alberta chose a regionalized management system in which 17 Regional Health Authorities (RHAs) replaced numerous hospital, public health and other boards and committees. As was the intent, these authorities are strongly influenced by local socio-political contexts; therefore, a more disparate management and delivery systems is evident. At the same time, the province's Department of Health was reduced in size.

While financial considerations have been identified as the main impetus for regionalization initiatives in Alberta, these financial imperatives have also been couched in discourse around local control, de-institutionalization and community – giving people control over health and health care decisions, recognizing the public as a partner in the health care system, and putting the "consumer"[1] at the centre of decision-making (Alberta Health Planning Secretariat 1993; Alberta Health 1991; Premier's Commission on Future Health Care for Albertans 1989a). This discourse is familiar to proponents of a more humane health care system and of a system more involved in the promotion of health and well-being. What is absent in government discourse, and openly resisted, is an analysis of the gendered impact of such reforms.

Alberta has a strong history in disease prevention, health promotion and population health. There is, however, a danger of making the economic goals of health care reform those of prevention and health promotion. As Noseworthy (1999) points out, disease prevention programs could be framed as a reason to reduce health care spending. Unfortunately, Alberta's expertise at the program level in delivering a cross-section of health promotion programs has not included attention to gender as a determinant of health. In a review of health promotion projects, none were identified that included this determinant (Thurston *et al.* 1999).[2]

In the face of a provincial budget surplus, the Alberta government has begun to discuss reinvesting in health care. For example, discussions have included the possibility of increasing frontline nursing staff in both hospital and community settings and introducing legislation that would expand opportunities for private, for-profit health care facilities. Discussions of increasing the role for private facilities have, however, been limited to exploring for-profit options and have neglected the role of the private, not-for-profit sector. The not-for-profit sector (e.g., community health centres) has historically played a role in the provision of health services in Alberta.

Discussions relating to health care reform and privatization initiatives in Alberta have included debate about the relative weight that specific policy initiatives give to objectives such as efficiency and equity. In spite of the budget surplus in Alberta, there are not infinite dollars available to finance the health care system. In a climate of limited resources, the interaction between equity and efficiency implies a trade-off. That is, if there are scarce resources, financial equity and equity of access may be ensured if efficiencies are compromised. In Alberta, health care reform has made a number of trade-offs; for example, provision of services in remote and in rural areas may compromise the objective of finding the "best ways" to produce worthwhile programs. Legislation introduced by the provincial government in the spring of 2000 (Bill 11 – the *Health Protection Act*) was purported to increase efficiencies in the system (i.e., shorter waiting lists). While there are questions about whether such efficiencies would be found through this legislation, there are also concerns that potential increases in efficiency would be at the expense of both financial equity and equity of access. Bill 11 would allow private surgical facilities to operate using both public and private financing; therefore, in such institutions, the provincial government would be permitted less control over the objectives that guide service provision. By giving up control, the government might not be able to ensure a balance between equity and efficiency.

Private health care providers bring many factors from the market sector into play in the health system. Taft and Steward (2000) point out that for-profit companies have added costs such as taxes, marketing, payments to investors and duplication of expensive equipment among competing providers. Conflicts of interest arise when private providers are also in decision-making positions within the public health care system. Several examples of this have been noted within one of the largest Alberta Regional Health Authorities, in Calgary. Private interests also conflict with public goals, such as a provincial breast screening program. Private radiologists fear loss of a profitable population of clients if the Alberta Cancer Board is permitted to institute such a program. These radiologists may believe strongly in the benefits of a systematic screening program, follow-up and research, but their business models demand that they be able to screen any woman who requests screening, regardless of practice guidelines, and that they maintain control of the case through records.

The private provision of health services in Alberta has existed for a number of years. Therefore, the argument that there is no room for private enterprise within the Alberta health care system will persuade few Albertans. Physicians and physiotherapists, for example, may be salaried employees within the public health system, private practitioners who work under contract to RHAs, or who directly bill Alberta Health and Wellness for their services. In each of these situations, the provider may be working privately, but her or his services have been financed publicly. This single-payer system is a tax-based public insurance system that pays for health services that are mainly supplied by the private sector (Fuller 1998). It is the expansion of private financing mechanisms (e.g., an individual paying directly for uninsured or enhanced health care services or paying for private insurance policies in addition to the public premiums) that threatens to undermine the principle of accessibility.

The discourse around efficiency sometimes represents public employees as greedy, inefficient or even lazy. McArthur, Ramsay and Walker (1996) compare many of the unionized jobs in hospitals (excluding nurses, technicians and lab assistants) with those of unionized hotel workers as evidence that public sector health care workers are overpaid relative to their private sector counterparts. People who work in hospitals, however, are at greater risk of exposure to germs, sometimes need to provide non-clinical assistance to patients, such as helping them to use phones or call for a nurse (Armstrong and Armstrong 1996), and serve a population that is generally much more stressed than in the hotel industry.

When it comes to professionals, what is absent from the analyses of labour costs is the context of the historically low pay and status of nurses prior to the 1970s (ibid.) and the lengthy struggle for better pay and working conditions. As noted by Renouf (1995), health care wages in Alberta rose faster than both average incomes and inflation during the 1980s; however, these increases addressed prior pay inequities:

> These gains did not come without struggle, exemplified by province-wide strikes of unionized nurses in 1980, 1982, and 1988. Health care unions fought to increase pay levels which, in real terms, had been very low for their predominantly female membership. Compensation increases in the 1980's were neither unjustified nor the product of a lax and free-spending provincial government. Primarily, they reflected pressures to address longstanding pay inequities. (229)

The government actively opposed the wage adjustments that occurred (Renouf 1995).

PUBLIC PARTICIPATION

The government's commitment to privatization of the health system has also been accompanied by a trend toward increasingly limited and controlled public participation in the planning processes. Alberta Health has held various types of community consultations (e.g., the Rainbow Report in1989, Partners in Health in 1991, Roundtables in 1993, the Health Summit in 1999). In addition, the Alberta Advisory Council on Women's Issues held a public consultation process in 1996 and the Provincial Health Council of Alberta held public consultations in 1997.

Although these avenues provided opportunities for input and feedback to decision-makers, it is not clear how the data gathered was translated into policy decisions by Alberta Health and the health regions. While the early consultations associated with the Rainbow and Partners in Health Reports appeared to be open and responsive to the concerns of the public (as we shall show), more recent consultations have appeared much less responsive.

In contrast, the Provincial Health Council consultations reported diverse feedback about the health care system, both positive and negative. For example, public meetings and focus groups reflected concerns that health care reform has focused too much on cost control to the detriment of quality; that there has been little citizen involvement in the decision-making of their RHAs; and that providers are not always sensitive to patient needs. They also supported an emphasis on prevention. In addition to these face-to-face meetings with members of the public, the Council also visited health authorities, interviewed former board members about their experiences with health care reform, and conducted a province-wide survey of Albertans. From these various consultations, the Council concluded that:

> cost containment through government expenditure has largely been achieved, although there has been an increase in cost to individuals, employers and communities. (Provincial Health Council of Alberta 1997a, 17)

On a more positive note, the Council also found more recognition of the linkages among lifestyle choices, social and economic policy and better health. It emphasized that integration of health and other sectors was needed to move health care reform forward, as well as better use of provider skills and health facilities, and better prevention programs. This example illustrates how public and other forms of consultation by a government body can be used to provide both positive and critical feedback on policy and make constructive suggestions for change. In 1997, the Council was examining ways to further expand its process for consulting with Albertans, particularly Aboriginal people. The Council was eliminated in 1998.

Shortly before its demise, the Alberta Advisory Council on Women's Issues (AACWI) carried out a public consultation process with women across Alberta. This consisted primarily of focus groups of women from diverse backgrounds, as well as opportunities for written or telephone submissions. In their discussions of their attempts to communicate with the government, most who participated felt their efforts had minimal results in terms of effecting change. When discussing barriers to effecting change and having impact, women identified lack of awareness of women's issues (including on the part of government); fear of consequences in their communities for speaking out; a belief that the government does not listen, especially to women; as well as more practical barriers like lack of time, money, knowledge and comfort in speaking out (AACWI 1996b).

Though a minority of women favoured discontinuing AACWI, many believed its closure "would weaken the government's ability to create legislation, regulation and policy that were sensitive to women's needs and concerns" (AACWI 1996b, 28). Most either supported continuing AACWI or developing a replacement structure that would still provide opportunities for women to work with government. Of all the options that were put forward, the government chose to follow through with its intent to close AACWI. While women's organizations have struggled to provide services where government cutbacks created gaps, their ability to engage in consultation at the provincial and local levels has been restricted. Given the anti-feminist stance of the current government, there is little trust that women will even be listened to, let alone heard.

Health care was the most frequently raised major concern in the AACWI consultations. Specific concerns relevant to the present discussion of privatization included:

- the impact of cuts on quality and availability of medical treatment;
- the increased use of users' fees and potential for limited access to adequate health care by poor women and their families;
- government and community expectations that women will be long-term caregivers at home for family members;
- the skill levels and quality of training for home care staff and other out-of-hospital care providers; and
- the future availability of abortions, given recent discussions regarding de-insuring abortions from health care coverage (the government decided not to de-list abortions from health insurance coverage, and covers full costs of abortions performed in private clinics as well as hospitals). (AACWI 1996b)

Progressive discourse is often used to mask regressive directions in social policy initiatives in Alberta. For example, Kline (1997), in discussing the Action Plan for the decentralization of children's services to regions (prior to its implementation), describes how the government uses the discourse of community to promote private responsibility for children's needs (in the family and done primarily by women), rather than collective community responsibility. Kline notes that early intervention is presented as an individual issue of skills training for parents, and social issues such as "low income" and "family violence" are seen as family and community issues that are not the responsibility of government. Thus, there is no recognition of the relationship between social and economic inequalities and individual actions.

Kline (1997) does not view the formation of RHAs as giving more power and control to local communities. She notes that such structures actually insulate the government of accountability, and also observes that in Manitoba and Ontario local decision-making structures were disbanded when they became critical of government policy and demanded change, including more funding and expanded services. This is a pattern that has been repeated in Alberta with the disbanding of the AACWI, the Provincial Health Council and decreased funding for women's organizations.

Privatization of Health Care in Alberta
The Current Vision
The provincial government's vision for the health of Albertans has evolved over the years and, in the course of this evolution, has facilitated the shift toward policies that emphasize greater private responsibility for health care. While the language of privatization has become more explicit, the gendered implications of this shift remain absent from the discussions of health care reform.

The 1999-2002 business plan from Alberta Health (now called Alberta Health and Wellness) focuses on access to quality health care services; promoting and protecting the health of individuals; and the contribution to health of healthy social, economic and physical environments (Alberta Treasury 1999). The plan opens the door for privatization through options for the provision of "benefits in excess" of the Canada Health Act and "better approaches." The present 2000-2003 business plan, while emphasizing consistency to the principles of the *Canada Health Act*, is explicit about the private sector as a partner:

> The achievement of this vision requires individuals to take responsibility for their health in their communities, in collaboration not only with the Ministry and providers of health services, but with a wide variety of parties including other Ministries, other levels of government and the private sector. (Alberta Treasury 2000a, 3)

Adding a statement about collaboration that includes individuals collaborating with the private sector suggests the government's intention to allow expansion of the private sector, including the ability of private clinics to market non-insured services to Albertans. On the other hand, the statement could be read to mean that people should take a more active role in their insured health care treatment that is provided by physicians by joining private physical activity programs, for example. Though policy documents usually are written in broad terms, further definition at the operational level is needed to define the intended roles for the private sector in Alberta's health care system.

Key Policy Initiatives
The emphasis on private responsibility for health care has been a consistent theme in the Alberta health system since the 1930s. For a brief period during the 1980s the force of this underlying ideology was diminished and policies that reflected the objective of equity were able to emerge (e.g., the legislation that enabled the creation of the AACWI). In the late 1980s, there was again a shift back to a focus on individual responsibility for health. This emphasis has continued to develop in policy documents throughout the 1990s.

In this section, we use a gendered lens to examine a number of key policy documents generated during the early stages of health care reform in Alberta. While they reflect an understanding of the need to clarify the roles of individuals, organizations and sectors in the health care system, they do not deal with the differential impact of such roles on men and women.

The Rainbow Report

In December 1987, Premier Don Getty established the Premier's Commission on Future Health Care for Albertans. The Commission's mandate recognized the need to maintain quality and accessibility of health services while clarifying the roles of the public and private sectors in health care delivery and funding, including the roles of individuals and community agencies.

Chaired by Lou Hyndman, the eight-member Commission (three women and five men) had two years to complete its task. Throughout 1988, the Commission used extensive means to gather information – including town hall meetings, public hearings, interviews, written submissions and toll-free telephone submissions. The resulting *Rainbow Report: Our Vision for Health* contained 21 major recommendations, which distilled down to the following six directions for change:

- Legislation that ensures that the health of individual Albertans is in balance with economic development and other initiatives is needed.
- There should be more individual responsibility for health – 1 per cent of the total Alberta Health budget needs to be allocated to targeted promotion and prevention programs.
- The authority for decisions affecting the relevance of health services should return to people within the communities familiar with local needs and priorities.
- Individual Albertans and/or their designates should have the responsibility for disbursing and managing the funds required for their health and health care needs.
- The government of Alberta should provide matching grant funds for the establishment of a publicly accessible Ethics Centre to assist Albertans facing complex issues which require deliberation and discussion (e.g., dying with dignity).
- The vision of "healthy Albertans, living in a healthy Alberta" needs an advocate who would communicate with Albertans and the government about health and health care.

In the years since its publication, *The Rainbow Report* has been heralded as the foundation for many of the current reforms. In reality, few of the recommendations have been implemented as envisioned. Although the province has moved toward a regionalized health system, the Regional Health Authority boards remain appointed, not elected. The Provincial Health Ethics Network has been established.

Despite the Commission's emphasis on the development of a health system based upon a common vision and values, there has been no explicit discussion of the values underlying the vision. *The Rainbow Report* describes the need to balance individual rights with the societal good and for the government to assist, support and protect individuals in achieving their individual health goals

(Premier's Commission on Future Health Care for Albertans 1989a). The central role of the government is reflected in the suggestion that the provincial government support individual responsibility for health by dedicating a percentage of the budget to health promotion and disease prevention initiatives.

The Commission highlighted the need for government to provide special support to some individuals or groups who may face barriers to accessing health care services (i.e., young people, women, the elderly, aboriginal Albertans and persons with disabilities). The report links the special support required by women to the multiple roles that women play (i.e., "homemakers, parents, breadwinners, career people, care givers" and "maintaining the primary role in decision-making about child health care matters") (Premier's Commission on Future Health Care for Albertans 1989a, vol. 2:52). Thus, while the final recommendations are couched in gender-neutral terms, the substance of the report reflects some understanding of differential access to health care services for women and men even though women's roles were primarily in the realm of caregiving. The same understanding was not apparent in the section of the report that dealt with health care providers, which emphasized the need for building positive relationships among health care providers and between health professionals and the individuals to whom they provide care.

In the appendices to *The Rainbow Report*, the Commission commented on the importance of volunteers in the health sector. While the report identifies that 60 per cent of volunteers are women, using volunteers is seen as a strength of the system. There is no analysis of the impact of this voluntarism on the lives of women, or the changes occurring in voluntarism and implications for the future. Dependence on unpaid labour that may not be available as more and more women enter the labour force could be seen as a weakness of the system.

Partners in Health

The government of Alberta established a Cabinet Task Force to assess the findings and recommendations of *The Rainbow Report*. Chaired by Minister of Health Nancy Betkowski (MacBeth), the Task Force solicited and analyzed submissions from 200 individuals and 179 interest groups from across the province. The only two women's organizations on the list were the Catholic Women's League of Canada and the Alberta Association of Homemaker Services. The AACWI is conspicuously absent. The Task Force supported, to varying degrees, 17 of the 21 specific recommendations arising from *The Rainbow Report*. In many instances, the Task Force supported recommendations in principle, but identified the need to collaborate with other sectors to develop appropriate strategies (e.g., education, justice, the environment).

The recommendations not supported by the Task Force included the suggestion that the government allow Albertans to manage the funds required for their health care needs, the creation of a provincial Health Advocate (this was felt to be the role of the Minister of Health) and the establishment of RHAs. The government endorsed the need for coordination and cooperation on a regional basis, but not through RHAs. At this time, the government still espoused the need for a strong provincial role in the coordination of the health system. The public responses argued against RHAs on the grounds that they would create another level of bureaucracy, reduce local autonomy, and have uncertain effects on accountability mechanisms. It is interesting to note that within three years, the provincial government had reversed its opposition to RHAs.

Starting Points

One of the first documents of the Klein government to outline health care reform directions was *Starting Points: Recommendations for Creating a More Accountable and Affordable Health System* (Alberta Health Planning Secretariat 1993). This report, prepared by MLAs Dianne Mirosh and Lyle Oberg, respectively the Chair and Co-chair of the Public Roundtables on Health, built on a process of public forums, written submissions, visits to hospitals, consultations with health officials in other provinces, and a review of past reports on health system issues.

The report's first recommendation is that "the new system adopt a service-oriented attitude that places the needs of the consumer as the highest priority" (Alberta Health Planning Secretariat 1993, 13). This recommendation addresses maximum access and choice, involving a range of providers and locations. One-stop shopping, where a person can access the range of providers and options when entering the system at any point, is recommended. The report assumes that not all services will be covered by Alberta Health Care and that "consumers will recognize that they will need to pay for services considered *non-essential* under a newly created definition of basic health services" (p. 13).

The second recommendation builds on this last point and calls for the establishment of a "definition of *basic health services*" that will "clarify health needs and health wants" (p. 15). This recommendation does not necessarily promote privatization, though the intent to "provide maximum value to the consumer" is consistent with a market perspective. The report uses the language of best practices to say that the result will be a definition of basic health services which ensures taxpayers only fund those services that meet established standards for quality health, and provide maximum value to the consumer (long-term benefit) and the taxpayer (cost-effectiveness).

The report acknowledges that "cost-effective" does not always mean the lowest cost service, and that occasionally, a more expensive service may be required to achieve a better long-term result. It also states that defining basic health services will restrict the number of publicly funded services offered, and that the "consumer first" approach demands that consumers have access to an optimum number of non-essential services. It also states that:

> We must understand that the consumer's *right* to a maximum choice of non-essential services will include the consumer *responsibility* of paying for those services. (Alberta Health Planning Secretariat 1993, 15)

A subsequent recommendation is to establish a commission to define essential services. The *Starting Points* report concludes with a number of challenges and questions. Some of these relate to the potential for various forms of privatization (e.g., health regions selling services to non-Albertans; contracting out food, laundry and maintenance services; partnerships between public and private sector x-ray/diagnostic labs). This section also raises the issue of shorter hospital stays and more outpatient services, but does not acknowledge the likelihood of an increased role for informal caregivers (who are most often women). Although the five principles of the *Canada Health Act* – public administration, comprehensiveness, universality, portability and accessibility – appear in an appendix, there is no explicit reference to them in the report's recommendations, and no reference to the appendix in the body of the report.

Health Goals for Alberta

In late 1993, *Health Goals for Alberta: Progress Report* (Alberta Health 1993) also mentions links to the private sector. In a discussion of maintaining quality and accessibility of the health care system, this document states:

> Partnerships between those who provide services, those who use health services and those who pay for health services, will be needed. Only in this way can we allocate our resources for the greatest benefits of all Albertans. (12)

The general wording of the document could include many meanings for "partnership." If partnership is intended to involve patients and their families in more meaningful ways as they deal with the health system, it would not be inconsistent with woman-centred models of care (see Horne, Donner and Thurston 1999 for examples.) If partnership, however, means informal caregivers being expected to take on more responsibilities as health care staff are cut or to pay a greater share of their health care costs, then partnership would be more akin to cost shifting.

The document goes on to address health service delivery and lays some early groundwork for the approach to health care reform that followed with the development of health regions. It addresses when and where services are provided, by whom, how they are integrated to improve accessibility, and cost-effectiveness. The report proposes new ways of delivering services focusing on the individual consumer and the particular needs of each community, and offers strategies to support people with health limitations to remain in their own homes, partnerships with groups outside the traditional health system and cost-effective service delivery.

The Regional Health Authorities Act

In 1993, despite earlier indications that the government did not favour RHAs, the concept re-emerged. Based on the Provincial Roundtables on Health held in September and October 1993, the Health Planning Secretariat recommended that "a regional structure be created for local decision-making" (Alberta Health Planning Secretariat 1993, 17).

The language used to describe the anticipated impact of regionalization is clearly the language of efficiency (e.g., "accountability," "customize delivery," "streamline," "economies of scale"), with little emphasis on equity. Members of the Secretariat endorsed regionalization for these reasons, yet it is unclear that mechanisms were set in place to ensure that these outcomes could be achieved. RHAs were not, for example, supported by mechanisms to assist with accountability (i.e., a health information system).

One proposed mechanism for customizing delivery was to mandate the creation of Community Health Councils (CHCs) in each RHA. However, their formation has been inconsistent across the province, and there are no specific guidelines for diversity of representation within the CHC regulations (Government of Alberta 1997). Women have not had much success in customizing the health system to meet their needs. Increased numbers of female medical graduates have helped (e.g., women tend to choose female physicians) but of the leaders in medical education and medical research, only 20 per cent are women even though medical classes are 50 per cent female. In addition, these women tend to be in the lower ranks of academia (McKenna, Hanion-Dearman and Yassi 1999).

It is interesting to note that between 1991 and 1993, the government reversed its interpretation of some of the potential impacts of regionalization. In the *Partners in Health* report (Alberta Health 1991) some of the reasons for rejecting the concept of regionalization included the uncertain impact on accountability, added bureaucracy and the impression that improved coordination of health services was not necessarily linked to "boundary lines on a map" (40).

The Regional Health Authorities Act (Government of Alberta 1994) legislated the formation of 17 RHAs and their links with two existing boards (the Mental Health Board and the Alberta Cancer Board). The 17 regions replaced over 200 separate boards of hospitals, health units and other health service institutions. Initially, RHA boards were appointed with the provision within the Act for having locally elected Boards, but this has yet to happen. The Act legislates that the RHAs shall:

- promote and protect the health of the population in the health region and work towards the prevention of disease and injury;
- assess on an ongoing basis the health needs of the health region;
- determine priorities in the provision of health services in the health region and allocate health resources accordingly;
- ensure that reasonable access to quality health services is provided in and through the health region; and
- promote the provision of health services in a manner that is responsive to individuals and communities and supports the integration of services and facilities in the health region.

The interpretation of this legislation has varied from one RHA to another and is easily influenced by the socio-political context within the region, such as differences in rates of eye surgeries (Armstrong 2000).

Five years after the implementation of regionalized health management in Alberta, its benefits have yet to be demonstrated. Donna Wilson (2000a) highlights several features of regionalization that have added to the cost of managing the health system. Wilson also suggests that:

- regionalization has not improved health care planning and delivery;

- citizens feel more disenfranchised from health care than they did prior to regionalization;

- regionalization has not improved communication and coordination of care between and among regions (there is actually greater diversity in programming); and

- RHA boards have become responsible for issues that are provincial government issues.

In sum, Wilson states that "a fragmented system, with considerable duplication of health care issues, has developed through regionalization" (Wilson 2000a, 13). She concludes that until it is determined that regionalization is a successful format for managing health care planning and delivery of health services, "it would be unwise to expect Regional Health Authority boards to assume the responsibilities associated with contracting out major surgery to for-profit firms" (14).

In 1997, rural women who participated in focus groups indicated that the creation of 17 RHAs and the development of funding barriers between regions had resulted in a competitive environment and in limitations in access to services for rural Albertans (Thurston, Scott and Crow 1997). For example, participants stated that even though some rural people may live closer to the major centre of a neighbouring region, they were discouraged from accessing services outside of their own region and in some cases, were refused service. One participant "indicated her dismay that the Alberta health care system was reverting to a dysfunctional regionalized system that had existed in the province in the 1940's and 1950's" (17). Related changes in long-term care services have meant that people who are elderly or disabled may be placed anywhere within a region depending upon where the long-term beds become available.

Wilson (2000a) discusses the implications for the regions of the population-based funding scheme that was introduced in the 1997-98 fiscal year. Regions may receive reduced funds because patients have received care in other regions (i.e., patients who are transferred to tertiary care institutions). The associated lack of funding permanence is especially problematic in rural regions where staff layoffs are the most viable method for achieving short-term savings. As the majority of health care workers are women, the consequences of such layoffs will have a greater impact on women either as paid or unpaid caregivers.

More recently, the Alberta Health 1999-2002 Business Plan describes the role of RHAs as follows (Alberta Treasury 1999, 2):

- RHAs will plan and deliver health services based on evidence of needs, with input from residents and community health councils and directions from the Minister of Health;
- services will be provided, when appropriate, *in homes and communities* (emphasis added), not just in hospitals;
- health services will be integrated with better linkages between hospital care, home care, community services, mental health services, long term facility-based services, rehabilitation services and public health;
- RHAs will work with other organizations in their communities to address social, economic and environmental issues that affect health.

The statement that services will be provided in homes and communities and not just in hospitals contains underlying assumptions regarding who will provide such care.

The Delegated Administration Act and The Government Organization Act

The current provincial government has favoured private delivery of government services since early in its first mandate. For example, *The Delegated Administration Act* (Bill 57) was introduced in the Fall of 1994 by House Leader Stockwell Day (Legislative Assembly of Alberta 1994a). Bill 57 was designed to facilitate private delivery of government services by either for-profit or non-profit organizations. Critics were concerned about diminishing legislative authority and accountability as well as the potential for favouritism in the awarding of contracts (Harrison 1995). *Edmonton Journal* columnist Mark Lisac (1995) wrote:

> The bill confused public and private business in many ways. One of the certainties seemed to be that cabinet ministers would not answer in the legislature for anything done by corporations to whom they had delegated responsibility, though the ministers would retain significant control over these corporations. And the province's auditor general would not have free access to review any of the agencies. (157)

The government eventually withdrew the bill, blaming the withdrawal on "a very public misinformation campaign" by the Liberals (Crockatt 1994). The government re-introduced Bill 57 in the Spring of 1995 and it was withdrawn a second time. However, *The Government Organization Act* (Bill 41) was an omnibus bill that included creation of government departments, boards, committees, councils, inter-ministerial and intergovernmental relations, and ministerial authority, as well as several pages of amendments to various Acts (Legislative Assembly of Alberta 1994b). The openness of some sections caused concern. For example, section 9(1) stated that "A minister may in writing delegate any power, duty or function conferred or imposed on him by this Act or any other Act or regulation to any person." Bill 41 not only authorizes the Minister or the Minister's department to charge fees "for any service, material or program the performance of any function or the doing of any thing," but also allows fees to be charged "by any board, commission, council or other agency for which the Minister is responsible" (section 12(1)). Section 14(3) allows disposal of government property.

Bill 41 was passed in 1994. The open-ended wording of section 9 in particular appears to make it possible for the government to accomplish many of the aims of the defeated *Delegated Administration Act* with even less public scrutiny. According to one critic, Bill 41 "allowed ministers to create programs and services, change regulations, make loans, sell public property, or transfer programs and services to the private sector which could in turn set fees – all without legislative approval" (Harrison 1995, 126). An unidentified government insider pointed out that the intent of Bill 57 could be accomplished through Bill 41 (Crockatt 1994).

A Better Way (I)

Over the next three years (1994-97), a number of other government documents furthered the government's plans for the health system. *A Better Way I: A Plan for Securing Alberta's Future* (Alberta Health 1994) cites principles and criteria that include individual and community responsibility, consumer focus, affordability and appropriateness of services (i.e., need- and evidence-based), and reduction of the cost of health care providers. The document is committed to public funding, but also states that "additional health services not based on significant need will be available, but will require a partial or full direct financial contribution from the consumer"(5).

In addition to downsizing and rationalizing the system, the section on "Strategies for Achieving the Spending Targets" addresses shorter acute care stays and shifting various types of care (pre- and post-operative, long-term palliative) to "the community." Though privatization of formal service delivery is not explicitly mentioned, the strategies include rationalizing and restructuring of diagnostic services – many of which have been privatized (see Taft and Steward 2000). The document also mentions the need to define basic services and the conditions under which they will be publicly funded. This raises the question of whether the document views basic services as different from those that are "medically necessary," as they must be publicly funded.

Strategies for "consumer focus" included improvements in home care and long-term care services. The new home care services would address complex or long-term health needs. Additional long-term care services included several independent living options, as well as respite and education for family caregivers.

The document focused on shifting an increasing proportion of health care costs to individuals by seeking "financial contributions regardless of age" (Alberta Health 1994, 7) for universal health programs. Seniors would be required to pay health care premiums, where before they were exempt. Income thresholds for premium assistance for other Albertans would also be increased.

The report recommended health care premium costs rise by 20 per cent (only Alberta and BC still have premiums).

Strategies for the emphasis on personal accountability and responsibility for health included health promotion initiatives, research and evaluation, information systems, ethics and information, and training. The primary focus was education and skill development for individuals, particularly to encourage independence, healthy lifestyles and appropriate use of the health care system. These are all important for helping people take actions to improve and maintain their own health. However, an individualistic approach to promotion and prevention assumes health is the responsibility of individuals, rather than recognizing that individual behaviour and health status are embedded in a broader social context.

A Better Way (II)

A follow-up document, *A Better Way II: Blueprint for Building Alberta's Future 1995/96-1997/98*, was presented as a business plan, and discussed the progress on the goals and strategies from the earlier document (e.g., regionalization, wage rollbacks, premium increases, reallocating $110 million to community-based services). The second document also mentions "de-insuring medically unnecessary services" as part of an omnibus agreement reached with the Alberta Medical Association, along with developing clinical practice guidelines, lab restructuring and reduced spending on physician services.

The second document was more attentive to diversity (i.e., age, urban/ rural, Aboriginal and immigrant populations, disabled persons) than previous documents, but gender was not mentioned other than in reference to performance measures concerning in-patient hospital days and home care for new mothers. There was more mention of collaboration with other sectors to address social issues such as unemployment and underemployment, neighbourhood safety and substance abuse. The new document also added "the impact of socio-economic and environmental determinants of health" (Alberta Health 1995, 7) to its principles and criteria. Many of the strategies under the four main goals were the same or similar to those of the 1994 document.

In discussing characteristics of the health system in the future, *A Better Way II* states that "not-for-profit organizations, volunteers, volunteer organizations and private for-profit operators will continue to make significant contributions to the health system" (Alberta Health 1995, 15). It also mentions private alternative approaches to health services, dealing mostly with complementary therapies and counselling. Individuals would contribute to or cover the costs of such services.

What is the present state of some of the user charges discussed in the *Better Way* documents? In 1999, premium assistance for health insurance for non-seniors was such that single individuals with incomes over $7,560 per year and families (two or more people) with incomes over $12,620 per year paid full premiums. Full subsidy is available only for singles under $5,000 and families under $7,500 (Alberta Health 1999a). Thus, only those with extremely low incomes qualify. Premiums are at a flat rate regardless of income once the relatively low subsidy thresholds have been exceeded – meaning that lower income families pay the same premiums as higher income families. The gender implications of government policy are that women are more likely to benefit from the subsidies than men. However, for non-seniors in particular, the thresholds are low and more women than men will "fall between the cracks" by having too much income to qualify for subsidy, but not enough to be able to afford the full premium amount. High-income earners, more likely to be men, will spend a lower proportion of their overall income on premiums than lower income earners who are above the threshold cut-offs.

Current home care policy states that assessment, case coordination, direct professional and personal care (e.g., meals, bathing assistance) services are provided free for nearly two-thirds of clients. For those assessed fees, homemaking is $5 per hour and meal services are $5 a piece (Alberta Health 1999a). The gender implications are that unless there is adequate funding for trained staff to spend time in these community settings, the shift to the community will require more work by family caregivers, most of whom are women. User charges for homemaking and meal services could be seen as financial barriers for some families, even though they are on a sliding scale based on income and number of dependents. This could lead to more work for unpaid caregivers who feel they must make trade-offs between the fees and other living expenses (e.g., seniors on fixed incomes who encounter rental or property tax increases or home repair expenses).

Action on Health

Government documents from 1993 and 1996 focus heavily on cost saving (which is often cost shifting although it is not acknowledged as such). *Action on Health: Access, Quality, Stability* argued that the cuts of 1993 to 1996 were necessary because "costs were spiralling out of control" (Alberta Health 1997, 13). The document indicated that because the government had taken action on the deficit and debt repayment, it was now possible to address problem areas (e.g., waiting lists) and put in place a stable, predictable funding base for health. The assertion is questionable, considering that total Alberta public sector health care expenditures per capita in 1999 dollars increased by just $107 between 1990 and 1993 (i.e., the four years preceding the start of major restructuring efforts). This is compared to the average increase for Canada as a whole of almost $176 per capita.[3] Thus, the rate of public cost increases was declining prior to the major restructuring of the mid-1990s (CIHI 1999).

The *Action on Health* document reiterates a commitment to public sector control of the health care system and coverage of medically necessary services without user fees, extra- billing or other barriers. Waiting lists were a concern for both specialized province-wide services and services at the regional level. One of the commitments to address waiting lists was to hire frontline health care staff.

There was little specific mention of gender in this document, except for performance measures pertaining to female-specific diseases (i.e., breast cancer screening rates and cervical cancer deaths), low birthweight newborns, and the population funding formula which would account for age, gender and socio-economic status. Health education for parents of young children, which is most likely to reach mothers, was also mentioned.

The focus on reinvesting funds in health care had the potential to benefit women, as they make up the majority of health care workers and informal caregivers. The question is: to what extent did the proposals of *Action on Health* actually happen?

According to Alberta Health's website section on health care providers, an additional $22 million was added in 1996-97 and $43 million in 1997-98 to hire more nurses and other frontline staff – leading to a total increase of 1,401 full-time equivalent positions (1999a). According to the Canadian Institute for Health Information (CIHI 1999), the number of registered nurses employed in nursing in Alberta rose from 20,751 in 1996 to 21,428 in 1997. There was an increase in both full-time and part-time positions, and in the number of nurses per 100,000 population (from 751 to 763). During any given year, women form approximately 97 per cent of the registered nursing workforce in Alberta (AARN 1995, 1996, 1997).

Total public sector health expenditure per capita in Alberta increased from $1,674 to $1,791 between 1996 and 1997 (CIHI 1999). After percentage decreases of 6.5 per cent and 5.8 per cent in 1994 and 1995, there was a 3 per cent increase in spending by the end of 1996, and a further 7 per cent increase by the end of 1997. After being considerably below the national average (by $100 dollars or more) from 1994 through 1996, 1997 expenditures brought Alberta close to the national average. CIHI presented projected public expenditure increases for 1998 and 1999 (to $1,982 for 1999), but actual numbers were not available at the time of writing.

Although there has been some reinvestment in Alberta's health care system, health care workers question whether it has been adequate. For example, the United Nurses of Alberta's contract bargaining of 1999 addressed not only wage and salary issues, but also workload, overtime requirements, weekend and shift work, and parity of facility and community-based nurses. UNA documents suggested that managers had unrealistic expectations and did not recognize the stressful working conditions of nurses. Despite averting a potential strike and winning wage increases and some improvements in working conditions, the union's concerns about staffing and workload remain (UNA 1999). This reinvestment focus continues with the 2000-01 budget, particularly for the hiring of more nurses (Alberta Treasury 2000b). It is too early to determine the extent to which this will benefit providers and users of the health care system.

The Provincial Health Council of Alberta[4] (1997a) also expressed concerns about strain on health care providers:

> Many individual service providers have been profoundly affected by job loss, fear of job loss and job change. Staff resignations and reassignments have, in some cases, led to frequent changes in personnel. This creates

difficulties in maintaining standards of care. Staff are sometimes performing unfamiliar roles without the support that was available before restructuring. We have been told that many providers feel uncertain, devalued and highly stressed. Many of these feelings are brought on by frustration resulting from loss of control or any sense of participation in decision-making. (11)

The Council noted that low morale and job satisfaction affects the availability and quality of care through absenteeism, long-term disability leaves, turnover, recruitment difficulties, and low levels of trust. It acknowledged that in some cases staff reductions have led staff to collaborate in new ways.

The Health Statutes Amendment Act

Bill 37 (*The Health Statutes Amendment Act*) of 1998 was the first attempt by the government to regulate the provision of surgical services provided outside of public hospitals. Much of the bill addresses accreditation of facilities and qualifications of practitioners, as well as information required to make decisions about the use of surgical facilities. The term "non-hospital surgical facility" (defined as a "facility at which insured services, together with related facility services, are provided"), was so open-ended that it was difficult to see how it would prevent the mixing of insured and uninsured services within a facility – and thus, the charging of fees for services that might normally be covered. A panel commissioned by Alberta Health to review Bill 37 concluded that the bill and its amendment were complex pieces of legislation that could be easily "misconstrued." The government eventually withdrew this bill in the face of strong opposition (Taft and Steward 2000).

Health Summit 1999

Provincial Health Council reports released in 1997 expressed concern about the strains created in the health system (Provincial Health Council of Alberta 1997a, b), and indicated that while some elements of the system had been reorganized, health care reform had not taken place. Following the release of these reports, Minister of Health Halvar Jonson announced Health Summit 1999. Two hundred participants were invited to Calgary on February 25-27, 1999 to debate four questions and to strategize the future of the health system. They included 100 representatives of people working in the health system, as well as 100 randomly selected members of the public. The four questions debated were:

- What is essential in Alberta's health system?
- What changes should be made in how health services are delivered and managed?
- What responsibility do individuals have for their own health?
- How much money is enough to sustain our publicly funded health system? (Alberta Health 1999c, 4)

Participants strongly reaffirmed the principles of the *Canada Health Act* with particular emphasis on public funding and administration and equality of access. They chose not to identify specific components of the system as essential or non-essential. The general conclusion was that "priorities cannot be placed on essential components: all components are important to different people at different times" (Alberta Health 1999c, 20). There was general agreement on the need to expand primary health care, and prevention and promotion strategies. The report from the Summit also indicated that participants saw responsibility for health as a responsibility shared among "individuals, families, the health system, communities, different levels of government, and other sectors outside the health system" (Alberta Health 1999c, 26). There was no consensus on the appropriate level of funding for Alberta's health system, which is necessary "before decisions can be made about how much funding is needed" (Alberta Health 1999c, 30).

Health Information Systems: The Health Information Act

In 1997-98 the government began to lay the groundwork for a new health information network called "alberta we//net." *The Health Information and Protection Act* (Bill 30) was first introduced in 1997. The Alberta Medical Association (AMA 1998) issued a position statement summarizing a number of concerns with the proposed Act, including:

- violation of the patient-doctor relationship;

- failure to protect personal identifiable health information; and

- profound operational and financial impacts for physicians.

In the face of strong public opposition, which centred on the lack of control that individuals would have over the release of personal health information, the government withdrew the Bill. It was again introduced to the legislature in November 1999, this time as *The Health Information Act* (Bill 40). The change in the name of the legislation is worthy of note. Although there is a stated commitment to the protection of personal privacy within the summary documents, the conditions under which information could be accessed without consent may be broadly interpreted. For example, the "custodian" may access information without an individual's consent to determine if someone is eligible to receive a health service, that is, to see if they are registered for Alberta Health Care Insurance or other benefits (Alberta Health and Wellness 1999). There was heated debate in the legislature over the bill. The Official Opposition proposed a number of amendments that would increase the level of control over personal health information and ensure that the legislation covered private as well as public health care providers (*Hansard* 1999). Critics were concerned that access to the government's health information database might allow private funders and providers to screen out people who are at higher risk. This would affect people who earn low incomes (e.g., women, people who are disabled). The government closed debate on the bill and it was passed in the legislature on December 9, 1999 with few amendments.

Bill 11: The Health Care Protection Act

With *The Health Information Act* in place, the government proceeded to introduce Bill 11, *The Health Care Protection Act*. The introduction of this legislation sparked substantial federal and provincial debate.

In late 1995, the federal government began to withhold transfer payments to penalize Alberta for allowing private clinics to charge facility fees to people receiving medically insured services. In 1996, while attempting to resolve this issue, the federal and Alberta provincial health ministers agreed to 12 principles outlining the Alberta approach to health care management (Alberta Health and Wellness 2000a).[5] Seven of the principles specifically discuss issues related to private purchase and provision of health services, but it is principle 11 that is perceived to have put in place much of the groundwork for the introduction of Bill 11. This principle, as stated originally, recognized that "physicians can receive payment from both the publicly funded system and fully private systems" (Alberta Health and Wellness 2000b).

The primary focus of Bill 11 is on practices related to acute care (i.e., care provided in public hospitals and approved surgical facilities). A departure from this focus is found in Part 4 of the Bill, which addresses the formation of the Premier's Advisory Council on Health. The mandate of the Council would be "to provide advice to the Premier on the preservation and future enhancement of quality health services for Albertans and on the continuing sustainability of the publicly funded and publicly administered health system" (Alberta Health and Wellness 2000b, 14). It should be noted that this does not state that the Council will provide advice on the preservation and future enhancement of the public health system.

The preamble to the legislation reaffirms the government's commitment to a publicly funded and publicly administered health system and to the principles of the *Canada Health Act*. However, the section of the Bill that deals with the designation of surgical facilities includes a clause that would permit the Minister to consider "any other factors the Minister considers appropriate" (Alberta Health and Wellness 2000b, 9). These "other factors," left to ministerial discretion, could override concern for whether the provision of such services would have an "adverse impact on the publicly funded and publicly administered health system or impair the government's ability to comply with the *Canada Health Act*" (Alberta Health and Wellness 2000b, 9). In a legal opinion obtained by the Canadian Union of Public Employees (CUPE 2000), the law firm of Arvay Finlay states that "the Bill's provisions violate *Canada Health Act* requirements dealing with universality, accessibility and comprehensiveness and may threaten the public administration requirement" (1). In addition, the bill states that "no decision made by the Minister in the exercise or purported exercise of power...under this Act may be questioned or reviewed in any court" (Alberta Health and Wellness 2000b, 11). The level of ministerial control and the exemption of the Minister from legal questioning were raised as concerns in public discussions about the bill.

The opening section of the bill states that "no person shall operate a private hospital in Alberta" (Alberta Health and Wellness 2000b, 3) and that surgical services may only be provided in public hospitals or approved surgical facilities. "Approved surgical facilities" are distinguished from public and private hospitals by stipulating that the primary function of such facilities is to provide a limited range of surgical services. It is also stated that major surgical services can only be provided in public hospitals (ibid.). The distinction between what is major and what is not is not clearly defined. Bill 11 gives the College of Physicians and Surgeons the authority to decide which procedures can be safely provided in surgical facilities, but offers some parameters for such decisions. For example, "uninsured in-patient surgical" services may be provided in such facilities and are defined as services that require "a medically supervised post-operative period of care exceeding 12 hours" (ibid., 18). Dr. Tom Noseworthy, former head of the Royal Alexandra Hospital in Edmonton and Chair of Public Health Sciences at the University of Alberta points out that minor procedures are now done primarily as day surgery and people are not admitted to hospital overnight unless their surgery is major (Pederson 2000a). Noseworthy generally favours a role for private service delivery with public financing (as currently exists), and yet he raises concerns about extending private delivery to include surgical facilities with overnight stays, noting that such clinics would no longer be doing minor surgery.

Although Bill 11 states that it will allow neither direct billing for medically necessary service nor "queue-jumping," private clinics will be able to bill for uninsured extra services. Thus, there appear to be incentives for physicians practising in both public hospitals and private clinics to direct people to the private side.

Under Bill 11, approved surgical facilities will be able to provide insured surgical services under contract to an RHA. Given the need to generate profits for shareholders, it is questionable whether such private facilities would be willing to share in the costs associated with negotiating, implementing and monitoring contracts with RHAs (Wilson 2000b). In fact, Bill 11 specifically states that the money for contracts will come out of the RHA budgets (Alberta Health and Wellness 2000b, 7). Money that is required for such contracting services will not be available for direct service provision. It is equally unlikely that it will be a priority for such facilities to assume responsibility for linking patients to services provided through the public health system (e.g., home care, diagnostic and intensive care services). This implies that patients who require assistance during or following surgery will have to acquire such services themselves. These implications have obvious consequences for caregiving responsibilities of family members, primarily women.

Bill 11 also raises concerns about de-insurance of more services that could then be picked up as uninsured user-pay procedures, or further privatization of public services. An existing example of privatization of public services in Calgary is the transfer of the Grace Hospital (which focused on women's health)[6] to the private sector. This previously public facility now houses the

Health Resources Group (HRG), a private clinic that is particularly interested in contracting with the RHA for overnight stays (Taft and Steward 2000).

A study of hospital utilization patterns in Alberta found that reductions in hospital separation rates (i.e., cases admitted to hospital and average lengths of stay) led to a 40 per cent decrease in Alberta's age-sex standardized hospital days rate between 1991-92 and 1996-97 (Saunders, Bay and Ahbhai 1998). The study also indicates that the reduction of the hospital days rate slowed in 1996-97 because average lengths of stay increased even though the separation rate continued to decline. The researchers noted that average case-intensity increased over that time period, "suggesting that sicker, more resource-intensive patients were admitted to hospitals"(15). The researchers also pointed out that hospital utilization was already on a downward trend in the five years prior to 1991-92 (a 26% drop in the standardized days rate) and that health reform and associated funding reductions accelerated the trend. Concerns have been raised about the impacts on women of short hospital stays and the shift from acute care institution to community care. There is some doubt that these concerns will be addressed in the shift toward private facilities (i.e., that private clinics would allow, at no charge, longer stays than public hospitals).

Concerns have also been raised about the implications of Bill 11 for the North American Free Trade Agreement (NAFTA). Rachlis (2000) states that under this agreement, "health care is protected only to the extent that it is considered a social service carried out for the public good" (5). That is, health care in Canada may be open to global competition which, once it occurs, may be irreversible. It has been argued that private for-profit hospitals already exist in Canada (e.g., the Shouldice Clinic in Ontario) and therefore the NAFTA has already been tested and proven innocuous with respect to health care. These arguments do not acknowledge that the Shouldice Clinic and other small facilities existed before the *Medical Care Insurance Act* (1966) and were grandfathered into private hospital legislation. New, for-profit facilities have not been licensed in Ontario, for example, since 1973 (Rachlis 2000).

In their critique of Bill 11, the authors of "Decline Klein's Medicine" (Barer *et al.* 2000) state that private payment shifts costs of care disproportionately to those with lower incomes. In Alberta, we know that the majority of people living on low incomes are women (CSWAC 1999).

In April 2000, the government began discussing amendments to the Bill, including tightening procedures to prevent "queue-jumping" and addressing conflict of interest (Geddes 2000). Shortly thereafter, the federal minister of health suggested more substantive amendments, including restrictions on insured and uninsured services being offered by the same providers and banning overnight stays (Pederson 2000). On April 11, 2000 Premier Ralph Klein's government announced that it would introduce a motion to block any further amendments and force a vote on second reading of the Bill as early as that night (Johnsrude 2000b).

Community-based Care and Home Care

In 1997, Casebeer, Scott and Hannah explored strategies for shifting service delivery patterns towards increased community-based care in one RHA in Alberta. At the time of the study, regionalization had been in place for two years and it was clear that the management team in the region had yet to define community-based care.

The Provincial Health Council of Alberta (1997a) indicated that despite the government's indications that there had been more funding for community and home-based services, it had no details on how the funding was being used. Although the Council recognized off-loading and its potential negative impacts, it did not acknowledge that women bear a disproportionate share of informal caregiving. It took family caregiving as a given, rather than questioning it. As the Council was a ministerially appointed body, it did not have a mandate to go beyond monitoring and reporting on reforms as defined and implemented by the government. Within that mandate, it did provide a more critical analysis than other bodies within government.

More recent studies have demonstrated that a substantial percentage of adult Albertans are providing health care support to a family member. A provincial survey commissioned by Alberta Health and Wellness and conducted by the University of Alberta Population Research Laboratory, found that 44 per cent of females and 32 per cent of males provided such support in 1999 (Northcott and Northcott 1999). Of those providing support, 44 per cent said it was a minor inconvenience and 12 per cent said it was a major disruption of their normal activities. Women were more likely than men to say that providing support was a major disruption. The survey did not assess the amount or level of support provided, so we are unable to examine hours and types of work by sex which might explain gender differences in perceptions of inconvenience. Other researchers (Armstrong and Armstrong 1996), however, have pointed out that in most cases women take on a greater proportion of caregiving tasks than men.

By examining Alberta Health annual reports between 1996 and 1999, Wilson (2000a) illustrates that, despite a commitment to increased support for home care and community health, the proportion of health system funds devoted to these areas has remained relatively constant (4.7% in 1996-97, 4.9% in 1997-98, 5.1% in 1998-99). At the same time, hospital downsizing resulted in the removal of approximately one half of all inpatient acute care beds across Alberta (i.e., from 12,000 beds to 6,260 beds in 1998-99). Wilson notes that a consequence of hospital downsizing has been the "shift of caregiving and cost of care to the family" (4). Morris *et al.* (1999) cite statistics from the Canadian Home Care Association noting that in the early days of health restructuring in Alberta, the government cut $749 million from acute care but added only $110 million to home care over three years.

There is also the issue of out-of-pocket costs. For example, Morris *et al.* (1999) expressed concern about home care recipients and their unpaid caregivers picking up costs (e.g., meals, drugs, medical devices) that would be covered if the recipient was in a hospital. The limited hours and services for which recipients are eligible for home care also lead to them having to pay fees for services beyond that level. This may be reflected in the sudden upward trend in private coverage in Alberta which, in 1997, showed an 11 per cent jump, more than double the increase for the national average and most other provinces.

Another area where provider strain is reported as high is among paid home care staff. Morris *et al.* (1999) found low wages, irregular hours, inadequate training and high turnover among workers (mostly women). Workers observed that these conditions resulted in a lack of continuity of care, staff shortages, waiting lists, health risks to both workers and recipients, and impoverishment. Some home care workers reported working at several jobs to make ends meet, and others were living below the poverty line. Morris *et al.* also discuss the "deprofessionalization" of home care work, isolation of workers, lack of adequate training, exposure to violence or harassment, and the absence of professional associations or unions. They found some examples of home care workers, as well as family members, picking up out-of-pocket costs (e.g., equipment, meals, drugs) for low-income clients, costs that would be covered in hospital. Morris *et al.* point out that as there is more competition between for-profit and not-for-profit providers (e.g., VON) there is likely to be continued downward pressure on wages and that for-profit providers will not reinvest money back into service provision.

Representatives of provincial health ministers have indicated that they prefer to have transfer payments restored to use as they wish in their existing health care systems, rather than develop expanded home care and community care, which they call "boutique programs" (Mackie and Sequin 2000). Given the government's record of expecting women to put their families first and volunteer unpaid labour as public services, it is unlikely that Alberta would use extra funds to design a home care program that did not rely to a large extent on the unpaid or underpaid work of women.

Conclusion

Alberta has long been committed to enhancing the role of the private sector in health care – and strong legislative and public opposition to the privatization agenda has done little to alter the course or the pace of change. Despite the level of public discourse regarding recent legislation, there has been little public discussion of the gendered impacts of the move toward privatization. Our analysis of health policy between 1989 and 2000 highlights the serious implications for women of increased health care privatization – lower wages, less secure jobs, out-of-pocket costs, informal caregiving obligations. Before any further legislation is introduced, the implications for all citizens, particularly women, must be comprehensively examined, using strategies for meaningful public participation in decision-making.

Notes

1. During the 1990s, the term "consumer" has been increasingly used in the literature to refer to people who access health services. The term embodies the market model of health care and the notion that health care and the social relations of health care are commodities (i.e., products rather than services).
2. This included a substantial but not complete sample of Alberta program reports.
3. Per capita expenditures are rounded to the nearest whole dollar.
4. The Provincial Health Council was established by the Minister of Health in 1995 to monitor and report to the legislature the progress of health care reform in Alberta. It was disbanded in 1998. There is a new Premier's Advisory Council on Health in the planning stages. It will be chaired by former Deputy Prime Minister Don Mazankowski (presently chair of the Institute of Health Economics) and will advise the premier and the government on health system sustainability (Alberta Health and Wellness 2000b).
5. After several attempts, we were able to obtain an original copy of these principles from Alberta Health and Wellness. It was indicated that it was just by chance that someone had kept a copy. We appreciate the cooperation of the staff person who shared this public information with us.
6. The Grace has since been relocated to the Foothills Hospital site and renamed the Grace Women's Health Centre

References

Alberta Advisory Council on Women's Issues (AACWI). 1996a. *A Decade of Challenge and Change: A Review of the Activities of the Alberta Advisory Council on Women's Issues.* Edmonton, AB: Alberta Advisory Council on Women's Issues.

—. 1996b. *Breadmakers and Breadwinners: The Voices of Alberta Women.* Edmonton, AB: Alberta Advisory Council on Women's Issues.

Alberta Association of Registered Nurses (AARN). 1995, 1996, 1997. *Membership Statistics.* Edmonton, AB: Alberta Association of Registered Nurses.

Alberta. Legislative Assembly. *Debates and Proceedings (Hansard).* 1999. 32nd Legislature, 4th Session. Vol. 33, no. 88 (July 11). Edmonton, AB: Queen's Printer.

Alberta Health. 1991. *Partners in Health: The Government of Alberta's Response to the Premier's Commission on Future Health Care for Albertans.* Edmonton, AB: Alberta Health.

—. 1993. *Health Goals for Alberta: Progress Report.* Edmonton, AB: Alberta Health.

—. 1994. *A Better Way I: A Plan for Securing Alberta's Future.* Edmonton, AB: Alberta Health.

—. 1995. *A Better Way II: Blueprint for Building Alberta's Future.* Edmonton, AB: Alberta Health.

—. 1997. *Action on Health: Access, Quality, Stability.* Edmonton, AB: Alberta Health.

—. 1999a. *Health Services for Albertans: Community-based Services.* <www.health.gov.ab.ca/services/sercomm.htm>; *AHCIPC Premiums and Rates,* <www.health.gov.ab.ca/ahcip/premiums.htm>; *Health care providers,* <www.health.gov.ab.ca/about/boutprov.html>. April 5, 2000.

—. 1999b. *Report of the Bill 37 Review Panel.* Edmonton, AB: Alberta Health.

—. 1999c. *Health Summit 1999: Final Report and Recommendations.* Edmonton, AB: Alberta Health.

Alberta Health and Wellness. 1999. *A Summary of Alberta's New Health Information Act.* Edmonton, AB: Alberta Health and Wellness.

—. 2000a. "Private/Public Health Services: The Alberta Approach." Edmonton, AB: Alberta Health and Wellness.
—. 2000b. *Bill 11: Alberta's Health Care Protection Act.* Edmonton: AB. Alberta Health and Wellness.
Alberta Health Planning Secretariat. 1993. *Starting Points: Recommendations for Creating a More Accountable and Affordable Health System.* Edmonton, AB: Alberta Health.
Alberta Medical Association (AMA). 1998. *Alberta Medical Association Comments to Bill 30: Health Information Protection Act.* Edmonton, AB: Alberta Medical Association.
Alberta Treasury. 1999. *Budget 1999: The Right Balance: Fiscal and Business Plan.* <www.treas.gov.ab.ca/comm/budget99/health.html>.
—. 2000a. *Budget 2000: New Century, Bold Plans. Health and Wellness Business Plan 2000-2003.* <www.treas.gov.ab.ca/comm/bud2000/health.html>.
—. 2000b. *Budget 2000: New Century, Bold Plans . Highlights and Accountability Statement.* <www.treas.gov.ab.ca/comm/bud2000/highli.html>.
Armstrong, Pat and Hugh Armstrong. 1996. *Wasting Away: The Undermining of Canadian Health Care.* Toronto, ON: Oxford University Press.
Armstrong, W. 2000. *The Consumer Experience with Cataract Surgery and Private Clinics in Alberta: Canada's Canary in the Mineshaft.* Calgary, AB: The Alberta Chapter of Consumers Association of Canada.
Barer, M., R. Evans, S. Lewis, M. Rachlis and G. Stoddart. 2000. "Decline Klein's Medicine: Alberta's Premier Has Made a Completely Wrong Diagnosis of What Ails Our Health System." *The Globe and Mail,* 7 March.
Bubel, A., and D. Spitzer, D. 1996. *Documenting Women's Stories. The Impact of Health Care on Women's Health.* Edmonton, AB: Prepared for the Edmonton Women's Health Network.
Calgary Status of Women Action Committee (CSWAC). 1999. *Watering Down the Milk: Women Coping on Alberta's Minimum Wage.* Calgary, AB: Calgary Status of Women Action Committee.
Canadian Institute for Health Information (CIHI). 1999. National Health Expenditure Trends (1975-99), <www.cihi.ca/medrls.execnhex.htm>.
Canadian Union of Public Employees (CUPE). 2000. *The Medicare Destruction Act,* <www.cupe.ca/arvay/summary.asp>, April 5, 2000.
Casebeer, A. L., C.M. Scott and K.J. Hannah. In press. "Transforming a Health Care System: Managing Change for Community Gain." *Canadian Journal of Public Health.*
Crichton, A., D. Hsu and S. Tsang. 1990. *Canada's Health Care System: Its Funding and Organization.* Ottawa, ON: Canadian Hospital Association Press.
Crockatt, J. 1994. "Tories Back Down on Controversial Bill." *The Edmonton Journal,* day month, A1.
Dacks, G., J. Green and L. Trimble. 1995. "Road Kill: Women in Alberta's Drive Toward Deficit Elimination." In T. Harrison and G. Laxer, eds., *The Trojan Horse: Alberta and the Future of Canada.* Montreal, QC: Black Rose.
Fuller, Colleen. 1998. *Caring for Profit: How Corporations Are Taking Over Canada's Health Care System.* Vancouver, BC: New Star Books.
Geddes, A. 2000. "Province to Amend Private Health Bill." *The Edmonton Journal,* 7 April, A1.
Government of Alberta. 1994. *Regional Health Authorities Act.* Statues of Alberta, 1994, Chapter R-9.07 with amendments in force as of August 1, 1996. Edmonton, AB: Government of Alberta.
Government of Alberta. 1997. Alberta Regulation 202/97. *Regional Health Authorities Act, Community Health Councils Regulation.* Edmonton, AB: Government of Alberta.
Harrison, T. 1995. "Making the Trains Run on Time: Corporatism in Alberta." In T. Harrison and G. Laxer, eds., *The Trojan Horse: Alberta and the Future of Canada,* 118-31. Montreal, QC: Black Rose.
Horne, T., L. Donner and W.E. Thurston. 1999. *Invisible Women: Gender and Health Planning in Manitoba and Saskatchewan and Models for Progress.* Winnipeg, MB: Prairie Women's Health Centre of Excellence.
Johnsrude, L. 2000a. "Klein Calls Out 'Truth Squads.'" *The Edmonton Journal,* 11 February, A1, A6.

Johnsrude, L. 2000b. "Government Forces Vote on Bill 11." *The Edmonton Journal*, 11 April, A1.
Kline, M. 1997. "Blue Meanies in Alberta: Tory Tactics and the Privatization of Child Welfare." In Susan Boyd, ed., *Challenging the Public/Private Divide: Feminism, Law and Public Policy*, 330-59. Toronto, ON: University of Toronto Press.
Legislative Assembly of Alberta. 1994a. *Delegated Administration Act*. Edmonton, AB: Government of Alberta.
—. 1994b. *Government Organization Act*. Edmonton, AB: Government of Alberta.
Lisac, M. 1995. *The Klein Revolution*. Edmonton, AB: NeWest Press.
Mackie, R. and R. Seguin. 2000. "Health Care Crisis, Leaders Warn." *The Globe and Mail*, 4 February, A4.
McArthur, W., C. Ramsay and M. Walker. 1996. *Healthy Incentives*. Vancouver, BC: Fraser Institute.
McKenna, R., A. Hanion-Dearman and A. Yassi. 1999. "Practice Patterns of Women in Medicine: Implications for the Medical Profession." *Prairie Medical Journal* 64 (1):16-19.
Morris, M., J. Robinson, J. Simpson, S. Galey, S. Kirby., L. Martin and M. Muzychka. 1999. *The Changing Nature of Home Care and Its Impact on Women's Vulnerability to Poverty*. Ottawa, ON: Prepared for the Canadian Research Institute for the Status of Women, funded by the Status of Women Canada's Policy Research Fund.
Northcott, H.C. and B.R. Northcott. 1999. *The 1999 Survey About Health and the Health System in Alberta*. Edmonton, AB: Conducted for Alberta Health and Wellness through the Population Research Laboratory at the University of Alberta.
Noseworthy, T.W. 1999. "Reconciling the Past and Shaping the Future: Health and Medicare." Keynote Address to Health Summit 1999, 25 February, Calgary, AB.
Pederson, R. 2000a. "Doctor Accuses Government of Clouding Health Care Issues." *The Edmonton Journal*, 10 March, A7.
—. 2000b. "Rock Wants Alberta to Drop Patient Fees." *The Edmonton Journal*, 8 April, A1, A12.
Premier's Commission on Future Health Care for Albertans. 1989a. *The Rainbow Report: Our Vision for Health*. Vols. 1-3. Edmonton, AB: The Government of Alberta.
—. 1989b. *What You've Said Newsletter Special Edition*. Edmonton, AB: The Government of Alberta.
Provincial Health Council of Alberta. 1997a. *Health Check-up on the Journey to Health Reform: Report Card on the Status of Health Reform in Alberta*. Edmonton, AB: Provincial Health Council of Alberta.
—. 1997b. *Annual Report to the Legislature*. Edmonton, AB: Provincial Health Council of Alberta.
Rachlis, M. 2000. *A Review of the Alberta Private Hospital Proposal*. Toronto, ON: Caledon Institute of Social Policy.
Renouf, S. 1995. "Chipping Away at Medicare: 'Rome Wasn't Sacked in a Day.'" In T. Harrison and G. Laxer, eds., *The Trojan Horse: Alberta and the Future of Canada*, 223-38. Montreal, QC: Black Rose.
Saunders, L.D., K. Bay and A. Alibhai. 1998. "Regionalization and Hospital Utilization: Alberta 1991/92 to 1996/97." Report #98-0001, prepared by Health Information Unit, Department of Public Health Sciences, University of Alberta.
Taft, K., and G. Steward. 2000. *Private Profit or the Public Good: The Economics and Politics of the Privatization of Health Care in Alberta*. Edmonton, AB: Parkland Institute.
Thurston, W. E., C.M. Scott and B.A. Crow. 1997. "Social Change, Policy Development and the Influence on Women's Health." Paper read at the Fifth National Health Promotion Research Conference, July 4-5, Halifax, NS.
Thurston, W. E., B.A. Crow and C.M. Scott. 1998. *The Role of Women's Organizations in Health Policy Development, Implementation and Dissemination*. Ottawa, ON: Health Canada.
Thurston, W. E., D.R. Wilson, R. Felix, G. MacKean and M. Wright. 1999. *Health Promotion Projects in Alberta 1993-1998: An Overview*. Edmonton, AB: Alberta Health and Wellness.
Trimble, L. 1997. "Feminist Politics in the Alberta Legislature, 1972-1994." In J. Arscott and L. Trimble, eds., *In the Presence of Women: Representation in Canadian Governments*. Toronto, ON: Harcourt Brace Canada.

United Nurses of Alberta (UNA). 1999. *UNA Stat* (Newsletter July): 3-7.

Wilson, D. M. 1995. *The Canadian Health Care System.* Edmonton, AB: Donna M. Wilson.

—. 2000a. "Regional Health Planning and Delivery in Alberta: A Basic Cost-Benefit Analysis in Response to a Health System Performance Issue." Paper presented to the Standing Policy Committee on Health and Safe Communities. Faculty of Nursing, University of Alberta.

—. 2000b. "Bill 11CA 10-Point Critique." E-mail communication to author, March 15.

The Information Gap: The Impact of Health Care Reform on British Columbia Women

Colleen Fuller

THE BC PROCESS OF HEALTH CARE REFORM

British Columbia was one of the first provinces in Canada to initiate major reforms in the health care system during the 1990s. Many of these reforms followed the recommendations of the Royal Commission on Health Care and Costs whose 1991 report, *Closer to Home*, attributed problems in the health care system to structural, administrative and funding practices. These practices, the report concluded, were responsible for growing disparities in health across the population and inequities in access to health services. The lack of an overall plan for health services delivery throughout the province and misplaced priorities in health spending also pointed to a system in need of an overhaul. The report asserted that the current health system could and should be changed to produce better health results for the same or lower overall costs (HIMCC 1996).

In response, the Ministry of Health initiated an extensive consultation and review process and outlined five interrelated themes to deliver more health care services outside the acute care sector and in a more efficient manner. These themes were: better health; greater public participation and responsibility; bringing health closer to home; respecting the caregiver; and effective management of the health system. The ministry's report, *New Directions for a Healthy British Columbia*, was released in March 1993, sparking a vigorous reform effort in the sector.

The first phase of health care reform took place from 1993 to 1996, and involved the establishment of 102 Regional Health Boards (RHBs) and Community Health Councils (CHCs) throughout the province. An important focus during this phase was the movement of non-acute care services out of hospitals and into the community, a reduction in the hospital workforce by up to 10 per cent, and reduced utilization rates in the hospital sector (to 850 beds per 1000 population). To minimize the impact of the resulting hospital layoffs, the province initiated discussions with the three main health care unions, leading to an agreement on labour adjustment and retraining covering 60,000 members. The agreement contained some of the most progressive job security language for health care workers in North America and has since been incorporated into the collective agreements covering most members of the BC Nurses' Union (BCNU), the Hospital Employees' Union (HEU) and the Health Sciences Association (HSA) (Health Canada 1997).[1]

In mid-1996, the Minister of Health placed health care reform on hold pending a review by a Regionalization Assessment Team, made up of four Members of the Legislative Assembly (MLAs). Another round of meetings and consultations took place, and in November of that year the second phase of health care reform was initiated. *New Directions* became *Better Teamwork, Better Care*, and the framework for governance was modified. Instead of 102 boards and councils, transfer of authority for the delivery of health care began on April 1, 1997 to 11 RHBs in major urban centres, 34 CHCs in rural and geographically isolated areas, and seven newly established Community Health Services Societies.

HEALTH CARE GOVERNANCE

Regional Health Boards in British Columbia are responsible for the direct management and delivery of health care services, while Community Health Councils have responsibility for acute care and continuing care residential services at the community level. Community Health Services Societies have responsibility for public health, mental health and some continuing care at the community level. These new roles have been redirected from the Ministry of Health and from some municipal governments. The 52 regional and community health structures have effectively replaced 700 boards that were solely responsible for the management and governance of hospital societies and other health facilities throughout the province. Residential care facilities and agencies run by religious organizations (such as Catholic hospitals) operate under affiliation agreements or service contracts with boards or councils.

For women, the establishment of regional and community governance structures opened up new opportunities for participation in key areas of decision-making in BC's health sector. In 1995, 53 per cent of the members appointed to RHBs and CHCs were women, compared to 25 per cent who were elected as MLAs, and 24 per cent of mayors and local government representatives who were women (British Columbia 1996). On the surface, the devolution of authority to boards and councils would appear to enable women to ensure that their collective and common gender interests are being met. However, without information about how women are affected generally and specifically by health care reform, it is questionable whether or not women can play the advocacy role they might wish to in policy development, planning and budget allocations.

The 1996 Report of the Provincial Health Officer said the Ministry of Health must give a high priority to developing better information about the outcomes, effectiveness and cost of health services. The report also cited the need to develop better data to track income equality/inequality and its impact on health. Yet neither the 1995 nor the 1996 report acknowledges a lack of information on the impact of health care reform on female utilization and on women as paid and unpaid caregivers (British Columbia 1995).

In 1996, British Columbia became the first and only province to incorporate the principles of the *Canada Health Act* in legislation banning the imposition of user charges for hospital and physician services. However, the province did not adopt then federal Minister of Health Diane Marleau's policy that the definition of a "hospital" included *any* facility that delivered medically necessary acute, rehabilitative or chronic care services (*Medicare Protection Act* 1996).

That same year, the province enacted the *Community Care Facilities Act*, establishing a branch responsible for the development and implementation of legislation, policy and program standards for licenced child day care facilities, and child and adult residential care facilities. These facilities were defined as those providing "care, supervision, social or educational training or physical or mental rehabilitative therapy, with or without charge." A community care facility might also provide food and lodging, and services to pregnant women – again, with or without charge (*Community Care Facility Act* 1996).

The legislation enacted by the province since 1994 has defined many of the terms within which health care reform is taking place. A preoccupation with the structures required to manage a reformed system (including those controlling governance) is reflected in most of the language contained in the new legislation. Public concerns about maintaining or even increasing access to health services have been addressed in the government's commitment to ensuring that adequate funding is available. The positive role such a commitment plays in the health care system cannot be underestimated. In addition, the BC government has attempted to ensure that legislation provides the tools needed to protect the non-profit nature of health care delivery. But it is unknown how the various pieces of legislation will fare as more and more authority is transferred to regional health boards, or what will happen now that a new provincial government with a different policy agenda is installed.

A revolution will be required, beginning at the level of information gathering, to develop an accurate picture of how health care reform leads to an increase in the number of for-profit providers, and how such developments impact on women at home and in the workforce. Without such information, policies that adequately protect access to vital services by women regardless of where they live, their ability to pay or their health status will be insufficient and implemented haphazardly, if at all. The circumstances of paid and, especially, of unpaid caregivers will remain unknown by the vast majority of the public, including those responsible for developing and implementing standards and policies in the health sector. Women are affected disproportionately by restructuring that results in reduced access to health care services. But even among women, the effects of reduced access are felt unevenly. Women of colour, Aboriginal women, women from ethnic minority groups, elderly women, lesbians, low-income women and women with mental and physical disabilities experience a multitude of impacts from actions that limit their ability to use the health system when and how they need to. This is because sexism combines with race discrimination and stereotypes about specific groups to further undermine the efforts of these citizens to achieve good or better health and increase their independence and autonomy. Information that reflects this diversity among the female population and the differences in how women are affected by health care reform and privatization is urgently required.

Women are entitled to information about their own conditions in order that they can better defend and exercise their rights and responsibilities as primary users and providers of health services in British Columbia. Such information needs to be collected and maintained in the public sector (within the context of privacy legislation) and protected from commercial exploitation and use by profit-making entities.

HEALTH CARE JOBS

Health care reform in BC was kicked off with the 1992 closure of Shaughnessy Hospital, located in an upper middle-class neighbourhood of Vancouver, with 350 acute care beds and 1700 staff. Although hospital staff and their unions, as well as a number of patient groups, physicians and others were fiercely opposed to the closure, the province worked diligently to ensure service levels would not be eroded. Despite fears throughout BC that the Shaughnessy closure would soon be followed by others, this has not happened. The majority of both staff and beds were relocated to other facilities within the region, and the provincial government fulfilled a commitment to establish a facility that would target its services at women. The old Shaughnessy site now houses the British Columbia's Women's Hospital and Health Centre and BC's Children's Hospital, as well as the BC Centre of Excellence for Women's Health.

The closure of Shaughnessy Hospital was the beginning of BC's effort to implement radical reforms to the health care system. The goals of the government were to reduce utilization rates throughout the province, transfer authority for the health care system to local levels of governance, and develop a more integrated approach to health care delivery. Downsizing in the hospital sector promised to be controversial, however, and the government took steps to minimize the impact of bed and staff reductions on nurses, paramedical health professionals and health services and support staff.

Like other jurisdictions in Canada, the health care workforce in British Columbia is overwhelmingly female. Women make up between 85 per cent and 87 per cent of those employed in the hospital sector and in the delivery of health-related social and community services. Not surprisingly, therefore, the announcement by the Ministry of Health that services would be devolving to the community sent shock waves through the highly unionized hospital workforce.

The hospital sector had provided women with opportunities for mobility, career advancement, education and secure incomes: job characteristics that were and are rare for most female workers. In addition, wage and benefit comparisons between the acute care sector and the largely unorganized community or social services sector were not promising. Unions that already had been concentrating some of their organizing efforts in the community had found that publicly funded, non-profit entities with small budgets and staffing levels of three to ten people were difficult to organize and expensive to service. Those who worked in the community sector, however, were among those most in need of the benefits of a collective agreement.

An important part of the health care reform process was the redistribution of union jurisdiction in the hospital, community and social services sectors and the establishment of multi-union bargaining associations in each area. The Health Sector Labour Relations Regulations established new bargaining units in the summer of 1995, sparking a lengthy review process among unions, employers and the Labour Relations Board to determine which employees belonged in which unions. In mid-1997, the regulations were scrapped and replaced with Bill 28, which modified the structures created by the "old" regulation. This process is ongoing, but bargaining associations were established in Bill 28 for paramedical professionals in both the hospital and community sectors, health services/support staff in the facilities sector, health services/support staff in the community sector and nurses (both registered and psychiatric nurses) in both the hospital and community sectors.

In April 2001, BC's Minister of Health, Corky Evans, tabled Bill 23, *Health Authorities Amendment Act*, integrating bargaining units representing workers in health services facilities and those employed in community health settings. This long-held objective of health care workers and employers passed just days before an election was called. At the time of writing it was not known how the Liberals, who have formed the new government, would view the new law.

The Health Labour Accords

As Shaughnessy wound down its operations, the government initiated talks with the BC Nurses' Union, the Hospital Employees' Union and the BC Health Sciences Association to reach an "accord" on job security and retraining. An agreement was concluded in 1993, establishing the Health Labour Adjustment Agency (HLAA) and provisions for province-wide seniority that allowed "bumping" from one facility to another. Although the accord did not initially ensure that as employees moved into the community, the job security provisions would go with them, it was an innovative approach to addressing the fears among hospital workers that "closer to home" would bring an abrupt end to their employment.

Under the health labour accord, the reduction in hospital staff was projected at up to 10 per cent, while the bed to population ratios were to be reduced to 2.75 beds per 1,000 population.[2] Among some employee groups, particularly in highly specialized areas, the prospects for alternative employment appeared slim. In part, this was because the community-based facilities envisioned for the future would be oriented towards more general levels of care. The HLAA, which registers and matches available positions to qualified health care workers whose jobs have been slated for elimination, has worked closely with employers and unions to ensure that as many layoffs as possible are "voluntary" (e.g., through early retirement incentives or retraining). But among some groups, such as medical laboratory technologists, the increasing use of robotics technology in the health sector and the amalgamation of hospital labs were combining with the province's downsizing efforts to severely reduce job opportunities. The HLAA initially had less success in relocating these employees to other jobs in the sector. Recent shortages, however, have boosted the demand for certain skills in the hospital sector and increased competition with the private sector for workers in key areas.

One clause in the health accord designed to protect unionized jobs prevented hospitals from closing outpatient diagnostic and rehabilitation services if such a closure resulted in a shift of funding for those same services to private providers within the same region. This was an important tool in the unions' collective agreements, but it did not stop the outflow of outpatient rehab and diagnostic services from the hospital sector. Many outpatient rehab departments have been closed and there has been a sharp increase in the use of private companies by the Workers' Compensation Board (WCB) and the Insurance Corporation of BC (ICBC).

In 1998, the Health Sciences Association (HSA) and the Hospital Employees' Union (HEU) negotiated what was referred to as a "side accord" agreement to address this problem. The accord established a joint union/Ministry of Health committee to advise the government on ways to enhance the role of public providers in two areas: laboratory services and breast cancer screening; and rehabilitation services and programs for clients of the WCB and ICBC. The committee would meet four times annually.

There are almost 3,000 laboratory technologists registered with the Canadian Society of Laboratory Technologists, 2,333 physical therapists (PTs) registered with the College of Physical Therapists of BC, and about 880 registered occupational therapists (OTs). The gender breakdown for lab technologists and their primary place of employment are not known. However, in physiotherapy women make up 1,928 of the total, while among OTs, women number 827. Among PTs, 785 are employed in private practice, while a majority of the remainder work in hospitals, long-term care, community health and other publicly funded programs.[3] Thus, the side accord promised to affect up to 4,000 people employed in non-profit, publicly funded facilities, approximately 85 per cent of whom would be female employees.[4]

The agreement won support from ICBC, which agreed to explore partnerships with HSA and HEU, regional health boards and community health councils to provide a variety of rehab services to their clients. Similarly, the WCB expressed interest in partnering with hospitals to look at ways these facilities could better meet the needs of injured workers requiring rehabilitation services, including, where necessary, skills upgrading among caregivers.

BC's two largest private lab companies were not so enthusiastic about the "Strengthening BC's Public Health Care Services" accord. MDS Inc. and BC BioMedical said the accord could lead to the disappearance of "community labs" and launched a province-wide petition campaign, netting some 65,000 signatures. Newspaper commentators charged incorrectly that the value of MDS shares on the Toronto Stock Exchange had fallen steeply because of the "lab accord."

The accord between the government and the two unions established a basis for discussion of a new bloc-funding system with the following elements:

- The "funding envelope" for all laboratory services would be transferred to regional health authorities to allocate within their geographic areas;

- Health authorities would be able to determine the appropriate number and location of outpatient and inpatient laboratory facilities, including collection stations;

- Health authorities could be expected to rationalize the provision of laboratory services and capture the savings potential from technological change.

As a condition of the new funding, health authorities would be required to plan and manage diagnostic services in a manner consistent with Section 3 of the *Health Authorities Act*.[5] For clarification, the accord stated "specifically, this means giving preference to the provision of services through the public sector and ensuring optimal utilization of existing and future public investment in laboratory services." This provision would also apply to any future changes to breast cancer screening (Health Sciences Association of BC 1998).

Side accords were also negotiated with other health care unions as a way of mitigating the impact of the government's "zero-zero-two" per cent wage guidelines over three years. But while the other negotiated accords provided a range of benefits to union members, the HSA/HEU/government accord was the only one that fully addressed the issue of privatization in an important area of the health care sector.[6]

Wage Parity

Wage parity is a central issue for unions representing support workers in hospitals and the community. In the so-called "facilities sector" (covering non-nursing and non-professional hospital staff, including activity workers, care aides, LPNs, nursing assistants, cooks and food service supervisors), unions won pay equity adjustments worth $64.1 million in wage increases, applied in 1998, 1999 and 2000 (BCGSEU 1998). The agreement covering these workers has been recognized as the "target agreement" – that is, those employed in the community sector will have achieved parity when their wages, benefits and working conditions match those that exist in the facilities sector collective agreement.

There are approximately 15,000 community social services workers in BC who work in approximately 5,500 community facilities offering community living, family and children's services, services to women, and child care. According to the unions representing these workers (BC Government and Services Employees' Union, Canadian Union of Public Employees, HEU and HSA) community social services workers earn up to $8 an hour less than hospital workers who do the same or similar work. But union demands for parity for community social services workers by 2003 are proving to be elusive. In 1998, a general wage increase of 30 cents an hour was won for all community caregivers, and extended and dental benefits established to match those in the facilities sector. But the government's offer of $12 million to address the wage gap will not move community caregivers up the income ladder as quickly as these workers would like.

In 1997, unions won an extension of employment security provisions to members working in the community, provisions that were further improved during bargaining in 1998. Community caregivers now receive a 12-month period of job security following a notice of layoff. During this period, caregivers can register with the Health Labour Adjustment Agency to obtain alternate employment and receive their full wages and benefits.

Home support workers waged a strong campaign during the 1998 round of bargaining to win improvements for a large pool of casual workers. The new agreement sets out clear parameters for regular job postings that will enable casual employees to convert their hours into regular positions. Health employers must demonstrate that changes in scheduling are needed to meet operational requirements, and they must take into consideration "the personal circumstances of caregivers." Home support workers in jobs whose primary focus is client/resident care received wage increases to between $14.50 and $16.00 an hour. Where client/resident care is not the focus of the job, a caregiver will receive between $12.50 and $13.50 an hour. Home support workers will also be folded into the unions' community agreement in the future (HEU 1998).

Despite the mammoth changes in the structure of health care bargaining begun in 1993, and the continuing tension over issues of wage and benefits parity, unionized health care workers in both the hospital and growing community sectors have fared better than their counterparts in other provinces. Unionized women employed in non-profit, community-based and unionized health care are seeing major improvements in working conditions and have developed a long-term agenda for establishing parity with hospital employees. However, the wage gaps between organized and unorganized workers are not being adequately addressed. Unorganized workers face huge challenges – first, to obtain representation and second, to convince employers in the community to accept the principle of parity. The number of providers operating on a for-profit basis is increasing in BC, and these will have greater resources to withstand pressure to increase wages above the minimum set in employment standards legislation.

NURSING: THE BURDEN OF CARE

The nursing profession is undergoing tremendous change as health care reform measures are implemented in both the acute care and community sectors. Approximately 31,000 RNs are employed in general, rehabilitation, extended and long-term care facilities, mental health centres, home care and community health agencies in BC. Another 150 RNs are employed in private business. This compares with more than 5,200 LPNs, of whom almost 3,800 work in a hospital setting and the rest are employed in home and community care, private businesses and physician offices. Only 1,095 RNs are males, while among LPNs only 381 are males. Within the health care workforce, the nursing profession is the most female-dominated area, and offers some of the widest opportunities for career mobility.

Workload issues topped the agenda during nurses' bargaining in 1998. This is not surprising, since early discharge policies in hospitals and the increase in outpatient surgeries mean higher levels of acuity and higher workloads for nurses. In a 1998 poll conducted for the BC Nurses' Union, more than 80 per cent of members reported that their patients/clients/residents were more seriously ill than they were five years earlier. The results were particularly marked among nurses in acute care and the community. Despite rising acuity levels, however, almost one-third of nurses surveyed reported a decline in the number of RNs delivering direct care (BC Nurses' Union 1998).

Many health care employers have attempted to cut costs by replacing higher-skilled RNs with lower-paid personnel with less training and experience. This is a controversial strategy for a number of reasons. First, many people feel LPNs are capable of performing many of the duties traditionally carried out by RNs, while many employers have identified the transfer of duties to lower-paid staff as an acceptable way to save money. Some of the exchanges between LPNs and RNs on this issue have been tense, since for both groups jobs are at stake. Second, because acuity levels are rising, the demands on nursing staff with higher skill levels to provide direct care also increase. Inadequate staffing levels in some areas exacerbate the problem.

Statistics support the BCNU's position on inadequate staffing levels in the nursing profession. In 1994-95, BC had the lowest number of staffed hospital beds per 1,000 population in short-term care units – 2.2 beds per 1,000 population, compared to the Canadian average of 2.8. BC patients also stayed for the shortest period of time in hospitals without long-term care units – 4.9 days compared to the Canadian average of 6.6 days. Overall hospital utilization in the province declined in 1997 to 645 beds per 1,000 population, a 40 per cent decline from 1991 (Statistics Canada 1997). A 1997 study by the Advisory Committee on Clinical Resource Management concluded that although many patients may not require acute care services, most require some form of care and attention, and that many forms of alternate care were simply not available in BC (BC Ministry of Health 1997).

Early discharge and delayed entry into hospital places increased demands on nurses employed in the community sector, including those working in home care. The BCNU charges that the number of community nurses is inadequate for the increased burden of care required in the home. If the number of home care nurses is inadequate it is likely that the care received by patients discharged early from hospital is inadequate as well – and that the burden of care is falling on those mainly female "informal" caregivers in the home.

The BCNU survey also indicated that a growing number of younger nurses are choosing to leave the profession, often because of high stress levels and heavy workloads leading to "burnout." These workloads are reflected in an increased rate of injury, with some 30 per cent of hospital nurses and 24 per cent of nurses in long-term care reporting that they had suffered a workplace injury during the previous six months. The BCNU survey also indicated that as many as half the number of members polled would leave nursing for another profession "if they had the opportunity." This was particularly true among younger nurses.

The promise of more federal cash transfers delivered in the 1999 federal budget and a threatened strike by the BCNU led the Minister of Health to announce an increase in nursing staff of 10,000 in early 1999. This promises to alleviate some of the workload problems experienced by RNs, although it is too soon to know where those RN positions will be concentrated.

Two initiatives in 1995 dealt with the roles of unpaid caregivers in British Columbia. According to the BC Ministry of Health, unpaid caregivers provide the majority of care at home and in the community. A committee established by the health minister looked at ways of strengthening support for informal care – identified as a priority in the *New Directions* strategy. The report, submitted to both the health and human resources ministries, stressed the need for respite services for unpaid caregivers. In another initiative, Nanaimo was selected to participate in a national demonstration project to improve services for caregivers. The pilot project is to focus on finding better ways to use community services to meet the needs of unpaid caregivers who require respite services.

However, support services for unpaid caregivers – the majority of whom are women, many of them elderly – are sorely lacking. The focus on respite care, as opposed to home support and nursing services, suggests the continuation of policies that will place increasing burdens on women providing care to spouses, children or other family members in need. Studies documenting the impact of health care reform, early discharge policies and evidence-based practices on women in unpaid caregiving roles are primarily anecdotal. Further study is needed in this area to ascertain the gaps in the health care system and to provide services that are required by patients who choose to remain outside an institutional setting.

HEALTH CARE REFORM AND PRIVATIZATION

Regionalization is at the core of BC's health reform strategy and involves a devolution of budgeting, planning and decision-making authority from the provincial to the community or regional level. Regionalization has also meant the transfer of some planning and governance functions from hospitals to regional health authorities. At the same time, a key objective of health care reform is the movement of many non-acute care services out of the hospital sector and into more accessible community-based facilities.

As in other provinces, the BC government vowed to locate a growing number of services in the community. But, unlike many other provinces, BC had not developed a network of publicly funded community-based health centres during the 1970s and 1980s to deliver non-acute care services. Thus, the plan to transfer services to the as-yet few community health centres caused consternation among caregivers and the public alike.[7]

The transfer of services outside of the hospital sector does not necessarily lead to privatization. But unless steps are taken to ensure these services are captured on the public health plan, privatization is the result. This is happening in BC as outpatient services move out from under the insured umbrella of the acute care sector into a non-insured, partially insured or privately insured arena often referred to as the "community." Since the question of whether a hospital service is fully covered under public health plans appears to depend on the location of delivery, this movement may impede access by patients seeking outpatient hospital services. This is especially true for some outpatient rehabilitation services provided by individuals or companies that derive a growing portion of their revenues from user fees, as well as from private and workers' compensation insurers.

Privatization also results from the removal – or de-listing – of services from the Medical Services Plan. BC has de-listed some services and prescription drugs, and increased deductibles in some areas. In 1998, for example, the deductible for Pharmacare, excluding seniors and other eligible enrolees, was increased from $600 a year to $800. A year earlier, user fees for physiotherapy and other supplementary health services delivered in a private clinic increased from $7.50 per visit to $10.00.

Services that have been de-listed are very few, but this may change in future. The agreement between the provincial government, the Medical Services Commission (MSC) and the BC Medical Association (BCMA) includes an undertaking to develop Protocols and Practice Guidelines for physicians, hospitals and other billing institutions in order to "contain utilization." The agreement defines insured benefits as "medically required services which fall within defined, approved Protocols and Practice Guidelines, and those medically required services where no Protocols or Practice Guidelines exist." Under the agreement, the MSC is required to give "priority attention" to proposals developed by the BCMA and, should the government fail to carry out the recommended cost-saving measures, it must add the amount "which would otherwise have been saved" to the total allocated to physician services (Government of British Columbia 1996). Thus, it appears the government will have powerful incentives to implement future de-listing that may be recommended by the BCMA, a vocal proponent of increased private sector funding for health care services.

Private insurers are expanding the scope of services offered on their health plans, both as a consequence of de-listing and in response to new commercial products and services marketed by health companies. Insurers are also benefiting from the movement of outpatient services from the acute care sector to the community. In addition, many individual providers in private practice are being encouraged to "opt out" of the Medical Services Plan, which in the view of some caregivers, maintains inadequate reimbursement schemes.

All of these activities threaten to impose financial barriers on patients who require services, and technically and legally summarize the nature of "privatization" in the health sector.

Barring Access

Barriers that impede access to health services insured by private companies are numerous. In addition to the economic barriers imposed by premiums charged by the private insurance industry, insurers maintain exclusions or higher premiums based on the age, sex, health status and employment history of subscribers. Women above the age of 14 years access health services – both on their own behalves and on behalf of children or elderly parents – far more frequently than men. Data for 1996-97 indicates that females in British Columbia accessed medical services on average 1.5 times more frequently than males. Female access to medical services was higher in 35 categories out of 46, and significantly higher in speciality areas such as obstetrics and gynaecology (which would be expected), massage and physical therapy, naturopathy, osteopathy, pathology, radiology, geriatric medicine and general practice medicine. Furthermore, as women age, their use of medical services increases even more sharply relative to men (Medical Services Plan 1997).

Therefore changes that result in the privatization of insured health services inevitably have a greater impact on female patients. The lack or inadequacy of public health insurance coverage for long-term and home care services also affect women disproportionately. One study in the United States indicated that on average females pay 68 per cent more in out-of-pocket expenditures for health care than males (CRLP 1998). This occurs for two reasons: first, more of the services women use are not covered by either private or public health plans and second, more women are likely to be excluded by eligibility criteria on private plans because of pre-existing conditions (including pregnancy).

While similar studies have not been undertaken by the province of BC, existing data indicate that some of the same conditions or pre-conditions exist here. According to a report of the Physiotherapy Association of British Columbia (PABC), 58 per cent of physiotherapy users were female in 1998, and overall a growing number of people who visit a physical therapist do so in the private sector. According to a 1998 PABC survey, the use of private clinics increased from 69 per cent of all those who used physiotherapy services in 1994 to 93 per cent who visited a physiotherapist in 1997-98. Of those who visited a physical therapist in 1997-98, 57 per cent said they would visit less often if they had to pay for the entire visit (in 1998, they paid a $10 user fee to visit a physical therapist in a private clinic) (PTABC 1998).

As the number of physical therapists practising in private clinics or employed by private companies increases, the manner in which practitioners identify their interests may also change. In other words, for some physiotherapists in private practice, their commitment to providing care may be compromised by legitimate concerns about their economic well-being.

Hospital Reform

Following the pattern established across North America, hospitals in BC began reassessing the way in which they delivered care in the early 1990s. At the same time, the consulting industry was developing a relationship with the hospital sector, selling re-engineering schemes that promised to incorporate an industrial model of health care delivery.

In 1993, Chilliwack General Hospital became the first facility in BC to implement a new and radical approach to patient care, a move that was closely watched by other hospitals in the province. The approach chosen by the hospital was Patient-Focused Care (PFC), a model developed in the United States by Booz-Allen and Hamilton, a consulting company. PFC was introduced to Canada by American Practices Management (APM), Inc. in Winnipeg. The program resulted in the elimination of 403 positions at St. Boniface General Hospital and Winnipeg's Health Sciences Centre, which rang alarm bells among the staff at Chilliwack's hospital.

PFC advocates claim that the program will reduce operating costs by 5-10 per cent, operating space by 15-20 per cent, and staff by 10 per cent, while providing care that is focused on patients rather than providers. The PFC approach uses "multi-skilled health practitioners" – some of whom have had as little as 11 days' training – to perform nursing tasks. The BCNU, HSA and HEU contracted the Trade Union Research Bureau to survey members at the Chilliwack facility to ascertain how the new health delivery program was affecting both employees and the quality of care. The survey found that 75 per cent of employees felt the system compromised patient safety, 89 per cent reported increased stress and workload and only 20 per cent said their work had become more interesting due to multi-skilling.

The BCNU accused the hospital of compromising the quality of care and of "replacing highly skilled workers with unlicensed, unregulated and underpaid workers." All three unions waged an intense campaign against PFC, leading to the appointment of a hospital-union-community team by the Ministry of Health to investigate the unions' charges. The committee was unable to reach a consensus on whether the "evidence" pointed to a compromise of quality care and the investigation creaked to a halt without resolving the issues. Job security issues were resolved in the health labour accord, but employees continued to express frustration and unhappiness with the changes in their work and the standards of care they were able to deliver at Chilliwack General Hospital.

These re-engineering efforts were occurring across the country, and in 1994 the Canadian Council on Health Services Accreditation introduced its new "Standards for Acute Care Organizations," which required hospitals to implement a "client-centred approach" to receive its stamp of approval. Consequently, hospitals in BC that wished to become accredited with the Council began adopting a variety of programs to meet the new criteria. Most of the data available on the impact of such programs is resident with the organizations that represent employers, employees and physicians, but very little, if any, is publicly available through the Ministry of Health.

Outcomes Measurement

BC hospitals are moving quickly to embrace health care delivery management systems that promise to achieve what are referred to in the United States as "patient-centred outcomes measures." Outcomes measurements are used to determine appropriate clinical practices and have been heavily utilized by the insurance industry to evaluate the validity of claims for medical, hospital and other health services. Paul Ellwood, architect of former President Bill Clinton's "managed competition" health care reform proposals, defines outcomes management as "a technology of patient experience designed to help patients, payers, and providers make rational medical care-related choices." He states that this technology "consists of a...national database containing information and analysis on clinical, financial, and health outcomes that estimates as best we can the relation between medical interventions and health outcomes, as well as the relation between health outcomes and money" (ACEP 1996-99).

In theory, outcomes assessments begin by measuring patient status and developing treatment plans, monitoring patient progress and evaluating clinical effectiveness, and conclude with outcomes information being fed back to improve the structure and process of health care services. In reality, as Armstrong and Armstrong (1996) have argued, the combination of outcomes measures and programs that change the delivery of health services are more cost-centred than patient-focused, and are used to enable health care managers to deny care – and limit the ability of caregivers to deliver care.

While such strategies seek to establish appropriate models to determine the clinical effectiveness of care delivered in BC hospitals, there appears to be no acknowledged need to measure whether new programs and practices designed to facilitate outcomes measurements will lead to reductions in service and autonomy for frontline caregivers. This would be an important step, given the experiences in U.S. jurisdictions, where more than 1,000 pieces of state legislation were introduced in 1996 alone to protect patients, most of them female, from guidelines that produced a litany of horrifying practices, including "drive-through mastectomies" (Merline 1996).[8]

Outsourcing

Health care reform is affecting the way hospitals deliver care, and the relationship between the acute care and corporate sectors. Many companies have supplied hospitals with a range of products for decades, and in the past hospitals often have worked to ensure that supply contracts are awarded to local companies. In the current environment, corporations have stepped up their attempts to negotiate "outsourcing" agreements with hospitals, and hospitals are being urged to narrow their "core missions" to areas of clinical care. A growing list of non-clinical services – such as laundry, maintenance, food services and health records management – are being contracted out to multinational corporations, despite studies that suggest the long-term savings from "outsourced" services are illusory.

The terms "outsourcing" and "contracting out" are used interchangeably with "partnership" and "alliance," and cover a variety of arrangements. Selective outsourcing is used to farm out specific jobs, for example, food preparation or maintenance. Facilities management (a service captured in NAFTA) occurs when a team is hired to oversee all operations at a hospital. Transitional outsourcing brings in an "outsourcer" for a few years, after which the operations are returned in-house when the hospital has learned how to run them. And finally, full-service outsourcing turns over an entire operation, such as information systems, to outside companies. Contracting out services often displaces hospital employees, reducing the facility's labour costs while providing new opportunities for big corporations.

Outsourcing, which companies say will assist the integration of health care delivery, is itself an important element in the integration of Canada's non-profit hospital and for-profit corporate sectors. Outsourcing represents a strategic and tactical alignment of interests in the health sector between publicly funded hospitals and the corporate sector. In Ontario, longstanding partnerships and outsourcing relationships between acute care facilities and corporations (many of them U.S.-based) have evolved into more formal "joint venture" arrangements in for-profit entities that provide "alternative sources of revenue" to cash-strapped hospitals.

Hospitals are targets of corporate sales strategies, and many believe that outsourcing will lead to substantial savings. But comparisons of costs in the United States, where corporate outsourcing contracts escalated by up to 46 per cent from 1995 to 1996, and Canada, where most hospitals continue to supply their own needs, cast doubt on these assumptions. Studies between the two countries show that higher costs among American hospitals relate primarily to the use of more expensive non-patient care services. Hospital support services in the United States (e.g., laundry and linen departments, dietary, housekeeping, equipment maintenance and plant operations) cost 24 per cent more per day than they do in comparable Canadian acute care facilities. Overall, hospitals in Canada were 41.6 per cent less expensive per discharge in 1995, with a 47.9 per cent longer average length of stay (Weil 1995).

As several hospitals in BC have discovered, outsourcing and other strategies to funnel tax dollars to corporations do not necessarily result in lower overall expenditures. However, many BC hospitals continue to adopt strategies used in other provinces to shift so-called non-core – and by implication, non-essential – functions out from under their umbrellas. The move to quality or outcomes measurements is leading some hospitals – such as St. Paul's and Vancouver Health Sciences – to develop information systems that will gather, organize and submit data on quality – and increasingly, they are outsourcing those systems to meet the demand (Compensation & Benefits Review 1997; Chin 1997).

Outsourcing companies achieve their cost savings almost entirely by reducing the cost of labour: maintaining low wages and benefits and fighting attempts to unionize. An assessment of "product costs" by The Toronto Hospital (TTH) found that, because hospitals are labour-intensive organizations, most of the savings that would accrue from outsourcing "will be derived from this category." TTH decided in 1993 that "the support services functions of the hospital could be carried out at less cost" by private companies. Hospitals, said TTH, "simply cannot compete with the economies of scale enjoyed by business" (Stenhouse, Hudson and O'Keefe 1996). BC hospitals have been vulnerable to the same temptations, and contracting out has increased in the province's acute care facilities, despite union charges that contracting out services often occurs in violation of collective agreement provisions. This is one reason why health care unions in BC – and across the country – have mounted vigorous campaigns to oppose contracting out of so-called "non-core" services.

Amalgamations

Hospitals are also amalgamating their services, and this promises to be a more acceptable way both to save money and maintain services in the non-profit sector. It also will avoid the transfer of services to lower-paid workers in the corporate sector. These amalgamations are occurring in laboratory, food and laundry services in the Lower Mainland. In other areas, hospitals are adopting more industrial and private sector models of efficiency, methods that many analysts say are inappropriate in a health care setting. For example, some urban and suburban hospitals are establishing areas of medical speciality, both to improve efficiencies and to secure their funding base. In 1999, residents of Mission, BC voiced concerns that their local facility would no longer offer maternity care seven days a week if the hospital in Abbotsford, some 30 minutes away, became the "maternity hospital" for the Fraser Valley health region. Mission Memorial Hospital provides services to several smaller communities that may be inaccessible to Abbotsford, critics charge, if a ferry across the Fraser River stops running. While it may be more efficient and less costly to establish a hospital specializing in maternity care for the whole Fraser Valley, residents were worried that not all deliveries can be planned to coincide with visits of the Abbotsford obstetrician to their community.[9]

The movement of service delivery from a non-profit environment to a for-profit and more commercialized setting is as significant to women as the actual privatization of funding for health care. The problems associated with maintaining adequate public funds for health services are compounded when the delivery of those services shifts to institutions primarily concerned with meeting the expectations of investors and shareholders. In this context, the provision of service relative to income received becomes paramount – that is, companies must ensure that the cost of providing services remains well below the level of revenue income. This is accomplished by reducing the number and/or quality of services, and by minimizing the cost of labour.

If patterns established elsewhere in Canada and in North America hold true, community-based non-profit providers in British Columbia will have an increasingly difficult time in a competitive health services market. Non-profit facilities dependent on public funding are often unable to establish the economies of scale in which large global corporations are able to function, and are unable or sometimes unwilling to achieve the "efficiencies" of industrial model providers. Added to this is pressure from the health care workforce to achieve parity with their acute care counterparts, and similar demands from community social services workers involved in health-related fields such as the provision of home care.

More information is required to determine the impact of hospital reform and the adoption of evidenced-based practices, utilization protocols and outcomes measurements on patients and health care providers. While some information is available, it is widely scattered, anecdotal, very subjective and not easily accessible. The impact of contracting out or outsourcing also requires more serious, in-depth study as the information that does exist often is unavailable due to company demands for confidentiality.

THE INFORMATION GAP

Information about how health care reform is affecting women is minimal, and much of what does exist is kept in holdings outside of the Ministry of Health, or outside of public view altogether. The Centre for Health Services and Policy Research (CHSPR) at the University of British Columbia publishes a province-wide and regional breakdown of the health care workforce by place of employment, gender and age. Gender statistics are not available before 1992-93. Some information can be obtained from the Medical Services Commission, which provides a breakdown of utilization and fee-for-service statistics that includes gender-based data. However, this information is not easily accessed. Information about programs and services offered to women by the Ministry of Health is available on-line, but most of this lacks statistical detail and can be described as promotional.

Unions representing BC health care workers probably have the most detailed and up-to-date information about their members' wages, benefits and working conditions. Unions also track the rate of privatization in the health sector, but once members shift their place of employment to locations outside the unions' jurisdictions, the data cease to be collected. Most professional associations lack the necessary funds to establish a sophisticated source of information, but some of what is available is useful.

Private companies operating in the health sector maintain data that enables them to plan their investments. Much of this information is extremely useful, but disclosure laws at both the provincial and federal levels place much of it beyond the reach even of shareholders.

For policy-makers and women to obtain an accurate picture of how reform efforts are affecting or could affect the primary users and providers of health services, information is key. There is no database in the province devoted exclusively to information about how women interact with the health system – either public or private. The Ministry of Health, while promoting public-private partnerships, does not track information about the use of private health services, although some of this data is available at the Workers' Compensation Board and the Insurance Corporation of BC because both are publicly regulated institutions. But there is no data available, for example, about the amount of out-of-pocket expenditures incurred by women who seek services in the uninsured health services sector.

The United States, by comparison, has logged a broad array of data on women and the health care system. Many of these databases should be examined to determine how the collection and storage of information about women as paid and unpaid providers and as users of health services in British Columbia might be organized. This is an urgent matter, since change continues at a rapid pace in the province, and there are few areas in which it is possible to establish a baseline prior to the introduction of health care reform.

If women hope to exert influence on the direction of health system reform – whether that influence is exerted at a governance, provider or patient level – we will need not only information, but guaranteed access to the data. Health care reform is leading to increased privatization of health-related information, both at the provincial and federal levels. One example is the Canadian Institute of Health Information (CIHI), a consortium funded in part by large corporations such as IBM, Hewlett-Packard, SmartHealth, SHL Systemhouse (a subsidiary of MCI), and several hospitals. The head of CIHI is Michael Decter, formerly Canadian vice-president of American Practices Management, Inc. CIHI collects useful data on health services and expenditures (including utilization statistics broken down by gender, age and location), and financial, statistical and clinical data, information which is provided to its members and usually for a fee to the public. Annual membership fees are between $1000 and $5000 annually, costs which are prohibitive for most of the population. Much of the information now stored with CIHI used to be available free from Statistics Canada, Health Canada and the Hospital Medical Records Institute.

In BC it is important that such data be protected from commercial use while being made available to the public free of charge. Provincial and federal discussions concerning patient medical records are now focusing on how to protect privacy while enabling private companies to gather, manage and distribute such information – for a fee.

Finally, companies that deliver health services, or which insure BC residents, should be required to submit utilization and cost information to a public data bank at no cost, since many will be operating on a fee-for-service basis paid entirely or subsidized by public expenditures.

Notes

1. The "Health System Reform in British Columbia" document is part of an ongoing review of health care reform in Canada begun in spring 1995 and conducted by Health Canada's regional offices, with the cooperation of provincial and territorial Ministries of Health.
2. The bed to population ratio in BC hospitals had fallen to approximately 2.2 beds per 1,000 population by March 2000, while the reduction of hospital staff has been minimal. These falling utilization rates are not unique to British Columbia (see Canadian Institute for Health Information 1999).
3. This number was arrived at by calculating approximately 2,200 lab technologists employed in hospital laboratories (based on HSA membership figures), plus 925 physical therapists and virtually all 880 occupational therapists employed in public or publicly funded institutions.
4. These figures are archived from Rollcall Update '97, Centre for Health Services and Policy Research (CHSPR), <www.chspr.ubc.ca/hhru/rollcall/1997> "Introduction," Tables 3 and 4; "Physical Therapists," Tables 2 and 4; "Occupational Therapists," Table 2, "Introduction," Table 3; "Licensed Practical Nurses in British Columbia," Tables 2 and 4; "Registered Nurses in British Columbia," Tables 2 and 5.
5. Section 3 of the Health Authorities Act (Provincial standards) states that:
   (1) The minister may, by regulation, establish Provincial standards for the provision of health services.
   (2) The minister may, by regulation, specify a health service, or the level or extent of health service, that must be provided in a region or community.
   (3) The minister must ensure under subsections (1) and (2) that health services in British Columbia continue to be provided on a predominantly not-for-profit basis.
   (4) The minister must not act under subsection (1) or (2) in a manner that does not satisfy the criteria described in section 7 of the Canada Health Act (Canada) respecting public administration, comprehensiveness, universality, portability and accessibility.
   (5) Any grant to a board or council by the government must be made on condition that the board or council complies with all applicable regulations made under subsections (1) and (2).
6. Currently the Medical Services Commission is responsible for licensing both private and hospital laboratory collection sites. Hospitals have experienced problems obtaining licences from MSC, which has expressed a preference for licensing private labs. In 1996-97, $54.7 million was paid in lab fees to hospitals for outpatient services, compared to $117.4 million paid to private companies in BC. From 1992-93 to 1996-97, billings for outpatient lab services grew by four per cent in the hospital sector and by 22 per cent in the private sector. Up to 80 per cent of private sector outpatient lab services are used to provide a relatively short list of routine services. Furthermore, fee for service billings ignore whether or not a test is performed in a highly automated environment (see BC Ministry of Health 1998).
7. Community health centres are characteristically those facilities that provide a broad range of integrated services, rather than community facilities that focus on specific and segregated areas of care.
8. "Drive-through" mastectomies refers to breast removal surgery done on an outpatient basis – on old treatment guidelines enforced by cost-conscious U.S. insurers utilizing outcome meseasurements.
8. These comments are drawn from my notes from a meeting in Mission, BC, organized by the Council of Canadians, March 9, 1999, on regionalization and health care reform in the Fraser Valley.

References

American College of Emergency Physicians (ACEP). 1996-99. "Quality of Care and the Outcomes Measurements Movement." Dallas, Texas: ACEP.

Armstrong, Pat, and Hugh Armstrong. 1996. *Wasting Away: The Undermining of Canadian Health Care*. Don Mills, ON: Oxford University Press.

BC Government and Services Employees Union (BCGSEU). 1998. Bargaining Update #12, Facilities Sub-Sector. 21 September.

BC Ministry of Health. 1998. "Province of BC Fact Sheet: Laboratory Services in BC." 16 October.

BC Ministry of Health. 1997. "Better Utilization Management of Hospital Beds Recommended." News Release. 11 March.

BC Nurses' Union. 1998. "Working Too Hard." *The British Columbia Nurses' Union Magazine* (September).

British Columbia. Provincial Health Officer. 1995. *A Report on the Health of British Columbians: Provincial Health Officer's Annual Report 1994*. Victoria, BC Ministry of Health and Ministry Responsible for Seniors.

—. 1996. *A Report on the Health of British Columbians: Provincial Health Officer's Annual Report 1994*. Victoria, BC Ministry of Health and Ministry Responsible for Seniors.

Canadian Institute for Health Information (CIHI). 1999. "Hospital Utilization, 1996/97."

Canadian Medical Association. 1996. "Regionalization." *Canadian Medical Association Journal* 154: 572A-572B.

Center for Reproductive Law and Policy (CRLP). 1998. "Reproductive Freedom News." Contemporary Women's Issues Database (12 December 12).

Chin, Tyler L. 1997. "Outsourcing." *Health Data Management* (August 19).

Community Care Facility Act. RSBC 1996, c. 60. Updated to 31 October 1997.

Compensation & Benefits Review. 1997. "Measuring Value in Healthcare: The Quality Factor." 18 September.

Government of British Columbia. 1996. Article 6: "Utilization and Cost Saving Measures." Renewed Working Agreement Between the Government of the Province of British Columbia, the Medical Services Commission and the British Columbia Medical Association. 3 May.

Health Canada. 1997. "Health System Reform in British Columbia." Ottawa: Health Canada.

Health Information Management Co-ordinating Council (HIMCC). 1996. *Strategic Plan for Health Information Management in British Columbia*.

Health Sciences Association of BC. 1998. "HSA Lab Campaign Pays Off with 'Accord' On Lab, Breast Cancer Screening and Rehab Services." *News Bulletin* (September 1998).

Hospital Employees' Union (HEU). 1998. "HEU Community Members Urged to Vote No in Contract Ratification; Absence of Firm Future Parity Pledge From Government the Problem." *Hospital Employees' Union Bulletin* (September 17).

Medical Services Plan. 1997. "Fee-for-service Payment Statistics, 1996/97." *MSP Information Resource Manual*. Vancouver: MSP, Information and Analysis Branch.

Medicare Protection Act. RSBC 1996, c. 286. Updated to 31 October 1997.

Merline, John. 1996. "The Backlash Against Managed Care." *Consumers' Research Magazine 79* (11 November).

Physical Therapists Association of British Columbia (PTABC). 1998. "1998 Market Research." Highlights of a Poll by MarkTrend Research. <www.physiobc.ca>.

Statistics Canada. 1997. "Hospital Downsizing." *Health Reports* 8 (4) (Spring). Catalogue No. 82-003.

Stenhouse, James H., Alan R. Hudson, and Michael J. O'Keefe. 1996. "Private-Public Partnerships: The Toronto Hospital Experience." In Peggy Leatt, Louise Lemieux, Charles and Catherine Aird, eds., *Strategic Alliances in Health Care: A Casebook in Management Innovation*. Ottawa: Canadian College of Health Care Administration.

Weil, Jim. 1995. "How Do Canadian Hospitals Do It? A Comparison of Utilization and Costs in the United States and Canada." *Hospital Topics* 73 (1 January).

Conclusion

These reports from across the country expose the extensive privatization of health care in Canada and lead to several conclusions:

1. All the provinces have moved to shift health care costs to individuals, to shift care delivery to for-profit concerns, to shift managerial practices to for-profit approaches, to shift care responsibility to households and care work to unpaid caregivers. Our definition of privatization is useful in revealing the multiple forms privatization is taking in Canada.

2. Although there are similarities among provinces, there are also significant differences. The process is uneven across the country. Indeed, some provinces have reversed privatization in some areas and others explicitly forbid certain forms of privatization. Manitoba, for example, has returned the management of home care to the public sector and Saskatchewan requires non-profit care delivery in specific areas.

3. Health care reform is happening so quickly, and with so little public information on the changes, that it is difficult to draw a full picture. More research on health care privatization is needed. We need to know more – both about the many forms of health care privatization and about its consequences for individuals and the system as a whole.

4. Outside the Centres of Excellence for Women's Health, there is little research being done to examine the impact of health care reforms on women. There is even less research that considers differences among women in terms of how they are affected by health care reforms.

5. The research that does take women into account suggests many health care reforms are having a negative impact on women. Those doing paid health care work are facing increasing workloads and increasing stress. More women are being "conscripted" into unpaid health care work, without training and with few supports. Those sent home quicker and sicker are finding it more difficult to get care – and important questions need to be

asked about the quality of care they are receiving not just at home but in institutions. The research on differences among women, although hard to find, suggests that those who have traditionally been most vulnerable are facing deteriorating conditions of care.

6. These reports clearly demonstrate the need for research on the impact of health care reforms that is gender-sensitive and woman-specific, research that begins with the recognition that women and men connect to the health care system in different ways and that there are also important differences among women.

7. Finally, the research demonstrates that there are real choices in how health care is reformed. Women need the evidence and the means to participate fully in making those choices.

AGMV Marquis
MEMBER OF SCABRINI MEDIA
Quebec, Canada
2001